Chicago Today

MAP
OF
COOK COUNTY
ILLINOIS

N

COMPLIMENTS
OF
RICHARD J. DALEY
COUNTY CLERK

Fabulous Chicago

Books by Emmett Dedmon

DUTY TO LIVE

FABULOUS CHICAGO

Emmett Dedmon

"I wish I could go to America if only to see that Chicago."

> Bismarck to General Philip H. Sheridan (1870)

"Good Americans are said to go to Paris when they die; but it appears to depend on whether they have been to Chicago first."

> Among the Americans, by George Jacob Holyoake (1881)

"Sir, Chicago is the boss city of the universe."

> An anonymous brakeman on a train coming into the city (1881)

Fabulous Chicago

RANDOM HOUSE

NEW YORK

FOR *Claire*

MY FABULOUS CHICAGOAN

Acknowledgments

WITHOUT the resources of The Chicago Historical Society this book could not have been written; without the cheerful co-operation of the Society's staff its writing would have required twice the time. I am particularly indebted to director Paul M. Angle for suggestions on procedure; to Elizabeth Baughman, who was both helpful and creative in guiding me among the society's source materials; to Grant Dean for checking the manuscript; to H. Maxson Holloway and Walter Krutz for help in obtaining illustrations and to Violett Richardson for help with manuscripts. At Newberry Library, Ben C. Bowman gave important help in securing prints of drawings from the library files.

An uncounted number of books were consulted but there is a special obligation to mention the following which include first-hand material not available elsewhere: *Stormy Years* by Carter Harrison II (Bobbs-Merrill); *Come Into My Parlor*, the authorized biography of the Everleigh sisters, by Charles Washburn (Knickerbocker); *My Thirty Years War*, by Margaret Anderson (Covici-Friede); *Always Room At The Top*, by Ganna Walska (Richard R. Smith) and *Mary Garden's Story*, by Mary Garden and Louis Biancolli (Simon & Schuster).

Many Chicagoans participated in the making of this book by giving generously of their time and information. Mr. and Mrs. Cyrus Adams, Mr. and Mrs. Edward McCormick Blair and Jack McPhaul read the entire manuscript and made many helpful suggestions. For help on special sections of the book, I wish to thank Mrs. William McCormick Blair, Felix Borowski, Earl Gross, Harry Hansen, Maurene Hudgin, Ogden Ketting, Herman Kogan, Mrs. Potter Palmer II, Mrs. Higinbotham Patterson, Denton Sparks, Vincent Starrett and Lloyd Wendt. The executives of the Chicago *Sun-Times*, the Chicago *Tribune* and the Chicago *Daily News* were all generous in making the facilities and resources of their newspapers available to me. The final responsibility for the choice of material and its treatment is of course my own.

EMMETT DEDMON

Contents

List of Illustrations

PART ONE *The Garden City*

1835=1871

Frontier Town

"INTERESTING women are in demand here," a correspondent wrote from Chicago to the New York Star in 1837. "I understand that when the steamboats arrive from Buffalo and Detroit that nearly all business is suspended; and crowds of desolate, rich young bachelors flock to the pier and stand ready to catch the girls as they land." The description was hardly an exaggeration. In the winter of 1834 there had been only two girls of marriageable age in the small village of Chicago. The town's first fashionable wedding, which had such touches of style as printed wedding invitations, was that of an Indian chief's daughter, Josette LaFramboise, and Thomas Watkins, the post-office clerk who handed every Chicagoan his mail. The Reverend Isaac W. Hallam of St. James Episcopal Church performed the wedding ceremony in the chief's house while outside a group of Indian braves with tomahawks, clubs and even human scalps at their belts punctuated the sentences of the Episcopal Book of Common Prayer with the whoops and shrieks of tribal dances. The noise of the Indian dances brought echoes of terror to the white guests at the wedding. Only a few years before they had lived in fear of an Indian attack after Blackhawk and his warriors paddled across the Mississippi to reclaim lands taken from them by treaty. Runners brought word almost daily of massacres on outlying farms. Refugees from western Illinois streamed in to the protection of Fort Dearborn, reactivated because of the Indian menace after having been abandoned several years earlier. When Blackhawk won an initial skirmish against a band of untrained troops the panic increased and did not subside until the brave but foolhardy chief was put to flight after a battle in Wisconsin.

Until 1835 Chicago had been essentially an Indian town. Pelts, furs, guns, blankets, kettles, knives, hatchets, vermilion and whiskey were the principal commodities of commerce and Indians the chief customers. Blackhawk's escapade led to a renewal of demands that this large Indian population be moved west of the Mississippi. This was made possible in September of 1833 when the government called a grand council at Chicago of seventy-seven chiefs of the Chippewa, Ottawa and Pottawatomie tribes. On the 26th of the month a treaty was signed to which seventy-six Indian chiefs affixed their marks and one—Sau-Ko-Noek—his name. Under the treaty the Indians were dispossessed of lands later to be valued at hundreds of millions of dollars; in return they were given an annuity that for the first two years was to be paid at Chicago. By 1835 they were to be west of the Mississippi.

In 1834, when the first of the annuity payments was made, four to five thousand Indians, far outnumbering the population of Chicago, camped outside the town. The village traders were looking forward to the event greedily, but the majority of the townfolk thought nervously of the Black-hawk uprisings and hoped for the best. The distribution of the payments was primitive and haphazard. The whole quantity of goods to be given the Indians was piled in a heap on the west side of the river near the modern corner of Randolph and Canal Streets. The Indians were made to sit down in a circle around the pile with their squaws behind them. A group of half-breeds and traders who had been appointed to pass out the merchandise grabbed it up by the armful and started tossing it to the Indians. There was no system or fairness about this method and the Indians soon made a rush for the pile, snatching at the goods in a disorderly turmoil until the final piece had disappeared. When the merchandise was gone, the Indians headed for the traders to swap blankets and clothing for whiskey. The one unsatis-factory note for almost everyone but Chicago's pioneer preacher, the Rever-end Jeremiah Porter, was that several ships bearing cargoes of whiskey were not able to land for sixteen days because of high winds.

The performance of the Indians at the final annuity payment in 1835 was more awesome. Aware that this was their final stand before leaving the country of the Illinois forever, the Indians were brightly decorated with scarlet, yellow and blue paint. For several weeks after receiving their goods and money they lingered around town, encouraged in their reluctance to leave by traders who had been amply foreprovisioned against any such ill winds as had marred profits the previous year. On the final day set by the government for their departure, a thousand warriors assembled at the govern-ment council house on the north bank of the river. All were covered with vivid daubings of paint and naked except for a breechclout. Their faces were covered with curved stripes of red or vermilion and edged with black points to give the impression of a ferocious grin. Their long black hair was tightly gathered in scalplocks that bore decorations of hawk and eagle feathers, some of them strung together until they touched the ground. All were armed with tomahawks and clubs. Soon a band of music makers striking sticks and clubs together and beating on Indian drums took up positions for a war dance. The long column of the shrieking, dancing Indians started moving toward the center of the town. The column paused at every house and log cabin, while Indian warriors rushed up to the door or gate brandishing their primitive weapons. The morning was hot and the muscles of the perspiring Indians glistened like cast bronze as they moved in a torrent of motion down the narrow streets.

John Dean Caton, later to be a Chief Justice of the Illinois Supreme Court, watched the spectacle from behind closed curtains at the Sauganash Hotel. To him it seemed that "all the worst passions which can find a place in the breast of a savage—fierce anger, terrible hate, dire revenge, remorseless cruelty—" were to be seen in the demonstration of the Indians. Finally the passion of the warriors was spent and they filed away to the west and to an oblivion which the United States Government had arranged for them. To Caton it had been a scene "to try the nerve of the stoutest." The question of what might have happened if the Indians, "in their maddened frenzy," had turned the sham warfare into a real attack forced itself even on those who had seen the Indians most. It would have been easy, Caton thought, for the Indians to have massacred the entire town and left "not a living soul to tell the story." That there was no massacre was in part the difference of a generation between these Indians and those who had ravaged Fort Dearborn in 1812. Another factor was the leadership of the Indian Sauganash, known also to Chicagoans as Archibald "Billy" Caldwell.

Sauganash was born in Detroit in 1780, the son of an Irish colonel and a Pottawatomie maiden. As a boy he had attended the Jesuit school in Detroit

CHICAGO IN 1838, by *Francis Castleneau*. Earliest known contemporary view of Chicago and learned to write English and French. His fine, slim figure led the Indians to call him "Tall Tree" but he was more often known as Sauganash, which meant Englishman. Sauganash was a loyal follower of Tecumseh who had served on Tecumseh's staff until the chief's death and who had come to the region around Chicago for the first time as a messenger to the Pottawatomies shortly before the Fort Dearborn massacre. It had been through the efforts of Sauganash that the family of John Kinzie had been saved. In 1820 he settled near Chicago and in 1827 was credited with preventing the Winnebagoes and Pottawatomies from staging an uprising which might have repeated the tragedy of 1812. When the Indians were forced to move west, Sauganash volunteered to go with his people and direct migration, though the government had specified he was free to remain. It was a gesture which gave meaning to Mark Beaubien's explanation, when he was adding the frame addition to his Eagle Exchange, the first building in Chicago not a log cabin, that he would name his new hotel "after a great man: Sauganash."

Beaubien himself contributed much to early Chicago, including an imposing total of twenty-three children (borne by three wives). He had arrived when an Indian trail was the only route into the city and had hired an Indian guide to show him the way. In addition to running a hotel, he was charged with the operation of the free ferry across the river, though the records show that on several occasions he was fined because he was off racing his horses against the ponies of young Indian sports rather than at his post of duty. In the evenings Mark was more easily located. He would play his fiddle for any who cared to dance. In his own words, "I play the fiddle like the devil and keep hotel like hell." When his hotel was crowded, Mark gave a traveler a blanket to cover himself on the floor, warning him to be careful that the Indians did not steal it. Then when the guest was asleep, Mark carefully removed the blanket and held it for the next arrival. In this way, he said, "I always had beds for all who wanted them."

Chicago's social life had its origins in the public balls held at Mark Beaubien's hotel. These were dances arranged by a board of managers from among the town's leading citizens. Everyone of respectability was invited. Servant girls danced in the same sets with their mistresses. (Many of the servants were daughters of new families "working out" in order to help the family get extra money to invest in Chicago real estate.) It was already a tenet of the town that there was "no place for drones or luxurious idlers in Chicago." Industry and frugality were alone respectable. Families came to the balls in wagons or oxcarts sufficiently sturdy to cope with Chicago's mud. The men walked alongside in heavy boots which they exchanged at the door of the hotel for dancing slippers. The carts were usually filled with hay and buffalo robes. An early visitor reported that while one lady was

OLD BARRACKS OF FORT DEARBORN AND LAKE HOUSE

sufficiently wealthy to wear a five-hundred-dollar gown, she arrived like all the rest—"in a cart, sitting upon the straw."

"At these Chicago cotillions," wrote Charles Fenno Hoffman, in an account of a journey to the West, "you might see a veteran officer in full uniform balancing a tradesman's daughter still in her short frock and trousers, while there the golden aiguillette of a handsome surgeon flapped in unison with the glass beads upon a scrawny neck of fifty. In one quarter, the high placed buttons of a linsey woolsey coat would be *dos-à-dos* to the elegantly turned shoulders of a delicate southern girl; and in another, a pair of Cinderella-like slippers would chassez cross with a brace of thick soled broughans, in the making which, one of the lost feet of the Colossus of Rhodes may have served for a last. Those raven locks, dressed à la Madonne, over eyes of jet, and touching a cheek where blood of deeper hue mingles with the less glowing current from European veins, tells of a lineage drawn from the original owners of the soil; while these golden tresses, floating away from eyes of heaven's own color over a neck of alabaster, recall the Gothic ancestry of some of England's born. How piquantly do these trim and beaded leggins peep from under that simple dress of black as its tall nut-brown wearer moves, as if unconsciously, through the graceful mazes of the dance."

Reminders that Chicago was a frontier town were everywhere. Yet there were already those who were predicting that one day Chicago would be a great city. They pointed to the fact that more than half the continent lay to the west, still undeveloped. The timber for the houses on the western prairies would have to pour through the funnel of Chicago from the wide forests of Wisconsin and Michigan. The manufactured goods from the East would have to be channeled through the young port at the end of the lake waterway. Nor were the prospects for trade one-sided. Already from the West were coming wagonloads of grain and livestock to be shipped to eastern markets. Wagon trains entering the city from the south after bending their way around the tip of Lake Michigan carried other vital cargo. By this route came families and whole communities which hoped to find their promised land in the West. Chicago was not always their stopping point. In 1849, when the gold-rush fever fired adventurous imaginations, many of those who had first chosen Chicago yielded to the greater lure of gold. The makers of covered wagons worked overtime and the price of guns for defense against the Indians rose as much as 50 per cent.

A vacant field south of Fort Dearborn had been set aside as a camping ground for the wagon trains and every evening it was filled with new arrivals. At twilight, the air above the river to the north was marked by a red glow from the reflections of the multiplying campfires. Chicagoans often stopped to watch and listen as the subdued excitement of a hundred conversations rose like a murmuring zephyr from the crowded prairie. Chicago's town crier, carrying a lamp and a bell to aid his quest for lost children, was frequently to be seen peering dutifully at the faces of the children in the throng around the camp ground. Every morning camp was broken early and the wagons started moving slowly down the town's main streets toward one of the roads leading over the prairie and swamp to the west. On the sides of the sturdy, big-ribbed wagons were the familiar slogans of "We'll Get Thar," "Reach It or Die," the ambitious "Pike's Peak or Bust" and, by one scribbler more ambitious than most, a line from a popular tune—"Plenty of Gold in the World I'm Told—On the Banks of the Sacramento."

The more prosperous among the arrivals preferred to come on a lake ship rather than put up with being bounced over "2,000 miles of connecting routes" of the Frink and Walker stagecoaches. The lake traffic was of such importance that most hotels were equipped with cupolas on the roof from which observers watched for incoming vessels and dispatched the hotel omnibus to the dock to pick up incoming guests.

Chicago's first hotel of any elegance was the Lake House, constructed of brick (then a rarity) at the corner of Rush and North Water Streets. It brought for the first time the novelties of napkins, toothpicks, printed menus and a French chef. Such touches of style were not without dangers. In 1838, the hotel manager announced a party for "the whole set of 200 North Side aristocrats." There was Bordeaux claret, champagne and oranges and grapes it required weeks to get from the East. (One early restaurateur made a buggy trip to Cleveland and waited two weeks to get a supply of fresh oysters.) The last dish which the Lake House manager put before his guests was new to most of them—it consisted of a piece of lemon peel floating in a tumbler of water and was served with a small glass bowl. Most of the guests thought it was an effete form of lemonade and drank it. To their consternation, they saw Mrs. John Kinzie, literally the first woman of Chicago, dip her fingers in the glass and let the water trickle over her hands in the bowl. Such incidents had not been eliminated by the 1850's. A visiting magazine correspondent, dining at the Briggs House where young Philip Henrici was introducing the city to fancy pastries, found that he might have as his "confectionery" or dessert a dish described by the printer as "Glass E. Jenny Lind." Pointing out that the same dish existed elsewhere as "Glace Jenny Lind," the writer nonetheless conceded the Chicago version was more "phonographic, Websterian and independent."

During the 1850's, the Lake House was replaced in popular favor by the Sherman House at the corner of Randolph and Clark and the Tremont House that seemed reasonably secure at Lake and Dearborn after having been burned down twice in the preceding ten years. Among the guests who stopped at the Sherman House was Ralph Waldo Emerson, who found it fit for a philosopher. He wrote his friend Thomas Carlyle that "it shows no signs of the rough and uncouth." On a later visit he added that the people who came to the hotel were "very earnest and active." He found many of them "quite intelligent," a fact he explained by their "being brought up in the East." Emerson also reported to Carlyle that the rooms at the Sherman House were lighted with gas, "and so, unlike English taverns, there is no charge for candles. I am told there is a bathroom on every floor and the hotel is four stories high. These bathrooms are at the disposal of the guests, a nominal charge being made for towels and soap; but if you supply your own soap and towels, there is no charge for the use of the water."

When elevators, or vertical railways as they were then called, were first

LAKE STREET FROM DEARBORN STREET, 1839, *by N. Roswell Gilford.* The building on the corner is the Tremont House

CHICAGO IN 1845

introduced, they were restricted to the use of the guests; luggage was not permitted. Trunks and suitcases still had to be carried by porters up and down five or six flights of stairs. To summon the elevator, guests had the choice of shouting down the shaft or banging on the wire cage with their room key. In less elegant hostelries, there was no central heating and an overnight guest was required to pay a special fee for a fire as well as for his soap and towel. Often he would have to retire by the light of a kerosene lamp. In such hotels, if warm water were desired, it was necessary to tip the chambermaid who would then fetch a pitcher from the kitchen. The frontier quality of life in Chicago was dramatized for one fair visitor when she found on the table in the "ladies' parlor" of her modest hotel "two rifles, a pistol and a powder flask." In her room, a buffalo skin took the place of the customary blanket.

The portrait artist, G. P. A. Healy, who arrived in 1850, found all the city "in a somewhat rough stage." Healy penned a Lincolnesque portrait of Chicago as "an overgrown youth whose legs and arms are too long for his clothes and who scarcely knows how to dispose of his lank awkward body. The city stretched along the lake shore and out on the prairie, unfinished, ragged and somewhat uncouth as yet." He found "The streets were abominably paved; the sidewalks, raised high above the level of the streets, were composed of rough planks, often out of repair so that one had to pick one's way carefully for fear of accidents. Big nails seemed placed there on purpose to catch in the women's dresses; and as the hideous fashion of crinolines or hoops as they were called, had just reached the Far West, many were the falls occasioned by these nails. The mud was so deep in bad weather that from side to side rickety boards served as unsafe bridges and the unfortunate hordes waded laboriously along as best they could."

The mud was probably the most famous topic of conversation in early Chicago. It was also a barrier to the development of a genteel society. The wheels of carriages could not always cope with the persistent muck. When the ladies went calling, it was frequently necessary for them to gather up their finery and huddle in the back of a sturdy wagon or a potato cart whose wheels would not break in the mud. On arrival, the cart or wagon would be backed up to the doorstep so that the visitor could step directly into the house. One frustrated young lady, confined to her house by the mud, composed her own soliloquy that compensates in graphic detail for what it lacks in poetic virtues.

March 7, 1868

Dearest Cousin

I should have written long before
But trouble entered at my door
And with it I am quite bowed o'er,
                    The mud.

I strove to visit you last week
But went no farther than the street
Ere I was buried up complete
                    The mud.

All whom I met wore faces new
Bespattered all and sad to view
With skirts most heavy laden too
                    The mud.

As home from school the children came
I durst not call them one by name
To tell my own I tried in vain
                    The mud.

Indoors all things with blackness spread
E'en to our butter and our bread
And out doors nigh up to your head
                    The mud.

I looked within the glass today
But frightened, hasted fast away
My beautous face was inky clay
                    The mud.

Afflictions not from ground arise
If that is so, I have no eyes
You'll not see me until it dries,
                    The mud.

With the exception of the high ground around Fort Dearborn, most of Chicago was located on a drained marsh. In earlier years, when the lowest sections were covered with flood waters, Indians paddled canoes from the Desplaines River to the South Branch of the Chicago River and down that sluggish stream to Lake Michigan. In the winter, it was still possible to skate for miles over the frozen prairies and swamps to the west. The entire city was cut by gullies and inlets leading to the river. In some seasons enough water stood in the gully at State Street for guests at the Tremont House to sit on the front steps and shoot the ducks that swooped down on the water.

With the rapid growth of the city, various plans were advanced to defeat the mud. None was successful until a decision was reached to build an entirely new surface. The South Division, as the South Side was known, was about ten feet higher than the downtown area and provided much of the dirt for elevating the business streets. Fort Dearborn, the only high spot in the central district, was torn down so that the land on which it stood could be carted to Randolph Street and bring that thoroughfare up to the new level. Some streets were raised as much as ten feet in a process that required twenty years to complete and left Chicago with a legacy of uneven sidewalks for another generation.

But as the streets went up, the buildings appeared to go down. The effect on the two-story courthouse was so depressing that a new third story and cupola were added so that it would rise far enough above the new surface to achieve a suitable height and dignity. Such expensive alterations were not practicable for most buildings and many viewed the raising of the streets as a calamity. A young man who saw it as an opportunity was a Yankee cabinet-maker, George M. Pullman. He had heard of the problem while he was helping to move buildings to allow for the widening of the Erie Canal. Shortly after coming to Chicago, Pullman undertook (with two other contractors) to raise an entire block of buildings on Lake Street at the same time. Pullman and his collaborators placed six thousand jackscrews under the buildings in the block and hired a small army of six hundred men to turn the screws. At a signal, each man gave the eight or more screws of which he was in charge a half-turn, raising the buildings a fraction of an inch. As the block rose slowly into the air, it was shored up by timbers. In this way the block, with its sidewalk, was raised four feet into the air in a period of four days without interrupting the business of any of the stores in the block. When the new foundations were ready, the buildings were lowered by the same gentle method. Acting alone, Pullman later engaged five hundred men and raised the Tremont House by the same means.

Others were also employing these same methods. All over the city buildings rose out of the holes into which the new street grades had plunged them. Not all the buildings were lifted up. Some were shifted to new locations and the sight of a building rolling down the street was a normal part of the day's street traffic. A visitor counted nine houses in one day being shifted out of the business district. One of the peripatetic dwellings was partially occupied by a cigar store whose proprietor stood in the entryway puffing a

ENTIRE BLOCK ON LAKE STREET BEING RAISED TO A HEIGHT OF FOUR
FEET, 1857, *by Edward Mendel*

cigar and ready to serve his customers while the move was under way. Uncertainty about how high the street grades might go led many builders to erect foundations that rose high above either the new or the old level. A result of this practice was the development of the "Chicago cottage" with the front porch and main entrance at the second-floor level. Long after there was any possibility that the street grades might catch up to these elevated houses, the style continued to be a popular one in Chicago.

Uncertainty over the height of the streets led to a notorious capriciousness among Chicago sidewalks. Builders with varying ideas about the height of the new grade constructed their walks at different levels. Frequently it was necessary to walk from one sidewalk level to another several times in a single block, a hazard not without problems for the hoopskirted women. It was with justification that periodic signs warned the pedestrian to "Use Your Intellect." In a small visitor's guide, aptly titled "Tricks and Traps of Chicago," feminine tourists were cautioned about "sidewalk oglers" who loitered near these sidewalk stairs hoping to catch the sight of a lady's limb. The author gave a hint of some keen scrutiny on his own part by saying that "it was the remark of observant travelers that in no American city do the ladies present more divine charms of limb than those of Chicago." He attributed this on the basis of "strictly scientific principles" to the fact that Chicago ladies had so much exercise in going up and down the steps in the sidewalks. The space under the sidewalks was used for a number of purposes, though in popular conversation this area was chiefly noted as the abode of gargantuan rats. On the lake front, where the waters touched Michigan Avenue, the area under the walk was used as a mooring and shelter for rowboats. On the North Side, one ambitious citizen was found by a revenue officer to have dislodged the rats and installed an illicit distillery under the walk.

FRINK & WALKER STAGE OFFICE, by W. E. S. Trowbridge

The streets were always crowded with a motley and colorful traffic. Carriages drawn by handsome horses passed side by side with creaking wagons drawn by stolid oxen. On almost every street were to be seen the horse-drawn omnibuses of Franklin Parmelee. Parmelee, who a few years before had been a clerk on a lake steamer, first introduced his coaches on Wabash Avenue. Successful in this enterprise, he formed another company which provided baggage vans to pick up luggage for the hotels. Soon he was a wealthy man. Conscious of his new eminence, he ordered the portraits of the members of his family painted on the panels of his coaches. They were soon dubbed "Parmelee's family coaches"; when all of them were drawn up before the Sherman House, Chicagoans pointed out Mr. Parmelee and all the little Parmelees, one of them a young girl whose luxuriant tresses covered half the side of the bus.

Riders on horseback were a common sight, among them hunters who rode powerful and spirited horses held in check by large metal bits and a tight rein. Most of these frontier men had pistols in their holsters; they rode in high-peaked saddles with short stirrups and long Spanish spurs shining against highly polished saddles and boots. Frequently knives were stuck in their belts and light rifles slung over their shoulders. The hunter and his game bag were as common as the truck farmer and his produce wagon. Wild fowl hung in the doorways of the meat commission houses on South Water Street in profusion—teal, partridge, jacksnipe, quail, prairie chicken and grouse—all of it to be bought for at most $2 a dozen while on the walls nearby hung the carcasses of deer and bear.

The buildings which lined the streets could not be identified by any dominating style of architecture. A correspondent of the London *Times* described them as "an extraordinary melange of the Broadway of New York and little shanties—of Parisian buildings mixed with backwoods life." Most of the store fronts were covered with signs distinguished more for their boldness and noticeability than style. Frequently only the first floor of the building was used for business purposes. The upper floors were converted into dormitories for the young men who were crowding into the young city with the hopes of making a fortune. That the streets were not completely bleak was attributable to the trees, of which there was an abundance even in the business district.

Looking down upon the city from the new Courthouse tower the visitor saw frequent patches of green among the buildings. Houses and churches alike were set in the midst of wide lawns or under the sheltering shade of elm, cottonwood, ash and linden trees. The land at the edge of town burst forth each summer with a profusion of prairie flowers. To Sarah Margaret Fuller these brilliant flowers, "which gemmed and gilt the grass . . . between the low oakwood and the narrow beach near the blue lake, stimulated a sort of fairyland exultation." Frederika Bremer, another early tourist, told of seeing the prairies splendid with sunflowers "four yards high" and asters which "grew above my head." Each month the prairies were covered with a different class of flowers—"in spring white, then blue and (in summer) mostly of a golden yellow."

The pastoral quality of the surrounding prairies was in direct contrast to the hustling commerce of the rapidly growing town. With the accumulation of greater wealth there were changes in the social life as well. "There is a good deal of style here," a newly arrived young lady reported to her cousin back East, "and considerable rivalry among the leaders of the town—the two most prominent don't speak." A hint of other improvements is also given in the letter. "Things are not so bad now," the correspondent cheerfully concluded. "The walking is pretty fair and ladies do not apprehend, in stepping out of doors, the loss of a shoe." For Chicago, it was a step in the right direction.

The Yankee Out West

In 1847, Chicago was ready for its first great convention. The leaders who sent out the call for the meeting called it The River and Harbor Convention, but its purpose was much wider than that of attempting to persuade President James K. Polk to develop the rivers and harbors of the Northwest. On the opening day three thousand delegates from eighteen of the twenty-nine states in the Union assembled in a huge tent erected on the courthouse square to consider "whatever matters pertain to the prosperity of the West." The resolutions the delegates passed had little effect on President Polk who thought it unconstitutional to use Federal money to develop the country's internal resources. But in the dispatches which the editors at the convention sent back to their papers was the first recognition of the importance of the port at the foot of Lake Michigan.

Thurlow Weed, a big man in New York politics and journalism, wrote to his Albany *Journal* that the Chicago meeting was the "largest deliberative body ever assembled" and predicted that "in ten years Chicago will be as big as Albany," a boast which was no more than an understatement. Equally enthusiastic was another New York editor, Horace Greeley, who was most impressed by Chicago's hospitality and particularly by the grand parade. He wrote the New York *Tribune* that "though the route traversed was short in deference to the heat of the weather, the spectacle was truly magnificent. The citizens of Chicago furnished the most imposing part of it—the Music, the Military, the Ships on Wheels, ornamented Fire Engines, etc. I never witnessed anything so superb as the appearance of some of the Fire Companies with their Engines drawn by led horses, tastefully caparisoned. Our New York firemen must try again; they have certainly been outdone." Among those whose presence was particularly noted by Greeley at the convention was Abraham Lincoln, "a tall specimen of an Illinoisan, just elected to Congress from the only Whig district in the state."

The stories of Chicago's progress were confirmed by the conversation of travelers returning to the East through the Erie Canal. It had been the opening of the Erie Canal in 1825 which had actually started the great migration to Chicago. The canal was the principal link in a new water route for commerce that was obvious to the eye on any map. It led from the Erie Canal through the Great Lakes to the Chicago River and then by the Illinois and Michigan Canal to the Illinois River and down the Mississippi to the great ports of St. Louis and New Orleans. Chicago, the gateway to the canal, lay at the natural junction of the two great inland waterways of the United States. The stories of the fortunes that were to be made in the rapidly growing city stirred the imagination of such ambitious New Englanders as George M. Pullman. Throughout New York State and New England other young men were heading west. Not all set their goal for Chicago but most planned at least to take a look at it. The greater part of those in this migration traveled light. Their assets were a small sack of savings, a letter of recommendation and a yen for adventure, preferably profitable. More than a few were resolute, tight lipped and tighter fisted, bent on making a killing in the city where millionaires could be made overnight. Quill pens at registry desks in the second- and third-floor dormitories of the business district scratched the names of the eastern seaboard's first families among those of more humble origin. So great was the influx that the newly-elected county commissioners established ceiling prices for the protection of travelers. Tavern keepers were ordered to charge no more than 25 cents for a half-pint of wine, rum or brandy; 12½ cents was the top price for a half a pint of whiskey or a night's lodging and 25 cents the limit for breakfast or supper. It was the city's first melting pot and into it went all sorts of men, including horse thieves, land speculators, and, as one chronicler put it, "other birds of passage—mostly vultures." Most of the new arrivals from New England were not "birds of passage" but eager young men whose leaving led one Yankee editor to protest the loss of the "most vital elements of progress and our future good condition."

Throughout the 1850's, this Yankee Exodus, as Stewart Holbrook was to call it, continued. Many a New England village was to see the prospects of its own future sacrificed to the greater promises of the West. The character of Chicago early reflected the objectives of these New England emigrants. The "Anglo-Saxo-Yankees," as they were called by the Chicago newspapers, ranged in viewpoint from stern moralists indoctrinated with the precepts of Puritanism to sharp speculators whose ethical antecedents were traceable to the Yankee horse trader. These men more than any others were the leaders of Chicago. When a visitor talked of meeting a Chicagoan, he usually meant he was talking to a transplanted Yankee. Of the first thirty-two mayors, twenty were from New England.

A Yankee who came early to Chicago was William Butler Ogden. He came west in 1835 as a representative of his brother-in-law Charles Butler, who had invested $100,000 in Chicago property he had never seen. Ogden found the land ankle deep in water and wrote that the purchase had been one of the "grossest folly." Determined to salvage what he could, he made a methodical survey of the land; by the time the summer sun baked the area dry, he was ready to auction it off. The sale caused him to revise his original opinion of the investment; one-third of the property sold for more than the original cost. Ogden decided to abandon an incipient political career that had already won him a term in the New York legislature and to cast his lot with a city where even swampland could be made to produce a fortune.

Two years later Ogden was elected Chicago's first mayor and throughout most of his life he was to remain its foremost citizen. Self-reliant, he was not willing to wait for the city to act when improvements were needed. He designed and built the first swinging drawbridge over the Chicago River. To enhance the value of the real estate he owned, he and his clients constructed nearly a hundred miles of streets on the North and West Sides and put in bridges where they were needed, including two over the Chicago River. He was preparing to dig a tunnel under the river at Washington Street when the city agreed to do it. Chicago's growth could be measured by his investments: in 1844 he bought a tract of land for $8,000; eight years later he sold it for three million. When work on the Illinois and Michigan Canal was stopped for lack of funds, he saw that the necessary bonds were issued and the money raised. Then, in the same year the canal was opened, he was ready with another project that within a generation was to render the canal obsolete: he built Chicago's first railroad.

The year 1848 had been an important one for the city. For the first time it had been linked with the East by telegraph. Then, after twelve years of intermittent construction, had come the opening of the Illinois and Michigan Canal and the realization of Louis Joliet's dream of a continuous waterway to the Mississippi. Finally, in the fall, had come the first railroad; a second-hand locomotive and two cars made a run of five miles to the west over the tracks of Ogden's Galena and Chicago Union Railroad. Ogden had

CHAMBER OF COMMERCE, 1865

not waited for the railroads to reach Chicago from the East but had shipped in his locomotive by water so that he could start his trains running toward the West in the future of which he so confidently believed.

Another of the Anglo-Saxo-Yankees was Potter Palmer, who made his fortune in a dry-goods store before he was forty and sold out to another new arrival from Pittsfield, Massachusetts, named Marshall Field. Not content to be idle, Palmer invested in real estate along State Street and by his leadership made it the main thoroughfare of Chicago. From Blandsford, Massachusetts (by way of Michigan City, Indiana), came three Blair brothers; Chauncey, Lyman and William. Washington P. Brink, a Yankee from Vermont, set himself up in the business of delivering parcels of any value. A newcomer from Maine was William Wallace Kimball, who thought there was a need in the young town for another dealer in pianos and organs. A Yankee packer, Philip D. Armour, found Milwaukee too small for him after the Civil War and moved to Chicago. He made a trip East in 1865 to sell pork for future delivery at $40 a barrel to eastern speculators who thought the war was nowhere near an end and that pork was due to rise to $60. After Appomattox, Armour delivered the pork and collected his $40 a barrel on meat he was buying for $18. In a single stroke of business, he had become a multimillionaire and lent credence to the legend that the smart Yankees had gone West.

Many of the migrant Yankees were first settlers in Chicago. The first lawyer, Russell E. Heacock, came from Litchfield, Connecticut. The first city prosecutor was John Dean Caton, who had come West via boat and wagon from New York, only to have the town's first law violator jump bail bond and disappear so that the city's first law case could never be prosecuted. The first druggist was Philo Carpenter, who came from the Hoosac Mountains of Massachusetts and brought with him a conviction that alcohol should be taken only for medicinal purposes; he also became one of the town's earliest temperance crusaders. One of the early meat packers as well as the first ship owner, the first lumber dealer and the first insurance salesman was Gurdon Saltonstall Hubbard of Middletown, Connecticut, who passed through Fort Dearborn initially in 1818 when he was on his way to the Mississippi as a sixteen-year-old fur buyer for John Jacob Astor and the American Fur Company. The New England lawyers could scarcely be counted, though outstanding among them was Jonathan Young Scammon from Lincoln County, Maine, whom history credits with introducing the boutonniere as an acceptable article of masculine wearing apparel in Chicago.

The newspapers and magazines, many of them Yankee owned or edited, were fond of speculating on the causes of this dominance of Chicago by a relatively small group of men. *The Chicago Magazine* said it thought "The Yankee out West is an enlarged and improved edition of a specimen of the species man. . . . Had there first been no East, rigid, stern, homes strict and puritanical, a land where industry is made a prime virtue and accumulation like unto it there could have been no West, fertile, expansive, liberal . . ." It was the magazine's opinion that when the Yankee "departed the home of his maturity he carried with him his outfit of religion, morality, perseverance, cuteness and tact; and when transferred to the area of favorable circumstances it is enlarged to the attitude of the best specimen of man." The definition of a "real genuine Yankee" by the Chicago *Times* was less respectful. The editor found the Chicago Yankees "full of animation, checked by moderation, guided by determination and supported by education." A Yankee, "just caught," he said, "will not be deficient in the following qualities:

He is self-denying, self-relying, always trying and into everything prying.

He is a lover of piety, propriety, notoriety and temperance society.

He is a dragging, gagging, bragging, striving, thriving, swiping, jostling, bustling, wrestling, musical, quizzical, astronomical, philosophical and comical sort of character, whose manifest destiny is to spread civilization to the remotest corners of the earth, with an eye always on the lookout for the main chance.

It was this interest in the "main chance" that characterized the early

Chicagoan in all that he did. Joseph T. Ryerson, son of a pioneer lumber merchant, was to recall later that "each one seemed to have but one object in life and that was to strive for the main chance, the means to live and get along, so that in this respect all were very much on a level." Frugality and hard work were the only virtues recognized. Very little was spent on outward show. A man's character was of more importance than the size of his bank account or his business. Banks that refused to extend credit to the city of Chicago or the Galena and Chicago Union Railroad handed over money readily in return for no more than William B. Ogden's personal note.

The life and philosophy of Ogden were in many respects typical. In a terse autobiography he recorded that he had been "born close to a sawmill, was early left an orphan, graduated from a log schoolhouse and at fourteen fancied I could do anything I turned my hand to and that nothing was impossible." There was very little in his later life to dispute this early appraisal of his potentialities. When Ogden had been refused capital for his first railroad by both the bankers of Boston and the merchants of Chicago, he drove up and down the Fox River valley with his Yankee friend, Jonathan Young Scammon, persuading the farmers to buy stock in the railroad that would be serving them.

A southern exception to the Yankee rule among the early builders of Chicago was Cyrus H. McCormick, who was born on a farm in Rutland County, Virginia. Even McCormick had his debt to the Yankees, for when he brought his reaper plant to Chicago it was William B. Ogden who advanced $25,000 to get the factory started. And the woman the reaper king

CHICAGO IN 1849 as seen from the top of St. Mary's College

eventually married was Nettie Fowler, whom he brought West from Jefferson County, New York.

Because of the few women in the community and the much smaller number who had matrimonial qualifications, "going East for a bride" was a regular occurrence. When Dr. William Mason, the Boston pianist, visited Chicago in the 1850's, he was surprised to be greeted at a reception by a crowd of predominantly young girls. "Where are your married women?" he asked. His youthful reception committee told him they represented the married women; they had been girls in New England, but were all married now to "our fellows." The arrival of a new bride was an event of special significance for the local dressmakers, who were frequently among her first callers. Having examined the bride's trousseau, a seamstress would then go from door to door, like a census taker or tax collector, soliciting orders based on the latest fashions from the East.

Though these early Yankees believed in "everything at high pressure" in their business lives, they tried to create in their home surroundings some of the atmosphere of the New England communities they had left. There was a large colony of Anglo-Saxo-Yankees on the North Side, living in large frame houses situated amid spacious yards and lawns. The residents prided themselves on their gardens and shade trees and spoke with proprietary pride of the motto in the city's seal, "Urbs in Horto." This, they explained to the Latinless or curious, might be translated freely as "The Garden City."

The house of William B. Ogden dominated this area much as its owner dominated the business community. The house was the only one in the block; from its place in the center of the square it looked south over another block-square area of trees and grass known, not surprisingly, as Ogden's Grove. A broad piazza extended across the south front of the house and on the north was a conservatory always bright with flowers. Near the large stables was a fruit house in which Ogden raised exotic grapes, peaches, apricots and figs in a perpetually maintained artificial climate. Around the house, maple, oak, cherry, elm, birch and hickory trees were festooned with climbing vines. The entire grounds were handsomely landscaped with ornamental shrubs, climbing roses and other flowers. Ogden's home was a stopping place for many of the celebrities who passed through the city— Daniel Webster, William Cullen Bryant, Margaret Fuller, Ralph Waldo Emerson and others were entertained there. The artist G. P. A. Healy, whom Ogden had persuaded to leave the court of France for the crude conveniences of early Chicago, ranked Ogden as a conversationalist with the three best Healy had ever known—Louis Philippe of France, John Quincy Adams and Dr. Orestes A. Brownson, the New England religious polemicist and iconoclast.

Adding to the pastoral quality of the neighborhood was the custom of

RUSH STREET BRIDGE IN 1861, by *Edwin Whitefield*. McCormick's works are at the center left

keeping a cow for the family milk supply. Each day the cows would be led to and from free pasturage at the edge of town. The city's wealthiest citizens had their own herd of bovine commuters—though the herdsman of this Yankee flock had more the aspect of a Cossack than a cowherd. His coat and cap were in the Cossack style and a generous beard plus an untrimmed crop of long black hair gave him the appearance of wearing a beard both fore and aft. With his trousers tucked in his rough boots he rode north on Rush Street each morning blowing a brass horn as a signal for his patrons to let their cows into the streets. As the herd was driven home in the evening, each cow turned from habit into her own dooryard. Almost every family of any affluence had its own cow. The penchant for milk extended to the boarding houses where an early guest found that "any man who calls for milk at breakfast or supper is generally called 'a cussed Yank.'"

Soon after Cyrus McCormick had successfully established his reaper factory, he sent for his brother Leander to help him in the business. Leander and his wife were also to provide a home for Cyrus, who had not yet found his own bride. Mrs. Leander McCormick was not long in recording her impression of Chicago. "A great many Yankees here," she wrote. "Mrs. Hamilton [a Kentuckian], does not like them much. She says that we must have a Southern society and let the Yankees, Germans, Irish, French all alone." Even though the McCormicks were among the wealthiest of Chicagoans, their home was furnished on utilitarian principles rather than for ostentation. Mrs. McCormick wrote proudly to Virginia that there was "a beautiful flowered red and green carpet in the chamber and parlor, and when the folding doors are open the stove in the chamber will heat both rooms . . . I would like to have a sofa and a pretty lamp in the parlor and think likely we will get them before long. The stairs are carpeted and the passage floor

MICHIGAN TERRACE (Terrace Row), looking toward the Central Depot, 1863, by *Edwin Whitefield*

has oilcloth on it. The dining room is not furnished except with nice chairs and tables; my dishes and eatables are kept in the pantry. There are three rooms upstairs, one finely furnished for Cyrus, the others will not be furnished till we get our boxes of beds and bedclothes."

The most elaborately landscaped of the North Side residences was that of S. H. Kerfoot, a real-estate dealer, whose carriage drives were said to be more solidly constructed than the city's streets. The grounds around his house were ornamented with artificial ponds, rustic bridges, fine greenhouses and all the other accouterments of new wealth. Another of the elegant homes was that of Julian Rumsey, an early mayor, who moved to the Near North Side shortly after his marriage in 1848 in the face of the strenuous objections of his father-in-law, who felt the location at 40 East Huron was "too far out in the woods."

A hazard to be faced by all who lived on the North Side was the crossing of the Chicago River on bridges manned by notoriously unreliable bridge tenders. The river skyline was thick with masts of vessels. The frequent passage of these ships in and out of the river made the bridge tender a functionary with considerable power. He was the most unruly member of the city's staff and until 1868 the city had no control over him. In that year an ordinance was passed limiting the amount of time a bridge could be open to ten minutes, but the boats still ruled as tyrants of the river. An intoxicated skipper who, according to the official report, "was coming up the river with full sheet besides his own three sheets in the wind" had sailed directly over a low float bridge. Another time James Dole was driving across the Rush Street Bridge at the same time a herd of cattle was passing in the opposite direction. The bridge tender swung open the bridge in response to the whistle of a tugboat and stampeded the frightened cattle toward one end of the bridge. Their combined weight tipped the bridge, dumping Dole, his fine buggy and span of horses and the cattle all in the water. Dole was rescued, but the bridge was ruined. In a lawsuit against the city a plaintiff complained that another bridge tender had delayed so long in opening a bridge that a damaged vessel being towed up the river had sunk for a second time.

Rivaling the North Side as a fashionable residential area was Michigan Avenue. From Dearborn Park at Randolph and Washington, south to Park Row at Twelfth Street, the avenue was a succession of imposing residences. A large number were constructed of Athens marble, a deceptively named limestone that had been discovered during excavations for the Illinois and Michigan Canal. The most exclusive area on the avenue was Terrace Row, a group of three-story buildings largely occupied by pioneer families. The showplaces of the street were the large new home of William Blair and the "Bishop's Palace," the home of the Reverend Dr. O'Regan. Chicagoans claimed that "in architectural proportions" the latter was not "surpassed by any residence in the West."

Probably the most unusual residence of any of these early Anglo-Saxo-Yankees was that of "Long John" Wentworth, who made his home on a five-thousand-acre stock farm near Summit and tried to pattern his way of life after that of Mount Vernon and Monticello. Before he retired to his life of statesmanlike detachment, however, he was to stride in giant steps through an important part of the Chicago story.

JOHN WENTWORTH

3

Long John and His Devils

LONG JOHN WENTWORTH was for twenty-five years editor of the Chicago
Democrat, twelve years a member of Congress from the Chicago district
and twice mayor of the city. The Yankee virtues and shortcomings were not
concentrated in Long John but rather expanded. He was a giant of a man,
six feet six inches in height. He had been too impatient to wait for a wagon
to carry him into Chicago in 1836. He preferred to stride barefoot into
Chicago carrying giant shoes fourteen inches long and six inches wide and
clinging to a jug of whiskey "with which to bathe my blistered feet."

On his first day in the city, Long John observed everything that a Yankee
might be interested in, from morality to economics. "Land is worth $40
per square foot," he reported to his sister. "The young men are mostly those
who have made a fortune out of nothing and are consequently quite dissipated. Such a place for smoking I never saw. Out of 150 boarding at this
house, not ten refuse to smoke. Here, as also at Detroit, ardent spirit is
always put upon the table for dinner and most all take their drink."

In the history of Chicago there was never another man cut to so individual a pattern as John Wentworth. He said bluntly he refused to be "one

of your bell livers." He said he "never had and never will live on time. Got no use for call bells, dinner bells or alarm clocks. My doctrine is this: eat when you're hungry, drink when you're thirsty, sleep when you're sleepy and get up when you're ready." It could be said of Long John that he was thirsty fairly often; his favorite beverage was brandy and he drank from a pint to a quart of "ardent spirit" every day of his long life. He spent more time in Chicago hotels than he did in his Summit home and the best table in the hotel dining room was always reserved for him alone. He planned his meals in his room, placing a mark on the menu before each dish he wanted. When he was ready to eat, he went down to the dining room expecting to find every dish he ordered—sometimes there were as many as thirty or forty—on the table ready for him. That the soup was cold or the ice cream melting did not bother him; most important was the fact no time had been spent in waiting, which he regarded as an intolerable waste.

When Long John was a member of Congress during the controversy over the Oregon question, there was some fear that in a war with England the British might take Fort Mackinac, use it as a base and attack the Lake Michigan towns. As Long John proudly and publicly traced his ancestry back to Thomas Wentworth, Earl of Stafford (who through the weakness of Charles I had been beheaded on Tower Hill), his political enemies began to make an issue of this English connection. Long John, who said he was "desiring to show my constituents that I was fully alive to their interests," made a speech in Congress so vigorously opposing the English view that the New York *Herald* printed a caricature showing the British lion being chased by Long John Wentworth. It was the first show of hostility between Chicago and the British Empire.

Although Wentworth was elected to Congress for six terms as a Democrat, his greatest exploits occurred during the two terms he was in the mayor's chair as a Republican. He was completely independent and honest, though his yearning for prompt action on every issue sometimes led him to ignore the normal forms of the democratic process. He was the city's first "strong-man" mayor; if he did not change Chicago's heart, at least he made a considerable difference in its face. His predecessor as mayor had been Thomas Dyer, whose inaugural parade had included a group of "female convivials" in open carriages, escorted by what the newspapers reported as "a miscellaneous crowd of men." The scandalized city, wishing to correct the situation but not wanting to be distracted from the more important business of making a dollar, voted Wentworth into office with a confidence that he would take care of the matter personally.

The new mayor immediately enunciated a tougher policy for criminals. He said that prostitutes posing as the mothers of large families had in many cases secured pardons for known criminals and warned that no such tricks would get his sympathy. He did not think criminals merited the luxury of idleness in jail and put them to work upon the city's streets, wearing a ball and chain and supervised by an armed overseer. The city had not wanted to go quite this far in setting an example for criminals and public protests forced him to abandon the practice. His political opponents were never to let him forget it.

The mayor's spear of righteousness was dulled but not broken. He next declared war on The Sands, a collection of tumble-down shanties along the lake shore on the North Side. The area housed a collection of the worst kinds of cheap lodging houses, saloons, gambling dens and bordellos. The pride of the community included such characters as Mike O'Brien, alternately a burglar and prize fighter; his son, Mike, Jr., a pickpocket and pander for his four sisters; John Hill and his wife, Mary, who are credited with being the first couple in Chicago to work the badger game on a gullible male. At Freddy Webster's, one of the worst of the houses, there was an inmate who, it was said, had been neither sober nor out of the house for five years and who had not had her clothes on for three. She died on March 8, 1857, from what the coroner called "intemperance."

Because the property in the area was involved in several lawsuits, none of the owners was willing to risk an eviction. Timidity gave way to boldness when the rights of one of the owners were purchased by the ever at hand William B. Ogden. He promptly told the occupants in his buildings to get

THE "LONG JOHN" FIRE ENGINE

out or he would tear their places down. At the same time, he offered to buy any of the other buildings in the area whose owners were willing to sell. The occupants turned down Ogden's bid, giving Mayor Wentworth a new opportunity to enter the jousting field as the representative of civic virtue.

Ignoring the legal procedures with which Ogden had been concerned, Long John told the residents to get out by April 20, 1857, or their houses would be burned down. The threat to set fire to the houses was a shrewd strategy that enabled the mayor to bring to the scene as his allies the members of the city's volunteer fire department.

A few of the fire companies were manned by scions of the first families and membership was as exclusive as in any private club. Others were made up of rough and ready volunteers who "ran wid de masheen" and worked the brakes, or the pumps. For their services this group enjoyed the privilege of chopping up the shanties of the poor or a discreet amount of looting in the property of better endowed citizens who needed their assistance. Occasionally the companies would fight over the honor of being first to the fire, stopping to carry on the battle for honors with little concern for the consequences to the flaming buildings of which they were the theoretical protectors. At a fire on Lake Street, which caused a million dollars in damage, the fire fighters were hampered because two engines had been so badly damaged in a battle for a prized silver trumpet that they were unable to be used.

Company No. 6 had its headquarters in the Silver Fountain saloon of its captain, Pat Casey. Casey dispensed a brand of whiskey known as "Casey's No. 6" which was warranted to get the imbiber drunker and incite him to more reckless deeds of daring than any other brand on the market. The company never went to a fire without a supply of its own "Casey's No. 6." Wentworth beamed with pride on all factions; when the city's first steam engine was acquired it was christened "Long John." The next two were named—in accordance with the principles of his political beliefs—"Liberty" and "Economy."

On the morning of April 20th, the mayor, with his fire department in support and flanked by a deputy sheriff and a semi-official posse, marched down to The Sands to carry out his threat. A few of the entrepreneurs had moved their businesses elsewhere but most of the inhabitants knew of no place else they could go. When the mayor arrived, many of the tougher members of the community were absent. They had been lured away by the greater attraction of a dogfight for a $500 purse at the Brighton race track between the dog of Dutch Frank, a Sands brothel owner, and the hound of William Galligher. According to the *Journal* the fight was witnessed by "a large crowd of pimps and bullies."

In the absence of masculine protectors, the girls in the area offered little resistance. They were given a short time to move their furniture into the

UNION STOCKYARDS, 1866

street. Their flimsy buildings were then hooked up to a strong chain and pulled down by a team of horses. A short time later, fire broke out in several of the remaining buildings. The newspapers reported it as an act of spite against the new owner of the property. Chicagoans thought it more plausible the fires had been set by members of the fire department anxious for a little sport before they went home. The spectacular nature of the raid, the notoriety of the area and the method used to tear down the buildings made the raid a subject of conversation all over the West. Local residents did not take such pride in it; they knew the evicted tenants were in business again in another part of the city.

The Sands was not the only vice area. Individuals of sufficient means could patronize Lou Harper's place at 219 Monroe. It was the finest brothel in Chicago, charged the highest prices and was invariably referred to by Madame Harper as The Mansion. Lou Harper's was not for the working-man but for the business and professional class and the rich young man about town. The proprietress attempted to give her business a show of style by attiring her girls in evening gowns rather than the customary chemise. She insisted that all should be introduced by name and did away with the practice of herding the girls into the living room and lining them up for the customer to make his selection.

The most flagrant of the town's "free and easies" was Roger Plant's Under the Willow at the southeast corner of Wells and Monroe Streets. This establishment expanded during the 1860's until it covered half a square block and was dubbed by the police "Roger's Barracks." Roger was a small

Englishman from Yorkshire. His wife, who had borne him twenty children, including several sets of twins, was a huge woman who had grown up on the waterfront in Liverpool and was the actual boss of the place. It was Roger, however, who had chosen the name Under the Willow as an expression of his sentimental side and it was Roger who had painted on every flaring blue shade in the entire series of buildings the large gilt question, "Why not?" a phrase that was repeated frequently on the streets every evening. The police seldom bothered Roger's place. He paid his toll "with extreme regularity" and there was also the practical consideration, as the police expressed it, that trying to raid the barracks would have been "like pulling in an elephant." During the Civil War, Roger made a small fortune. At its close he decided to become a landowner and farmer, explaining that "a country life was best for the children." He also became a patron of the most fashionable race tracks and otherwise "blossomed into respectability." To this Frederic Francis Cook, one of the city's ablest reporters, was to add as a postscript, "Well, why not?"

Still another collection of brothels was to be found on Wells Street. Long John Wentworth, attempting to stamp them out, thundered that "inefficient city officers allowed gamblers to settle and with them came the disciples of Potiphar's wife and that crowd of moral and social outcasts which gamblers instinctively draw around themselves wherever they go." The street was in

HOUGH HOUSE, 1866

such ill repute that the property holders away from the street's vice area sought to obliterate the disgrace to themselves and to Captain William Wells, a hero of the Fort Dearborn Massacre. They petitioned the City Council to change the name to Fifth Avenue, assuming that an affront to New York's most fashionable street was less to be censured than despoiling the name of a Chicago hero.

Another section of the city that Long John wanted to tear down was Conley's Patch, a collection of hundreds of the "dirtiest, vilest, most rickety, one-sided, leaning forward, propped up, tumbled-down, sinking fast, low-roofed and most miserable shanties." It was the worst of several "patches" which came to life during the winter months when the close of navigation on the Great Lakes added thousands of idle sailors to the town's population. Chicago was the foremost grain and lumber market in the country and much of this commerce was carried by water. During the 1860's more than thirteen thousand vessels a year docked at the port. Some of the sailors took winter work in the forests of Wisconsin and Michigan but a larger proportion found temporary quarters in such patches as that of Mother Conley, whom the Chicago Times felt it was in no danger of libeling when it said she was "one of those unfortunate individuals in whom love of liquor is the ruling passion."

Mother Conley was an aging virago who gave the patch its name but its ruler was a powerful procuress known only as the Bengal Tigress. In addition to her other pleasures, the Bengal Tigress loved to fight. When she was in a boisterous mood the men in the patch barred their doors and windows and stayed out of sight. She was reputed to have torn down, single-handed, several of the shanties in one of her rages. The police avoided her as much as possible and when it was necessary to lock her up a sizable squad was sent for the purpose. Fortunately, the police station was nearby in the old Armory at Adams and Franklin so the officers had only a short distance to transport their obstreperous prisoner. Patrol wagons were scarce and police had to bring their victims in as best they could. An officer in the Bridgeport district, faced with the problem of getting Jimmy Kilfoil, an Archer Avenue character, into a cell, loaded the inebriated Jimmy into a wheelbarrow and pushed him the two miles to the Armory.

Police raided the patches and brothels at intervals but with little effect. After one raid, the Tribune reported "police authorities invited a score or two of the demi-monde in the South Division, on Saturday night, to be locked up at the Armory till Sunday morning. The raids were not successful, as usual, many of the girls being absent in places of amusement." The concentration of brothels is indicated by a police report that in one night's raid they had broken up "fourteen dens of infamy and vice" in a two-block area on Clark Street. Gamblers were also targets of the mayor. A short time after the raid on The Sands, Long John led a raid on Burrough's Place, one of the local gambling dens. Two officers were sent around to gain entrance by a back door. When the surprised gamblers fled to the street they found the huge mayor and a squad of police waiting for them. Long John left nothing to chance. He personally supervised the booking of the prisoners. When the gamblers' attorney tried to speak to his clients through the bars of an open window, the mayor seized the lawyer and personally threw him into another cell.

Long John's war on the vice districts did not cause him to neglect what he considered the abuses of the more respectable elements of the city. First to catch his eye were the awnings and signs which the merchants had erected over the downtown sidewalk. It is not known if some of these were hung too low to permit the passage of the six feet six inches of Long John Wentworth, but more diminutive Chicagoans were in agreement that the signs were a menace and an eyesore. Businessmen had also added to the clutter with boxes and display cases on the sidewalks. The mayor decided to put an end to such practices. As his experience with reform had taught him to expect little in the way of co-operation, he undertook to correct the situation himself.

On the night of June 18, 1857, he summoned the police force and gave orders that every overhanging sign, awning, and all posts or other obstruc-

RESULTS OF LONG JOHN WENTWORTH'S SIGN RAID, 1857

tions in the downtown streets were to be removed immediately. As the police started down the street to carry out his command a series of express wagons he had hired to stand by for further orders began to appear out of nearby alleys and livery stables. All the loose signs, awnings and display cases were ripped off and loaded into the wagons. The mayor ordered all of the debris taken to the municipal market building in the center of Randolph Street north of State where the signs were piled up until such time as their owners could retrieve them. The next morning Chicago found the downtown streets free of every obstruction that had been blocking the sidewalks. The merchants complained about the violation of their rights but Long John sensed the public was on his side and refused to let them put the signs or awnings back up. One dentist lost a repulsive set of mechanical false teeth under a glass bell which were capable of "masticating the air for twenty-five days at a time." He refused to claim his property but took the opportunity to advertise that "Long John or one of his imps, or someone else, stole my sign away, but not my official instruments. I remain at 77 Lake Street, Tremont Block." The mayor was also charged with preparing the force for the raid by a generous distribution of bourbon. He admitted that whiskey had been given to the force but denied anyone had been given too much drink on the grounds that he had poured every man's drink personally!

The police who executed this raid were known as the leather-badge force. Their name was derived from the leather insignia that Long John had designed and required them to wear on the plain uniforms made to his specifications. The police were distinguishable only by the heavy canes which they carried during the day and the heavy batons they wielded at night. Instead of whistles, the police were provided with "creakers," such as had been used by the watchmen of London for three centuries.

When John C. Haines succeeded Wentworth as mayor in 1858, the police were given uniforms with a short blue frock coat, a navy blue cap with a gold band and a brass star. When Wentworth returned to the mayor's chair he stripped the force of its finery and restored his plain garb and leather badges. In the name of economy, he reduced the size of the force to a captain, six lieutenants and fifty patrolmen; they were to police a city of more than one hundred thousand. As a result of his refusal to reconsider his action and expand the police force, a law was put through the legislature setting up an independent police board and taking the control of the force out of the mayor's hands.

On the night the new board held its first meeting, Long John called the entire police force to City Hall. At about 2 o'clock in the morning, after the new board had adjourned, the mayor had the force called to attention and made a speech lauding the men as America's finest police. Then he had

CORNER OF LAKE AND STATE STREETS, 1866

a surprise for them. Having learned, he said, that the new board was going to fire them all, he wanted to spare them that humiliation by discharging them himself. The firings were to take place immediately. The mayor's action, which at a minimum was capricious, left the city without police protection until the following morning. The papers, in reporting the episode, charged that the city had been turned over to "burglars, robbers and incendiaries." However, as the lawless elements had no way of anticipating their good fortune, the night passed with only two robberies. The newspapers took consolation in the fact that one of the thefts had occurred at State and Van Buren, "one of the most frequented thoroughfares" in the city.

Early the next morning the police board was hastily called into a special session. A new superintendent of police was appointed and about two dozen patrolmen rehired. Requirements for members of the new force were published soon afterwards. All were required to be more than five feet six inches tall, were forbidden mustaches and required to wear their whiskers "à la militaire." The leather badges vanished forever and the police were given new uniforms, necessary, as the announcement explained, "to distinguish a policeman from a drayman or a baggage wagon driver."

There was never a full explanation from the mayor of why he had fired the force. The *Tribune* charged that it was a sly bit of sabotage to discredit the Republican Party before the impending election. As the police board was predominantly Republican, the paper charged Wentworth was trying to force it to act immediately on the fifteen hundred applications for police jobs. As "19 out of every 20" would have to be disappointed, the majority of the men would tend to side with the Democrats on election day. The *Tribune* concluded an editorial on the episode with the indignant comment that "the offense deserves punishment in the penitentiary, but unfortunately it has not been provided against by statute, for the reason it was not deemed possible that such an act would ever be committed on the same principle that the Spartans had no rule for the punishment of patricide."

In 1861, Long John retired temporarily to his farm at Summit, returning at intervals to serve on public commissions or give the city a bit of advice. He sold his newspaper when he retired from politics. If he wanted an audience he had only to rent a hall and advertise that he was to give a lecture. He always drew a full house. Chicago thought he was a big man, even if he had not been quite the size to change the operations of either the laws or the lawless.

Allan Pinkerton, who had been hired as Chicago's first detective nearly a decade before, also found the task of dealing with the formidable underworld too large. Within a year he said he was "impressed with the importance of establishing a detective agency which would be independent of political influence and by whose efforts the criminal could be punished without fear or personal favor." The city hall was not a favorable climate for such an agency, so he formed a private detective force. Within a short time, most of the buildings in the business district were guarded by a corps of watchmen under his direction. To Chicago's businessmen it was more practicable to buy honesty as they bought everything else than to try to improve the quality of law enforcement through the unpredictable channels of municipal reform.

Attempts at reform were small and sporadic. In 1863 the Chicago Erring Women's Refuge for Reform opened its doors. A few years later a special department of the Washingtonian Home was opened for "female inebriates" in what was formerly the large house of C. J. Hull at Halsted and Polk. By 1870, a need for more constructive measures was felt and a Society for the Promotion of Social Purity was formed to "help the fallen" and study the causes of prostitution. Despite these gestures, however, Chicago remained a place that an editorialist described in the St. Louis *Democrat* as a town of "fast horses, faster men, falling houses and fallen women."

Elegance on a Grand Scale

SOCIETY as it existed in the older communities of the East was unknown in Chicago until after the Civil War. Visitors frequently commented on the absence of any women on the streets. One traveler confessed that "as to the ladies, I did not see them in the West and have not a word to say respecting their beauty." An author in the *Atlantic Monthly* found the streets "very peculiar in not having a lady walking on them—by this I mean that I did not meet a woman who seemed to claim that title or any title much above that of an ordinary domestic."

The only social affairs with any pretensions to elegance were the Bachelors' Assembly Balls at the Tremont House. These were planned and sponsored by the town's young men to repay the families in whose homes they had been entertained (and who might have eligible daughters). The single girls were so few that it was impossible to make up a sizable party with them alone. As a consequence, a bachelor's invitation traditionally included all the feminine members of the family, including the mother.

If there were any divisions among Chicago society during the fifties, they were formed principally by the choice of a church. A few congregations were recognized as aristocratic. Membership or attendance in these was a valid passport to social recognition. On the North Side, fashionable worshippers attended either St. James Episcopal Church, where William B. Ogden was a regular occupant of a pew, or the North Presbyterian Church around the corner. North Presbyterian was known as McCormick's Church because it was so thoroughly dominated by the theology and philanthropy of Cyrus H. McCormick. The most select congregation in the South Division was that of the Second Presbyterian Church at Wabash and Washington. Among its members were such political adversaries as Long John Wentworth and William "Deacon" Bross, one of the owners of the *Tribune*. The church building was erected of tar rock, a blue bituminous limestone that exuded black pitch and resulted in a mottled appearance that caused it to be dubbed the church of the spotted saints.

Many members of the Second Presbyterian found the easy morality of Chicago alien to the principles of their New England upbringing. They were willing to concede the city was the place to make a fortune, but they were not reconciled to what they considered the horrors of living among so much wickedness. After talking the situation over with their minister, the Reverend Dr. Robert Patterson, they embarked on a trip north from Chicago in search of a location for a community where Presbyterian standards of morality would be less threatened. Finally, after following a deer path through heavy groves of trees, the group came to a site near the edge of Lake Michigan where nothing was visible but lake and forest. As the spot seemed to be satisfactorily isolated, it was chosen as the spot for the new village, to be called Lake Forest. Jed Hotchkiss, a landscape architect, was engaged to lay out the town as a model community; the new settlers counted on their own ideas to make it a model of moral rectitude.

The Methodists were also restive about the moral influences of the young city, particularly about the absence of a suitable school in which to train their children. In 1850, a group of young men, all under forty years of age, met in the offices of lawyer Grant Goodrich and outlined plans for a midwest university around which might spring "a community of desirable citizens." There were practical reasons for their hopes of success. Dr. John Evans, who with Orrington Lunt and Goodrich was a leader in developing plans for the university, estimated it would cost a thousand dollars less to educate a son near Chicago than at Yale or Harvard. Lunt thought he had found the ideal site for the university near a grove of oak trees on the lake shore north of the city. The trustees agreed with his choice and on January 28, 1851, the state granted the trustees a charter for the establishment of Northwestern University. It was not until 1855 that the first students were

NORTHWEST CORNER OF LaSALLE AND RANDOLPH STREETS, showing
  Courthouse Square, 1864

enrolled—only ten in number. The students wore a uniform cap while
their two professors appeared in Prince Albert coats and tall silk hats.

It remained to establish a community of desirable citizens. This was also
accomplished by the trustees; they purchased nearly three hundred acres
lying west of the University, laid it out in lots and gave it the name of
Evanston after Dr. John Evans. The original plan had been to name the
new suburb after Lunt, but he refused to leave his house in Chicago where
the waves of Lake Michigan washed almost up to his door. The early commuters from Evanston had little in the way of streets or sidewalks to aid
them. Those who worked in the city carried lanterns to and from the
Evanston station each day. When they boarded the Chicago and Milwaukee
train, pulled by a wood-burning locomotive, they left a row of lanterns
standing on the platform for their return in the evening. The Methodists,
strict believers in temperance, forbade the sale of liquor in the new community. The saloon keepers' association sued to set aside the ban on liquor,
but finally lost its case in the Supreme Court. The Methodists were inclined
to accept the final court hearing as an indication of intervention by Divine
Providence. The lawyer for the distillers and saloon keepers was too intoxicated to speak; Harvey Hurd, the attorney for Evanston, was required
to present both sides to the court. It would have been rather a severe set-
back if he had lost his own case.

39 ELEGANCE ON A GRAND SCALE

In Chicago, the outstanding date on the social calendar was New Year's Day, when the girls received gentlemen callers in a day-long ritual that began at 10 o'clock in the morning. Lists were kept of the number of carefully groomed visitors in white gloves and swallowtails and these records were minutely compared during the next twenty-four hours to see who had triumphed and who had failed. Every house had its own refreshments. This custom added to the arduousness of the day; the callers could eat only so much chicken salad or scalloped oysters, no matter by how lovely a hand it was prepared. Serving of wine was considered "fast," except in the West Division, where the large southern colony often augmented its mahogany sideboard with a decanter of madeira or a bowl of eggnog, a fact that had as much to do with the traffic in that direction as the charm of the southern girls.

Almost all entertaining was done at home. Every party of any size required such an expenditure of energy and planning that few were eager to play the role of hostess. Invitations had to be written in the hostess' own hand and delivered personally. Sending invitations by mail was considered to be the worst of form because of the danger of their getting lost. For many years, Chicagoans refused to trust a message of such importance as a party invitation to a paid messenger. The only concession was to permit the hostess to send the invitation up to the house by her coachman or footman while she sat in the carriage. On the day of the party all the food had to be prepared at home; caterers were not yet considered stylish. In the summer, the girls might wear corsages of prairie flowers but during the winter months flowers could be had only from the single florist who kept a shop and greenhouse south of the city near Cleaverville at Thirty-fifth Street.

Visitors were likely to describe Chicago society as a mushroom aristocracy. Because of the newness of local society, there were many opportunities for sophisticated witnesses to subject it to ridicule. One supercilious visitor from Albany, New York, complained that at a reception given by one of the most prominent men of Chicago, he met "out of a company of thirty-six men, ten pork packers, three butchers, four railroad men, two bankers, one lawyer, eight doctors and a number of clerks." He noted a "prominent fiddler" had come "dressed in swallowtails, a checked vest, green necktie and red gloves." At another party the same fastidious reporter was offended by the sight of "a young man whose parents do a large business in the retail boot and shoe trade who danced with one of the prettiest girls in the room, whilst his cheek was swollen with an enormous quid of tobacco."

There were evidences, however, that Chicago was trying to catch up to the times in both society and style. The German Cotillion, which Empress Eugénie had designed to take the place of schottisches, redowas and polkas for proper French young ladies and their escorts, found its way to Chicago

LaSALLE STREET FROM COURTHOUSE SQUARE, 1866

during the same season it was introduced in New York at the Schermerhorn costume ball. The intricate, formal dance was immediately popular and remained a favorite until the end of the century.

Simplicity was the theme of most of the local styles. Not many years before a good number of Chicago women were riding to church on horseback behind their husbands. They continued to be cautious in adopting fancier ways, particularly as their husbands' reputations in the business community might be damaged if people thought the family's money was going for fancy clothes and other luxuries rather than investments in land. When the *Chicago Magazine of Fashion, Music and Home Reading* was founded to bring culture to Chicago homes, the editors reminded readers its purpose was "to give home fashions; styles that do not involve a great outlay of money and which can be utilized by Western women in their homes." They added with provincial pride that "we omit mentioning many rose-colored or violet-tinted silks or point-lace sets; because the majority of our readers do not wear such articles and we do not want them to look upon such things as necessary either to their comfort or happiness. We would rather be the useful friends of the American representative woman in her family than the protégé of the greatest lady foreign soil ever produced."

The advice of the *Chicago Magazine* was usually of this practical nature. One report was written with special reference to the Chicago weather. "The uncertainty and inclemency of the spring weather interferes sadly with the permanency of a new toilet, since, if one day is warm enough for a parasol, the next demands a resume of cloak and furs." The fashion arbiter continued with a suggestion that a "warm underwaist" be worn with spring suits and warned against "entirely tight outside garments hardly suitable for the street [which] display the form too liberally for the promenade, especially upon ladies of middle age." If some ladies were too bold, others were perhaps not quite honest. The magazine suggested that the Greek bodice be worn by "flat-chested persons who desire a fuller outline of figure" and gave instructions for forming its shape with folds of velvet or muslin or silk.

Most of the town's fashionable gowns were styled by seamstresses from patterns in *Godey's Lady's Book*, the *Report of Fashions* or the *Dressmakers' and Milliners' Guide*. So complete was the reign of the dressmaker that the *Chicago Magazine* found it necessary to advance a series of arguments in favor of ready-to-wear clothing; the women were assured they could now go out in such a dress in a Chicago gale and not be afraid of unraveling "yards of ruffling and bolts of lace."

The informal nature of most social life was reflected in the popularity of skating and sleighing. It was around these activities rather than around formal balls and parties that most of the social events were centered. "Picknicking" was a favorite pastime; after collecting the members of their set, young couples clambered into a low, racy-looking sleigh piled high with hay and buffalo robes and drove north to a friend's house or an inn for a supper and a dance to music most frequently furnished by a German band. Skating was as popular as sleighing. Skaters patronized one of five rinks where the younger members of society were to be found curvetting, wheeling and freezing through the forward roll, the Dutch roll, the figure three, the double roll, the figure eight and all the other maneuvers so important in their vocabulary.

The severe Chicago winters did not catch the editors of the *Chicago Magazine* unaware. "Not less interesting," its fashion expert reported, "now that winter has shown its true colors and the cold breath of the lake visits us, is the study of the articles of comfort and underwear which combine no little elegance with their increasing utility. Colored trousers for street wear (under the dress) are a necessity in western cities, where soft coal leaves its tinges on everything that dares to be white. Ladies make up very loose Turkish drawers of opera flannel in pearl gray or ash color with embroidery of crimson or scarlet to draw on before walking out. The comfort of these garments cannot be estimated by those who have not worn them."

Less practical matters were in the minds of Chicagoans in 1860, when it was learned that Mayor Long John Wentworth had left for Montreal with an invitation for Albert Edward, Prince of Wales (later Edward VII), who was then on a tour of Canada, to visit Chicago. The city's numerous foreign

CORNER OF CLARK AND WATER STREETS, 1866

societies began polishing up their regalia and practicing special drills for the parade they were certain would be part of the celebration. Ladies who had hopes of being invited to the elaborate formal ball planned for the prince sent hastily to the East for special gowns. Disappointment was widespread when word was received that the prince had accepted the offer only if he could come incognito as Baron Renfrew. He stipulated there were to be no honors or attention other than those "any English gentleman might be given."

Some placed the blame on the mayor for such an arrangement, reasoning that he thought he would be able to dominate a civic reception much easier than a formal ball. On his side, the mayor used the editorial columns of his Chicago *Democrat* to justify accepting the prince's terms, explaining that the prince's wishes were really those of most Chicagoans, who did not like "kow-towing to royalty."

The morning before the prince was to arrive, Mayor Wentworth and a committee of citizens took the Michigan Central train for Detroit to meet the prince and his party. There were no ceremonies, according to the reporters who were present, not even the customary introductions all around. Finally, everyone climbed aboard the prince's special train—but with the British and Americans traveling in separate cars. Every precaution had been taken for the prince's safety and a special pilot engine preceded his train by about ten minutes to be sure that no accident should mar his visit.

Chicago's enthusiasm for his appearance could not be entirely restrained. The railroad station was brilliantly illuminated for his arrival and a crowd of about five thousand was pressing about for a view of the royal tourist. Many wore special medallions which had been prepared in honor of the visit. The satisfaction of the group at the station was slight. The prince was taken quickly to a carriage and driven to the Richmond House, where the entire second floor had been redecorated and refurnished before his arrival. The following morning the prince stayed behind the closed shutters of his apartments while crowds milled around the hotel in the hopes of catching a glimpse of him.

During the morning, a committee of Mayor Wentworth, William B. Ogden, William Bross and E. W. McComas called on Lord Lyons, the British minister accompanying the prince. They presented the nobleman with an address of welcome for the prince that was equally a document of surrender for Chicago's hopes of carrying out its elaborate plans. "Learning that his lordship's fatigue arising from the exciting scenes through which he so recently passed would render such attention undesirable to him, we have forborne from every demonstration calculated to disturb his privacy and repose," the committee promised. If this forbearance excluded a grand ball, it was not taken to rule out a parade. The prince, who had agreed to a tour of the city, could hardly escape when his route took him down Wabash Avenue and back up Michigan while a crowd of fifty thousand—then about half the population of the city—lined the sidewalks to watch. Nor was he able to protest effectively when the city's fire department fell into line behind him with its new engines decked out in flowers and followed by the usual floats representing the town's industries.

A NEW YEAR'S DAY CALLING CARD

After the parade the prince was taken to see the Courthouse, the pumping works which kept the water flowing in the Illinois and Michigan Canal, the Chicago Historical Society and other points of civic pride. He expressed some disappointment that he had not been allowed to visit one of Chicago's towering grain elevators, so an additional excursion to one of these was undertaken with Fernando Jones, the city's unofficial host to distinguished guests, acting as guide. In the evening, the prince left on his special train for Dwight, where he was to do some shooting, leaving a nervous and divided Chicago to appraise the success of his visit.

The uneasiness with which the young city had anticipated its first experience with royalty, especially English, was reflected in the editorial columns of the *Tribune*. It was able to record "with great thankfulness that the visit of Baron Renfrew and his party did not bring out, in this city, the exhibition of vulgar curiosity and a more vulgar flunkeyism which many feared. On the whole, the people behaved very well. There was, as Princes are rare in this country, a general desire to get a glimpse of royalty, but we have not heard that anyone forced himself upon the distinguished strangers nor that any outrageous breach of propriety was committed."

In this respect, Chicago counted itself ahead of New York, where the young ladies pressed about the prince at a grand ball in a manner which the Duke of Newcastle observed was "not in strict accordance with good breeding." When Long John Wentworth was asked how it felt to sit next to the future King of England, he replied: "I was not sitting beside the prince. He sat beside me."

Eight years were to pass after Chicago's disappointing experience with royalty before the city staged its first society function of any magnificence. The occasion, actually the birth of Chicago society, was a Charity Ball at Crosby's Opera House, suggested to Chicagoans by P. G. Gilmore, the Boston band leader who was never happier than when dealing with the colossal. Society columnist Peregrine Pickle stated the subject of the grand ball in a style that was at least succinct:

> Let them [in the East] learn that Chicago can do enough business in hogs and horn cattle on Saturday to make them dizzy, hear better sermons Sunday and pay more for them, array herself in a manner on Monday that would make the lilies sick, not to speak of Solomon, and drive a fiddler *in articulo mortis* either of himself or the last strand of his catgut Chicago now proposes to show them the finest men, the handsomest women, the most elegant toilets, the largest ball floor, the handsomest ball room, the best music and the best supper ever known in this country. . . . The reputation of Chicago should henceforth rank as high for balls as for wheat.

The arrangements for so important an affair were not entrusted to the

ladies but were taken over by such men as Joseph Medill, George M. Pullman, Isaac Arnold, Mahlon D. Ogden and Jonathan Young Scammon, the
same group which directed the other phases of Chicago life. The price of
tickets was set at $20 but the Yankee influence was so strong in this city
of new millionaires that loud cries of protest went up over this extravagance.
The committee, who were mostly Yankees themselves, were aware that not
to attend was to be out of society, and saw no reason for lowering the price.
The preparations were so elaborate that the affair had to be postponed in
order to allow time for the decorations at the opera house to be completed.
As the time for the ball approached, Chicagoans forgot the importance of
being practical. The tickets, which had sold slowly at first, were suddenly
not to be had at any price. Gowns were chosen without respect to cost and
"tearful were the faces of many" whom economy or lack of funds reduced
to the Flora McFlimsey dilemma of "Nothing to Wear." At the milliners
and mantua-makers there was "mounting in hot haste." Many dresses were
ordered from London, Paris and New York while Chicago dressmakers
found themselves floundering in mazes of gores and flounces. The hair-
dressers sent emergency appeals to the East for more hair to build up the
elegant "waterfalls" with which every fashionable lady hoped to top her
coiffure.

The ball was scheduled to begin at ten o'clock. As "there was no distinction in being late," the opera house was crowded early in the evening. Many
Chicagoans arrived in carriages but those who lived near the opera house
strolled over from their Michigan and Wabash Avenue homes as though
they were attending a neighborhood party. There were some who walked
because the livery operators had raised their prices for the evening and it
was not considered good business to pay more than the market price. The
stage of the opera house was decorated with flags from the world's nations,
standing in front of a stage-high backdrop that had been painted for the
occasion. Over the center of the stage hung a chandelier forty-five feet in

circumference and holding ninety-five lights festooned with flowers and leaves. An artificial platform from the stage extended out into the auditorium to form the dance floor. Overhead a chandelier seventy-five feet in diameter hung beneath a double canopy of fresh flowers, extending in festoons to the far corners of the auditorium and populated by an inanimate flock of stuffed doves.

As elegant as the decorations was the supper arranged by caterer John Wright, whose restaurant under the opera house was the city's most fashionable eating place. In the music hall next to the opera house, a table was spread with delicacies and ornamented with such architectural-gastronomic features as "a Swiss chateau in color, a church, *Charlotte russe de la Reine*, *pyramids d'Espagnol*, pagoda temple, four illuminated ice baskets in colors, two nougat temples and ornamental prairie chicken patties, boned turkey, boneless hams, a boar's head, patties of quail" and other luxuries. The bewilderment with which the guests must have viewed the skyline of their supper table extended to the grand march. Gilmore neglected to tell the committee that the "grand old march" would precede the "grand march" and the leaders had to be called back for consultation with the band leader. Two orchestras furnished the music, Gilmore's Boston Band playing for the dances while a reed orchestra provided the accompaniment for the promenades.

Generally, Chicagoans preferred more robust entertainment than Gilmore's Charity Ball. The most popular event of the year was one which excluded the ladies entirely—the annual Thanksgiving Day game dinner given at the Tremont House (and later at the Grand Pacific) by hotel man John B. Drake. The menus for these affairs suggested the continuing identification of Chicago with the frontier. The number of dishes dwarfed the traditional Thanksgiving Day feast. To be invited to one of these dinners was a sign that a young man had been accepted by the business community—which in Chicago was identical with being accepted socially.

A menu from one of the dinners is a measure of the host's liberality:

THE NEW TREMONT HOUSE, corner Lake and Dearborn Streets

Venison, Hunter Style   Game Broth

FISH

Boiled Trout with Shrimp Sauce
Baked Black Bass with Claret Sauce

BOILED

Leg of Mountain Sheep. Ham of Bear. Venison Tongue. Buffalo Tongue.

ROAST

Loin of Buffalo. Wild Goose. Quail. Mountain Sheep. Red Head Duck.
Jack Rabbit. Blacktail Deer. Coon. Canvasback Duck. Prairie Chicken.
English Hare. Bluewing Teal. Partridge. Widgeon. Saddle of Venison.
Pheasant. Mallard Duck. Wild Turkey. Spotted Grouse. Black Bear.
Opossum. Leg of Elk. Wood Duck. Sandhill Crane. Ruffled Grouse.
Cinnamon Bear.

BROILED

Bluewing Teal. Jacksnipe. Blackbirds. Reedbirds. Partridge.
Pheasant. Quail. Butterball Ducks. English Snipe. Ricebirds.
Redwing. Starling. Marsh Birds. Plover. Gray Squirrel. Buffalo Steak.
Rabbits. Venison Steak.

ENTREES

Antelope Steak with Mushroom Sauce. Rabbit, Braised with Cream Sauce.
Fillet of Grouse with Truffles.   Venison Cutlet with Jelly Sauce.
, Ragout of Bear, Hunter Style. Oyster Pie.

SALADS

Shrimp.   Prairie Chicken.   Celery.

ORNAMENTAL DISHES

Pyramid of Game en Bellevue. Boned Duck au naturel. Pyramid of
Wild Goose Liver in Jelly.   The Coon at Night.   Boned Quail in
Plumage.   Redwing Starling on Tree.   Partridge in Nest.   Prairie
Chicken en Socie.

As the menu makes plain, the standards of Chicago were those of the
gourmand rather than the gourmet. From charity balls to game dinners,
everything had to be on the grand scale.

S. O. Douglas Politics

The Little Giant and the
Rail Splitter

IF MAKING money was Chicago's vocation, politics was its hobby and pursued with equal dedication. The language of political argument was either eulogistic or vituperative; the reaction to such incendiary oratory was violent nearly as often as it was reasonable. Among the political issues of the day none caused greater indignation than the dominance of the South in national politics. One measure after another for the improvement of the Northwest had been defeated by southern votes in Congress. Throughout the Midwest there was a growing determination to break up the power of this southern bloc.

In the vocabulary of the transplanted Puritans who were the leaders of Chicago, rightness and righteousness were the same. Motivated by a practical desire to achieve political recognition, the midwesterners found inspiration for their crusade in an abhorrence to the institution of slavery maintained by the southern states. Joseph Medill, the editor of the *Tribune*, began to talk of a new Republican Party that would break the power of the South and East by forming a new coalition of North and West. The new party was not to be formed on political and economic principles primarily but on the moral issue of slavery. As the new party took form, Chicago became the testing ground for ideas that were to divide the country in civil war but ultimately to form the framework for reunion on a basis better suited to a free nation.

Anti-slavery sentiments were popular in Chicago. It had been an early stop on the Underground Railroad that transported fugitive slaves to Canada and freedom. Only perfunctory efforts were made to enforce the Fugitive Slave Law and it was not uncommon for runaway slaves to be loaded aboard Canadian-bound lake ships in large groups of twenty or thirty. One of the managers of the Underground Railroad was Allan Pinkerton. His house on West Adams Street often was surrounded by groups of petitioning Negroes seeking help for a trembling relative or fugitive friend.

Another leader of the anti-slavery movement was Dr. C. V. Dyer, a physician who was credited with helping the first slave to come to Chicago make his escape. He was always ready to aid the fugitives. On one occasion he heard a commotion outside his office and saw that an owner had just captured a runaway slave and was dragging him down the street. A crowd had gathered but was afraid to interfere because of the penalties of the Fugitive Slave Law. Dr. Dyer rushed down from his office, slipped through the crowd until he was behind the southerner and then cracked the slave owner over the head with a heavy cane. As the owner fell to the ground stunned, his slave escaped down the street. Dr. Dyer made no effort to flee but shouted "Make way here! There's a man hurt!" The southerner, slowly regaining his wits after the hard jolt to his head, willingly accepted the fortuitous offer of first aid from the sympathetic doctor.

Dr. Dyer's cane was itself the memento of another exploit. A plantation owner who had tracked down his slave and lodged the Negro in the city jail for safekeeping registered at a downtown hotel to spend the night. The doctor, hearing of the incident, assembled some friends and together they called on the southerner at his hotel. What they wanted, they said, was to offer him protection from the mob that was gathering to run him out of town. The victim of the hoax, unwilling to test the veracity of a story that might easily have been true, left Chicago that night without attempting to collect his property from the jail. For his part in the hoax, Dr. Dyer was given an inscribed cane by his friends. In a similar episode, a Missourian with the miserly name of Uriah Hinch was reported in the papers to have left town without his slave when city authorities "refused him protection."

The founding of the Republican Party presented a confusing issue to the unsophisticated voter, who was as firmly Democratic in politics as he was anti-slavery in his morals. The choice was made more difficult when the great spokesman for the Democratic Party in its efforts to preserve its own unity and that of the nation became Stephen A. Douglas. "The Little Giant," as he was known, was popular in Chicago and an infallible hero to the Irish, who made up about 20 per cent of the population. During the ten years before the Civil War, when public opinion swayed first toward Democratic compromise and then firmly away from it toward Republicanism and abolition, Douglas was to experience the gamut of political fortune.

He came into his greatest disfavor immediately following the passage of the Kansas-Nebraska Act, which allowed the settlers in the new territories to make their own decision about slavery. Traveling westward after his support had resulted in passage of the bill in Congress, he said he was able to go from Boston to Chicago by the light of his burning effigies. He refused to evade the problem, and on his return announced he would speak the evening of September 1st from the steps of Market Hall. On the afternoon of the day scheduled for his speech, the flags on the ships in the harbor and river were lowered to half mast. For half an hour in the evening the bells of many churches tolled mournfully as a sign of their displeasure at the compromise with slavery embodied in the law. Because of this hostility, a rumor circulated that Douglas would appear with a bodyguard of five hundred Irish.

That evening an uneasy crowd of about ten thousand filled the streets, windows and rooftops of buildings near Market Hall. When Douglas stepped to the front of the platform, his voice was smothered by a wave of hisses and groans and an answering volley of shouts and cheers. William "Deacon" Bross, sitting by the platform as a reporter for the *Tribune*, hurled what the crowd considered a taunting question at Douglas. According to another reporter, "it was a firebrand in the midst of the combustibles." The audience became a mob and for nearly four hours drowned every attempt of Douglas to speak. Added to the hoots and jeers were rotten apples and other fruit thrown at the platform where he stood. Convinced at last that no speech was possible, Douglas hurled his final words at the crowd: "Abolitionists

SHERMAN HOUSE looking west on Randolph Street with Courthouse on the left, by *Edwin Whitefield*

CHICAGO IN 1853

of Chicago! It is now Sunday morning. I'll go to church and you may go to Hell."

Another source of hostility toward Douglas was the Know-Nothing or Native American Party that resented his alliance with the Irish. In the year following the Market Hall riot, the Know-Nothings, who feasted on a chauvinistic hatred of all foreigners, were able to elect their candidate, Dr. Levi D. Boone, mayor of Chicago. It was not a wise choice for a city in which almost 50 per cent of the population was of foreign origin. Boone's first administrative act was to decree that all policemen must be native-born Americans, a blow which more than decimated the force and was a particular insult to the city's Irish. Not satisfied, Boone next turned on the Germans, who made up about 25 per cent of the population. The issue over which he picked a quarrel was beer.

Before the rapid growth of the German community, beer was almost unknown in Chicago, which showed a marked preference for whiskey. But when the Germans arrived, they brought their own customs with them and tended to preserve their traditional way of life in a series of somewhat segregated communities within the city. They patronized their own German theater (probably the best in any language in the city), German churches, German trade unions and even showed a liking for patent medicine bearing German labels. They also established their own beer gardens, though at least one of these—across from St. James Episcopal Church—was Americanized in name to a tea garden. Initially, all of the beer was imported from Milwaukee, as engineers thought it impossible to construct the subterranean vaults needed for brewing in the swampy soil of Chicago. Adolph Mueller thought it could be done, however, and soon was brewing Chicago's first locally produced beer.

Mayor Boone, who regarded beer drinking as a foreign and un-American custom, set out to stop it. His first action was to raise the liquor license fee by 600 per cent and to recommend that no license be issued for more than three months. Both these proposals would have put most of the small saloon keepers in the German neighborhoods out of business. As the next step Boone ordered the enforcement of a half-forgotten law closing the saloons on Sunday. The Sunday closing, which the mayor made plain applied only to beer emporiums and not saloons that sold only whiskey, caused an uproar on the North Side which was so predominantly German it was known as the "Nord Seite." The first Sunday about two hundred Germans were arrested for violation of the ordinance and their trial set before Squire Henry L. Rucker, a justice of the peace whose office was opposite the Courthouse.

The case was called the morning of April 21, 1855. At the hour for the hearing, a tumult was created as the saloon keepers with about three hundred of their friends marched into the Courthouse Square accompanied by the music of a fife and drum. After threatening and defying the judge, the column retreated to Randolph and Clark and took possession of the intersection in front of the Sherman House. The police arrived and forced the mob north across the river where it disbanded. By afternoon, another crowd larger than the first had gathered and was supported by a group of Irish volunteers. It was armed with shotguns, rifles, pistols, clubs, knives and shillelaghs. Rumors of an intended raid reached City Hall and about 150 special deputies were sworn in to fight the Germans.

At 3 o'clock the mob made its way down Clark Street but was disrupted temporarily when the mayor ordered the bridge tender to swing the bridge open after half the crowd was across. Using the added time to place his forces in strategic spots, the mayor confidently ordered the bridge closed. The crowd surged forward and was soon battling the police and deputies in an effort to force its way to City Hall. One member of the mob blew off the arm of a policeman with a shotgun blast and was shot down and killed. Firing broke out on both sides until the defeated rioters retreated across the bridge carrying their wounded with them. That evening cannon were placed at the approaches to the Courthouse but the worst of the disturbances were over. The effect of these "lager beer riots" was to lessen the mayor's zeal for closing the German saloons and prohibiting beer drinking. Though he did not pursue his quarrel with the Germans, the violence during the riots discredited his party and the Know-Nothings were never again a factor in Chicago politics.

CHURCH OF THE HOLY FAMILY, 1866

Political turmoil of a different kind continued to surge through the city as the young Republican Party boldly stated its credo of no compromise with slavery. In 1858, the Republicans nominated Abraham Lincoln as their candidate for the United States Senate. His opponent was Stephen A. Douglas, who had regained a considerable part of his earlier popularity. The candidates began their campaigns with speeches from the balcony of the Tremont House on succeeding nights. Later they were to meet on the same platform in a series of debates whose significance was fully appreciated by those who heard and read the arguments of the two speakers.

Lincoln was nearly as well known as Douglas and each man had the physical vigor, political background and power of expression to state his case forcibly and well. Douglas had the greater experience of the two. For years in the House of Representatives and the Senate he had debated with the country's ablest orators. It was said that no matter how many speakers were arrayed against him, he had never been discomfited. He was bold, aggressive and when necessary, defiant. He had tremendous moral courage and with it a confidence in himself as well as his cause. Lincoln, though his experience had been more limited than that of Douglas, was also a thoroughly trained speaker. Because of the greater reputation of Douglas, Lincoln welcomed the chance to meet him in debate; he knew it was as rigorous a test as he would ever face. When the two met, each put forth his utmost strength.

Both men were conscious that Illinois was no more than an arena for their contest; their real audience was the nation. Isaac Arnold, Lincoln's friend and biographer, described it as "not a single combat" but a competition that "extended through the whole campaign [as] the American people paused to watch its progress and hung, with intense interest, upon every movement of the champions." As is always the case with those who bear the burden of compromise, Douglas had the poorer cause; he argued it with an eloquence which made the impossible seem necessary. Because of the large Democratic vote in Chicago his party won control of the state legislature (which still elected United States Senators) and he was sent to Washington. More important to the backers of Douglas was the fact he was in a good position to win the party's presidential nomination in 1860. Lincoln's friends were of a similar mind; the debates had established the ability of their candidate to deal with national issues. They said it was of small importance the Republican Party had been unable to win a place in the Senate; Lincoln would have the presidency instead.

Joseph Medill, the editor of the *Tribune*, who had shrewdly foreseen and encouraged the alignment of forces out of which came the Republican Party, was convinced that it could win in 1860 only by nominating a westerner. Lincoln did not seem an ideal candidate to Medill but because of the debates with Douglas was the logical choice to oppose the "Little Giant" whose nomination by the Democrats was taken for granted. The favorite for the Republican nomination was William H. Seward of New York. As the Republican National Committee met to select a convention site the contest appeared to be Seward against the field. This expectation enabled Illinois committeeman Norman B. Judd to persuade the committee to hold the convention in Illinois as neutral ground. Once the decision to hold the convention in Chicago was reached, the spring of the trap was set. Medill then declared for Lincoln and the *Tribune* began a sustained campaign to win the nomination for him. As a basis for Republican Party policies, Medill took the ideas outlined by Lincoln in the debates with Douglas.

To house the convention, the Republicans of Chicago erected a rectangular wooden building at the southeast corner of Lake and Market (Wacker) and named it the Wigwam. Its acoustics were so remarkable that speakers could be heard in any part of the building with little difficulty. As the opening day of the convention drew near, straw votes on the trains coming into Chicago gave Seward a tremendous lead over the other candidates. The ardent Seward supporters called themselves the Irrepressibles. After their arrival they paraded the streets behind brass bands and passed out champagne and cigars in the hotel lobbies. Medill, Judd and Arnold, who had set up headquarters in the Tremont House, ignored

THE REPUBLICAN WIGWAM WHERE LINCOLN WAS NOMINATED, 1860

the noisy demonstrations; with other members of the Illinois delegation they employed their trading abilities in dickering for votes. Lincoln had given orders there were to be no deals but he was safely out of the way in Springfield. At the political huckster shop in the Tremont there was lively bargaining. In the columns of the *Tribune*, Medill doubled his barrage of arguments in support of nominating "The Westerner," Abraham Lincoln.

The meeting at the Wigwam was Chicago's first national political convention, but there was nothing amateur about the arrangements. Medill and Judd, who were in charge of seating the delegates, put New York at one end of the hall and surrounded it with other states that were conceded to be for Seward. Pennsylvania, an important state in the doubtful column, was placed at the opposite end of the hall where it would be nearly inaccessible to New York representatives. In between as a buffer were placed the Lincoln delegations from Illinois, Indiana and New Jersey. With these arrangements perfected, the Lincoln supporters outlined a plan to assure their control of the galleries. Judd arranged with the Chicagoans who controlled the railroads to bring in Lincoln men free of charge. On the night preceding the day for the nominations the committee distributed hundreds of tickets to Lincoln boosters. All were instructed to report early to the Wigwam and jam it to the doors before the Seward supporters, who had scheduled a grand parade, could arrive to claim their seats. The next morning while the Sewardites were marching from their headquarters at the Richmond House behind an elegantly uniformed band, the Lincoln "shouters" were pouring through the three doors of the Wigwam to pack the galleries. The "shouters" did their work so effectively that reporter Murat Halstead wrote in the Cincinnati *Commercial* the nomination of Lincoln was followed by a sound "like all the hogs ever slaughtered in Cincinnati giving their death squeals together and a score of big steam whistles going." Adding to the pandemonium was a "stamping that made every plank and pillar in the building quiver."

The first two roll calls after the nominating and seconding speeches were concluded did not give any candidate a majority, but Lincoln's strength continued to grow. On the third ballot he lacked only a vote and a half of the total needed for nomination. Then a delegate from Ohio, a group so badly split it was considered to be without influence, asked to be recognized. He was David Kellogg Cartter, who spoke hesitatingly because of a speech impediment while a taut convention listened. "I rise (eh), Mr. Chairman (eh)," he said—the impatient delegates bent forward in their chairs—"to announce the change of four votes of Ohio from Mr. Chase to Abraham Lincoln." Halstead wrote his paper in Ohio that after a moment's silence, "there was the noise in the Wigwam like the rush of a great wind in the van of a storm—and in another breath, the storm was there. There were thousands cheering with the energy of insanity." On the roof of the Wigwam the sly and confident Lincoln men had mounted a cannon. An observer who had been shouting the results of the balloting to those outside gave the signal that Lincoln was nominated and the cannon boomed forth in a salute that spread the news to all Chicago.

The nomination of Douglas, the city's native son, by a divided Democratic convention in Baltimore came as an anticlimax to all but the city's Irish. The split among the Democrats assured the Republican Party of its first President. Jubilant Chicagoans joined the Republican Wide Awake marching clubs and, protected by oilcloth caps and capes, carried dripping oil torches through the streets. In November Lincoln was elected President and a new era of American politics and a somber chapter of American history had begun.

The Lincoln triumph had its bitter taste for his Chicago backers. Norman B. Judd who maneuvered to bring the convention to Chicago and nominated Lincoln, was passed over for the cabinet post he expected. He was later given a consolation prize in the form of a ministerial post to Prussia. Medill fared better. He wanted the postmastership for John L. Scripps, one of the partners in the *Tribune*. Charles Ray, another of the partners, said it was not wanted "wholly for the money there is in it, but as a means of extending and insuring our business and extending the influence of the *Tribune*." The argument consisted of the same combination of public interest and private gain that Chicagoans considered infallible. Medill reasoned that if Scripps received the appointment, the country postmasters of the Northwest would work to extend the newspaper's circulation; since it was a Republican newspaper, this in turn would "benefit the party," which in turn was best for the country. Scripps received the appointment and one of the foundation stones of an American newspaper empire was set into place.

Patronage, however, was overshadowed by the great question of secession. Medill counseled his readers to accept a "bloodless separation" but his candidate was not of any such mind. When the Confederate forces fired on Fort Sumter, Lincoln stood steadfast by the principles of "no compromise" that had led to the founding of the Republican Party. The first call for troops to preserve the Union was issued and Chicago prepared to take up arms.

The Civil War and the Chicago Conspiracy

THE PRIDE of Chicago's military forces in the years before the war had been the Zouave cadets of Colonel Elmer Ellsworth. Impressed by the valor of the French Zouaves in the Crimean War, Ellsworth had organized his own company of cadets in Chicago, modeling the uniforms after those of the French troops. Ellsworth was a fanatic about discipline. To qualify for membership in his corps, the cadets were required to sign a pledge of monastic severity. A cadet could be expelled from the group for "entering a drinking saloon at any hour day or night"; entering "a house of ill fame under any circumstances or pretext whatever"; entering a gambling saloon or gambling for any sum of money or even for playing billiards in a public hall or saloon. The latter, the pledge explained, was "interdicted not because of any objection to the game but because it is a step toward the other offenses named, and the excitement and associations of the billiard saloon naturally lead to drinking."

The cadets were famous for their precision drill. In 1860, challenging any similar organization to match their skill, they made a tour of the East for a series of contests. After appearances at West Point, New York and other eastern cities, the Chicago Zouaves returned undefeated, marching from the railroad station with their uniforms adorned with ladies' gloves, lace

MONUMENT TO STEPHEN A. DOUGLAS, 1866

handkerchiefs and dried and faded flowers as well as epaulets, swords, pistols, plumes, badges and medals. Shortly afterward, Colonel Ellsworth left the cadets to study law in the office of Abraham Lincoln in Springfield. When Lincoln was elected President, Ellsworth followed him to Washington. After the firing on Sumter, Ellsworth took a commission with the New York Fire Zouaves. Serving with them, he became the first Union officer to fall in the Civil War.

Without Ellsworth, Chicago's Zouaves disbanded for lack of leadership. The outbreak of war found the city with almost no well-trained troops. When Governor Richard Yates sent word that Chicago should raise as strong a force as possible and have it armed and equipped to march immediately, the city was in a state of alarm. There were already fears that the southern part of Illinois might try to secede to the Confederacy; the public interpreted the call for troops as a sign that Rebel forces were preparing to invade the state. A stock-taking of the city's arsenal reassured no one. The four hundred members of the militia who had been mustered into service were without arms. To meet the crisis, the city borrowed fifty muskets from a Milwaukee company. The remainder of the troops were a pawnshop army equipped with squirrel rifles, shotguns, single-barreled pistols or any other weapon that could be obtained from a gun store or pawnshop.

Only eight days after the beginning of hostilities at Sumter, the troops were ordered aboard a special train at the Illinois Central station—"destination unknown." The commander alone knew that the troops had been assigned to Cairo, in "Egypt" to guard the confluence of the Ohio and Mississippi Rivers. With only four cannon and assorted small arms, the poorly organized companies were expected to prevent supplies from being shipped to the Confederacy over the river route and to guard against an invasion of Illinois. Extensive security precautions were made necessary because of pro-slavery sentiment in the southern part of the state and the possibility that armed groups sympathetic to the South might already be secretly formed. Through skillful planning by the officials of the railroad, the troop train ran the length of the state without advance notice of its coming. The regular trains preceding it had left on schedule and been sidetracked by prearrangement. After leaving a small force to guard the wooden trestle over the Big Muddy River a short distance to the North, the expedition arrived in Cairo "to the astonishment of all and the rage of many."

Back in Chicago, Bryan Hall on the east side of the Courthouse Square was crowded for a loyalty meeting. Resolutions were adopted supporting the Union and the inevitable committee of business leaders that was part of any Chicago activity appointed. Most Chicagoans, who considered the war a crusade to stamp out the evils of slavery (and destroy the political and economic power of the South), gave it unqualified support. The Irish community, because of its sympathies for the South through the common bond of the Democratic Party, was the only area of the city where the war was unpopular. In the Irish areas of Archer Road and Bridgeport, Rebel victories were more likely to be celebrated than those of the northern armies. The possibilities of any active resistance from the Irish died away, however, when their great hero, Stephen A. Douglas, appeared before a crowd of ten thousand to pledge his support to Lincoln and ask his audience "never to permit the government to be destroyed."

Though the Irish felt themselves stubbornly bound to disapprove of the war, individually they enlisted as rapidly as any other group. And it was the Irish troops of Colonel James Mulligan's Brigade who were Chicago's first heroes of the war. On the day after Douglas spoke to his Irish followers, an announcement appeared in the papers of a rally of patriotic Irish to form a regiment of volunteers. The regiment was immediately filled. As more companies had been formed than the government could equip, the regiment was not mustered into service until June. Once accepted, it was sent to Lexington, Missouri. There the army neglected to reinforce or supply it and allowed the men to be cut off by Confederate forces. After a long and hopeless stand, the troops surrendered. Colonel Mulligan refused to give his parole that he would not fight again and was kept a prisoner for several months until exchanged for a Confederate officer prisoner. Upon returning to Chicago, Mulligan formed a new brigade to replace the one captured in Missouri. He fought at its head throughout the war until July 24, 1864, when he fell fatally wounded near Winchester, Virginia. Then, seeing that his aids' concern over his condition was increasing the danger that the colors of his troops might be captured a second time, he gave his final command: "Lay me down and save the flag."

Colonel Mulligan's dying phrase, sent home to Chicago in a hundred letters, was the inspiration for the city's patriotic song writer, George F. Root, to write a war ballad taking its title from the gallant colonel's command. Root's war songs, among them "The Battle Cry of Freedom," known as the "Northern Marseillaise" and "Tramp, Tramp, Tramp" were known by every Union soldier. The composition of a new song was an important event for Chicagoans. A crowd would gather in front of the courthouse steps to hear it sung for the first time by the city's favorite singers, Frank and Jules Lumbard. The Lumbard brothers would sing it over and over until the crowd knew the words by heart. In this way the song was widely circulated before it was printed. The tunes could not be called folk music, but their popularity was born in much the same manner as that of folk songs. Another Chicagoan who kept the Yankees singing was Henry C. Work, who wrote "Marching Through Georgia," as well as the famous temperance ballad, "Father, Dear Father, Come Home with Me Now."

Patriotic fervor was high in Chicago. Early in the war vigilance committees had been formed to watch for traitors and guard against attempts to blow up the city's powder magazines. The courthouse square was filled with tents of organizations recruiting soldiers for volunteer companies. Theater owner J. H. McVicker offered a silk flag for the first company raised in Chicago and gave it to Fred Harding's company at the Tremont House on the day the group started for Cairo. On it were the words "Retaliation! No mercy to traitors." The Board of Trade put as its first order of business the enlistment of new troops. One ardent supporter of the war, Solomon Sturges, equipped an entire regiment, The Sturges Rifles, out of his personal fortune. Letters were mailed in patriotic envelopes with pro-Union slogans emblazoned on red, white and blue borders.

The Germans' thrifty patriotism took the form of scraping large quantities of grease from under the ice on the Chicago River, which they cooked with lye to make soap. Everyone in the city boasted of McCormick's reaper factory; the newspapers promised that these new reapers, by freeing young men from the farm for the battlefield, would eventually give the North its coveted victory.

The first major break in Chicago's patriotic ranks came after the Emancipation Proclamation. Democrats who had supported the war as necessary to preserve the Union now felt its purpose had been subverted by the

Abolitionists. The leader in speaking out against the continuation of the war for such a purpose was a six-foot, forty-five-year-old editor, with "the grace of an Apollo" and snowy-white beard and hair. He was Wilbur F. Storey, editor of the Chicago *Times*. Storey had purchased the *Times* from Cyrus McCormick in 1861, intending to use it to support the conciliatory views of Stephen A. Douglas. The start of the war and the death of Douglas shortly afterward left Storey with no political champion. As the city soon learned, however, Storey could speak for himself.

The newspaper philosophy of Storey was "to print the news and raise hell." He followed it to the letter. It was Storey's newspaper which announced the execution of four murderers with American journalism's most famous headline, "Jerked to Jesus." Subheads immediately beneath this alliterative summary explained that "Two of Them, in Louisiana, Died with the Sweet Confidence of Pious People," and continued "While Yet Two Others, in Mississippi, Expired Exhorting the Public to Beware of Sisters-in-Law." During the war Storey spent money lavishly for news from the front. His instructions to his correspondents were simple: "Telegraph fully all the news you can get and when there is no news, send rumors."

It was not surprising that when Storey chose to oppose the war, he did it in the most vehement fashion possible. As his newspaper was the semi-official spokesman for the Democratic Party which controlled the City

GROUNDS OF THE CHICAGO SHARPSHOOTERS ASSOCIATION

Council and had recently elected a mayor, his views carried added authority. His diatribes against Lincoln and the war plus the relationship of his paper to the party in control of the city's administration ultimately were brought to the attention of General Ambrose E. Burnside, then in command of the military district which included Chicago. Burnside, "famous for his sideburns, his inventions in firearms, his nobility of character and his military mistakes," made one of his more illustrious errors by ordering General J. B. Sweet at Chicago to suppress the *Times*. Simultaneously, he ordered the anti-war New York *World* excluded from the mails within his military jurisdiction.

The order from Burnside against the *Times* was based on its "repeated expression of disloyal and incendiary sentiments" such as the paper's charge "the war, as waged by military satraps of the administration, is a subversion of the Constitution and the people's rights under the law." Storey, who knew another man's mistake when he saw it, accepted the news of the proposed suppression calmly. He dispatched a rider to Sweet's headquarters with instructions to report back when the troops left for the *Times* building. Meanwhile, he succeeded in getting most of the day's publication off the press and into a safe place for later distribution before the troops arrived.

When the news was circulated that the *Times* had been suppressed a crowd gathered in front of the paper on Randolph Street to protest this arbitrary military intrusion into Chicago's political differences. Shouts for Storey failed to bring the editor to the window. He sat in his office unperturbed, confident that the order would not be upheld and satisfied that meanwhile it would create a schism among the Abolitionists. The crowd continued to grow until it had reached twenty thousand—which meant it was the equal of all the Chicagoans who had voted in the previous election. The Democratic sympathizers were in a majority and the threat was frequently heard that "If the *Times* is not allowed to publish, there will be no *Tribune*."

To calm the crowd a series of Democratic speakers made talks urging patience until Burnside's order could be countermanded. Wirt Dexter, a prominent Republican lawyer, appeared to promise that his own party was urging the President to nullify the edict. Away from the scene of the demonstration a group of Republican and Democratic leaders sat down together in a tense meeting called by Judge Van H. Higgins, a large stockholder in the *Tribune*. The Republican delegation was headed by Senator Lyman Trumbull and Representative Isaac Arnold. The leader of the Democrats was the omnipresent William B. Ogden. Being practical men, the conferees did not argue about principle or the justice of the cause. Rather they adopted a cleverly worded resolution asking President Lincoln to lift the ban against the *Times* "upon the ground of expediency alone."

That night the correspondent of the New York *Herald* closed his dispatch from Chicago with the words, "At this hour the *Tribune* still stands." The streets during the night were full or rumors about the measures the *Tribune* had taken for its own defense. One of these was that Colonel Charles Jennison, a lieutenant of John Brown during the Bloody Kansas days, had enlisted a corps of gunmen and smuggled them into the lofts of various buildings about the *Tribune*. Jennison was something of a poseur who dressed cowboy fashion and was usually to be found swaggering down the street with a retinue of admirers. The crowd had no doubts that if he were about the premises of the *Tribune*, there would be no hesitancy about shooting anyone who attacked.

The tension remained high until shortly after midnight when Judge Henry Drummond of the United States District Court issued an order directing the military authorities to take no further steps in carrying out the Burnside order. "I desire to give every aid and assistance in my power to the Government and to the administration in restoring the Union," he said. "But I have always wished to treat the Government as a Government of law and a Government of the Constitution and not as Government of mere physical force. I personally have contended and shall always contend for the right of free discussion and the right of commenting under the law and under the Constitution upon the acts of officers of the Government."

The next day it was the radical Republicans who crowded around the courthouse. They were angered by the judge's ruling and by the action of their party leaders in appealing to the President to rescind the Burnside edict. Senator Trumbull tried to speak but was interrupted with cries of "Traitor" and "We want Jennison." The meeting broke up after demands for the resignation of Senator Trumbull and Representative Arnold. The next day President Lincoln revoked Burnside's order against both the *Times* and the New York *World*. Wilbur F. Storey went back to editing the *Times* as calmly as was possible for an individual of his temperament; his enemies had given his newspaper a new fame and started it on the path to prosperity.

More southern sentiment came to the surface when the government converted Camp Douglas, an induction center at Thirty-third Street and Cottage Grove, into a prisoner of war camp for Rebel troops captured at Fort Donelson. When the prisoners arrived, hopes of an early victory were raised by the sight of the southerners marching through the streets. They carried ragged old bed quilts and pieces of carpet for blankets and were clothed in homespun pants colored simon's blue or "oilnut bark." To others the sight of the bedraggled Confederate soldiers was a cause for sympathetic concern. Later a free hospital known as St. Luke's was founded where the sick of both Confederate and Union forces might be cared for by qualified nurses and physicians. Some of the captives had visited in Chicago before the war; others had relatives in the city and about 10 per cent of the prisoners were Irish. Many of the women whose homes were originally in the South formed committees to distribute food and clothing to the prisoners. On Sundays a visit to Camp Douglas became a regular part of the schedule for an afternoon drive. The situation soon became too much for the ardently patriotic Board of Trade. It passed a resolution stating that it "frowns upon and condemns any attempt to make lions and distinguished visitors of any of the prisoners now among us. We recommend to the citizens of Chicago to abstain from offering those polite and marked attentions that make [the prisoners] heroes to the manifest degradation of ourselves."

As the war progressed, the population of the camp increased to about seven thousand and the uneasiness of Chicago grew correspondingly. So few soldiers were available for guarding the camp that a special force of volunteers was enlisted to help keep watch at nights. One mass break from the camp was tried but an informer revealed the plot to the camp officials. When the prisoners rushed the wooden fence and knocked it down they found a regiment of Pennsylvania troops waiting for them. A volley from the soldiers drove most of the prisoners back to their barracks and the few who did escape were soon recaptured.

A more serious threat to the city was the "Chicago Conspiracy" in which the prisoners at Camp Douglas were to play an important role. In the spring of 1864, Jacob Thompson, a member of the Confederacy who had been

CAMP DOUGLAS, 1864, by Albert E. Myers

DEMOCRATIC NATIONAL AMPHITHEATER ON MICHIGAN AVENUE, 1864
Lithograph by Charles Shober

Secretary of the Interior under President Buchanan, went to Canada with $250,000 in sterling exchange for the purpose of organizing an expedition to release prisoners of war at camps in the Northwest. The plot had two purposes. One was to strike at the enemy far behind the front lines. The other was to increase the sentiment in support of the Democratic Party and defeat Lincoln for re-election in the fall.

Arms were to be supplied to the prisoners through the Sons of Liberty and Knights of the Golden Circle, two secret organizations sympathetic to the South. Both were heterogeneous collections of Copperheads, riffraff and solid citizens who resented the super-patriots of the Republican Party and their "petty tyrannies." The plan was to stage a mass break during the excitement and confusion of the Democratic national convention, to be held in Chicago late in July. The released troops were to do as much damage as possible by burning and pillaging. Chicago was still a city of wooden buildings and there was reason to believe that properly located incendiary fires could destroy an important part of the business district. As another part of the plot, armed men were to be introduced into the city under the guise of convention delegates. These men would join with the escaped prisoners for a drive on Camp Morton in Indianapolis and free the southern captives there.

As the convention opened, men characterized by "bad whiskey and seedy homespun" clothes hung about the street corners. They announced in loud voices they had come to nominate a "peace President" but brandished ominous bowie knives and guns. For the second time an informer prevented a serious conflict by relating the plot to the commandant at Camp Douglas who wired for reinforcements. Within a day a thousand additional troops arrived to guard against the uprising. The leaders of the conspiracy, realizing they had lost the secrecy which was an essential part of their plan, passed the word during the third day of the convention that the project had been temporarily abandoned. Though it is probable the more grandiose parts of the plot would have been impossible to achieve, the insurrection could have caused great damage in the city and would have created wide demoralization throughout the North if even a part of it had been realized.

In November, information was allegedly obtained that the conspiracy was under way again. The purpose of the new plot, according to a report issued by the United States Judge Advocate General on the eve of the presidential election between General George C. McClellan and Lincoln, was "a general uprising in Missouri" and similar uprisings in Indiana, Ohio, Illinois and Kentucky. The plan in Chicago was for a thousand men to attack Camp Douglas, liberate the prisoners there and march to the Court-house Square where they would be joined by five thousand Sons of the Illinois, another organization supporting the southern cause. This much of the plot might have been credible, but the report continued with an allegation there is reason to believe was based more on political inventions and motivations than on fact.

The government claimed confessions had been obtained from southern officers of a plan "to attack Camp Douglas, release the prisoners there, with them to seize the polls, allowing none but the Copperhead ticket to be voted and stuff the boxes sufficiently to secure the city and state for General McClellan; then to utterly sack the city, burning and destroying every description of property, except what they could appropriate for their own use and that of their southern brethren." The idea of creating a revolutionary force to stuff the ballot boxes and then burn up the ballots along with the rest of the city was farcical. But there was hardly time to point out the absurdity of the charge before the election; the army quickly took action on the basis of the judge advocate's report before any doubts could be raised about its accuracy.

In a series of arrests, soldiers brought in a group charged with the con-spiracy, including Colonel G. St. Leger Grenfell and J. T. Shanks, two of the actual leaders of the earlier conspiracy. Chicagoans Charles Walsh, a Brigadier General of the Sons of Liberty, and Judge Buckner S. Morris, the second mayor of Chicago and treasurer of the Sons of Liberty, were also arrested. The arrest of Judge Morris was the worst injustice of the fiasco. Although a stout Democrat and opposed to the war, he was completely innocent of treason, as even his persecutors later were anxious to concede. His fault had been not one of the law but of matrimony. He was married to a Kentucky woman who was in charge of distributing clothing and goods to prisoners and frequently sheltered escaped prisoners in her house. Morris

THE GREAT NORTHWESTERN SANITARY FAIR, 1865

was acquitted at his trial but his reputation was never restored. As a pathetic epilogue, his wife, whose actions had involved him in the repercussions of the plot, left him and went to live with her family in Kentucky. Walsh and two others were convicted on charges of conspiring to release the prisoners and destroy the city of Chicago. All the others picked up in the pre-election raids were found not guilty. The case of the Chicago Conspiracy was over but it left the city puzzling over one question: Had it ever existed?

More on the creditable side among Chicago's war activities was the Soldier's Fair of 1863 to raise money for the Sanitary Commission. The Commission was a deceptively titled organization which did relief work among the soldiers. One feature of the fair was the sale at auction of the original Emancipation Proclamation for $3,000. But the center of most attention was Old Abe, the eagle mascot of the Eighth Wisconsin Regiment and a veteran of "twenty battles and sixty skirmishes." Both the eagle and the regimental "eagle bearer" were granted special leave for the fair and all Chicago paid them honor. In a city of about one hundred and fifty thousand more than one hundred thousand photographs of the bird were sold. The traffic was nearly as heavy for the sale of feathers, real and false, which were supposed to have been shot from his tail in battle. A purchaser of one of the genuine feathers was Joseph Medill. He had it made into a quill pen and kept it above his desk over the legend, "The pen is mightier than the sword."

The fair of 1863 had been little more than a grandiose bazaar and a much bigger exposition was planned for 1865. It was to have its own buildings and exhibit halls in Dearborn Park, east of Wabash between Washington and Randolph Streets. The war was over before the doors of the fair were open, but the plans were carried out to raise funds for returning veterans. Both

General Grant and General Sherman visited the fair. They were not, however, as loquacious as Old Abe, who at the first fair would respond to any resounding cheer or even a political speech with a loud screech. General Grant had been exptected to speak, but when he was introduced he declined. General Sherman was then asked to talk but demurred with the explanation, "I have always been willing to do anything the Lieutenant General asked me to do, but he has never asked me to make a speech." To this Grant replied, "I have never asked a soldier to do anything I couldn't do myself." Both of the generals were tremendously popular in Chicago, Grant because he had lived in Galena and Sherman because many Chicagoans had been among the force of "yellow-haired Germans and dark-haired, blue-eyed Irish, Scotch and English" that had marched with him to the sea.

INTERESTING The end of the war found Chicago counting with pride the number of volunteers it had provided for the Union forces. But in 1864 this same arithmetic had produced resentment against Lincoln when the President issued an extra call for the drafting of more troops. Chicagoans felt that because of the number of volunteers the city had provided its draft quota should not be so high. A mass meeting was held and a committee headed by Joseph Medill deputized to go to Washington to get a change in the quota. In Washington, the committee was turned down first by Secretary of War Stanton and then by Lincoln himself. The President did consent to go along for a second meeting with Stanton and listen to the arguments of both sides. After the discussion had gone on for some time, Lincoln suddenly lifted his head and turned on the committee a "black and frowning face."

"Gentlemen," he said in a voice full of bitterness, "after Boston, Chicago has been the chief instrument in bringing this war on the country. The Northwest has opposed the South as New England has opposed the South. It is you who are largely responsible for making blood flow as it has. You called for war until we had it. You called for Emancipation and I have given it to you. Whatever you have asked for you have had. Now you come here begging to be let off from the call for men which I have made to carry out the war you have demanded. You ought to be ashamed of yourselves. I have a right to expect better things of you. Go home and raise your six thousand extra men. And you, Medill, you are acting like a coward. You and your *Tribune* have had more influence than any paper in the Northwest in making this war. You can influence great masses, and yet you cry to be spared at a moment when our cause is suffering. Go home and send us those men."

Medill later told Ida Tarbell, "We all got up and when the door closed one of my colleagues said, 'Well, gentlemen, the old man is right. We ought to be ashamed of ourselves. Let us never say anything about this but go home and raise the men.' " Medill recalled that the six thousand additional men made a total of 28,000 at war from a city of 156,000. "There might have been crepe on every door almost in Chicago," he said, "for every family had lost a son or a husband. I lost two brothers. It was hard for the mothers."

The grief over the loss of sons, husbands and brothers at the front was submerged in a mourning that gripped the entire city when news was flashed of the assassination of Lincoln. The funeral train was to pass through Chicago on its way to Springfield and the city began making preparations for the reception of the body of the President. One of those who was able to offer a suggestion was George M. Pullman, who with the financial help of Marshall Field had completed the first of his new palace cars. Would it not, he asked, be appropriate for the funeral train to carry the most elegant railroad car in the country? Those in authority agreed, even though it meant that bridges along the route had to be altered to accomodate the wider Pullman car. Indirectly, the Lincoln funeral train became the showcase for America's first Pullman car.

In Chicago no group was more indignant about the assassination than the actors who felt the crime had disgraced their profession. In a special meeting at the Sherman House, the companies then at Wood's Museum and at McVicker's, where assassin John Wilkes Booth had been a local sensation several years before, voted to express "their detestation and abhorrence at him who has spread the somber pall of sorrow over our land." As a further

LINCOLN FUNERAL PROCESSION AT CHICAGO, MAY 1, 1865

mark of respect they agreed to close the theaters until after the funeral services.

The funeral train arrived in Chicago on May 1st, the last stop before its final destination at Springfield. Both the engine of the train and the pilot engine which preceded it were adorned with portraits of Lincoln. Black blankets trimmed with silver stars were draped over the boilers in simulation of the mourning gear worn by the horses that pulled the funeral hearse. The train came to a stop on the pilings of the Illinois Central tracks at the lake's edge and, as the *Tribune* reported the next morning, "The waters of Lake Michigan, long ruffled by the storm, suddenly calmed from their angry roar into solemn silence as if they too felt that silence was an imperative necessity of the mournful occasion." From the train the casket was carried slowly to the Courthouse while three dozen high-school girls scattered flowers along the way. For a day and a night Lincoln lay in state in the Courthouse where every window and doorway had been draped in black. A crowd that had been pouring into the city for two days stood shoulder to shoulder with Chicagoans until nearly 125,000 people had passed through the double line into the Courthouse.

The tribute to Lincoln in death was to be followed within a year by a tribute to his chief adversary in the great debates, Stephen A. Douglas. The Little Giant had died in 1861, shortly after pledging his life and support to Lincoln and the Union cause. With the pressures of the war gone, Chicago remembered Douglas again. Funds raised through thousands of pledges were used to post a tall monument on the lake shore near Thirty-fifth Street. The statue was on land that Douglas had once owned; he had purchased it as he had the land much farther to the south on the shore of Lake Calumet, because he had confidence it would one day be part of a great city. The dedication ceremonies for the monument were attended by President Andrew Johnson, General Grant and Admiral David G. Farragut. Before them spread a crowd of one hundred thousand who by lifting their eyes toward the sky could see the figure of Douglas on his towering pedestal. At the base of the pedestal on the sarcophagus were his final words to his sons: "Obey the laws and uphold the Constitution." It was the platform which had lifted the debates of two sons of Illinois to greatness.

MOLLIE COSGRIFF ("Irish Mollie")

Everyone Comes Here: Anything Goes Here

VIOLENT CRIME was rare in early Chicago, if the scarcity of judicial executions may be taken as an index. The first official hanging took place in 1840 in a prairie south of the city, now Twenty-ninth and South Parkway. The second execution, which did not occur until after a lapse of seventeen years, was staged at the corner of Jackson and Ashland Boulevards. The new location was for the greater convenience of the public, which was permitted to attend in the absence of more delicate forms of amusement. By 1865 the atmosphere of the growing city had changed; it was sophisticated enough for a double hanging (conducted in private).

There were several explanations for the rarity of crime during the first period of Chicago's growth. One of these was that anyone with the initiative to commit armed robbery could with less risk make a fortune speculating in land. A writer for *Leslie's Illustrated Weekly*, after commenting on the city's "broken down adventurers, real estate sharks, fast men [and] fast nags," described Chicago's capital as city lots and its currency as bonds and mortgages. "Every man owes five times the amount he can pay," he reported, "and is considered a 'poor cuss' if his collateral don't foot up to a hundred thousand."

In such an atmosphere, where everyone "from your bootblack to your hack driver . . . put on real estate airs," the highest stakes were to be found in the gamble over land. Professional bettors found only a limited market. There was no reason to risk a stake at cards when anyone who enjoyed "skinning a sucker" could wander down to the comparatively unregulated Board of Trade where he would find any number of similarly minded individuals willing to match wits with him. The extent of the hazards for the unwary was illustrated in the case of one speculator who bought two hundred barrels of pork. Later, the speculator from whom he had purchased it refused to buy it back on the grounds that it had been short in weight. At least one visitor to the city had the impression that "the secret actions of some of the most prominent men, who under the praise of performing what was considered a smart transaction, were literally conniving at open fraud and robbery" explained Chicago's increasingly indulgent attitude toward official corruption and even crime. David MacRae, an English tourist, was surprised to find that "in the case of a downright swindle, the criminal, in public estimation, seems to be the man who has allowed himself to be swindled." Though the swindler might be called a rogue, it was MacRae's observation that the so-called rogue usually would be recommended when there was "a keen stroke of business to be done."

It was the Civil War, accentuating a number of forces which had been building up since the opening of the Illinois and Michigan Canal, that finally brought the professional gambler to Chicago. He was strictly an imported product. The Illinois and Michigan Canal had always been an important part of the city's history. The first streets of Chicago had been laid out and named by a surveyor of the canal commission. The continuous waterway which the canal provided from the Great Lakes to the Mississippi and the port of New Orleans had contributed much to Chicago's burgeoning prosperity. Silent cargoes of wheat and cotton moved north and south along this waterway and with them went loquacious sailors and travelers to tell of the tremendous fortunes being made in the young city by the lake. With the outbreak of the Civil War, the South could no longer afford the luxury of gentlemen gamblers or of the afternoons of idleness that brought customers to their tables. It was time for a smart man to be on the move—and what was more natural than to come to Chicago where big fortunes were certain to grow larger during the fat war years? It was at least worth a single pass of the dice.

The gamblers—affluent, picturesque and bold—added color and gaiety to somber streets ordinarily dominated by the stern faces of the hustling Yankees. Some of the gamblers affected the mannerisms and toggery of their favorite victim, the loquacious and elegantly attired plantation owner. Others sought to surround themselves with a romantic air by dressing as plainsmen. Still others were obviously the end result of social devolution—degenerate

A GAMBLING DEN ON RANDOLPH STREET

scions of old families who prided themselves on distinguished ancestry, real or imagined. They came from every port of call along the Mississippi and almost all of them prospered. The Chicago *Times* had cause to complain that "our country cousins need to be more than ordinarily on the lookout, as in these times that try men's souls, there are a greater number than usual of those who try the depths of men's pockets." Any hope there might have been of dislodging the newcomers rapidly faded as they established a proprietary claim to their own special area of the city.

On Randolph Street, where most of the gambling dens were located, the new arrivals were the kings of the street. The subjects who paid them the allegiance of admiration and imitation were the single men living over stores in barrack dormitories, soldiers on leave, bounty-jumpers in a hurry to spend their bounty money before the law put them back in the army, veterans celebrating the end of their enlistment or sailors whose vessels had just tied up in the harbor. Day and night this transient population crowded the wooden sidewalks of Randolph Street to try its luck. The hero of every man around a card or dice table was the "sport" with the Mississippi River antecedents. His sayings and doings were the most widely quoted topics of conversation on the street. His feuds, which erupted in so many shootings that the block between State and Dearborn was known as Hairtrigger Block, evoked violent partisanship and demonstrations of loyalty among his followers.

Late afternoon was a good time to see most of the gamblers, who appeared regularly to do a bit of sidewalk strutting. At about the same hour, the gaudy hats and brightly colored gowns of the *nymphes du pave* and girls from the more prosperous bordellos would join the promenade, either singly or in the company of a "gentleman friend," as the phrase went in any introduction. The wealthier gamblers could be seen riding down the street in open carriages, often accompanied by bejeweled and brilliantly dressed consorts who advertised the gambler's prosperity and, in some cases, good taste. The consort of a successful gambler was usually the mistress of a brothel; if she were not already in such a position of business eminence, the gambler customarily provided the capital so that she could have her own "establishment." Like most aspects of Chicago life, this arrangement was directed toward practical ends; the reputation of one partner in each of these highly specialized fields added luster to the name of the other.

The most famous of such romances was that of George Trussell and Mollie Cosgriff, proprietress of a parlor house with pretensions to gentility. Mollie, who was equally well known as "Irish Mollie," was a handsome woman who chose her clothes with care and wore them with chic. Trussell, according to a contemporary reporter, was "tall, straight as an arrow and might have stood as a model for one of Remington's Indian-fighting cavalry officers. As a gamester he was 'top sawyer' among the highest rollers with the record of many broken banks to his credit."

After the Civil War, when Trussell was in a mood for expansion, he bought the famous trotting horse, Dexter. The horse held several track records and was of sufficient distinction to merit a portrait by Currier and Ives. With the acquisition of Dexter, Trussell spent an increasing amount of time at the stables and track preparing the horse for the opening day's races at the Chicago Driving Park. Mollie, whose experience with racing had been limited and who did not have a high opinion of the fascinating qualities of the equine species, grew increasingly suspicious of her lover's frequent absences. She appeared to bear her new loneliness in good spirit, however, and even acquiesced to George's request that she plan a champagne dinner to celebrate his approaching debut as a racing manager. To her chagrin and

DEXTER, the famous trotting horse that figured in the George Trussell shooting, 1857

embarrassment in front of her guests from the "select" sporting houses, the guest of honor did not appear for the dinner. After her guests were gone, Mollie was left alone with her humiliation and champagne. A brief soliloquy convinced her that George needed a lesson in the practices of domesticity. Still wearing the white moire gown she had put on for dinner, Mollie equipped herself with what the next day's paper described as the means of "enforcing the new household ordinance about stay-out-lates." She found George in Seneca Wright's saloon on Randolph Street, adjoining Price's livery stables where Dexter was quartered. George was standing at the bar listening with approval to a rendition of the "Limerick Races" by a singer from North's Circus. Mollie, relieved to find him at such an innocent pastime, rushed into the saloon and threw her arms around his neck. Then, for reasons never fully explained but possibly having something to do with her charms being less than those of a four-footed beast, she shot him dead.

The shooting occurred in Hairtrigger Block and at first caused little excitement outside the saloon. In the offices of the Chicago Times across the street, the city editor who presided proudly over a staff of "two ex-convicts, ten divorced husbands and not a man living with his own wife," didn't bother to send out a reporter. A moment later the shrieks and cries of the bereaved Mollie gave notice that the shooting was more than an exchange between two gamblers. The Times reporter rushed across the street to find Mollie bending over her lover and crying "George! Have I killed you? Have I killed you?" George didn't say; but the coroner, who did, called it murder. A jury set Mollie free after the gun inexplicably disappeared and her counsel pleaded "temporary emotional insanity," an excuse which a few nervous males thought might set an unhealthy precedent. Meanwhile, the court listed the estate of George Trussell as containing, among other items, "five gold watches, two diamond pins, one revolver, one single barrel pistol, five hats and twelve pairs of cassimere pantaloons."

ARMORY AND GASWORKS showing police herding prostitutes, 1866

The Chicago Driving Park continued to be under a jinx after the death of Trussell. It was closed by a second and equally sensational scandal only a month later. A race for a $5,000 purse for the best three out of five heats was scheduled between the trotters General Butler and Cooley. Although Cooley was the underdog, he won the first two heats with his trainer, Bill Riley, driving. Then William McKeever, the owner of General Butler, took the reins of his horse away from the trainer and pushed to victory in two heats to deadlock the contests. By the end of the fourth race it was dark and Riley wanted to quit. He charged that McKeever had broken the rules by running Butler instead of trotting him on the far side of the track out of sight of the judge's stand. So much money had been bet that the judges insisted the fifth race be run; to satisfy Riley they sent watchers to the far side of the track. The fifth race started with the horses even but as they thundered out of the darkness into the home stretch, the judges saw McKeever was missing from the racing sulky behind General Butler. After a brief search, McKeever was found lying on the backstretch, his head crushed by a piece of fence rail. The coroner's hearings in the case dragged on for days, with all of the testimony reported word for word in the newspapers. No flaw could be found in any man's account of the accident which might point to a possible murderer. Finally, the jury called it the work of "persons unknown." The killer, whoever he was, gained nothing. There was justice among gamblers if not under the law—all bets were off.

After the death of Trussell, the slain gambler's foremost rival, "Cap" Hyman, emerged as boss of Randolph Street. When both men were alive, an exchange of shots was commonplace when they met. Trussell when sober was quiet and usually managed to avoid Hyman. But when Trussell was loaded with whiskey, his own temperament was a good match for that of his more excitable adversary. As far as police records show, both men consistently missed their target. It was not for lack of practice, for it was Hyman who caused the *Tribune* to issue its famous editorial complaint that "the practice of shooting people upon the most trifling provocation is becoming altogether too prevalent in this city." Occasionally public indignation forced the police to clamp down on Cap's rampages. At such times, Hyman would vanish from the streets for a month or two and wait patiently until the public's mood had returned to its customary indifference.

During one of Hyman's obstreperous moments, he paid an afternoon visit to the Tremont House. To amuse himself he drew a pistol and held everyone in the hotel prisoner. Walking back and forth at the top of the high steps at the Dearborn Street entrance, he refused to allow anyone to leave or enter the hotel. The street was soon deserted. The officer on the beat and the house detectives were all afraid of trying to shoot it out with Hyman and an appeal for help was sent to Captain Jack Nelson at the detective bureau. Nelson strode into the deserted street and abruptly ordered Hyman to put up his gun. Hyman, without any show of defiance, complied and surrendered. When he was asked why he had not threatened Nelson as he had the others, Hyman had a practical reply that was possibly a clue to his longevity. "Jack can shoot too quick for me," he explained.

With this combination of bravado and discretion, Hyman was destined to prosper. He acquired as his mistress Annie Stafford, reputedly the fattest madame in town and for reasons somewhat obscure referred to as "Gentle Annie." Like Mollie Cosgriff, Annie was given to worrying about her lover's fidelity. Frequently she suggested that a matrimonial alliance would have the desired effect of letting others know Cap was marked property. The prospective groom evaded all suggestions until after the shooting of George Trussell. Annie, inspired by the effectiveness of Mollie's direct action methods, armed herself with a rawhide whip which she was confident would be effective without being lethal. Storming into Hyman's gambling house, she found her lover asleep on the sofa. Waking him up with a crack of the whip, she chased him into the street. No record can be found of the end of this curious pursuit but its effectiveness cannot be doubted. It was announced soon afterward that Cap and Gentle Annie were to become husband and wife.

MICHIGAN AVENUE FROM PARK ROW, 1866

The newspapers called the wedding of Cap and Gentle Annie the "swell-est show" Chicago had seen. It was attended by members of the sporting set from as far away as St. Louis, Cincinnati, Louisville and New Orleans. The wedding was not the only cause for celebration. The same day the newlyweds opened a roadhouse in Lake View for which they had chosen the radiant name of Sunnyside. The advent of Sunnyside had been well advertised and the opening-night party was the most important social event of the year for the gambling fraternity. The guest of honor was to be the same Captain Jack Nelson who had subdued Cap Hyman at the Tremont House and who had since been elevated to deputy superintendent of police. This curious role for a member of the law-enforcement detail was explained on the grounds he was to be present "by no means in his capacity as a keeper of the peace." Other city officials had also promised (unofficially) to be present and there were even a few businessmen with "a tincture of sport in their blood" who had invitations.

There was a heavy snowfall on the day that Gentle Annie succeeded in her ambition of becoming Mrs. Cap Hyman. The snow only added to the evening's prospects. The town was well supplied with sleighs and that evening the fanciest among them were to be found speeding northward to the merry jingle of the bells on the horses' harness. In the city most of the gaming dens were dark as their owners headed toward Sunnyside with a "most particular feminine friend" snuggling beside them in their sleighs.

The bolder men from the Board of Trade who acknowledged they had invitations gathered for a preliminary celebration at the Matteson House. Shortly after eight o'clock, amid a fanfare of horns and the shouting of a sizable crowd, the group made its start in a gondola-shaped sleigh pulled by four horses and filled from prow to stern with boisterous celebrants.

Cap Hyman, who reputedly had a college education and a better-than-average social background, planned the details of his party with meticulous care. He invited the members of the press to act as moral censors and gave them a suitable briefing beforehand. "I would like you gentlemen of the press to understand that the affair will be straight to the wink of an eyelash," he said. "All the ladies are here on their honor and Mrs. Hyman will see to it that nothing unseemly will take place. We want the best people in town to patronize Sunnyside and will make them welcome."

As the guests arrived, Hyman presided with the air of Ward McAllister. Gentlemen were ceremoniously introduced to the ladies, engagement cards were consulted, and all the rest of the formalities which are characteristic of similar functions in a more sedate society were observed. A few of the feminine guests gave evidence of earlier social training, a reminder that there were then no gradations to the glamorless substrata of prostitution; one false step and the victim was precipitated straight to "the depths." For this reason many of the "boarders" of the more sumptuous establishments often played a leading role in the romantic dramas of the period. Most of the guests at Sunnyside's premiere, however, had been culled by Gentle Annie with an eye for their abundant physical charms (too often marred by an excess of cosmetics). For these the role of intellectual companion was awkward, even when quoting carefully memorized sentences about Lord Byron. Efforts to "do the lady business" resulted in embarrassing breaks. Several of the hostesses made it plain they were getting impatient for the moment when "this honor business" would be over. There was an intermission for supper, or rather a banquet, at which Jack Nelson took his seat of honor. Each male guest was assigned a female companion to "take in"—clearly a reversal of the role to which most of the feminine guests were accustomed. As the banquet started, everything seemed to be agreeable, so much so that the *Tribune* reporter found it "portentous." What it portended was recorded in his story the following day:

> About midnight a group, consisting of several ladies(?) and gentlemen(?) [the question marks are the reporter's], became quite animated in conversation. Something was said which was construed by the person addressed to be a reflection upon her character as a lorette. The person addressed replied she was as good as the rest, she thought, and clinched the observation with a very strong epithet. These researches into character naturally shocked those whose sensibilities were most tender and

BRIGGS HOUSE, 1866

it was but a few moments before some of the more ingenious in the use of language, uttered expressions provocative of blows. One of the young women, Eileen McMasters, residing on West Madison Street, was constrained to wear her eyes in mourning for the remainder of the evening. Another, whose name was not ascertained, is represented to have her face left in the condition of dissolving views, the red, white and blue each striving to be the predominant color, a third is reported to have had her nose changed from a pug to a Roman. How much hair bestrewed the floor, what became of the waterfalls and hoop skirts in the conflict, will never be known.

A footnote indicating that the social impact of the party was not confined to a single night was provided by Frederic Francis Cook. "For many days after the event, police justices were worked overtime issuing warrants of arrest for assault and battery," he wrote in *Bygone Days In Chicago*. "On successive mornings the old Armory Court exhibited such varied facial disfigurement that the reporter's psychologic interest was completely lost in the shock to artistic sensibilities, when one recalled how these animated canvases, now so streaked and splotched, but a few nights before had dazzled the beholder with their deftly composed color schemes."

Happily for the peace of the city not all gamblers had the social ambitions of Cap Hyman. A gaming proprietor who stayed close by his tables was Frank Connelly, proprietor of the Senate gambling den. The Senate was known as a "high-toned game" and no small-money players were allowed. The dealer was George Holt, known as the "gentleman par excellence" of Chicago gamblers. The place was raided periodically but the guests were never taken to the station in police wagons. They were driven in carriages at Connelly's expense. After he paid the fines of the entire party, Connelly would have the carriages return the players to the Senate and resume the game.

Chicago became a completely wide-open town with the introduction of Keno. It was argued that the game was not gambling but only another name for an innocent German game called lotto. At first, the police couldn't come to any conclusion in the matter—presumably, said a reporter at the time, because of the regularity of the pay-off. But Keno also had the effect of moving gambling further into the open. Faro had been played at least one flight up and with some pretense of closed doors. Keno transformed the stores of Randolph into a gambling midway. Buildings were renting at exorbitant prices and still the gamblers could not accommodate all who wanted to play. On Saturday nights the crowds pushed out into the street from every Keno game and above the din of those outside could be heard the voice of the proprietor calling out the lucky numbers as they were drawn. An order from police headquarters would have been sufficient to close the games but the police authorities avoided such direct action in order to stage a massive raid. (Knowledgeable Chicagoans pointed out that the raid would produce a record volume of bail-bond business, with the professional bond operators cutting the captains and sergeants in on the night's profits.)

A major part of the police force was mobilized for the raid. Because the Keno players far outnumbered the raiders, the police first blocked the outlets of the various buildings and kept the players prisoner until enough transportation could be found to haul them all to jail. The raid began shortly after 10 o'clock but it was not until two hours later that the last of the players had been taken away. The three-story Armory Court and jail were soon packed with victims and part of the overflow jammed into a large barn at the rear. When the barn would hold no more, a temporary camp was set up in front of the armory and the prisoners surrounded by a corral of blue-coated policemen. The process of setting bond and getting bail was started immediately and went on through the night and all day Sunday. When the supply of bail blanks was gone, the sergeants ordered the patrolmen to write out the necessary wording on blank sheets of paper. As a move to close down Keno, the raid was effective. But its only effect on the gamblers was to cause them to move back upstairs.

The Finer Things of Life

THE BEGINNINGS of the theater in Chicago were not auspicious. The first permanent theater was established in 1837, in the converted dining room of the Sauganash Hotel. In the following year the managers planned to move to a building nearer the center of the business district but ran into opposition based on a combination of New England conscience and Yankee thrift. A group of the town's businessmen presented a petition to the City Council asking that no license for a theater in such a location be permitted. They argued that "Theaters are subject to take fire and are believed to be dangerous on that account to property in their vicinity . . . insurance cannot be obtained on property in their vicinity except at greatly advanced premiums." They were alarmed, they said, over the danger to "the property and lives of your petitioners," giving their property a significant precedence over their lives in their concern. Grant Goodrich, a member of the council committee which considered the petition, felt that the danger to the moral welfare from the establishment of a permanent theater was even more to be abjured. In a minority report, filed after the majority of the committee had voted to grant the license, Goodrich called the tendencies of the performance of "modern theaters" to be "grossly demoralizing, destructive of principle" and "nurseries of crime."

The theater which produced this contention was no more than a make-shift auditorium that had formerly been an auction hall. Among the players at the first performance were Mr. and Mrs. Joseph Jefferson. A special attraction of every evening's show was a curtain song by their son, Master Joseph Jefferson, whose favorite appears to have been a number called "Lord Lovel and Lady Nancy." Master Joseph saw the theater during these many curtain appearances as one of "stuffed seats in the dress circle and planed boards in the pit." In his autobiography he recalled that the new drop curtain contained "a medallion of Shakespeare suffering from a severe pain in his stomach over the center." The dome of the theater was pale blue, with pink and white clouds surmounted by four awkward ballet girls representing the seasons and presumably strewing flowers, snow and grapes over the unsuspecting audience. At the heads of the seasons were four fat cherubs, which Jefferson found to be in "various stages of spinal curvature."

The theatrical season was unorthodox by modern practices. It began in the spring and continued only through the summer months. This eliminated both the problem of heating a building susceptible to fire and the hazard to the audience furnished by Chicago's muddy streets. The theaters drew a large proportion of their audiences from visitors. The most regular patrons were prosperous speculators attracted to the city by the opportunities in real estate (which always rose in value during the summer when the sun had dried up most evidences of its swamplike character). The local press was divided about the theater. One editorialist argued that it was no more proper to allow young people to sample the pleasures of the theater than any other form of vice. Others, under the guise of helpfulness, offered ideas to improve the respectability of the plays and therefore make them more palatable. The Chicago American suggested that managers bring to an end "the habit of throwing out extemporaneously obscene witticisms, which, while they catch the laugh of some, are very offensive to ladies and gentlemen in attendance." It then offered its own rather puzzling formula for wit, which it said should be "chaste and salty enough to preserve its purity," a remarkable use of salt as a preservative. The same arbiter of moral propriety, more than anxious to be of service, advised the ladies that if they were waiting for "fashionable precedents" he could tell them that, at Springfield, the theater was attended generally by the "beauty and fashion of the fair sex and by all the gentlemen of the town, from Supreme Court judges down."

Various means were used to "bend the devil round the stump" in circumventing transplanted Yankee prejudice against frivolous entertainment. One of these was to establish a theater as part of a museum. The museums had, in addition to a series of exhibits labeled educational, an adjoining lecture room for both plays and speakers. Chicago's leading museum was that of Colonel Joseph H. Wood. The Wood's Museum, according to its proprietor, contained "150,000 curiosities of every kind," including a ninety-six-foot fossil caled Zeuglodon, a sea lion, a lighted panorama of the city of London and a hall of paintings. The quality of the art exhibited was not high and the Tribune critic complained that "the drawing and anatomy of some of the Indians was at fault." He did, however, find something to approve in "the marble and moonlight beauty of the slaughtered maidens." An adjoin-

COLONEL WOOD'S MUSEUM, 1866

ing lecture room was large enough to accommodate fifteen hundred people and during the season a stock company offered plays there.

The first theater to be patronized in large numbers by respectable Chicagoans was that built in 1847 by John B. Rice, a theatrical manager from Buffalo. Rice erected a new building on the south side of Randolph, following the plan of the old Coliseum for his seating arrangement. For the first time Chicago saw boxes elegantly fitted up with carpets and comfortable furniture. A competent company of actors and sedate surroundings enabled Rice to overcome much of the resistance to theatrical performances. It was not long before the Chicago *Journal* was reporting that "a large number of ladies—the beauty and fashion of the city—are in nightly attendance." Respectability was also maintained by a line in the advertisements to the effect no females would be admitted unless "accompanied by gentlemen." This precaution was considered necessary to exclude foot-weary prostitutes who might consider the admission fee a suitable price for finding a more comfortable situation in which to interview their prospects.

It was at Rice's theater that opera was first presented in Chicago in a season notable for its brevity. The bill was Vincenzo Bellini's *La Sonnambula*

(*The Sleepwalker*). A visiting company of singers took the leading roles, assisted by a "home chorus" and supported by a local orchestra. Before the hero, Elvino, could discover what force had taken his somnambulant Almina to another man's bed, the performance was interrupted by cries of "fire" outside the theater. Rice, who was his own manager, stepped to the front of the stage and shouted "Sit Down! Sit Down! Do you think I would permit a fire to occur in my theater?" Such was the confidence of the members of the audience in Rice, who was twice to be mayor of the city, that they took their seats. A voice—appropriately from the prompter's box—startled the manager with the information that the theater was in fact on fire from flames that had originated in a livery stable across the alley. The theater was cleared and Chicgo's first opera season brought abruptly to an end; but only after an inebriated opera lover, who sat applauding the holocaust on the stage as the best imitation of a fire he had ever seen, had been dragged to safety. Rice was undaunted and constructed another theater in which he offered Chicago its first full season of Italian opera in 1853.

Concert music was provided for the most part by touring singers and musicians. In 1850, Julius Dyhrenfurth conducted an aggregation of twenty-two musicians in a symphony concert to dedicate the music hall at the Tremont House but did not attempt anything as ambitious as a symphony. Three years later, during a visit of the Germania Orchestra, the young city heard a performance of Beethoven's Second Symphony—which by that circumstance became Chicago's first.

McVICKER'S THEATER, 1866

It was in the music hall at the Tremont House in 1853 that Chicagoans became acquainted with Adelina Patti, who as a "somewhat delicate, pale-faced, dark-browed child with thick glossy hair hanging in two long braids down her back, dressed in rose-colored silk, pink stockings and pantalettes," was singing bravura airs at the age of twelve. Patti was always to be a favorite of listeners who might also remember it was at her debut that such evidences of sophistication as numbered tickets and ushers appeared for the first time. When Patti returned in 1855, she was in the company of Ole Bull, the famous Norwegian violinist. The concert was billed as the "farewell to America" concert of Ole Bull. However, on June 29, 1857, he was back for "one farewell concert" and the following evening was up to giving a "positive farewell." It would have seemed to him poor form to describe his subsequent visits in 1868, 1869, 1872 and 1877 as anything but "farewell concerts," an invention in which he appears to have anticipated Buffalo Bill.

Ten years passed after the erection of Rice's Theater before the opening of another playhouse of comparable importance. Then James H. McVicker, who had been among the most popular of Rice's performers, established McVicker's Theater on Madison Street west of State. It was the most costly and impressive theater in the West and McVicker made it a hospitable place for distinguished drama. On the McVicker stage Chicagoans saw E. A. Sothern, Edmund Keane, Edwin Forrest, Jane Coombs, Mrs. John Drew, Ada Rehan and Joseph Jefferson, no longer singing his curtain song, but now starring in *Rip Van Winkle*. It was at McVicker's that the touring company of America's first musical comedy, *The Black Crook*, attained a run of fifty-six nights, considered extraordinary for the time.

John Wilkes Booth, whose murder of Lincoln evoked a terrible denunciation from his fellow actors, had achieved a personal triumph in Shakespeare's *Richard III* when he played at McVicker's in 1862. During the run of the play he had attended a charity party and was asked for his autograph to sell. He demurred on the grounds that his signature was worthless, but a young girl convinced him that she could sell all he would provide at 25 cents each. When Booth's murder of Lincoln assured the actor of a prominent if villainous role in American history, many Chicago families spent hours trying to salvage these autographs from attic trunks and cluttered bureau drawers.

Edwin Booth, the assassin's brother, also acted at McVicker's. Playing Juliet to Booth's Romeo was Mary McVicker, the daughter of the theater's proprietor. The romance was carried over from the stage to life and Mary later became Mrs. Edwin Booth. In one of Booth's performances at Mc-Vicker's, the actor was shot at by an insane clerk named Mark Gray. The bullet missed Booth and lodged in the framework of the scenery. The imperturbable Booth later had it removed and encased in a gold cartridge

CROSBY'S OPERA HOUSE, 1866

which he wore on his watch chain. On it was engraved "From Mark Gray to Edwin Booth."

All the theaters which Chicago had seen up to the end of the Civil War were eclipsed by the splendors of Crosby's Opera House. Uranus H. Crosby was a young Cape Cod distiller shrewd enough to anticipate the wartime tax on liquors. By building up his supplies before its imposition he had become rich. He was determined to use his money to erect a magnificent building for grand opera that would be a "temple of the arts." He selected a location on Washington Street west of State and at a cost of $700,000 erected a combination opera house, art gallery, and office building. The first floor was rented by W. W. Kimball's piano store, John Wright's restaurant that later became H. M. Kinsley's "celebrated and elegant confectionery, ice cream and dining establishment," and George F. Root's music-publishing firm. The second and third floors overlooking the street were occupied by offices. On the fourth floor was an art gallery and ten artists' studios, including that of G. P. A. Healy. The opera house auditorium was in the rear of the building. It had a seating capacity of three thousand, including a dress circle of fifty-six private boxes. A special wing, with an entrance on State Street, was occupied by a music hall for smaller concerts.

The fortunes of Crosby's tremendous showplace were erratic. The grand opening, scheduled for April 17, 1865, had to be postponed because of the mourning for Lincoln. At the end of a year, Crosby realized that he had falsely calculated the demand for grand opera as well as the cost of producing it. For the first time he was aware that the symbolic statues of Painting, Sculpture, Music and Commerce which stood above the entryway to the opera house were not comfortable neighbors. However, if Crosby was not on intimate terms with the first three arts, he was with the fourth. He soon had conceived an audacious plan to retrieve his fortune: he would give away the $700,000 opera house and the most valuable of its art treasures in a lottery.

The emphasis in his plan, as it had been in the construction of the opera house, was cultural. He did not sell the chances directly as a lottery, but formed the Crosby Art Association, which offered buyers a lottery ticket along with the purchase of one of a series of engravings of popular paintings. Art catalogues took the place of lottery books and even those who were opposed to gambling could with good conscience participate in the lottery on the ground that they had acquired a valuable engraving. The drawing was first announced for October 11, 1866, but not enough of the 210,000 chances had been sold by that date; the drawing was postponed to January 21, 1867. During the intervening months, thousands of people who expected their five-dollar ticket would make them the owners of the imposing edifice strolled through the corridors of the opera house with a proprietary air. Between acts of the opera they were to be found gazing condescendingly at the paintings which less fortunate ticket holders might hope for as a consolation prize. Sales boomed. On the day set for the drawing, all the tickets had been sold except 25,593 which Crosby retained as his own.

For several days before the drawing the trains were bringing in ticket holders who had come to claim their prize. The hotels were filled and temporary barracks were set up in the saloons. The night before, ticket holders too excited to sleep roamed the streets, stopping only long enough to take a little sustenance from an ubiquitous carpetbag. Early in the morning a long line had formed in front of the doors to the opera house. The city slowed almost to a halt. The rooms of the Board of Trade were deserted. Not a single spectator was in the only courtroom that opened for business. At 11 o'clock, the doors of the opera house were thrown open and the crowd surged in, kept under control by an extra force of police. The excitement was so great that a few women dared convention to fight their way to places in the gallery. For the most part the audience was made up of men, some of them on the "fancy order" as one newspaper observed.

On the stage of the opera house were two wheel-shaped cages. The larger contained the numbers of the 210,000 lottery tickets. In the smaller was a list of 302 prizes, ranging in value from the opera house itself to worthless paintings from the art gallery's storage bin. A committee that included representatives from Detroit, St. Louis, New York, Boston and Philadelphia, had been appointed to take charge of the drawing. A total of 112 prizes had been drawn from the prize wheel when the ticket of the opera house was drawn. From the other wheel a judge drew ticket number 58,600. As the numerals were read out the hushed audience waited for the owner to rise and identify himself. When no one rose there were shouts for the committee to read the name of the winning ticket holder. These demands were ignored and the drawing continued, only a few noting in the continuing furor that Crosby himself had drawn two of the best paintings with a combined value of $26,000 as well as Volk's bust of Lincoln.

The drawing was finished with the name of the winning ticket holder a mystery. In a midnight bulletin attached to the end of its story, the *Tribune* began to suspect all was not as it should be. "It is asserted in the best informed circles that Crosby holds the tickets for the three chief prizes next after the first, and it is not certain that he has not that also. It also turns out that the opera house to be deeded is not the whole building as represented but only the audience room in the inaccessible center of the block. If this proves the biggest swindle of the season, no one will pity the victims." In later editions, the *Tribune* added the information that the winner was A. H. Lee of Prairie du Rocher, Randolph County, Illinois.

There were some who doubted if either A. H. Lee or Prairie du Rocher existed. As if to forestall such skeptics, a letter written to Lee's brother-in-law in St. Louis was reprinted with a suspicious alacrity in a St. Louis newspaper. The letter contained in great detail a picture of the scene when Lee was notified he was the winner after he "had undressed and was sitting in my long-tailed nightshirt." He then went on to the purpose of the letter: "I just say this to you; it is for sale. I suppose that somebody wants to buy it and I have to ask you to sell it for me. It is impossible for me to leave my wife in her present condition or I would go up to you at once." By the 25th of January, Mrs. Lee was sufficiently recovered for her husband to get to Chicago if not to his brother-in-law in St. Louis. Chicago was not to know of his arrival until after his departure. Then it was informed only through a letter to the editor in the Chicago *Republican*, a form of communication for which Lee showed continuing preference. In the letter to the editor he explained "it was my wish and request that I might come here and transact my business with Mr. Crosby without becoming the object of unpleasant notoriety and without having my name heralded in the newspapers; and I feel deeply indebted to him for the considerate manner in which the request has been observed, especially as it has cost him some embarrassment as well as occasioned invidious comment. Feeling that the opera house should properly be owned by Mr. Crosby, I made him the offer to sell it to him for $200,000 and the offer was accepted in a spirit which was most gratifying and the money promptly paid me."

The letter did not convince Chicagoans. They had only to figure out that Crosby had sold more than $900,000 worth of chances on a $700,000 investment. Apart from his expenses and even after the payment of $200,000 (which there was reason to doubt had been made) he still retained the total amount of his first investment, plus the opera house. The statue of Commerce must have been smiling broadly as Uranus Crosby passed through the portals of his "temple of the arts."

The question of whether Crosby had swindled the public was not quickly dropped. The promoter found it expedient to retire to a New England village and leave the management of the opera house in the hands of his uncle, Albert Crosby. Under the uncle's management, the opera house continued to be a showplace, though not always for grand opera. In 1867, the *Tribune* exclaimed belligerently that "the public will receive with feelings akin to indignation, the announcement that Mr. Maretzek of New York after his flourish of trumpets, has canceled his arrangements and decided not to give a season of opera here, offering the excuse for this breach of promise, that the season subscriptions are too small to warrant him in bringing an expensive troupe here. We need hardly say the excuse is a very flimsy one. We have only to chronicle the fact and inform Mr. Maretzek of New York that if he can do without Chicago, Chicago can do without him and that in all probability when Mr. Maretzek of New York demises, opera will still exist and be heard in Chicago as heretofore." On Thanksgiving Day of the same year, the opera house was used for a public reception for Edward Payson Weston, the great "walkist," who had walked from Portland, Maine, to Chicago at an average rate of fifty-two miles a day and in some days had traveled more than ninety miles. In 1868, music gave way to politics as the Republicans took over the opera house for their national convention and nominated General Grant for the presidency.

In November of 1869, the attraction at the opera house was not one Uranus H. Crosby had envisioned for his dwelling place of the arts. It was Lydia Thompson and her British Blondes, the large-limbed beefy specimens who introduced burlesque to America. The display of "personal charms" was rated far greater than that of the sensational *Black Crook* and denunciations of the show from the city's pulpits were followed by a rushing business at the box office. The hit of the show was a number called "Sinbad the Sailor," with Lydia, who specialized in boy parts, playing Sinbad. The company played a return engagement the following year and during its second stay incurred the ire of Wilbur F. Storey, the hot-tempered owner

REPUBLICAN CONVENTION AT CROSBY'S OPERA HOUSE, nominating
General Grant for President, 1868

of the *Times*. Storey thought the company immoral and was angry at its
success because he was in the middle of a feud with Crosby.

Storey published a daily attack upon the morality of the show. When this
had no effect he printed comments on the chastity, or rather lack of it, of
members of the company. The climax came in a one-line editorial: "Bawds
at the Opera House! Where's the Police?" Lydia vowed revenge for this
insult. That afternoon she, Pauline Markham, her featured dancer, Archie
Gordon, a press agent, and Mr. Henderson, her company manager, waited
near Peck Court on Wabash Avenue for Storey to come by on his customary
afternoon walk. When Storey came into sight, Henderson saw that Mrs.
Storey was with the editor and suggested the attack be postponed. "Not at
all," said Lydia. "So much the better. She will get an idea of what it means
to attack one of her sex."

As the Storeys approached, Lydia drew a riding whip from under her
wrap. Calling Storey a "dirty old scoundrel," she tried to beat him. He
caught the blow on his left arm and with his right hand seized Lydia by
the throat. Gordon sprang on Storey's back while Henderson pulled Lydia

out of Storey's grasp. During the affray the belligerence of Mrs. Storey for once exceeded that of her husband. "Wilbur," she shouted, "draw your pistol." A policeman arrived in time to help a group of passers-by disentangle the combatants and the next day the four appeared before Justice Augustus Banyon, a paunchy, swollen-nosed, red-faced celebrity of the day. He found Lydia and her companions guilty of charges brought by Storey, fined them $100 and then suspended the fine.

Plans were under way in the summer of 1871 for events of a more dignified character. Throughout the summer, the opera house had been redecorated and modernized at a cost of more than $100,000. Crosby announced he would inaugurate a new season on October 9th with a series of "ten grand symphony and popular concerts" by Theodore Thomas and his orchestra. Every effort had been made to make the new opening as resplendent as the manager's nephew had hoped the first opening would be six years before. But the fate which had pursued the opera house since it was built had one final irony to reveal. Theodore Thomas and his musicians were turned back in a scorching hot train at Twenty-second Street. The stage—that October 9th of 1871—had been set for far greater drama.

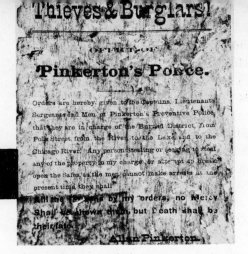

9

The Red Snow

To CHICAGO it appeared that Crosby's Opera House had a kinship with catastrophe. The first opening had been delayed by the assassination of Lincoln. Then, on October 8, 1871, less than twenty-four hours before the grand reopening, the city's eyes were turned anxiously toward the West Side as the Sunday papers headlined stories of "The Great Conflagration." For seventeen hours a fire stormed out of control over four blocks west of the river before Chicago's weary firemen could master it. The damage amounted to nearly a million dollars; if it had not been for the generosity of saloon keeper Daniel W. Quirk, the sum might have been ten times greater and the entire West Division destroyed.

Quirk owned a saloon on the southeast corner of Adams and Canal Streets, several blocks north of where "The Great Conflagration" had started. Throughout Saturday night and Sunday morning the fire moved steadily in a path pointing toward Quirk's saloon. Seeing that his business was doomed, Quirk announced to the crowd watching the fire that anyone who wished could help himself to a supply of liquor and cigars. After a sampling of Quirk's hospitality, the men in the saloon reassured their generous host that they would do all they could to save his buildings. Buckets of water were carried from the river to soak the walls and roof. The portable fire extinguishers that were to be found among the crowd at every Chicago fire were brought into use and sparks from the blaze were extinguished before they could do any damage. The fire, that had been pacing steadily northward, came to a halt before the stout defense of Quirk's volunteer fire brigade.

Spectacular fires were not an uncommon occurrence in Chicago. In 1868, a fire on Lake Street had done more than two million dollars' damage and hastened the exodus of stores to the new business district developing on State Street. By 1871, Chicago was paying more for fire insurance than was collected for state, county and municipal taxes. The city had sixty thousand buildings of which forty thousand were wholly of wood and only a handful of the remainder were fireproof. Roofs were made of felt and tar or of wooden shingles. Year by year the loss from fire was increasing. The *Tribune*, housed in a new fireproof building, was uneasy about the contrast between its own structure and most of the others around it. In an editorial in the summer of 1871, it warned that the city's marble fronts were only a "thin veneer" and the "dispensation of sheet iron and pine planks" had made of Chicago's buildings a "cheat, a snare and a lie." It also told of buildings with walls a hundred feet or more in height that were not more than "a single brick's thickness" and deplored the menace to pedestrians from cornices that "come rattling down to the street in a high wind." The fact was, as the editorialist noted, that the city had been debauched by its own prosperity. Its population had risen from slightly more than four thousand in 1840 to nearly three hundred thousand in 1870. In the haste to grow and prosper it was content to keep roofs over the heads of the newcomers; corrective measures could be taken later.

The summer of 1871 increased the hazards of flimsy construction. The weather was the driest in the city's history. From the fourth of July to the first of October, a period when there normally was a total of eight to nine inches of rain, less than an inch and a half had fallen; this was distributed over six different days. The city, its factories, its frame houses, wooden pavement and plank sidewalks were dry as tinder. Prematurely withered leaves from the trees of "The Garden City" covered the ground.

These omens were largely ignored, principally because of the city's pride in the new waterworks on the North Side. The opening of the waterworks in 1867 gave many Chicagoans the feeling that all the water in Lake Michigan was available on a moment's notice. Watching clear water pour from their faucets, they remembered the years when small fish squeezed through the city's filters and newspapers reported a "four-inch fish made its appearance through an office hydrant," or that "thousands of minnows have been found in Chicago water pipes this winter." The water tower, standing nearly one hundred feet high, was an assuring symbol of the city's readiness.

Only the scorched and weary members of the fire department, returning to their station houses after winning their desperate battle with the West Side fire, realized how inadequate a symbol it was.

At the station of the Little Giant fire company most of the men were near exhaustion when the equipment was finally put away about dusk Sunday afternoon. There was still a need to keep watch, however, and the fireman assigned to the station watch tower during the night hours took his post as usual. About 9:15 P.M. he saw flames leaping toward the sky about six blocks north of the station house. He sounded the alarm and the engine company was on its way toward the blaze as rapidly as the tired crews could harness the horses. As the company rolled out of the station, the fire alarm telegraph box began sounding an alarm. It was the signal of a fire nearly a mile south of where the watchman had seen the flames. The firemen ignored it.

The Little Giant company followed the beacon of fire to De Koven Street, about a half-mile south of the fire of Saturday night. Three barns, a paint shop and a shed were on fire and burning fiercely. Members of the crowd told the firemen the blaze had been going in the area of closely built wooden cottages and shanties for nearly an hour. Across the street in a vacant lot, his hair singed by flames and his face blackened by smoke, stood Peg Leg Sullivan. He was leaning on the neck of a badly frightened calf

THE CHICAGO WATER CRIB, 1866

he had rescued from the barn. Seeing the flames, he had gone into the barn to drag the calf out by the halter. In the struggle, his peg leg had plunged through a rotten board in the floor, catching the top of it so that he could not move. As quickly as possible he unfastened the straps, abandoned his peg and hobbled out with his arms around the neck of the calf. The rescued animal was not Sullivan's but one of the small herd of five kept by Mrs. Patrick O'Leary. She was explaining that a cow had kicked over a lamp when she had gone to the house to get some salt for an ailing animal.

The Little Giant company hooked up its hose and turned a stream of water on the fire, puzzled by the failure of any other company to arrive. Bruno Goll, a druggist who had turned in a fire alarm shortly after nine in the box outside his store and repeated it ten minutes later, watched anxiously for fire companies to be sent in response to his signal. The key to the puzzle lay in the Courthouse tower, where the city's fire watcher had sent out the alarm that rang at the Little Giant's station house. The watcher there had seen the flames but had misjudged their location by more than a mile. Then, as the blaze from the O'Leary barn increased, he realized his error and asked the operator to change the signal. The alarm operator refused to change it, compounding his stubbornness by repeating the wrong alarm a second time. As nearly as could be ascertained later, the alarm from Bruno Goll failed to register on the central board. By the time this accumulation of errors and mechanical failures could be overcome, the fire was moving swiftly northward toward the scene of Saturday night's blaze, urged along by a brisk southwest breeze.

About 10 o'clock a mass of burning material from one of the burning cottages or barns whirled four blocks through the air to the steeple of St. Paul's Roman Catholic Church. The flames that started in the steeple soon enveloped the church and burned over an adjoining factory into Bateham's lumber mill on the bank of the river. There the fire feasted on a thousand cords of kindling for Chicago stoves, half a million feet of furniture lumber and three-quarters of a million wooden shingles. Bateham, an early fire marshal, enlisted volunteers to fight the flames with pumps from the river, but was forced to abandon the attempt despite a fear that burning brands from the yard might ignite the entire South Division. By this time all the fire-fighting equipment of the city was mobilized against three separate fires that had gone out of control. Two separate columns of flame were moving northward from the O'Leary fire and it appeared that nothing could prevent their junction with the inferno in Bateham's mill. But before this consolidation could take place, the capricious fire struck unexpectedly east of the river.

The Parmelee Omnibus and Stage Company had just completed a new stable at Jackson and Franklin on the southwest edge of the business dis-

THE CHICAGO WATERWORKS, 1867

trict. The stalls were new and the lofts freshly filled with hay for the horses which were to be moved in two days later. It was on this target that a mass of blazing timber descended after hurtling nearly a quarter of a mile from the holocaust on the west bank of the river. The hay and newly painted lumber blazed up instantly. A short time later the gas works nearby were on fire. The heroism of a watchman who transferred the gas to tanks on the North Side prevented an explosion but simultaneously put out every light on the South Side of the city. The situation was suddenly desperate. The fire was in the heart of the city, while west of the river an inferno of flames three-quarters of a mile long and one hundred fifty acres in extent defied the best efforts of the firemen against it.

The new fire in the business district forced the fire companies to divide their efforts. Some of the engines, giving up the West Side as lost, rushed over to the South Division. There the fire, like a shrewdly commanded army, moved forward in a pair of flanking movements around the business area. One column moved north from the tinderbox shanties of crime and vice in Conley's Patch to the proud buildings of LaSalle Street. Another arm stretched eastward and south toward the lake. Wild flames hurled brands of fire high in the sky. The watchman in the wooden crib at the end of the lake tunnel—two miles from shore and three miles east of the fire—found the sky filled with a rain of sparks. With the help of his wife he began soaking the roof of the crib to keep it from burning down to the waterline.

At midnight Mayor Roswell B. Mason wired as far as New York City in an appeal for extra fire-fighting equipment. In Milwaukee, St. Louis and Cincinnati, fire engines were loaded on railroad cars to be rushed to Chicago. Meanwhile, as the moon rose dully through a thin pall of smoke, the fact became increasingly clear that a firebreak of some kind would be needed to stop the progress of the flames. James H. Hildreth, a former alderman, asked for authority to blow up buildings in the path of the fire and was granted it. His zeal was greater than his skill and his first effort in the Union National Bank did no more than blow out all the windows. About the same time, General Philip Sheridan, commander of the Army of the Missouri with headquarters in Chicago, also had the idea of blowing up buildings. Hildreth, however, had the powder and used his civilian prerogatives by refusing to share it with the general.

While Hildreth experimented with explosives, the fire continued its unpredictable leaps over the city. Shortly after one o'clock in the morning, a flaming beam landed in the cupola of the Courthouse and the fire soon spread to the lower floors. In the jail on the ground level the prisoners screamed for their freedom as the Courthouse bell pealed monotonously over their heads and the crackling of flames signaled the spreading of the fire. Finally most of the prisoners were freed, the exceptions being accused murderers who were led handcuffed to the lake shore. In the deserted building an automatic mechanism continued clanging the bell until the tower itself fell, to be quickly followed by the crash of the building.

The pace of the fire increased. At Jackson and LaSalle, the new Grand Pacific Hotel—six stories of olive-tinted Ohio sandstone, with a carriage court roofed over by a glass dome, five hundred rooms each equipped with an "electric annunciator" and "a vertical railway to connect all floors"—crashed to the earth before a single guest had scratched his name on its register. At Dearborn and Adams, the equally new Bigelow Hotel with its red carpeting, carved walnut furniture and art galleries disappeared in the flames before it could open its doors for a single moment of elegant existence. The Tremont House went up in flames for the fourth time in its history. Its intrepid manager, John B. Drake, was able to save only the money from the safe and a few pillowcases full of silver. Hurrying along the streets with his salvage, Drake heard men prophesying Chicago would never recover. He did not believe them. On his way to his home he paused in front of the Michigan Avenue Hotel at Congress Street. He saw that it was directly in the path of the flames but still untouched. He turned and strode into the lobby where he confronted the startled manager with an offer to buy the hotel's lease and furniture. The distraught proprietor, besieged by pleas for help from guests dragging their belongings into the street, could not believe the offer

THE GREAT FIRE, by *Currier & Ives*. Note that flames are going in the wrong direction

was a serious one. Drake handed him a thousand dollars in cash from the Tremont moneybox as an advance payment. Even a thousand dollars was a good price for a hotel that appeared destined to burn and the offer was accepted. Copies of an agreement to buy if the hotel survived were hastily drawn up and witnessed by guests at the hotel. With his copy in his pocket, Drake picked up his pillowcase of silver, and hurried down Michigan Avenue toward his home hoping for the best.

The flames by this time had lighted the sky almost to the brilliancy of daylight. From a distance the whole city appeared to take on the appearance of a lurid, yellowish red. The fire burned so intensely there was only a minimum of smoke. Everywhere in and around the burning areas there raged a blizzard of hot cinders, falling in a steady downpour that stung the skin like needles. In many places the red flakes and hot black ashes filled the air until it was impossible to see the distance of a block ahead. Adding to the terror was the danger from maddened animals, dashing through the streets in a torture of pain from the red snow that blistered even the toughest hide. In the heart of the fire, the heat was as intense as that of a welding torch. Iron columns two feet in thickness were burned into dust. Car wheels from the streetcars stood in the tracks half burned away while the tracks turned upward in grotesque patterns from the twisting force of the flames. Jets of fire consumed fireproof safes and bored holes of fire

BURNING OF THE CROSBY OPERA HOUSE

through fireproof walls. The noise was tremendous as the roar of the flames and the crash of falling walls formed a deep-throated chorus to the staccato explosion of barrels of oil and paint.

There were no passive spectators of the fire. The crowds were fleeing for their lives, trying desperately to save something which would provide the basis for a new start if they should survive. The streets between the buildings were narrow gorges of pushing, struggling mobs. People crowded upon such points of vantage as high sidewalks and fences only to have them collapse beneath the weight of harried refugees. Fifth Avenue (Wells Street) and Conley's Patch had already emptied their population into the streets. Debauched, pinched with misery, the flotsam of the city's slum floated along with the crowd. Some smashed windows with their bare hands and snatched what they could, ignoring bleeding hands that sometimes spoiled the fine clothes and silks before they could be taken from the displays. In front of Shay's dry-goods store a man loaded one of the company's trucks with silks and drove away, defying a store guard's command to halt with a curt, "Fire and be damned." A ragamuffin with white kid gloves on his hands and gold-plated jewelry in his back pocket was less fortunate; a falling marble slab from a burning building crushed him to earth.

Daniel Quirk's Saturday-night hospitality would have been wasted on Sunday's mob. At Chapin and Gore's restaurant and liquor store, men were hired to roll a hundred barrels of whiskey down to the comparative safety of the lake shore before the liquor could be seized by the looters who operated just ahead of the flames. Elsewhere beer and whiskey were to be had for the taking and the unruliness of the crowd in at least one instance forced the firemen to turn the hoses from the flames to the mob. The crowd only laughed and in a combination of hysteria and drunkenness taunted the firemen to do it again. The madness was increased by the desire of Chicago to save not only its life but its property. Express wagons, dirt carts and even coaches were used to haul goods to places of safety. One driver asked—and was given—a thousand dollars to haul a half million dollars of a bank's currency to a safe place on the far West Side. A frantic bride rushed along carrying her half-wrapped wedding presents. A round-faced man had seized a woman's turban to protect his hair from the cinders and pushed his way uncertainly down the street while a feather on the turban waved weirdly in the gusts of wind. Women, shrieking with hysterical laughter, dragged large Saratoga trunks slowly down the sidewalks. A red-faced German pushed a wheelbarrow full of clothing that did not obscure the keg of beer over which it was draped. A radical, who stood on top of an abandoned piano to declare that the fire was the friend of the poor and urge the crowd to help itself to what it wanted, was suddenly quieted by a well-aimed whiskey bottle. A woman kneeled in the street with a crucifix held up before her and the skirt of her dress burning while she prayed. Along the river, burning ghost vessels drifted with their masts aflame. Bridges that had caught fire teetered wildly on their centerposts like grotesque fireworks.

About an hour after the Courthouse crashed to the ground the flames leaped the river again, carrying the fire into the North Division where a group of railroad cars containing kerosene on the Chicago and North Western Railway tracks caught fire. From the railway the flames jumped to Wright's livery stables to form another column of fire. The fire rolled north on a wild revel through the neighborhood of frame houses and stately homes of Chicago's first settlers. A short time later a burning brand about ten feet long landed on the slate covering over the wooden roof of the waterworks. The entire building was soon on fire and the pumps destroyed. When the last reserve of water from the tower had been used there was no more water for the city's fire lines except where it could be pumped from the river.

Five separate fires were then eating at the heart of the city. Early Monday the fire on the North Side reached from LaSalle Street and the river to

Oak Street and the lake. The original fire on the West Side had stopped its spread at the firebreak formed by the burned-out area of Saturday's fire but the entire district was a smoldering ruin. In the business section, the flames continued to advance voraciously. During the morning the fire started to backtrack and those buildings that had been saved during the night were caught up and destroyed. At 9 o'clock the Palmer House burned and a short time afterwards McVicker's Theater and the "fireproof" *Tribune* building toppled to the ground. East of the business area, on Wabash and Michigan Avenues, the yards and sidewalks were heaped high with household goods, trunks and stocks of supplies from the stores along State and Lake Streets. At the lake front baseball park, at the foot of Washington and Randolph Streets, refugees from the fire sat despondently on piles of mattresses and clothing. As the circle of flames to the west was drawn more tightly around these temporary islands of safety the weary refugees had to move again. At the ballpark there were hurried attempts to bury silver and other heavy but valuable belongings while a lone policeman shouted purposeless threats about defacing the ball grounds.

On the North Side, where the extremes of wealth and squalor had been separated only by the commonplace barrier of Clark Street, the disparate classes huddled together without distinction on the lake shore. The once-notorious Sands were covered for a distance of about a mile with men, women and children in a variety of undress. Many of the women were in nightgowns

REFUGEES IN THE STREET

with a wrapper pulled tightly around them and the men had tucked their nightgowns hastily and inadequately in the tops of their trousers. Each family sat on an island of personal property—silver, boxes of valuable papers, chairs and even disjointed bedsteads. There was a mixture of the ludicrous and pathetic. Great plate-glass mirrors flashed back the illumination of the fire and elegant carpets served as temporary shelters. Mattresses and carpets continually caught fire from falling sparks and there was a constant procession to the edge of the lake for buckets of water to extinguish the smoldering flames.

Early Monday morning, when the great lumber mills along the river caught fire, the heat was so intense that those on the beach were forced into the lake to avoid being suffocated. A. T. Willett ordered his horses and wagons driven as far out as possible and many of the refugees clambered into these high-wheeled vehicles to wait out the fire. Others spent hours sitting on the backs of chairs, their feet resting on the seats in the water. Judge Lambert Tree and his wife stood knee-deep in water for fourteen hours. Others on the North Side sought protection in Lincoln Park, still in the process of being evacuated as a cemetery. For hours they sat gloomily among the open graves and upended tombstones keeping a death watch on the city. Later the shower of sparks was so thick that the park had to be abandoned. Even those who had been able to get to an artificial island in the middle of the park lagoon had to pour water over their clothes to keep from burning alive.

Meanwhile, the fire was moving among the frame houses and yards of dry leaves on the North Side with the force of a hurricane, lifting up whole buildings and throwing them on top of others. The terrific draft created by the heating of the air sent the fire hurtling along the tops of the buildings, skipping from one block to another. In front of the actual line of fire moved a zone of intensely heated air that cracked windows and sent black smoke pouring from walls and furniture until whole houses burst into flames almost as quickly as the flaring of a match. During the night the servants in the bigger houses had been burying such property as they could in the spacious yards, hoping that the fire would pass over it. Most remarkable was the number of pianos which were recorded as being buried, an indication of the social importance attached to these instruments as well as of the prodigal labors which were inspired by fear of the fire. Not all of those who buried valuables were able to save them. Mary Arnold Scudder, newly married daughter of Lincoln's friend, Isaac Arnold, buried her wedding presents only to have them fused and destroyed from the heat.

At the Chicago Club, whose membership was restricted to the wealthiest businessmen, the members toasted their defiance of the destruction of their businesses with a champagne breakfast. Before they could finish, the fire roared into their exclusive club. Hastily filling their pockets with cigars and taking along all the liquor they could carry, they picked up the red satin sofas from the lobby and took them to the lake shore where they sat down and finished their meal. The fire which destroyed the Chicago Club was on the south fringe of the flames and not burning as fiercely because of the prevailing southwesterly wind. At 11 o'clock Monday the final row of buildings to be destroyed in the South Division caught fire. It was Terrace Row, the fashionable collection of row houses on Michigan Avenue between Congress and Van Buren Streets. William "Deacon" Bross reported that the entire row vanished "quickly and grandly" as the flames "wrapped up the whole block and away it floated in black clouds over Lake Michigan." Bross's preoccupation with reporting the fire for the *Tribune* resulted in his being one of the best targets for plunderers. He sent his coachman to the lake shore with a buggy full of harness, coffee and other property only to have some friends foolishly turn it over to a stranger who said he had orders to drive it away. Bross never saw it again. Later, an express wagon pulled up to the door. Bross assumed his daughter had hired it and she assumed that he had. They both hurried to fill it; not until after the driver disappeared did they realize that they had been helping him rob them. Finding another stranger on his doorstep with "a considerable invoice" of his clothes and "the hunting suit outside," the usually volatile Bross could only comment, "Well, you might as well have them as let them burn."

The destruction of Terrace Row ended the threat of fire to the south but there was a new danger as the flames from the western edge of the business district threatened to backtrack across the river and destroy the West Division in the same way the area north of the river had been devastated. All the buildings on the west bank were soaked with water from the river; by Monday afternoon, while the business section was burning itself out, the fire continued to grow only to the north. By nightfall, the big fires were out except in the neighborhood of Clark and Fullerton on the northern limits of the city. The last house to burn was that of a doctor on Fullerton Avenue; it went up in smoke about 10:30—more than twenty-five hours after the start of the fire. Shortly before midnight a light rain started to fall. Between 2 and 4 o'clock Tuesday morning the fire died out, though from Harrison to Fullerton burning coal piles in the city's cellars cast a weird footlight of red on the panorama of the city's ruins.

In the area swept by fire only two homes had been saved—the mansion of Mahlon D. Ogden and the modest home of policeman Richard Bellinger. Ogden was away, but his friends kept the roof of his house covered with wet blankets and carpets, the same precautionary measure that had been tried and failed in hundreds of other cases. Bellinger was probably the only man to fight the fire directly and win. During the night he raked up his leaves and

BUSINESS DISTRICT AFTER THE FIRE, looking north from Harrison Street

burned his wooden fences and sidewalks. He kept a wet covering on his roof, first using water from his cistern and carrying buckets from a ditch two blocks away; then as a last desperate measure pouring his entire supply of cider over the roof and walls.

Tuesday morning Chicago counted its losses. The fire destroyed 2,124 acres in the central part of the city. It burned 17,450 homes, made ninety thousand homeless and destroyed property worth two hundred million dollars—one-third of the wealth of Chicago. At the customs house, James E. McLean waited forlornly for his "fireproof vault" to cool. Opening it, he found that a million and a half dollars in currency for which he was responsible had burned; it required an Act of Congress to wipe out his prodigious debt. There were more important tragedies. Nearly three hundred were known to be dead; how many more vanished in the crematorium of the city was never to be known. Parts of the picture of a sorrowing city appeared in the makeshift newspapers that were soon on the streets: "Mrs. Bush is at 40 Arnold Street. She lost her baby . . ."—"Henry Schneider, baby, in blue poland waist, red skirt, has white hair. Lost."

The destruction was comparable only to the great fires of London and Moscow. The London fire burned thirteen thousand houses and drove two hundred thousand from their homes but covered only five hundred acres of ground. That of Moscow burned over four hundred acres and destroyed twelve thousand houses. The area of the Chicago fire had been twice as great as the total of those of London and Moscow.

Chicago turned matter-of-factly to the problem of recovery. City offices were set up in the First Congregational Church and a relief program was started. In the first day, nearly five thousand special police were appointed to keep order and stop the looting. The badge of these new officers was a small white piece of cloth with the word "Police" printed on it. The badges had been printed on a boy's press by Allan Culver with the aid of Katherine Medill, whose father Joseph had already found a print shop from which to issue his *Tribune*. The mayor issued proclamations forbidding the sale of whiskey and fixing the price of bread. The army provided tents as temporary housing.

Most cheering were the immediate offers of help which came from over the nation. Two special trains with food and clothing were dispatched from New York. Special committees arrived from St. Louis and Cincinnati to find what was needed. From England came the offer of books to replace the library destroyed in the fire. Only one letter, published in the *Chicago Magazine of Music, Fashion and Home Reading*, showed little sympathy. It came from the literary editor of an Augusta, Georgia, newspaper: "I feel a deep interest in the misfortunes of your city and would fain help you all I can," the correspondent wrote. "And yet, do you know, we owe it—some of my friends and I—to the implacable temper of Chicago troops, during the war, that we are now exiles, impoverished and struggling, far from the sepulchres of our fathers and without a single heirloom sacred to past affection spared us. It was a Chicago soldier who threw into the flames the likeness of my mother, and tearing a box of invaluable literary memoranda from the person who held it, consigned the box to the same flaming bed." The fires of Sherman still burned.

Another Union hero, General Sheridan, was called upon by Mayor Mason after the fire to declare martial law and preserve order. During the first day several looters had been shot dead by angry citizens. The mayor's practical, if unconstitutional, action, angered Governor John Palmer. The governor considered it an invasion of state's rights and felt the city should have appealed first to the state government for aid. After an exchange of angry letters among the governor, mayor and President Grant, the troops were withdrawn. Then, within a few days, they were brought back without the accompanying onus of martial law.

One of the first Chicagoans to recover his composure and nerve after the fire was W. D. Kerfoot. While the ruins of the buildings were still too hot for handling, Kerfoot put up a wooden shack on the deserted street to house his real-estate office. Outside a sign proclaimed in black letters: "All gone except wife, children and energy." Chicagoans, conscious that during the same hours that they were having their ordeal, flash forest fires had killed 750 in Peshtigo, Wisconsin, and destroyed the Michigan towns of Holland and Manistee on the eastern shore of the lake, thought that Kerfoot had all that was needful.

John B. Drake, who had been considered so foolish as to pay an option on a hotel that was sure to be burned, walked down to the edge of the burned district; he found the Michigan Avenue Hotel still standing. He immediately wired New York for a loan and a few days later walked into the hotel lobby with the full purchase price in cash. The proprietor, who realized the hotel was the only one standing in the downtown district, refused to sell and said there was no law which could make him. Drake left and returned in a short time with three or four friends. He laid his watch on the proprietor's table and gave him five minutes to deliver possession. As the proprietor hesitated again, Drake's friends made some remarks about the proximity of Lake Michigan and the imminent possibility of the proprietor's bobbing about in the water. This show of determination settled the issue and the sale was completed. Drake renamed the hotel the Tremont House and kept possession of it until 1873—just one year before it burned down.

89 WASHINGTON STREET, *by W. P. Burton*. The first building erected after the fire

PART TWO *Enter the Ladies*

1871=1890

10

Puritans on Prairie Avenue

CHICAGO, having once raised itself out of the mud, turned optimistically to the chores of creating a new city over the ashes of the old. Poetic tributes from Bret Harte, Will Carleton, John Greenleaf Whittier and many an amateur were a spur to these efforts. From the city's prolific songwriter, George Root, came a series of tunes on the same theme—"Passing Through the Fire," "Lost and Saved" and "From the Ruins Our City Shall Arise." Those fortunate enough to have saved their pianos were diverted by a nocturne composed by Clara E. Saylor and given the clangorous title of "The Chicago Fire Bell." The city was determined that it would not be, as Sir Christopher Wren had disdainfully characterized the officials of London, "unworthy of a great fire."

Wagons hauled bricks from the ruins to the lake-shore basin to make ground for a larger lake-front park. Other teams dragged the ruins of the Courthouse north on Clark Street to provide a more solid base for that busy thoroughfare. Thrifty Presbyterians took the tar-stained stones of the Second Presbyterian Church and used them for their new church building in Lake Forest. New and more solidly constructed buildings began to appear above the jagged profile of the downtown area. In the Kendall Building, George H. Johnson used the first hollow-tile floor construction and thus made complete fireproofing possible. Architects flocked to Chicago, drawn by the rare opportunity to remake a city.

There was not always time to rebuild. Marshall Field & Co. opened its doors in a former horse barn of a street railway company. South of the fire area, on the elegant residential streets of Michigan and Wabash Avenues, "trade walked into the houses with a yardstick for its stiletto and domestic life took up its pack and retreated." Merchants who had lost their stores opened for business in the front parlors of their homes. The piano, the gorgeous sofas, the medallion carpet and the clock of ormulu were carted to the upper floors while temporary showcases took their places in the drawing and dining rooms. Servants accustomed to performing polite services at formal dinners were drafted as clerks to sell hats, furs, shoes and jewelry in the hurly-burly of the new domestic competition. Handsome bronze-hinged front doors were cluttered with business notices. Broad windows where canaries once chirped were blocked out by garish signs lettered with various degrees of skill (and spelling accuracy) by sign painters whose services were suddenly at a premium.

On the east side of Michigan Avenue in the burned district, temporary pine buildings were erected after the Board of Public Works abrogated the rule the lake front could be used only for a park. The city issued temporary leases for these lots and extracted a guarantee that all the barrackslike buildings would be torn down within a year. The former residents of the avenue, either burned out or forced away by the exigencies of business, sought more tranquil surroundings. Only a few had any desire to return to their old location. Most sought to avoid harsh memories and the fear that a southwest wind might bring with it another wall of flame. Some stayed permanently in Riverside, where they had summer homes. Others moved to new areas of the city.

The pattern for most of society's migration was set by three men who were referred to, more in reverence than irreverence, as the trinity of Chicago business: Marshall Field, George M. Pullman and Philip D. Armour. When these three established their homes on Prairie Avenue, that once deserted street became the most fashionable address in Chicago. Within an area of five blocks, forty of the sixty members of the exclusive Commercial Club had their homes. The pride and interest of the city in these new mansions was intense. When the food commission merchant and banker, J. W. Doane, erected his Chicago palace, the newspapers sent reporters daily for accounts of the progress in its construction. Within a few years after the fire the scene along Prairie Avenue changed from one of wild grasses and grazing cows to a vista of towered mansions with great bay windows and spacious yards. Those who could not find places in the exclusive precincts of Prairie Avenue lived either on adjoining Calumet Avenue or farther south in "Millionaire's

REBUILDING CHICAGO. View at Lake and LaSalle Streets, by *Theo R. Davis*

Row" on Michigan Avenue. In the construction of the expensive homes on Michigan Avenue, there was a tendency to imitate the boulevard system of Paris, with blocks of adjoining houses of similar style and arrangement. But the owners did not always allow their architects to follow the Parisian taste. Efforts to achieve individuality or excel all others soon led to an excess of ornamentation that, unhappily for the city's reputation, was known as the Chicago Style.

Life in these mansions took on an elegance previously unknown. Stern puritan living gave way to epicurean enjoyment, though many New England households still frowned on the practice of serving wine with meals. The hired girl was replaced by a downstairs maid and a butler. No longer was dinner served at noon with the head of the family coming home from the office to do the carving. Ladies' luncheons and formal dinner parties at which the hour was set "as late as 7 o'clock," became popular forms of entertainment. Before calling on friends, a lady scanned carefully the newly published *Bon Ton Directory*, giving the "Names in Alphabetical Order, Addresses and Hours of Reception of the Most Prominent and Fashionable Ladies Residing in Chicago and Its Suburbs." That there was a certain uneasiness about adopting the more rigid rules was evidenced in the frequent notation, "Friends Always Welcome."

The chief characteristic of Chicago society was its newness. Most hostesses had little experience in entertaining formally. A guest from Boston was horrified to find her Prairie Avenue hostess serving dessert ices in the center of

MRS. IRA HOLMES, 1866, *by George
P. A. Healy.* The mother of Burton
Holmes

calla lilies, a horticultural innovation more magnificent than appetizing.
More conservative hostesses relied on the catalogues of the fashionable
caterer, Kinsley, for instructions on how to manage a "Kettledrum" (a word
borrowed from English garrison life where the drumhead often served as
tea tray), High Tea, Coffee, or an At Home. Kinsley's was Chicago's most
fashionable restaurant and aspired to the title of The Delmonico's of the
West. H. M. Kinsley had first maintained a restaurant in Crosby's Opera
House. After the fire he erected a five-story Moorish castle on Adams Street,
making it additionally conspicuous with red-and-white striped awnings which
hung from every window. Here the diner might have a choice of a French
or German café, a Ladies' and Gentlemen's Restaurant, a Gentleman's
Restaurant or the option of using one of the private banquet rooms or the
large ballroom. From this headquarters Kinsley issued the catalogues which
determined the proper etiquette for Chicagoans in such matters as Afternoon Reception, Society Jewelry, The Art of Dressing and The Etiquette
of the Ballroom. For those wishing to remain *au courant* with fashionable
conversation or menus, Kinsley included a glossary of frequently used French
terms. One of Kinsley's most famous performances was in connection with
the driving of the golden spike which marked the completion of the Union

Pacific Railroad. Kinsley filled a baggage car with provisions, chafing dishes, cooks and waiters to serve a group of travelers which included Jay Gould, George Pullman, William H. Vanderbilt and other railroad kings going west for the ceremonies.

Summertime in Chicago found society activities at a minimum. Life along Prairie Avenue returned to an informality more like that of a small town than of a city approaching a population of half a million. On summer evenings the drawing room was moved to the front steps; the children sat on the family's stoop rug waving friendly greetings to passing friends while the adults sat in rocking chairs in the porch or vestibule. This flight from the drawing room may have been hastened by the styles in interior decoration which had been given a depressing tone by the Eastlake pattern popularized at the Philadelphia Centennial Exposition. In the name of art, houses were filled with ebonized furniture and fragile gilt chairs while flimsy curtains replaced traditional draperies. Under the influence of William Morris, many houses were given a dungeon gloominess by brown and green wallpapers applied in perpendicular patterns called picture screens and friezes. Another fad was for gilt milking stools, spinning wheels and chopping bowls which added an incongruous note to many a formal drawing room. Increasing the sense of melancholy were the dried cattails in upended sewer tilings which decorators preferred to more cheerful flowers. In personal dress, bangs and bangles were the fashion rule among debutantes, while their escorts tended to toothpick shoes and tight trousers. Matrons wore bonnets or mantillas, while men of substance identified themselves with massive rings in the pattern of their seals.

Culture was not neglected. The women of society formed a Fortnightly Club whose purpose was to be the dissemination of both "social and intellectual culture." Their husbands joined the Chicago Literary Club with much the same purpose. Both were to prove durable institutions. More transient was the Twentieth Century Club, patterned after the Nineteenth Century Club which Courtlandt Palmer had organized in New York. The newspapers, recording the founding of the Twentieth Century Club, said that "while there are many bright minds among its members, it is essentially a listening club and not a talking club, and in this respect it differs from any other social, scientific, or literary club in America."

Mrs. George Roswell Grant, who had the idea for the Twentieth Century Club, felt that "when a distinguished foreigner and people from other parts of the country come to Chicago, they want to meet the representative society people. They don't care about being bored with a lot of men who have a local reputation as men of genius . . . They want to meet people whose names are known as men and women of fashion." Despite such attractions as a lecture in Italian (reported as having been delivered "after a fashion like drawing long, tight-fitting corks"), the club was split by dissension. At the first annual meeting a group of rebels planned a protest against what they called "autocratic management" in the club's affairs. The women complained that only a few ladies such as Mrs. Pullman, Mrs. Doane and Mrs. Field had been allowed to entertain the club and that too many meetings had been held in the Art Institute. Speaking anonymously to a newspaper reporter, one of the insurgents explained the reasons for her stand: "Why did we go into the club if not to get a chance to entertain and be entertained by swells . . . What we want is to have a provision inserted in the new constitution that the club shall meet only in the homes of its members." The lady also expressed disappointment in the club's choice of speakers. "There has been absolutely nothing sensational or interesting in the slightest degree in the lectures," she said. "We might just as well have had Carmencita and people of her sort who would give us something to talk about." The reign of Mrs. Pullman, Mrs. Field and their cohorts was not easily disturbed, however, and the rebels went meekly along with the established order.

The Marshall Field house was one of the dominant mansions on the Avenue. It was designed by Richard Morris Hunt, the same architect who built the New York residences of William H. Vanderbilt and John Jacob Astor. Field did not pick Hunt because of his New York reputation but because the architect came from Brattleboro, Vermont, and could therefore be counted on to plan a building expressing the Yankee virtues of "dignity, simplicity and common sense." Field's instructions to the architect were succinct: "No frills." The result was a house extraordinarily plain in its exterior where Mr. Field ruled, but sumptuous in its interior where Mrs. Field had her say. A spectacular circular staircase of carved wood spiraled upward from the end of the central hall. The ivory and gold drawing room with its high ceiling would have formed an appropriate setting for state receptions in a royal palace. Though undistinguished in appearance to the outsider, the house was one of the most costly in Chicago and was the first to be equipped with electric lights. (The power came from a privately owned electrical plant in J. W. Doane's stables.) Every morning at a regular hour Marshall Field left his home in his carriage for his store. But on arriving at

GOING TO THE RACES

State Street, he would get out of the carriage a short distance from Marshall Field Co. and walk the rest of the way. He thought it both bad taste and bad business to arrive at work in a fancy carriage with a coachman on the box.

Marshall Field prescribed this stern regimen only for himself. With his children he was overindulgent. The first "grown-up" birthday party of Marshall Field, Jr., was the most magnificent the city had ever seen. For several years Mrs. Field had made it a custom to give a Christmas party for young Marshall and his sister, Ethel. In 1886, when Marshall was seventeen, his mother felt it was time for him to have a more adult party. She planned a "Mikado Ball" around the theme of the Gilbert and Sullivan operetta which was currently the most popular stage success in America. Decorators were called in to transform the house into a miniature Japanese village. Not even Kinsley's was considered adequate for the occasion. Sherry's was engaged in New York to bring all the supplies of linen, silver and food from the east in two private railroad cars. The cost of the party exceeded $75,000.

On the night of the ball, Prairie Avenue was illuminated for several blocks with special calcium lights. A long line of polished carriages drawn by meticulously groomed horses began delivering the first of the five hundred invited guests at 6 P.M. the hour that the friends of fourteen-year-old Ethel had been bidden to arrive. Everyone was in a Japanese costume. The carriages stopped at the side entrance as the front hall had been blocked off with a reproduction of Ko-Ko's garden, the setting for the second act of *The Mikado*. On one side of the hall was a miniature pagoda which housed the musicians of society's favorite band leader, Johnny Hand, who wore a black silk ribbon dangling from his glasses. Valicia and his mandolin orchestra, the first unit of its kind ever heard in Chicago, alternated with Hand's musicians. The drawing room had been converted to an octagonal Japanese court. The doors had been removed and replaced with swinging fringe curtains of beaded wood, ivory and glass such as were used in doorways by the wealthy people of Japan. The walls of every hall were obscured behind satin and bamboo screens and the ceilings hidden by a profusion of Japanese lanterns and parasols. Expensive bronzes, tapestries and porcelains had been purchased to carry out the oriental motif. At one end of the ballroom stood

CARRIAGES ON DERBY DAY, 1893

KINSLEY'S RESTAURANT (From Kinsley's catalogue)

two Japanese flower trees, their artificial foliage carefully arranged by a Japanese artist. There were imported favors for every guest, Mrs. Field having scored a social and diplomatic coup by persuading the iconoclastic James McNeill Whistler to design two of the favors that were distributed along with toy animals, lanterns, parasols, Japanese slippers and the currently popular ornamental storks. As the younger guests left the party, their older brothers and sisters arrived to dance to "I've Got a Little List," "Willow Tit-willow" and other Sullivan airs, which must have required complicated stepping. The dancing was managed by Eugene A. Bournique, whose parents ran the most fashionable dancing school in the city and where adults as well as children learned the intricacies of ballroom behavior.

Bournique's was more than a dancing school. Many society receptions were held in its richly furnished ballroom beneath brilliant crystal chandeliers flanked by a series of stained-glass windows. Most residents on Prairie Avenue had their own ballrooms but met at Bournique's for an exclusive dancing class organized by Mrs. Pullman. In this class were the first couples of Chicago's society, many of them in their fifties and sixties. They applied themselves to the problems of the schottische, the waltz, the polka, and a quadrille of local origin known as "The Prairie Queen" in the same methodical manner they had amassed fortunes. Among the students were the sons of two Presidents—Frederick Dent Grant and Robert Todd Lincoln. General Philip Sheridan was another member of the class. The hero of the Wilderness Campaign and the Battle of Five Forks, who had never learned to go any direction but forward and around the flank of the enemy on the battlefield, carried this military single-mindedness into the ballroom. When General Sheridan waltzed, he whirled his partner around and around without reversing his direction while the dizzying lady listened hopefully for the end of the dance. Jennie Otis Counselman confided after a series of turns with the general that "as he stepped on my toes and did not reverse until I was dizzy, I concluded many who were not heroes danced better."

As a feminine society began to develop, the men spent much of their time at the Chicago Club. Here a guest might see Marshall Field, George Pullman, N. K. Fairbank, John Crerar and T. B. Blackstone dining together or playing poker at the "millionaire's table"—which might more accurately have been called that of the multimillionaires. Many fortunes were still to be made. Gustavus Swift, who had come to Chicago to do the cattle buying for a packing firm and had since become head of the company, was to be found in the malodorous surroundings of his plant's sewage outlet watching for signs of fat that might indicate wastefulness on the production line. This frugality, engendered in part by ancestors who had fought an unequal battle with the miserly sands of Cape Cod, was to prove the basis of a fortune for this "Yankee of the Stockyards." It was also to give the industry a solid economic base and a notoriety for using everything of the hog but the squeal. Gustavus Swift had no reason to apologize for his role as sewer inspector. It was recognized as a sound business practice; and business success rather than an ancestral blood line was the only sure key to the portals of Chicago society.

One of those who dared to rebel against the stern rule of the city's business leaders was Mrs. Herbert Ayer, who "loved everything that was pretty and especially everything that was French." She was a student of ceramics and antiques. It was known—and discussed with disapproval—that she was fond of French novels and had even dared to act out French plays at parties in her home. She entertained unconventionally at Sunday-morning breakfasts, real French *déjeuners à la fourchette* at which she served *omelettes aux fines herbes*, chicken livers *en brochette*, *café noir* and a fine wine. Her guests were principally stage celebrities such as Edwin Booth, Lawrence Barrett and John McCulloch. If they found the breakfasts unusual it was only in the degree of pleasure they afforded. These violations of the social proprieties continued to disturb Chicago's society arbiters until Mr. Ayer's firm failed. It was felt this catastrophe carried a moral for the eccentric behavior of his pretty wife. But Mrs. Ayer was not prepared to accept an unhappy ending to her romance with life. Using her own name of Harriet Hubbard Ayer, she manufactured and sold a beauty cream of her own prescription.

She was soon the head of a prosperous cosmetics business. Moving to New York, she was hired as a columnist by Arthur Brisbane and became the highest paid woman journalist in the country. Although separated from her husband, she displayed a nobility worthy of a heroine in the French romances of which she was so fond. Learning that her former mate was dying, alone and without money, she returned to pay his bills and care for him. She sat holding his hand when he died. Gallic sentiment had given the story of Harriet Hubbard Ayer an ending of which not even transplanted Puritans could disapprove.

The most festive day for all of South Side society was Derby Day at Washington Park. The running of the American Derby was the signal for the fashionable world to display its summer finery. Shortly before noon the boulevards of the South Side began to fill up with lines of carriages. The horses' tails were docked and their heads held high; polished harnesses jangled cockily as the gay cavalcade of the best people, the finest horses, the handsomest phaetons, victorias, coaches, hansoms and even "just plain hacks" made its way south to the race track at Sixty-first Street and Cottage Grove Avenue. In the carriages sat the wives of the town's new millionaires, wearing summer gowns and holding brightly hued sun parasols over their heads. Frequently the women would be unaccompanied, their husbands preferring to ride out in one of the big drags or "Tally-ho" coaches filled with cronies from the Chicago Club or Calumet Club, the exclusive province of those who could claim a place among the first settlers. Mayor Carter Harrison usually galloped along on a Kentucky thoroughbred with Mrs.

RACECOURSE AT WASHINGTON PARK

Harrison and Carter, Jr., following more sedately in one of the small T-carts. The drivers of the fancier turnouts would frequently leave their female passengers at the clubhouse and spend another half-hour driving around the special paths to the left of the clubhouse. Here fancy-gaited animals were put through their paces, wheeling, turning, prancing high and flecking foam while an appreciative audience in the clubhouse applauded with discreet enthusiasm. Later the horses were driven to the rear of the club area where grooms unhitched the animals and took them to shaded stalls in the rear to cool and feed.

It was in their horses and carriages that fashionable Chicagoans first dared to compete for public attention. Hobart Chatfield-Taylor gave credit for this new air of sumptuousness to the English coachman who, "clean shaven and erect," sat upon the box where formerly there had been a mustachioed Scandinavian or a Negro with the sole responsibility of driving the horses. The English coachman, by his own impeccable attire and formally correct behavior, set a new standard for the occupant of the carriage behind him. To merit the approval of one's English coachman was the obsession of every socially ambitious Chicagoan, though more than a few among the city's first citizens found it difficult to resist grabbing the reins themselves. Their children were more adaptable and in many homes it was the children who insisted the coachman be added, proud to have him shout at less elegant modes of transportation, "Git out of the way and let the quality by!"

There was expensive competition to see who could have the flashiest horses and most expensive carriages. Charles Schwartz was the innovator, driving his Brewster drag and team of bays from one end of Michigan Avenue to the other. Hall McCormick was next in the contest with a London-built drag and a pair of roans. Both, however, were outdone by Potter Palmer, who surprised Chicagoans by appearing in a French char-à-banc with leopard skins spread over the seats. It was not the sole surprise Potter Palmer was to give Chicago.

MRS. POTTER PALMER AS A
YOUNG LADY, *by George P. A. Healy*

The Pride of Potter Palmer

IN THE summer of 1871, a few months before the great fire, Chicagoans learned to their astonishment that Potter Palmer had reserved the bridal suite of the Palmer House for himself. A bachelor of forty-four, Palmer had retired as a multimillionaire several years before when Marshall Field and a group of associates took over the management and a major interest of Palmer's dry-goods store. Palmer was not of a temperament to enjoy inactivity. After a short trip to Europe, he returned to Chicago and purchased a million dollars' worth of land along State Street. With typical audacity he set out to make it the principal street of Chicago. His first step was as far-seeing as it was unconventional: he chopped twenty-seven feet off the front of his property and added it to the width of the street. Then, to demonstrate his own faith in the future of the street, he began construction of his Palmer House with the determination to make it the most elegant hostelry in the city. Chicago heard Potter Palmer liked to make frequent trips to Saratoga, where he acquired a reputation as a playboy and free spender. Stories filtered back to Chicago of late dinners, dashing rides behind four-in-hands, rivulets of champagne and gold coins dropped freely by the Quaker dry-goods prince into waiting hands. Occasionally he would shock Chicago by driving his buggy down the street with his feet on the buckboard and a lady of the demi-monde at his side.

The city's surprise over Palmer's decision to renounce the pleasures of Saratoga and similar pastimes was compounded when he revealed his bride would be Bertha Honore, a beautiful twenty-one-year-old daughter of a family from the city's aristocratic Kentucky colony. The courtship had been brief; this was explained on the grounds that Palmer was decisive in his actions. Those who knew Bertha Honore were as firm in their belief that the quick culmination of the romance could be attributed to the bride. They knew her as a girl of firm will and in later years had cause to suspect she immediately foresaw the potentialities of a union that was to prove illustrious for Chicago, and, to all appearances, as happy as less splendid romances.

Potter Palmer and Bertha Honore were married in July in the new Honore home on South Michigan Avenue. The bride wore a Paris gown of rose-point lace and white satin; orange blossoms were looped over her shoulders and a crown of the traditional flowers rested on the small wave in her long, dark hair. More than seven hundred guests attended the reception. Kinsley had exceeded his own high standards, replacing the customary cut glass with a complete service of sterling silver. The wedding gift of the groom to the bride was on the same fabulous scale; it was the new Palmer House, then valued at half a million dollars.

Palmer was in the East when the great fire obliterated his State Street investments. He lost ninety-five buildings in the flames and rents totaling $220,000 a year. Because of his heavy holdings in land, he fell $15,000 short of having enough money to pay taxes on the charred earth that represented his total assets. He was able to recoup because an insurance company, whose faith in his abilities must have been devout, gave him a loan of $1,700,000 with no more collateral than his signature. With these funds the Palmer House was rebuilt, more imposing than before. Its design was grandiose; before it was finished, Palmer told his bookkeeper to enter no more charges as he didn't care to know the cost. Even so, he pared no magnificence from his plans. He insisted that the hotel set a new standard for being fireproof and shrewdly used the fact to publicize his accomplishment. He offered other hotel owners the option of starting a fire in any room in the Palmer House. If the flames spread beyond the room within an hour, Palmer would pay for the damages; if not, the other hotel keeper had to pay for them. There were no takers for the offer.

Another bit of showmanship, on a level with the earlier innovation when he offered to let women take goods home on approval against the advice of such established merchants as A. T. Stewart of New York, was his order to have silver dollars embedded in the floor of the Palmer House barber shop.

His silver dollars meant as much to the men as his courteous store policies had signified to their wives; generations of farm boys in the Midwest were to grow up dreaming of the day they could walk on the silver dollars in the Palmer House barber shop, known also as the Garden of Eden in honor of its proprietor, W. S. Eden.

As Potter Palmer set out to remake the city physically and commercially, his bride was busy trying to remake it socially. Her first opportunity for a display of her talents as an architect of society on a grand scale came with the marriage of her sister, Ida Honore, to Lieutenant Frederick Dent Grant, the son of the President. The wedding was at the Honore home, relocated on Vincennes Avenue at Forty-fifth Street, but its sumptuous plans were in the determined hands of sister Bertha. On the afternoon of the wedding, the Palmers arrived in an elegance exceeding that of President Grant and his wife. Mr. Palmer was sartorially exact in a gray topper with gray gloves and wore in his gray cravat one perfect pearl. Mrs. Palmer, wearing her collection of diamonds and pearls, made a spectacular appearance as the rays of the sun caught the edges of the diamonds among the pink tea roses in her hair and her sedate gray gown flared out in a bold fringe of cardinal red. Even the couple's first-born baby, Honore, eight months old, was brought in suitable elegance to the wedding. He lay with appropriate decorum on a beribboned satin pillow in a handmade dress three yards long. The bridal couple knelt under a canopy of white flowers—camellias, orange blossoms, Cape jasmine and carnations. The cut flowers were of such a variety that when antiquarians attempted to reproduce the wedding table in later years, they found many of the flowers unobtainable.

No bride's costume was ever more explicitly described than that of Ida Honore, who wore, according to the next day's paper, "a Paris gown of lace and supple white satin d'orange, underneath which was a corset of the same satin, made to order with one hundred bones in it." Her petticoats ranged from a top one of soft imported muslin with a long train to a short white flannel "inside" with four petticoats between these two. In the bride's trousseau, according to the knowledgeable scribe, were a dozen more corsets, including one of lavender foulard with "matching underwear" and endless pairs of stockings classified as opera, carriage, reception, morning and evening. The groom created his own sensation by dashing up to the house in an open wagon drawn by four well-curried army mules with jingling harness and burnished hooves. On the second floor, the young couple's wedding gifts were on display, including $10,000 worth of diamonds that Potter Palmer gave his young sister-in-law and the pearls she received from her mother-in-law, the first lady of the United States, with whom the bride was to live at the White House.

Detailed reporting of society events was so uniquely a Chicago practice that the Philadelphia *Evening Bulletin* blamed it for "the annual crop of divorces in Chicago." The *Tribune* took exception to this theory, explaining the reason so many details were made available to the local press was that "the gentlemanly reporter is indigenous to Chicago. Nowhere else do travelers find the calm repose, the insouciance, the neatness and elegance of attire, the quiet, unassuming manner, the soft, smooth voice, the graceful, languid gait that conspire in the construction of the Chicago reporter."

The reign of Mrs. Palmer over Chicago society, which began with the Grant wedding, coincided with the rise of the feminist movement. There was evidence that Mrs. Palmer was more closely attuned to the real aspirations of this social revolution than was Amelia Bloomer. "One hears so much about the 'new woman' that one is in danger of being bored by her unless she arrives quickly," Mrs. Palmer said. However, she was a vigorous advocate of greater education for women. In a newspaper article, she discarded the platitude that "the fact of sex in women, instead of being fixed and unalterable seems to have been a variable condition," changing for the worse if a woman were educated. It was her theory that women "in a lucky moment found that men did not really admire the stupid, superficial fools they had trained us to become. . . . Woman is no longer frightened by the thought that man may not admire and love her, for she feels that he can't help it." This confidence in her own abilities and those of the rest of her sex brought her often to the lecture platform, where she discoursed on any subject from politics to art. Her theories of art were characteristically individual. "You women know how it is," she said in explaining art to a culturally avid audience at the Art Institute, "the more you put on, sometimes, the worse you look, and the more you take off, the better you look." That her audience was

GENERAL GRANT IN LINCOLN PARK, with Carter H. Harrison and Thomas Hoyne, 1879 not more shocked by such theories was explained by a writer in *The Woman Beautiful* who reported "people are concerned not so much about what she thinks as they are about her aloof manner, her stunning carriage, the smooth pink and white unwrinkled skin, the perfect teeth, wonderful hair, velvet gowns, her world famous furs and the sumptuous way in which she conducts her ménage."

Mrs. Palmer's ménage, as the magazine writer described it, was an innovation of her husband's as important as his development of State Street and his sponsorship of Chicago's boulevard system on the South Side. In the 1880's, Potter Palmer turned his attention to the neglected lake front on the North Side, then a wilderness of small dunes, stunted willows and pools of stagnant water. In this inhospitable setting, he planned to build the most splendid house in Chicago. His first problem was to fill in the marshy land. He disdained the use of waste material as both unsatisfactory and unhealthy. He ordered sand from the lake shipped in, hoping by this means to do away with any danger of malaria or the other diseases that were (probably erroneously) attributed to locating buildings on land made from waste and garbage. For the privilege of dredging this sand from the lake, he deeded his riparian rights to Lincoln Park, setting the pattern for a lake front development that was to be world famous.

He was less original in the architecture for his new home, choosing to pattern it after the imitation Rhenish castles popular with the rich and homesick brewers of Milwaukee. A high brownstone mansion studded with turrets, balconies and minarets, the house was finished in 1885. In a defiant gesture toward less affluent imitators, Palmer constructed the house without exterior doorknobs or outside locks; it was only possible to enter when a servant opened the door. For a visitor the test was as arduous as a diplomatic ceremony; his card had to pass through the hands of twenty-seven butlers, maids and social secretaries before he could be admitted. Even Mrs. Palmer's closest friends were required to write for appointments.

Upon being admitted to the Palmer mansion, the visitor stepped into an octagonal hall three stories high, its floor a mosaic of marble and its walls heavily obscured by large Gobelin tapestries. From the hall he might be taken to a French drawing room, a Spanish music room, and English dining room with a shiny dark sideboard of solid Dominican mahogany or through a Moorish corridor into a Turkish parlor or perhaps a Greek or Japanese parlor. Intimates of the family rode in one of two private elevators—the first installed in a private home in Chicago; on arriving at an upper level they stepped out across inlaid parquet flooring past the bedroom where Mrs. Palmer slept in a Louis XVI bed ten feet high. However, Chicagoans did not appreciate Mrs. Palmer's jade collection which she considered one of the finest in the world. When her guests continued to show lack of interest in

ROOF GARDEN AT THE PALMER HOUSE, 1873

it, she sadly moved it to Paris, commenting that "There is no use having it here, as no one ever looks at it."

Members of local society were more appreciative of Mrs. Palmer's abilities as a hostess, when she entertained at formal dinners in the ballroom and banquet hall for as many as fifty guests. Gowned in velvet and wearing a $30,000 collar of diamonds and pearls, surrounded by her collection of Monets, Degas and Corots, Mrs. Palmer presided with the demeanor of a queen. Foreign visitors were pleased and impressed that she could converse in French with them. The walls were loaded with art treasures that were to form the nucleus of the Art Institute of Chicago. Mrs. Palmer was an early collector of French Impressionists. By the time her house was built she had enough of these French paintings to fill a gallery, with sufficient Monets remaining to form a frieze on the walls of her ballroom. Potter Palmer was not always present at these stately dinners. He excused himself on the ground that he was not a society man, and often spent the evenings alone in a room in a tower of the house. He preferred an afternoon at the races or an evening with his business cronies planning a greater—and richer— Chicago.

Everything Mrs. Palmer did showed the results of careful planning. Self-control was her fetish. She believed that through strict self-discipline anything could be accomplished. Despite the luxury of her own position, she was an early champion of the rights and welfare of working women. In these activities she won the respect of Governor John Peter Altgeld, who wrote her at length and with a warmth that was as much a tribute to her charm as her politics. One letter he concluded: "Now please do not ask why I have written this letter, for all I could say would be that 'I could not help it.' I believe, however, that this is always a good excuse, especially if one is willing to take the consequence. I made frantic efforts to see you in the fall but the fates were against me. They guarded you jealously and spared you the affliction . . . Assuring you of my high regard as well as admiration, I am very respectfully yours, John P. Altgeld."

Mrs. Palmer's interest in politics was more than that of dilettante. She encouraged her son, Honore, to run for alderman of the Twenty-first Ward and when he announced for the office she became his political manager. Honore applied himself to the task of getting elected with the same discipline his mother practiced. He studied Italian so he could address the voters in his ward who spoke no other language. To the Germans he spoke a precise Harvard German and managed a passable French for the few voters of French origin. Honore's rival attempted to ridicule these efforts to meet the voters on their own level by circulating the report that Honore had joined the waiter's union. Honore heard the joke and hurried down to the Palmer House where he had himself photographed in a white uniform carrying a tray, much to the pleasure of the waiters in every restaurant and saloon in the district. The climax of Honore's campaign was the reception given by Mrs. Palmer for the ward workers and others supporting her son's candidacy. Many of the guests were more familiar with the lodging houses and saloons in the southern part of the ward than with polite society, but the doors of the mansion were opened to all. It was an unusual reception. The guests arrived in force, five hundred strong and led by a band. Mrs. Palmer received them wearing her most elegant gown. She shook hands with every guest, entertained the crowd with a brief concert and served them supper. The opposition was helpless before such tactics and Honore was elected. Much to the satisfaction of his mother, he was a diligent alderman and subsequently was returned to the council for a second term.

The great indulgence of Mrs. Palmer was jewelry. Her collection of gems and stones was exceeded only by that of Queen Margherita of Italy, who had a considerable ancestral advantage over the American newcomer. One of Mrs. Palmer's collars—given the appropriate if degrading name of a dog collar—contained 2,268 pearls and seven large diamonds. At a ball given by the Countess of Stafford, Mrs. Palmer wore a diamond-studded belt, a circle of diamond stars around her throat and a standing collar of diamonds. During a transatlantic voyage, she stopped Alois Burgstaller of the Metropolitan Opera in the middle of an aria by suddenly appearing in the audience wearing a tiara of diamonds as big as Tokay grapes, a corsage pinned to a base of diamonds, a sunburst of diamonds nearly ten inches in circumference, a stomacher of more diamonds and a collar of pearls. Mrs. Palmer crossed the Atlantic every year; when she traveled as a passenger on the maiden voyage of the Lusitania, she sent back daily reports of the trip for the *Chicago Herald-Examiner*. It was through the trips to Europe of Mrs. Palmer that society there was made fully aware of Chicago's great wealth, a bit of knowledge which was to have repercussions a generation later when Chicago heiresses entered the market for European titles with the same aggressiveness that their fathers had shown in gambling over land.

Abroad, Mrs. Palmer made her own rules of behavior just as she did in Chicago. When the opera *Salome*, which Richard Strauss had fashioned around a poem by Oscar Wilde, was causing a sensational controversy in Europe, Mrs. Palmer arranged to have it performed in her Mayfair house in London. Among the guests who saw the opera's London premiere, given by a cast imported from Paris, were King Edward and Queen Alexandra. At another party the entertainment was Pavlova dancing. When Mrs. Palmer gave a reception for Honore and his wife in Paris, the guests were offered as a diversion a performance of the Russian ballet.

In Chicago, the court through which Mrs. Palmer reigned over society was her New Year's Day reception. To be invited to this annual event meant that one was accepted in society during the following year. There was always trepidation that Mrs. Palmer, who believed in pruning her lists every two years, might drop a name from the list. The invitations were never refused. Those admitted to the New Year's reception were also reasonably certain to receive invitations to Mrs. Palmer's annual Charity Ball, usually held about a fortnight afterward. These Charity Balls were regarded as civic institutions rather than society affairs and were given a proportionate amount of space in the newspapers. Each year, from five to seven columns of the front pages of the newspapers were given over to the details of the evening as the new aristocracy of Chicago stepped out of polished carriages and walked under special awnings and over specially laid oriental rugs into the Auditorium, where the ball was held. Very few dared to be late. The boxes which overlooked the dance floor were filled with a promptness considered correct by the "personified millions of the West." Looking around him at one of the Charity Balls, a *Tribune* reporter saw "good, easy men in their somber conventional garb of black and white . . . yet what rich city of the antique world—Antwerp or Venice in her palmiest days," he asked, "could have shown an assemblage of burghers rivaling in gold power and gold necromancy the achievements of these decorous merchants?"

The grand march at the Charity Ball was the opportunity for Mrs. Palmer to acknowledge the authority of her deputies who ruled over the subdominions within Chicago society. One wing of the formal promenade was always led by Mrs. Palmer herself, appearing on the arm of someone such as N. K. Fairbank, the president of the Chicago Club, or General Nelson Miles, the hero of the Indian Wars. Leading the other column of Chicago's wealth might be either Mrs. William J. Chalmers, who reigned over the West Division from her Ashland Avenue home, or Mrs. Horatio O. Stone, whose authority was generally accepted as pre-eminent in the South Division.

The West Division had been the early home of Mrs. Palmer's family and remained a predominantly southern community. Originally Ashland Avenue had been known as Reuben Street, but when "Hey Rube!" became popular as a term of ridicule, the residents of Reuben Street found themselves being called Rubes. This was intolerable and the property owners asked to have the name changed to Ashland, after the country estate of Kentucky's Henry Clay. Their petition was successful and southern hospitality and customs continued to prevail along Ashland Avenue. The houses were spacious and the grounds nearly the size of country farmyards. Most families kept their own horses, cows and chickens and raised their vegetables in back-yard gardens. The squire of the avenue was Mayor Carter H. Harrison, who kept his black bay in a stable near his house and liked to ride up and down the street in the manner of a plantation owner looking over his acreage.

A self-contained segment of Chicago society was to be found west of the Potter Palmer house on the North Side, centering around the forty-five-room mansion of Cyrus Hall McCormick. The McCormick house, which required five years to build, was predominantly French in style, with a high

TALLY-HO PARTY GOING TO THE DERBY, 1870. Third from left is Carter Harrison I. Next and reading to the right are General Philip Sheridan, Potter Palmer and General John A. Logan

mansard roof and elaborate cresting. The interior was impressively decorated with banded columns, garlands and other features easily traceable to
Charles Garnier's Nouvel Opéra, the architectural wonder of the world
in the reign of Napoleon III. There was a private ballroom with a full stage
in which the publicity-shy McCormick clan could enjoy its entertainment.
The private auditorium may have been suggested by the family's experience
during the Civil War; the former Virginians were so discomfited by the
bloodthirsty denunciations of their southern kin from the pulpits that they
finally quit going to church.

Around the mansion of Cyrus, the other members of the McCormick
family built their homes. William Sanderson McCormick lived in a large
house of yellow Milwaukee brick on Huron Street and Robert Hall McCormick lived a short distance away on Rush. When young Robert Sanderson
McCormick married Katherine Medill the couple lived close by at the
Ontario Hotel. Leander Hamilton McCormick, with whom Cyrus had
made his home before marrying Nettie Fowler, lived a few steps away at
Rush and Ontario. Passers-by, looking at the collection of the clan's mansions, named the area McCormickville.

The most ostentatious mansion on the North Side was that of Perry H.
Smith, a vice-president of the Chicago & North Western Railway. The
house was located on the northwest corner of Pine Street (now Michigan)
and Huron, just a few blocks north of the river. White marble walls, a slate-
covered mansard roof and the enormous size of the building gave it the
appearance of a public institution. Inside, guests found a small theater with
rising rows of permanent seats in the manner of commercial playhouses.
The rooms were tremendous and appeared more spacious at night when
tall mirrors were drawn across the high windows in place of the more conventional interior shutters. The highly polished mirrors, their edges con-
cealed by velvet draperies, were hazards for guests unfamiliar with the
house, who often took them for doorways. The housewarming for the mansion was scheduled for January 2, 1878, to avoid conflict with the traditional reception of Mrs. Palmer. Even with this gesture, Mrs. Palmer was
for once the loser. The Smiths, determined never to be outdone, monop-
olized the attention of fashionable gossip for weeks by showing their guests
three faucets in the butler's pantry—one for hot water and one for cold
water; while out of the third poured bubbly, sparkling iced champagne.

Few families could hope to compete with the munificence of a Potter
Palmer or Perry Smith. Competition among most hostesses took the form
of seeking unique favors to distribute at their formal parties. European
travelers sought original party mementoes with the same fervor they pursued antiques or shopped for Paris gowns. Frequently the favors were of
a nature to be used during the ball—parasols to be spun during a dance,

133   THE PRIDE OF POTTER PALMER

brightly colored hats for the girls, flower-trimmed harnesses with bells which tinkled delicately as the girls directed their escorts through the intricate patterns of a cotillion. On exceptional occasions, the men might also take home a remembrance such as the solid gold dresser boxes which Mrs. Pullman distributed at one of her parties.

Through these final decades of the nineteenth century and the early years of the twentieth century, the dominant figure who represented Chicago society to the world and whom the city itself recognized as its most illustrious hostess continued to be Mrs. Potter Palmer. One of the warmest tributes came from a newspaper in New York, a city that has never been lavish in its praise of things Chicagoan: "With levees, soirees and promenades now in the dim perspective, we can look upon Mrs. Palmer's time and see what will be missed in the new ensemble. For each age has its afterglow, and none more brilliant than the one just passed. Poets, painters, and novelists drew upon such as she to make lovely pictures of grandes dames."

MRS. POTTER PALMER,
1893, *by Anders L. Zorn*

GARDNER S. CHAPIN. A caricature
by T. Wust from the Chapin and
Gore Restaurant

12

The Sporting Life

A HISTORIAN of the police department, writing of Chicago during the 1880's, lamented that it had become known as a "fast" city throughout the land. "People of respectability tolerate things here," he wrote, "which are perfectly shocking to the moral sense of respectable people elsewhere. Men, reckless of public opinion, and women, regardless of feminine delicacy, are continually creating social sensations. . . . The painted woman drives an elegant equipage, paid for, perhaps, by some prominent citizen; whole thoroughfares are given over, nay abandoned, to bagnios and brothels." *Scribner's Magazine*, viewing Chicago about the same time, was in full agreement. "Chicago! The name has a strange fascination for the American people. The name is familiar in the remotest villages of all parts of Europe. The wickedness and piety of Chicago are in their way marvelous."

Perhaps most to be marveled at was the man who personified this combination of wickedness and piety—Carter H. Harrison I, who through four consecutive terms ruled over Chicago during the expansive eighties. Harrison's aristocratic background and southern upbringing, plus a period at school in Europe, had given him a sense of noblesse oblige toward the workingman and infinite tolerance for the weaknesses of all human beings. He believed that vice was as durable as virtue, that no law ever written could prevent gambling or prostitution and that a workingman had as much right to have a glass of beer on Sunday—his only day of leisure—as on any other day of the week. The mayor was not alarmed by charges that the city suffered from moral decay. He once declared in a burst of oratorical enthusiasm that "the young city is not only vigorous but she laves her beautiful limbs daily in Lake Michigan and comes out clean and pure every morning." Reformers, noting that in one year more than seven million bushels of corn were consumed in the manufacture of whiskey in Illinois, were not sure it was water which the city was using for its bath. But even Harrison's enemies, such as Senator John A. Logan, who charged that Harrison had made Chicago known as the Gomorrah of the West, conceded that the mayor had been good for business. His belief in progress and a wide-open town exactly suited the burgeoning city, where the aim of every citizen was "first to make money, next to spend it—how, where and when is nobody's business." Or as George Wellington Streeter observed shortly after he laid siege to the North Side lake front, "This is a frontier town and it's got to go through its red-blooded youth. A church and a WCTU never growed a big town yet." The city's tolerant and humorous view of crime was typified in a police-court item in the *Tribune* reporting that "Ben Hughes and George Carr, two youthful pickpockets, were sentenced to six months in the House of Correction by Justice Summerfield. They picked the pocket of Mrs. Alcina Riebeling in a bungling manner and were thus punished for their lack of skill."

There were so many vice districts that local baedekers were published to enable the visitor to find his way among the Black Hole, Little Cheyenne, the Bad Lands, Satan's Mile, the Levee, Dead Man's Alley or Hell's Half Acre. This last section of real estate was distinguished by the fact that every building was occupied by a saloon, a low gambling house, a concert saloon, an assignation house or a row of streetwalkers' cribs. It was not an area in which it was of much use to call the police, for they never entered it except in pairs and then only when on specific assignments. This caution was no reflection on the courage of the police. Applicants wanting positions on the detective force were warned that "the criminals of the Garden City are noted for their recklessness. They shoot quicker and with less provocation than in any other city and the detective who pits himself against these desperadoes and hopes to come out with a whole skin must be nervy to a degree and as quick as chain lightning in handling a gun."

One of the saloon proprietors of the day was an ex-pickpocket who owned the Lone Star saloon and Palm Garden at the southern end of Whiskey Row. His name was Mickey Finn. Among the drinks he offered to his patrons were a "Mickey Finn Special" and a "Number Two." The Mickey Finn Special was compounded of raw alcohol, water in which snuff had been soaked and a mysterious white ingredient Finn had obtained from a voodoo doctor. To those whose digestive apparatus was too sensitive for this fiery concoction, Finn serve Number Two, in which beer rather than alcohol was used to make the voodoo doctor's blackout pills more palatable. A Mickey Finn Special could render a victim unconscious for two or three days, enabling the ingenious Finn to stack up his dupes in the back room without missing a turn at the bar where other customers might be clamoring for one of the *specialités de la maison*. At his leisure Finn would rifle the pockets of the doped patrons and dump them into the street.

Another early entrepreneur was Johnny Harmon, who is credited with opening Chicago's first concert saloon at Madison and Peoria Streets. Here girls provided entertainment while dispensing drinks to thirsty patrons. Harmon fell victim to his own desire for efficiency. He placed a sign over the bar with the following legend: "Gentlemen will please keep their hands off the waiter girls, as it interferes with the discharge of their duties." This unamiable attitude caused a sharp drop in business and shortly afterward Harmon was forced to close his doors for lack of patronage.

Attempts to reform the city's vice districts either fell short of their mark or were sabotaged by the intolerant leaders of the temperance movement. The administration of Joseph Medill and his "fireproof ticket," elected to prevent the misappropriation of relief funds after the fire, was nearly wrecked by groups insisting that all Chicago's woes were directly attributable to the opening of the saloons on Sunday. However, one constructive reform was put through under Medill. A complicated tax-levy system was established which restricted the taxing powers of the city to only 2 per cent of the assessed value of the real and personal property. This tax program was based upon a combination of pessimism and realism—if the aldermen could not be kept from stealing, at least the city could limit the amount they could steal.

Political corruption was notorious. When a combination city hall and county building was constructed, the county-building portion cost a million dollars more than the city hall, though both were of the same dimensions and material. This was considered excessive graft, even for Chicago, and eventually several politicians were convicted for diverting the funds. One of these escaped before he could be taken to the penitentiary and fled to Canada. He did not die a fugitive but returned shortly thereafter to Chicago where he opened a saloon. As it would not have been considered sports-

A SUMMER CONCERT GARDEN

manlike to arrest him a second time, he was not bothered by the fair-minded representatives of the law.

In 1872, the city tried twice to establish a reform group, once with a Committee of Seventy and again with a Committee of Twenty-five. Both groups broke up in fights with the anti-liquor crusaders. When the temperance groups lost a public referendum on closing the saloons on Sunday, praying women began tours of the city's saloons. Kneeling in the sawdust and alternately weeping, singing and praying, the women implored divine assistance in leading the bartenders to repentance. When this widely dispersed attack failed, they marched in a body to City Hall to protest to Mayor Harvey Doolittle Colvin. As the mayor was no more than a hireling of the town's boss gambler, Mike McDonald, the mass demonstration only served to embarrass the clergymen whom the indignant ladies forced to accompany them on their foray. In 1874, another reform effort was made, this time with a Committee of One Hundred. Like its predecessors it dispersed without having disturbed the city's customary pattern of life. In 1877, the Citizens' Law and Order League, by concentrating upon the sale of liquor to minors and demanding court action against it, was able to accomplish some good in a limited area. But even these successes were achieved only because the saloon owners were willing to co-operate.

The ignominy of failure that haunted all Chicago reform efforts pursued the indefatigable Frances E. Willard, the devout lady who resigned as Dean of Women at Northwestern University to head the Women's Christian Temperance Union. Miss Willard's temperance crusade began modestly with a campaign to get Chicago women to replace the wineglasses on their parlor tables on New Year's Day with pledge books; in these gentlemen callers were to pledge their total abstinence. This crusade was to grow until it resulted in the passage of the Eighteenth Amendment, prohibiting the sale of alcoholic liquors. But Miss Willard, who was to have so much influence on American history, was to have less success in Chicago. She was not able to convert her own nephew, Josiah Flynt, to her cause. Flynt, who had been reared by Miss Willard, was a victim of what he called the "go-fever." He hopped a freight train for Buffalo, stole a rig, was caught, escaped from reform school and finally entered hoboland, where he became one of the important sources of information for Havelock Ellis in that author's *Studies in the Psychology of Sex*. From Josiah Flynt to Mayor Colvin, Chicagoans were more interested in the exploits of gamblers like Mike McDonald than in the earnest pleas of Frances Willard.

McDonald was the successor to Colonel Jack H. Haverly, who in the days following the Civil War had raised the gambler to the level of a business-man. Haverly preferred to refer to himself as an organizer or a promoter rather than a gambler. It was Haverly who expounded the idea that betting on the horses was no worse than gambling in wheat. As a demonstration of his principles, he sought to reduce betting on the races to a steady, dividend-paying basis. He formed auction pools to bet on the races precisely as the members of the Board of Trade formed pools to trade in wheat or pork. Soon the papers were sending reporters to the tracks to send back tabulated accounts of Haverly's "investments." These were reported in the same columns with statistics on the daily sale of carloads of wheat or cargoes of lumber. Unhappily, Haverly's system was no better than that of any other horse player—except on those days he had been given information on a fixed race.

McDonald went a step beyond Haverly. In addition to putting gambling on the same basis as a legitimate business, he entered into a working part-nership with the politicians. During the time that Joseph Medill was mayor, McDonald had enough influence with the board of police commissioners to persuade them to fire the chief of police for, among other acts of which McDonald disapproved, barring the gambler from police headquarters. Mc-Donald did not have any influence with Medill, however, and the mayor threw out the police board and rehired the police officer. The defeat was only temporary. When Harvey Doolittle Colvin was elected mayor, Mike McDonald became the boss of Chicago. It was during Colvin's regime that

McDonald built a four-story gambling house at the corner of Clark and Monroe Streets in the center of the business district and known as The Store. One of the gambler's partners was afraid that it might be too big. McDonald replied—in a phrase that takes a certain glory away from P. T. Barnum—"Don't worry about that. There's a sucker born every minute." Another reason for the gambler's confidence may have been the prowess with the dice of his one-armed brother-in-law, Nick Hogan. Gamblers said that if Hogan had two arms he would have all the money in the world. Throughout most of the 1870's and 1880's The Store was the largest of a group of thirty gambling houses which ran wide open on Clark, Dearborn, State and Randolph Streets. Anyone wanting favors from City Hall usually had to go first to the second-floor office of Mike McDonald at The Store. It was McDonald, along with Harry Varnell, who headed Chicago's first gambling syndicate. In a single year the pair made a profit of nearly a million dollars from the control of betting at northern Illinois and Indiana race tracks.

McDonald was also interested in boxing. It was he who gave John L. Sullivan the backing that enabled the Boston Strong Boy to make his bid for the world's heavyweight championship. Sullivan came to Chicago to ask the gambler to back him in a fight with Captain Dalton, then the leading contender for the heavyweight title held by Paddy Ryan. When McDonald said he didn't think Sullivan was big enough to whip Dalton, the fighter offered to take on three toughs from the stockyards at one time; he promised to lick all three in a bare-knuckle fight within an hour. Mc-

CHARLES COMISKEY. A caricature by William H. Schmedtgen from the Chapin and Gore Restaurant

Donald, who was sure of seeing a good fight one way or the other, agreed to the proposition. When Sullivan finished off his opponents in the specified period, McDonald gave the fighter the backing which enabled him to meet Dalton. After knocking out Dalton in the fourth round of a fight at Chicago, Sullivan won the world championship with a ninth round KO of Ryan in a ring in front of the Barnes Hotel at Mississippi City, Mississippi.

The favorite gathering place in Chicago for sports figures and gamblers was the restaurant of Chapin and Gore, on Monroe Street just west of State. Gardner Chapin and James Gore first met in California during the gold rush. Later they separated, Chapin coming to Chicago to open a small grocery store and Gore remaining in the West, where he grew wealthy as a salesman of mining stock. Gore visited Chicago later to repay Chapin a loan of $200 and stayed to go into partnership with his old friend. He persuaded Chapin to add a wholesale liquor store—which at that time meant selling whiskey by the jug—and in a short time the new branch was doing so well the grocery was abandoned. The liquor store was then expanded to include a restaurant where the finest steaks in Chicago were served. Behind the lunch counter was a series of ranges where the customers watched their meats roasting over the coals. If a patron failed to find a piece of meat that pleased him, manager Louis Pease hired a hack to go to the stockyards to bring back the desired cut. With such a high standard of service, Gore scoffed at all advertising, declaring that all he needed was a "walking ad," a satisfied customer. He would only break this rule, he told a salesman for Wilbur Storey's Chicago *Times*, if he could buy the entire front page of the paper. The salesman, either through shrewdness or lack of tact, told Gore he wouldn't pay the price for such an advertisement. "Name the price," Gore said indignantly. As a result of this conversation, the first full-page advertisement ever run in a Chicago newspaper made its appearance on September 4, 1875.

During the racing season the restaurant became the headquarters for the bookmakers. It was said that if a bookmaker wasn't at Chapin and Gore's, he must be either in the hospital or the morgue. As all transactions were cash, the bookmakers frequently found themselves with more money than it was wise to carry down a Chicago street. This money, locked in an individual tin box carrying the name of the gambler, was put in the restaurant vault. Often the vault contained as much as half a million dollars in cash. But in one of those uniquely inviolate agreements of the lawbreaking fraternity, it never was robbed. No women were admitted to Chapin and Gore's, but this was by choice of the proprietors and no reflection on its social status. The wealthiest Chicagoans were among its patrons. General Phil Sheridan, Long John Wentworth, Philip D. Armour, actor Joe Jefferson when he was in the city, the Pinkertons (when they were not looking for one of the restaurant's patrons), John W. "Bet-a-Million" Gates and Dr. Florenz Ziegfeld, the popular director of the Chicago Musical College, ate there often. Another popular table was that where General Nelson A. Miles and Colonel William F. Cody matched tales about Indian fighting during the times that Buffalo Bill's Wild West Show was playing Chicago. The wall of the restaurant was gaudily decorated with caricatures of famous guests and a painting of a fictitious "Chapin and Gore Butterfly Ball" which portrayed many of the town's more decorous citizens in undignified merry-making. The canvas included such incongruous couples as Wilbur F. Storey and Lydia Thompson, whose closest actual relationship had been at opposite ends of a horsewhip.

Neither Chapin nor Gore was afraid of competition. With the profits from their restaurant they financed the establishment of the genteel catering firm of Kinsley's. Another restaurateur who profited from the partners' generosity was Charles Rector, a former dining-car superintendent who had caught their attention when he was working at the Boston Oyster House. With the financial assistance of Chapin and Gore, Rector founded his own restaurant. Until Rector moved to New York, it was the most popular after-the-theater eating place in Chicago.

A notable and unusual eating establishment was that of Ambrose and Jackson, founded by two runaway slaves who had arrived during the 1850's. Neither could write but both could cook. They did one of the largest businesses in Chicago. Among their regular patrons were Democratic stalwarts Stephen A. Douglas, Cyrus H. McCormick and William B. Ogden.

The gamblers, like the city's more respectable millionaires, had moved away from the downtown area after the fire. Many of their elegant homes were located on Drexel Boulevard, a street never mentioned without a disapproving shrug by the residents of nearby Prairie Avenue. No fancier carriages or dresses were to be seen than those on display along this boulevard when the gamblers took the fancily attired mistresses of demi-monde mansions out to the races or for a Sunday-afternoon ride. No violence ever sullied the streets of this neighborhood and every effort was made to keep it respectable.

Nearer the center of town crime and prostitution had been organized with the same business efficiency that characterized more legitimate activities in Chicago. The organization of the vice district was the equal of any neighborhood in the city. It had its own newspapers, published under such titles as Chicago Street Gazette, Chicago Gazette, Chicago Life and Chicago Sporting Life. One entrepreneur felt the business establishments were sufficiently permanent to issue a Sporting and Club House Directory. The publisher's chief difficulty was with saloon keepers who were patronized by the "sporting-house trade" but who would not advertise in the directory. With

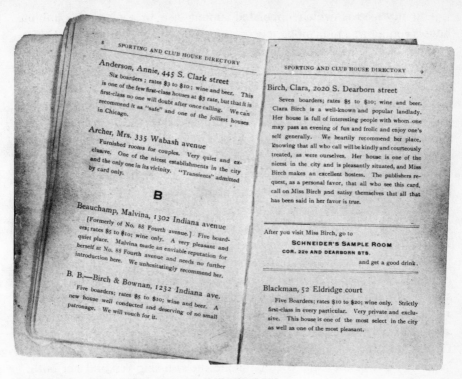

Anderson, Annie, 445 S. Clark street

Six boarders ; rates $3 to $10 ; wine and beer. This is one of the few first-class houses at $3 rate, but that it is first-class no one will doubt after once calling. We can recommend it as "safe" and one of the jolliest houses in Chicago.

Archer, Mrs. 335 Wabash avenue

Furnished rooms for couples. Very quiet and exclusive. One of the nicest establishments in the city and the only one in its vicinity. "Transients" admitted by card only.

B

Beauchamp, Malvina, 1302 Indiana avenue

[Formerly of No. 88 Fourth avenue.] Five boarders; rates $5 to $10; wine only. A very pleasant and quiet place. Malvina made an enviable reputation for herself at No. 88 Fourth avenue and needs no further introduction here. We unhesitatingly recommend her.

B. B.—Birch & Bownan, 1232 Indiana ave.

Five boarders; rates $5 to $10; wine and beer. A new house well conducted and deserving of no small patronage. We will vouch for it.

Birch, Clara, 2020 S. Dearborn street

Seven boarders; rates $5 to $10; wine and beer. Clara Birch is a well-known and popular landlady. Her house is full of interesting people with whom one may pass an evening of fun and frolic and enjoy one's self generally. We heartily recommend her place, knowing that all who call will be kindly and courteously treated, as were ourselves. Her house is one of the nicest in the city and is pleasantly situated, and Miss Birch makes an excellent hostess. The publishers request, as a personal favor, that all who see this card, call on Miss Birch and satisfy themselves that all that has been said in her favor is true.

After you visit Miss Birch, go to

SCHNEIDER'S SAMPLE ROOM
COR. 220 AND DEARBORN STS.

and get a good drink.

Blackman, 52 Eldridge court

Five Boarders; rates $10 to $20; wine only. Strictly first-class in every particular. Very private and exclusive. This house is one of the most select in the city as well as one of the most pleasant.

SPORTING AND CLUB HOUSE DIRECTORY

a fine feeling for delicacy, he avoided profanity and only quoted them as saying they didn't want their names in a "D——ed W—— House Directory." The book contained both the names of recommended houses and a listing of dives the publisher felt it was wise to avoid. There were advertisements for liquors, candies and for a medicine guaranteeing "the Opium Habit will be positively cured at home without interruption of business." Even with these gestures of co-operation, the publisher had to concede that "compiling a *Sporting and Club House Directory* is an undertaking beset with difficulties which are not to be met with in any other sort of compilation."

One of the directory's more eloquent listings was that of Mrs. M. J. Dean: "14 boarders, rates $5, $10, $15 and $20. Mrs. Dean's house is strictly first class . . . on the first floor besides three magnificently furnished parlors is the handsome and well equipped cue and billiard room. There are two music rooms on the first floor and one on the second. . . . The whole building from cellar to garret is pervaded with an atmosphere of quiet elegance. . . . Most of Mrs. Dean's boarders are eastern people and while they are modest and ladylike they are still full of fun and music and entertain callers with a grace all their own."

The newspapers which circulated among the brothels and gambling houses contained a piquant variety of news. There were columns on "Doings in Dixie" and "The Ups and Downs of the Gay Sports in the Crescent City"; a serial story, "Irish Mollie, the Courtesan Queen"; and news of billiards and boxing. An etiquette column on "Good Manners and Household Decoration" was a regular feature. Probably the most popular column was the one called "Hot Turnovers." Here the reader learned that "Lottie Maynard should not be so fresh with other girls' lovers or she will hear something to her disadvantage" . . . "Emma, at 17 Union Street," could read that she had "better let up monkeying after Charley Todd, for he has a perfect lady, and everybody knows he is dead stuck on her."

There were also warnings of shootings and feuds. To Kit Morgan, on December 9, 1882, was a message from "One That Knows"—"There is no law that you cannot go up and down Madison Street all you want and if you want to stand on the corner of Fifth Avenue and Madison, that you can do. Don't be bluffed." Dick Remington was told he "had better keep away from 26 and not be pulling that gun or he may get more than he got and lose the gun too." Another warning read, "Murphy, you want to stay away from 529 Clark Street. Stay away from that old cat." And "Mike the Lusher must stop his monkeying with May of the Bon Ton . . . if you don't leave that girl in the Leland Hotel alone she will slug you and her both." There were probably many young men interested in the fact "They have two new strawberry blondes at the Hotel de Goodrich," or who might agree "There is a lot of snide young tidbits at 376 State Street." In the *Chicago Street Gazette* of October 20, 1877, the reader was informed "Harry Robinson's nose lights up the avenue elegantly these dark nights. Have another cup of bean soup, Harry." A domestic report revealed "Anna Wright is again happy. The old man is best after all, ain't he, Anna?" The creatures of this underworld society were traditionally peripatetic and it was unquestionably important to some to read "Again she's moved. Miss Lollie Whitney is now one of the flock of angels who flutter their wings and oil their feathers at the cage of [Carrie] Watson."

Carrie Watson applied to her institution the same principles that had formed the basis for many another Chicago fortune. She regarded prostitution as the "natural result of poverty on the part of the woman and passion on the part of the man." For her, it was not a matter of morals but of economics. Carrie was only eighteen and a virgin when she came to Chicago. She entered her profession not through necessity, as many girls did, but because of its business potentialities. After a talk with Lou Harper, Carrie became an inmate of the latter's mansion with the express purpose of learning the business. She must have been an apt pupil. Within two years, she leased a house on South Clark Street and opened an establishment catering only to society trade. Five years later she was ready to remodel the house into a resort that Herbert Asbury has termed the finest in America at the time. It was a three-story brownstone mansion with five parlors, more than twenty bedrooms and a bowling alley and billiard room in the basement for those bored or satiated with other entertainment. The halls were hung with expensive paintings and wine was brought to the parlors in solid silver buckets. The girls received their guests in fashionable and expensive gowns while a three-piece orchestra headed by a character known as Lame Jimmy provided music of an appropriate mood. There was no soliciting with the exception of what Asbury describes as an "ornithological pimp"— a parrot trained to say, "Carrie Watson. Come in, gentlemen."

The publisher of the *Sporting and Club House Directory* required a page and a half to list the attractions of Carrie Watson's. She had:

> 20 boarders; rates $5 to $50; pool rooms, billiard rooms, wine and beer. In fact, everything and plenty of it. This is one of the most widely known sporting houses in the United States or Canada. Nothing west of the Alleghanies [sic] begins to compare with it in brilliance or magnificence. In the basement are the billiard and pool rooms with perfect appointments. On the 1st floor are 5 parlors and a music room (at the latter of which competent musicians are constantly in attendance) and these parlors defy description. . . . A moment in the brilliantly lighted corridor, resplendent with bronze and crystal decorations and one is ushered into the far and justly famed "Mikado" parlor with its 4 walls and ceilings composed of solid French plate mirrors . . . the English language is inadequate to describe the feeling of one who enters this enchanted bower for the first time . . . the hand that writes this grows palsied at the recollection and these lines if longer drawn out will end in an inky blur . . . Miss Watson's is the HOUSE of the West . . . Her boarders are of such variety that any taste is sure to be suited and no living human being ever went away dissatisfied.

Carrie Watson's public appearances were as spectacular as her place of business. When she went out she drove in one of two snow-white carriages with bright yellow wheels. The carriages were pulled by four glistening black horses, probably the handsomest in the city. A measure of both her financial prosperity and the dubious operations of political favoritism was the fact she paid a larger personal-property tax than most of Chicago's millionaire businessmen. Her assessment was exceeded only by that of Marshall Field, George M. Pullman, Potter Palmer and J. W. Doane; it was equal to that of the fast-rising traction magnate, Charles T. Yerkes.

That Miss Watson had no regrets about how she became a woman of property was revealed in an interview in *Sporting Life* on December 9, 1882: "Miss Carrie Watson says she would be willing to reform but she can't think of any sins she has been guilty of. She charges regular prices for

The Ball! The Ball!

The Annual Ball of Shang Andrews—the one that was "postponed for obvious reasons"—will be held next Tuesday Evening, December 4, at the Park Place Hotel, instead of Concordia Hall, as originally intended. The whole house has been secured for the occasion, including the large parlors, where the ladies can enjoy "solid comfort" when not tripping the fantastic toe with their partners in the dance. The ball room consists of the entire upper floor of the building, and is as large, if not larger than Concordia Hall. The floor will be waxed, and every effort will be made to secure the pleasure and comfort of every lady and gentleman who attends. The Park Place Hotel is what was formerly known as the Powell House, located in the town of Jefferson, half a block from the city limits. Those who do not go in private conveyances can take the Milwaukee avenue cars, which wi'l carry them to within about two blocks of the Hotel; but this distance they need not walk, for 'busses will connect with every car, and carry passengers to the door. There will undoubtedly be a good crowd, and we are sure everybody will have a good time.

Boys, the boss girl of the West Side can be found at 120 West Washington street. Her name is Jennie Comstock, and she is very much of a lady, and always the same. Give her a call, and convince yourselves. She's gay.

Cranky Liz, of 120 Washington, had better go North, or where folks take crankiness better than here.

Where, oh where is the ba'd eagle now?

Delia Leon, what were you doing around the corner Monday night? Brace up, old girl, for Pat will find out all. WATCHER.

Charley M. had better let up on that mash of his, or his French Emma, at 535 State street, will get on to the racket; then look out. ONE WHO KNOWS.

Edna M., who resides (sometimes) at 326 State street, is too stuff for her own good; everyone is not an ungrateful wolf, like yourself. You get left often, by choosing wrong. BALD-HEADED SPORT.

The old reliable, Blanche Reid, was out West lately. Come back to see your poor Tommy, MONTREAL.

We are glad that Em Gillas and Jack have made up again. Ida, you ought to have saved your hands, and not broke the glass, for you are no good with Jack. NIGHT HAWK.

Ida, won't you never take a tumble? When the land lady gives you the bounce, why don't you walk, and not beg to stay? BLUE EYES.

Johnnie Fresh, Charley the kid is in town again, so be very careful, or you will get left. ONE WHO KNOWS.

Black-eyed Amy, of 478 State, you had better let up on your foolishness with that married man, F., or you will think a freight train has run over you. DO YOU HEAR?

There is to be found at 47 Lasalle street a dive for the worst trumps in the city, both male and female. This dive is presided over by a female bulldozer named Stewart, who tries

to impress upon the public the purity of her chastity. She told it on Hill and got left, but if she continues trying to impress it on the Irishman she will rue it. Taking it all in all, as a bulldozer she is a failure.

Little Homer is lushed all the time. What is the matter? Is not business good with Jennie? Brace up; if she is broke, she always comes to the front. A FRIEND.

Since the R. brothers have taken their departure we presume that the blonde will give her partners the shake. We wonder who Belle will rope in for the third lover, now that Georgie is no more? Is emma still thinking of sending you to take music lessons? ONE OF THE GIRLS.

Fannie Wright says she is Irish to the back bone, nevertheless she cannot make herself solid with that Irish peeler.

Nellie Green, from Biler street, tried to boil a boilermaker for five dollars, but the man of iron could not be cooked, so easy, but he rivited her boiler with a broomstick and a pair of knuckles, for which he was taxed five dollars.

Josie Davenport was up again on Thanksgiving for the second time in a week, each time on the information of Ruby Bell, the Pittsburg graduate of rascality and thievery.

In our next issue we shall give an account of a sensational dream by a prominent young man connected with the police department. It was all about the necessary utensils and furnishing for house keeping. He must have marriage on the brain.

Della T., the self-made blonde, at 88 Fourth avenue, should not travel with a kicker when she asks her friends to go and take a drink; don't drink, Dell; 'taint nice, and muddles your clothes. Mattie B. says you are a b'ower. HELEN'S BABY.

We see that the two that were separated by one, are together again, and are happy, while the one is mourning her lost J. But never mind, C. all's well that ends well.

Frank, you should be ashamed of yourself to take Ed. out and get him full and then have fun with him; he is too good a feller to use that way; he'll turn the tables on you sometime. CORA L.

We think that Harry had better let up on G, as she is no more good on earth, except to chew beans and drink soda.

Mattie B, the kicker at 124 4th ave. should make it pleasant for the boys whether lush or not—kindness wins. How is the Cincinnati Doctor? TWENTY-SIXTH ST., N. Y.

Bell Jones feels much better since Billy don't come home every night. And I am sure Smith is quite well. SHINE ON.

Jennie Hamer has got so many lovers that she does not know what to do with them all; but there is only one she loves. We know who it is, if no one else knows. OVER THE RIVER.

Funny Dan, the b. t. and hard man, at corner State and Harrison streets, had better took a tumble ere 'tis too late. Ohio street is on—THE NORTH SIDE.

Jake Ellie says he is going to win Miss Annie, but we don't think he will, for Johnnie is the captain. LITTLE GIANT.

The pavements on Milwaukee avenue are all solid, and Madame Scott need have no fear of breaking through, when she goes to the ball.

Mattie Wilson has just returned from the Black Hills. Her trip was to be a profitable one, and she says that in a week or two she will boast a better collection of genuine diamonds than any other girl on the West Side. She resides on Clinton street. She

must not be confounded with Irish Mate, whose permanent home is the Bridewell, which latter place is at present graced by her presence.

Little Blondie had better pay that borrowed three dollars pretty soon, as we have heard the lender say that "there will be war on the avenue inside of thirty days;" and our advice is, wind won't go no longer.

Remember, the old tickets are good for next Tuesday night's ball.

"Boquet" had better cease his attentions to Kit. His strawberry blonde may catch him, and then the fur would fly; besides, 'tis not manly in him to covet his former master's girl.

Alice Revere had better cease wagging her back-biting tongue. She will make time, too, by paying less frequent visits to Canal street.

"Mollie, Bell, and John," exclaimed the Judge Friday morning. Drunk and disorderly—30 days." By the time you get out you will be sober. A FRIEND.

We are sorry to announce the departure this morning of Lottie Maynard and Sadie Mason, who have gone to see their Ma, but will return in three weeks. So, boys, be patient. HARRY.

There is no better place for a ball within a thousand miles of Chicago than the Park Place Hotel.

Personal—My four-eyed friend I met at the Adelphi last Wednesday afternoon, can have the pleasure of my company to the Tivoli for supper, by meeting me at the same time and place on this Saturday afternoon. Could not keep the last engagement on account of the party you saw and heard, who sat behind me. J. G.

Miss Jessie, at Costello's, as she is there is not an equal to her George, even if he is a counter jumper. Look out, Jessie; you will find a rival in Blanche, for she is in love with all the Georges and Willies.

The landladies talk of organizing a Protective Association, the object being to guard against being "bilked" by their boarders. The members of the association will pledge themselves to harbor no girls who are not square with their previous landlady.

We would like to know where Georgie Lee and Harry F. were going Tuesday night? George, you had better be careful, or Hairy Faulk will get on to you, and you will get another black eye. ONE WHO KNOWS.

Carrie and Georgie, the two blondes at 174 Fourth avenue, had better let up on trying to mash those two dry goods clerks, or their solid men will find it out. A FRIEND.

The "Pail" alluded to in an item in last week's GAZETTE was not Phil Kelly, of 4141 Halsted street.

Eddie, the barber, is still at 47 La Salle, doing the chores; although being but a brat of a boy, as Mrs. Stew art calls him, he still performs the work of a full grown man.

Our friends from Leland, Ill., paid us a flying visit last week; got gloriously full; took in the Academy of Music, and then the town in general; ordered one dozen more copies of the GAZETTE, and went home happy, saying—"Who can't enjoy Thanksgiving? AL.

Miss Susie Edwards, formerly of Goodrich's, is now with Miss Lizzie Moss, No. 90 Fourth avenue.

French Georgie has returned to Madame Costello's, 343 South Fifth avenue.

Fanny Cook, the keeper of a Canal street roost, is becoming savage with years. If one of her girls should happen to leave she pursues her with the malignity of a fiend. Her lying

tongue wags about her, and she has her beastly bullies beat her, if she is found. Fanny may yet get back to her old occupation—emptying slops; or she may learn a useful trade at the Bridewell. Who knows? Let us pray.

Last week a trunk was found in a barn in the rear of 56 West Madison street. Kit Anderson, a former boarder in a dignified hotel on Desplaines street, was discovered to be the owner. She had the trunk removed to Wabash avenue, as she did not find it necessary to utilize the barn as a bed room any longer. Kit, what will the former "solid" think of this?

Those two girls of 70 Wells street, had better keep away from that Franklin street engine house, and not be riding the hose that is stretched on the sidewalk. Now, girls, when you want to throw kisses to them firemen, don't do it on the public street. TA-TA.

Times are hard on Biler avenue. Well, we think they are when Belle Taylor goes two blocks to get two glasses of beer for five cents. Shame on you, Belle; can't that fellow of yours furnish you dust enough to buy your beer close at home? Now, Belle, take a tumble and don't make a show of yourself. running two blocks for two cents and a half. A NEIGHBOR.

Miss C.. the big dame, had better go to her solid man to borrow street car fare, and not be hanging around Pacific Garden begging 5 cents, and then think she has done something funny. Shame on you.

If the hacks and private carriages are all engaged, don't forget that you can take a Milwaukee avenue car, any time before midnight, and go within two blocks of the Powell House.

After the departure of a certain Stock Yard lady for Texas—which event occurs a week or two hence—we shall take occasion to write a brief Sunday school lesson for the edification of a South Side restaurant keeper. If he does not enjoy our little sermon, we are positive that he will at least be interested.

Joe, a nobby laundry keeper, had a rousing jollification at his home on Clark street a few days ago. There was more fun than you could shake a stick at. Long Wallace was there, and when he danced his ponderous hoofs made a noise like the rumbling of not-far off thunder.

Wonder if Mrs. Stewart has found out who that man with the ulster on was? If this drunken, big-mouthed old rip gives that party any further talk, she will wish that she had made up her bed in hell instead of at 47 LaSalle street. Now go for your old hatchet, you old rag.

There was a sensation at the corner of Clark and Randolph about 3 o'clock Friday morning. Some said it was an explosion of some kind, while others contended that it was Red Hot's sausage can that fell and blew up; but on investigation it was found to be only Big Tom, who lost his equilibrium and dropped on his haunches; and he said he was very glad that he did not grow his teeth in that part. OLD SORES.

Mr. J. B., a second hand furniture dealer, wants to bet ten dollars that his name cannot be published in the GAZETTE. Set 'em up, Joe, and keep your money.

Hump-back Jack is once more in the city. Halsted street is honored by his presence. He received a handsome and substantial present—which is he willing to show on invitation—from a lady in St. Louis during his brief residence there. Jack is going to Texas in a week or two. He says

NEWS ITEMS FROM THE Street Gazette, 1877

wine, never cheated a man or woman out of a cent, never told a lie, never starved her boarders, never got drunk, and never even took as much as a pinch of snuff. Now, what more could be expected of a good woman?"

Unique in this enterprising district was Waterford Jack, "the millionaire streetwalker." Like many another tycoon, she attributed her success to hard work and industrious application; it was her boast she had walked the streets every night regardless of the weather for more than ten years. Foot weary at last, she organized a company of streetwalkers and established them in a marble-front store, acting as their business manager. All the money the girls earned was turned over to her. She took a percentage for accounting and other expenses and banked the rest for the girls. If prudent enough to retire, they might have some reward to show for their labors. The *Chicago Street Gazette* paid this tribute to Waterford Jack early in her career: "Waterford Jack has $22,000 in the bank, every cent of which she has picked up on the streets of Chicago. Jack (her right name is Frances Warren) has made money. It is said to her credit that she never stole a cent and was never drunk in her life. She is a pug-nosed, ugly little critter, but for all that she has prospered in her wretched business and now stands before the world the richest streetwalker in existence."

No matter how illegal their business, the madames of the city's brothels felt entitled to the full protection of the law. One legal pioneer who called upon the law for assistance was Madame Hastings, who ran a notorious establishment where the girls were wakened in the morning with cocktails and usually followed this eye-opener with a breakfast of absinthe. The house was also believed to be a principal outlet for the white-slave trade. Even with such a reputation, Madame Hastings objected to being raided by police equipped with warrants made out against mythical personages such as Richard Roe or Jane Doe. She sued to have one such series of arrests set aside. A lower court ruled against her but upon an appeal to a higher court the warrants were ruled illegal and Madame Hastings took her historic place among the champions of law and order.

Among other famous houses of assignation was The Arena, on Michigan Avenue, distinguished by its many porches as well as by its reputation. Nearly as successful as Carrie Watson was Lizzie Allen, who ran a place known as the House of Mirrors. Lizzie Allen was famed for her liberal use of cosmetics as well as her business enterprise. In one of the district's newspapers it was announced that "Lizzie Allen has put on her fall coat of veneer and varnish and she is now the finest looking woman in Chicago." She remained in business for thirty-eight years before she retired. When she died, her estate was valued by a probate court at $300,000. She rests now in Chicago's Rosehill Cemetery under a tombstone inscribed "Perpetual Ease." Her house was taken over by two girls from Kentucky—the Everleigh sisters.

13

The Melting Pot Explodes

CHICAGO was restless. During the seventies and eighties it had been a principal beachhead for the suddenly rising flood of immigration from Europe. This tide of new workers, following upon the unemployment which resulted from the panic of 1873, forced wages dangerously low. Resulting economic pressures on both the immigrant and established families increased the difficulties of assimilating a large foreign population. Language was another obstacle. The lack of communication among the rapidly growing alien groups led to an increase in resentment. Chicagoans (some of whom were only a few years removed from Europe themselves) blamed the later arrivals for cheapening the price of labor. The new workers, faced with the same poverty they had hoped to leave behind them, were bewildered and without leadership. The economic pressures of unemployment and poverty, built up over a period of years behind this barrier of language, were to explode finally in the most tempestuous decade of Chicago's history.

More and more of the new families arriving in Chicago spoke varied languages of southern and central Europe. Their common tongue, if any, was not English but German, the universal Latin of European radicalism. For entertainment the immigrants had to find places where German was spoken; their own language communities had not yet taken form. Entertainment in the German theaters was expensive; even the beer gardens were beyond the means of an unemployed worker who had spent his life's stake on the trip to the New World. The only diversions accessible under these conditions were the free labor meetings, in reality socialist rallies, where skilled orators spoke eloquently in German of the worker's millennium. A dramatist could not have created a more roseate picture than the visions of these outdoor spellbinders, who captured both the hearts and minds of their audiences. If the men who heard these speakers had not been out of work or isolated by the barrier of language, they might have found other sources of amusement. But they were essentially a captive audience and soon came to believe the speakers on the platform were the only real champions of the workingman.

Older Chicagoans referred to these speakers and writers, whose ideas were vigorously advocated in the columns of the German-language newspaper, *Arbeiter Zeitung*, as anarchists. It was a description less valid in the beginning than it was to become later. Most of the so-called anarchists were originally German socialists; they did not turn to anarchism until after a series of frustrations during the frequent battles of these bitter years.

The first mob made its appearance in the winter of 1872 in front of the offices of the Relief and Aid Society on LaSalle Street. The mob had been brought into being by a rumor that relief money had been embezzled by members of the society and withheld from the rapidly rising number of unemployed. Because the mob lacked leadership, the police were able to disperse it by driving it north through the LaSalle Street Tunnel and forcing the men to divide along the streets running east and west from LaSalle. No shots were fired and the incident, known as the "Bread Riot," was not regarded as serious. During the winter of 1873 unemployment (and with it, poverty) spread to such a degree that the first floor of City Hall was given over to families who had no other shelter. There was no serious violence, but the desperate figures huddling under their rags in the corridors of every public building were a reminder of the size of the problem which had to be solved.

Four years later, there was a hint of impending trouble when the newspapers reported groups of employes were quitting work along the line of the Baltimore & Ohio to protest a cut in wages. These reports caused little alarm at first, but concern increased when the items reappeared with nagging persistency and reported the spread of the strike to Pennsylvania and West Virginia. Reports of riots were frequent. Then, in the third week of July, the railroads with offices in Chicago followed the lead of the eastern lines by cutting wages 10 per cent.

The following Sunday, newspapers issued extra editions hourly with reports of the spread of the riot fever. Railroad shops were burning in Pittsburgh and the city was in the hands of a mob; there was rioting in Philadelphia, trouble was threatening in Cincinnati and tempers in St. Louis were at a "fever heat." In Chicago, the downtown streets were as crowded as on a business day. There were rumors that local railroad workers were about to join the walkout. By Monday, most of the city's railroad employes were off the job.

The socialist leaders were quick to exploit the situation. A mass meeting of workers was called for Monday night at Market and Madison Streets. An audience of nearly five thousand heard a series of speakers urge a march through the streets in support of a general strike. No specific program of action was adopted, but on Tuesday morning the automatic telegraph alarm at police headquarters rang continually as officers reported the movements of half a dozen different mobs through the city. Strangely, there was no evidence at the time or later that the striking railroad workers formed any significant part of these crowds. Workers were compelled to leave their jobs and join the roving gangs. In many cases employers anticipated the mobs by closing their factories and sending the workers home.

One group of rioters marched up Canal Street armed with clubs and sticks taken from the lumber yards along the river. While the police were attacking this gang, another had made its way to Remington's gun store on State Street. It was preparing to smash the windows to get at the guns and ammunition when the police arrived to break it up. An hour later the mayor issued a proclamation asking gun-store owners and pawnbrokers to take all the firearms and ammunition from display cases and lock them away. The mobs continued to roam the streets. By late afternoon the city's factories were shut down from the lake to Western Avenue near the edge of the city.

CHICAGO IN 1883, by S. D. Childs

Every distillery, tannery and brick kiln on the North Side was closed. A circular was distributed calling a second mass meeting, but the police dispersed the crowd as it arrived and the meeting was never held. Mayor Monroe Heath ordered the saloons closed, but the proprietors interpreted the order as applying only to their front doors and a brisk business continued via the side entrances.

During the night the city prepared for civil war. More than three hundred special police were sworn in. Arms and ammunition were collected from the stores and an arsenal was established at City Hall. Cavalry companies were organized from private stables. Even the workhorses of the street railway company were saddled and used by police. In another proclamation the mayor asked the citizens to "organize patrols in their respective neighborhoods and to keep women and children off the streets." On the North Side, a group of young men from the town's wealthiest families formed a volunteer company and made their headquarters in the mansion of Perry Smith, hiding their guns in the basement coal bin. Military companies were organized by wards. On Wednesday morning the mayor was assured there were twenty thousand men under arms and ready to act if necessary.

The mobs had also gathered an arsenal and were brandishing revolvers, shotguns and rifles. Factories were set on fire. One crowd gathered at the McCormick reaper works, a favorite target for demonstrations. The police had to send twice for reinforcements before the men could be driven away. To increase the mobility of the police, the delivery wagons of Marshall Field & Co. and John V. Farwell were taken over as troop carriers. Even with this improvisation, it was difficult to keep up with mobs, who would disappear down a series of alleys and form again on another street.

The socialists, over the signature of "The Workingmen's Party of the United States," continued their strategy of calling a nightly meeting. Police who attempted to break up a crowd of about two thousand at Market and Madison were pelted with lumps of coal from nearby yards. Meanwhile, a more serious threat occurred at the shops of the Burlington Railroad, where a mob had joined with a group of strikers in an effort to burn the buildings. A crowd of about three thousand had ditched several cars and locomotives by the time the police arrived. When the police foolishly drove up in omnibuses and wagons they were beset with stones and pieces of brick. They opened fire in return and in a half-hour's fight seven of the rioters were killed and twenty-five seriously injured. Sixteen of the policemen were seriously injured and only two or three escaped without any injury.

While the police were battling the rioters, a mass meeting was being held in the Moody and Sankey Tabernacle. The mayor sent a message requesting the raising of "a force of five thousand good and experienced citizens," composed as largely as possible of ex-soldiers to put down "the ragged Commune wretches." Enlistments began immediately and the troops took up headquarters in the ornate surroundings of the Grand Pacific Hotel. More sensible was the action of the City Council. Realizing that the mobs were made up principally of unemployed workers, the aldermen voted half a million dollars to start construction immediately on a new Courthouse.

Thursday began quietly. The Workingmen's Party distributed a circular saying "the honest effort to increase wages depends entirely upon your good conduct and peaceable though firm behavior." Then came the unexpected arrival of two companies of United States troops, sent directly to Chicago from the Indian Wars. Every soldier wore a full cartridge belt at his waist and carried a rifle on his shoulder. The troops were tanned, grizzled and covered with dust, but as they marched down Madison Street to their headquarters at the Exposition Building, they were cheered more loudly than many a handsomer parade.

At police headquarters, Deputy Superintendent Joseph Dixon created his own mobile artillery by mounting a cannon on an express wagon. When a mob took possession of the viaduct over the railroad tracks on South Halsted Street, he rushed his new weapon to the scene of action. He found the mob stoning and firing upon the trains of both the Burlington and the Chicago and Alton as they passed under the viaduct. The police forced the mob off its vantage point and kept it away with the threat of Dixon's cannon. But the crowd continued to fight against a force of two companies of volunteer cavalry and two regiments of troops. The jails in the nearby police stations were full of rioters. Ten of those in the crowd were known to have been killed and nineteen of the police were injured or wounded.

That night another meeting was called for Turner's Hall. It had no significance, but the police decided to break it up on the grounds that "Poles and Bohemians were there in large numbers and the wildest threats were made." Two squads of police charged the meeting. A wild fight followed, with shooting on both sides. Stoves and furniture were thrown indiscriminately through windows to smash openings for emergency exits. Two policemen were wounded, one of the men in the hall was killed and an unknown number wounded. Later, those who held the meeting sued the police. The judge rendered a decision which said in effect that if every policeman in the attacking force had been killed, no member of the crowd could have been legally punished.

Possibly because of the arrival of the federal troops, the Turner Hall foray and the Halsted Street riot were the final outbursts of the week of disorganized violence. On Friday the riots stopped. After these defeats in the railroad riots, the socialists formed military companies and paraded the streets with their weapons under the banner of a red flag. A state law pro-

DRIVING THE RIOTERS FROM TURNER HALL, 1877

hibiting the marching in public of armed companies of men forced these activities underground. The groups continued to drill in secret, wearing rubber shoes so they would not be heard outside the gymnasiums where they trained and hiding their faces under black hoods so that no one could inform against his neighbor. About the same time the socialists turned to a weapon closely associated with the history of the anarchist movement— the bomb. They became in fact the anarchists they had been labeled. On week-end trips to the Indiana sand dunes, squads practiced with homemade bombs. Blast effects on the surrounding area of shrubbery and trees were carefully measured and recorded.

The opening of Chicago's new Board of Trade building was a symbol the anarchists were quick to seize as a provocation for a demonstration. The usual handbills were distributed—this time over the signature of the International Working People's Party—and a mass meeting called for the evening when the Board of Trade dedication was to be held. According to the circular, the plan of the evening was as follows: "After the ceremonies and sermons, the participants will move in a body to the Grand Temple of Usury, Gambling and Cut-Throatism, where they will serenade the priests and officers of King Mammon and pay honor and respect to the benevolent institute. All friends of the bourse are invited."

About five hundred men and women appeared for the meeting. After listening to denunciations of the Board of Trade, they started toward the building to break up the dedication ceremonies. Marching behind a group of red flags (for the common blood of humanity) and black flags (for starvation), the demonstrators sang the *Marseillaise* in English, French and German. At the head of the column strode Samuel Fielden, Albert Parsons and August Spies, a trio which Chicagoans suspected considered itself the Danton, Marat and Robespierre of the American Revolution. Because the column's intentions had been so well advertised, a force of two hundred police guarded the approaches to the Board of Trade, while another four hundred were being held in reserve. The police forced the singing and chanting paraders to turn north away from their objective. Unfortunately, the mob's surge trapped a late member of the Board of Trade and his wife. Their carriage was stoned and tipped over by the angry crowd in a scene reminiscent of the revolutionary days of Paris.

Later the same year the employes of the West Side Street Railway Company went on strike after the company violated an agreement. The public's sympathies were with the strikers. For several days Chicagoans from the West Division rode uncomplainingly to work in express wagons, hacks or other makeshift transportation. To break the strike, the company hired new drivers and attempted to run its cars along their regular routes. Almost immediately, mobs formed along Madison Street. They stormed the cars, stoned the drivers and conductors, and tipped over several of the company's vehicles. The mayor, faced with this recurrence of rioting, had no choice but to provide the police protection which the company demanded. Captain John Bonfield, who was in charge of the police in the district, believed the most practical solution to any problem was a show of force. He first tried a plan of stationing wagonloads of police at intervals along the route. This strategy was ineffective and drivers continued to be chased from their posts and cars toppled. Bonfield's next tactic resulted in a sight probably never duplicated in America—he formed an armored train of streetcars. From the company barns came a unit of three cars. The first was an open car loaded with armed policemen. The second was a closed car to be used either as a prison van or ambulance. Then came another car of armed men with their guns facing to the rear. As these cars moved away, another three followed, and then another three until there were about seventy-five cars in the line. Ahead of the leading car marched a force of police with the indomitable Bonfield out in front. The rioters, unable to attack the cars, piled obstructions on the tracks. On some corners barricades were erected and from behind them the mob threw stones as the police attacked with oversize billy clubs. No attempt vas made to pick up passengers; the maneuver was purely a tactic to cow the demonstrators. The unusual cavalcade fought its way slowly from Western to Ogden Avenue, with the police under orders not to fire unless they should be fired upon. The show of force had its effect and the defeated mob vanished into the alleys and byways. But it was still to be heard from again, and more fearfully than ever before.

Despite these humiliations, the anarchists continued to plan for the day they would seize power. They experimented with more homemade explosives. Maps of the city were studied and intersections marked where properly placed dynamite could paralyze traffic. In January of 1886 a bomb was left on the doorstep of Judge Lambert Tree. A few days later, another was found in the Burlington Depot. Impetuous practitioners of the doctrine of violence were growing bolder.

In February the workers at the McCormick reaper factory left their jobs in a walkout in support of an eight-hour day and increased wages. During the following few months, as the McCormick strike dragged on without a settlement, it was followed by other strikes as the agitation for the eight-hour day in all industries increased. By May, the trend to the shorter work shift was conceded by all but the most stubborn employers. Even the generally intimidated employes of Pullman City had gone out to wait for the shorter day. At the stockyards, seven thousand packing-house workers had gone on strike at 7 in the morning and had been back on the job at noon with their requests granted. The Knights of Labor, the union organization of the time, was cautious about making claims of universal success despite these favorable signs. But the anarchists, who had first been suspicious of the eight-hour day movement, now embraced it as their own cause. A universal eight-hour day was inevitable, they told their faithful audiences; by May 1st it would prevail throughout the country and labor strife would be at an end. The millennium was at hand.

Like most millenniums, that of May 1, 1886, was slightly postponed. Because of the high expectations engendered by the writings and speeches of the anarchists, the absence of any significant change caused an emotional reaction of bitterness and frustration. The disappointment was particularly severe among the McCormick strikers, whose jobs were being taken by other workers, and among the freight handlers and switchmen who were hard pressed by the effects of a long strike. This was the atmosphere when a mass meeting was called for Monday afternoon at a prairie lot on Blue Island Avenue, then known as the Black Road because of its black cinder surface. Nearly five thousand men were in the field when the quitting bell at the nearby McCormick reaper works sounded and the gates swung open to let out the non-union workers.

These were the men who were being denounced by the speakers on the prairie for "taking bread from the mouths of children." Through coincidence or shrewd timing on the part of those who had planned the affair, the crowd needed no urging to seek vengeance. Shouting "Scab!" the strikers swarmed across the prairie toward the gate, forcing the workers back inside the plant. A policeman standing near the entryway fell with a bullet in his thigh. The crowd laid siege to the plant and, even after patrol wagons with police reinforcements arrived, a second attack was launched. In this assault half a dozen of the demonstrators were killed. A striker who attempted to leap on a patrol wagon was shot down in the street. The volleys from the guards successfully scattered the strikers, who moved away in small groups to the nearby saloons. A few minutes later, Mayor Harrison came cantering by on his Kentucky mare. It was not the least remarkable event of the day that the men on the street, who had just been fired upon and had had some of their number killed by the mayor's police force, showed no hostility toward him. The only taunts were those of an occasional wit calling upon the open-handed mayor to "set 'em up" for the crowd.

While the workers brooded over their misfortunes in the saloons, the editors and printers at the *Arbeiter Zeitung* were busy exploiting the day's drama. Circulars were printed and a few hours later a man on horseback rode through the North and West Sides scattering packages of them where-

THE FIGHT AT THE HALSTED STREET VIADUCT, 1877

ever a group of workers could be found. "Revenge! Workingmen to arms!" the pamphlets urged. "They killed six of your brothers at McCormick's works this afternoon . . . To arms, we call you; to arms!" It was signed "Your Brothers."

The circulars produced no upsurge of violence. Tuesday morning the Black Road was quiet. There was only the sound of noisy conversation coming from the overcrowded saloons. (Except for one grocery and an undertaking parlor, saloons were the only places of business in the area.) About noon the tranquillity was shattered by the sound of a yelping dog, running at full speed down the middle of Black Road with a can of pebbles tied to his tail. No political pamphleteer ever produced action as quickly as the frightened dog, which had been the victim of a cruel boy's prank. From every swinging door along the street small groups of men rushed out to see what had caused the disturbance. The surge was simultaneous and the nearly deserted street was transformed suddenly into a scene of action. As if by some common thought, the men started drifting toward the McCormick works. There, as no one moved to assume the role of leader, they milled about impatiently and waited for someone to signal the next move.

An objective unexpectedly presented itself when one of the detectives mingling with the strikers attempted to arrest a man carrying a pistol. Only the proximity of the police at the McCormick gate saved the impetuous officer from being beaten to death. Frustrated in its attack on one victim, the crowd scented another when someone shouted that a police officer had been seen using the telephone at Samuel Rosenfield's drug store at Eighteenth and Center. To the belligerent and excited crowd, this information made Rosenfield an agent of the police. The men moved quickly to the drug store, sending a shower of bricks and stones through the plate-glass windows at the front of his shop. The police were able to rescue Rosenfield and his family from their living quarters in the rear of the building but because of the narrow streets could not break up the mob which soon had stormed into the store and emptied the shelves. The next objective of the angry rioters was Weiskopf's saloon, located under a hall where the anarchists occasionally held meetings. Weiskopf was accused of being an informer. His place was reduced to a shambles in a few minutes while the less ferocious members of the attacking force rolled barrels of whiskey and beer into the street and cracked them open for the crowd.

During the day the anarchists kept up their barrage of propaganda. In Tuesday's edition of the *Arbeiter Zeitung*, August Spies had written an editorial calling upon the workers to take up arms and "rise in your might and level the existing robber rule with the dust." In the afternoon another circular was on the streets; it called for a "great mass meeting at Haymarket, Randolph Street between Desplaines and Halsted" and promised "Good

TRADING ON THE BOARD, 1891

speakers will be present to denounce the latest atrocious acts of the police—
the shooting of our fellow-workingmen yesterday afternoon."

The night of the meeting—Tuesday, May 4, 1886—was a warm, damp
evening. Dark clouds moved quickly across a somber, starless sky. At the

time set, a crowd of about one thousand had gathered in the Haymarket. To the reporters the men seemed sullen and preoccupied. The boisterous, drunken outbursts which usually erupted in the early stages of such rallies were subdued and infrequent. A block away, at the Desplaines Street police station, officers and patrolmen were preparing for a battle. A force of two hundred men armed with new revolvers and "extra-long hickory clubs" was on the alert. A large number of detectives had been sent to mingle with the crowd.

The speakers who had called the meeting were late in arriving. Then, looking around for a suitable platform, they sighted an empty wagon standing near the entrance to the Crane factory half a block to the north. Following the speakers to the wagon, the crowd moved off of Haymarket Square and north on Desplaines Street. Finally the meeting got under way, though very much behind schedule. August Spies, the German-born publisher of the *Arbeiter Zeitung*, spoke first. He was followed by Albert Parsons, son of the famous Confederate general, W. H. Parsons. Last came Samuel Fielden, the Lancashire Englishman who made his living driving a stone wagon and who was as devout a Methodist as he was anarchist.

On the fringe of the crowd was Mayor Harrison. After listening to the first speeches he visited the police station and told the officers he did not think it necessary to break up the meeting. "I have no right to interfere with any peaceable meeting of the people," he said. "So long as they are orderly, I will not interfere." The mayor and chief of police then left the station, putting stubborn John Bonfield, now an inspector of police, in charge. Bonfield, without informing his superiors, had been making his own preparations for dispersing the crowd. When the detectives making periodic reports to the station told Bonfield that Fielden was saying "the law must be throttled, killed and stabbed," the inspector's temper gave way. Bonfield ordered his force into the street to break up the meeting. About the same time, rain started to fall and the crowd began to move away. But Bonfield insisted upon his victory. He turned his column of police from the broad Haymarket into narrow Desplaines Street, a maneuver which pushed the crowd back together.

A captain in the front rank ordered the meeting to break up. He was answered with a shouted reply from Fielden that it was a peaceable gathering. Then a bomb with a sputtering fuse appeared over the heads of the crowd and landed in the middle of the police. It exploded the instant it touched the ground and the front ranks of the police fell in pain and terror. Revolver shots rang out from both sides. Paul Hull of the *Daily News*, covering the meeting, said someone in the crowd cried "Charge" and the shots came "like the falling of corn on a tin pan or the roll of a drum." In five minutes the riot was at an end. The first Nihilist bomb in America—of the same pattern

ATTACK ON POLICE PATROL WAGON NEAR McCORMICK'S REAPER
WORKS, 1886

as the missile which had killed Czar Alexander II of Russia—exploded with
terrible effectiveness. Seven police officers died of their injuries and sixty
others were wounded. It was impossible to tell the casualties among the
crowd; most were dragged, helped or carried away by their friends. Best
estimates were that at least two hundred were wounded; there was no way of
registering the death toll.

The following day the police attempted to fix the responsibility for the
bomb. The offices of the *Arbeiter Zeitung* were closed when large supplies
of explosives allegedly were found there. August Spies of the *Arbeiter Zeitung*
and Michael Schwab, its assistant editor who spoke in German at the
anarchist meetings, were arrested. Albert Parsons, whose wife was to be
known as the Jeanne d'Arc of Chicago anarchism, fled but later surrendered.
Also arrested and accused of having a part in the plot was Louis Lingg, an
organizer for the carpenters' union who was believed to have manufactured
the bomb, George Engle, a painter, Adolph Fischer, a printer, Oscar Neebe,
an organizer for the beer-wagon drivers' union, and Samuel Fielden. The
police were unable to link any of these with the murder off Haymarket.
But such was the temper of the times—and the courts—that all were convicted of murder on the ground that their inflammatory speeches and pub-
lications had incited the throwing of the bomb. Luther Laflin Mills, the
prosecutor, erected a wire barricade at the second-floor landing of his home

to protect his family from creeping intruders. At the trial, two factors in the prosecution's case were the handbill urging the workers to take up arms and the fact that the meeting had been moved to Desplaines Street from Haymarket. It was the police contention that this had been done to form a trap for the police, though the events of the night the bomb was thrown did not bear out the charge.

After the conviction, Judge Joseph E. Gary imposed the death sentence on Parsons, Spies, Fielden, Schwab, Fischer, Lingg and Engle. Neebe, whose crime apparently consisted of owning stock in the *Arbeiter Zeitung*, was given fifteen years in prison. After a request for a new trial had been refused, the condemned men asked for the privilege of addressing the court. Their speeches reflected the variety of their character.

Fielden was eloquent and forgiving in his three-hour oration: "I have loved my fellow men as I have loved myself," he said. "I have hated trickery, dishonesty and injustice. If it will do any good, I freely give myself up. I trust the time will come when there will be a better understanding, more intelligence, and above the mountains of iniquity, wrong and corruption, I hope the sun of righteousness and truth and justice will come to bathe in its balmy light the emancipated world."

Spies charged the penalty against him was a conspiracy to "stamp out the labor movement." Schwab tried to tell the unsympathetic court and audience exactly what anarchism was; he called it "a state of society in which the only government is reason." Lingg was defiant. "I die gladly upon the gallows," he said, "in the sure hope that hundreds and thousands of people to whom I have spoken will now recognize and make use of dynamite. In this hope I despise you and despise your laws. Hang me for it."

Parsons called the trial "the sum totality of the disorganized passion of Chicago" and charged the jury had been bribed. He went on to explain why he and his companions had chosen the techniques of the anarchists over those of the early labor leaders who relied on the peaceful techniques of trade unionism. Dynamite, he said "is democratic; it makes everybody equal. The Pinkertons, the police, the militia, are absolutely worthless in the presence of dynamite . . . Dynamite is the equilibrium. It is the annihilator. It is the disseminator of authority; it is the dawn of peace; it is the end of war. It is man's best and last friend; it emancipates the world from the domineering of the few over the many, because all government in the last resort is violence; all law, in the last resort is force . . . Force is the law of nature and this newly discovered force makes all men equal and therefore free."

Spies, standing on the gallows on November 11, 1887, cried out "There will be a time when our silence will be more powerful than the voices you hear today." Parsons pronounced his own benediction in the words "Let the voice of the people be heard." But with the explosion of the first purposeful bomb, the anarchists exploded any chance they might have had for political effectiveness. The bomb was considered by Americans an indiscriminate and unfair weapon; even those who protested the unfair trial of the accused could find little to defend in this philosophy of dynamite as the equalizer.

Fischer and Engle went to the gallows with Spies and Parsons. Lingg, who had been under sentence of death, acted as his own executioner by exploding a dynamite cartridge between his teeth in his jail cell. Schwab and Fielden had their sentences commuted to life imprisonment by Governor Richard Oglesby.

The identity of the bomb thrower was never firmly established. Most evidence pointed to the fact that he was once picked up by the police but released after being interrogated as a "mere windbag." All those who could settle the question with historical finality are dead, but their descendants say they heard from their fathers and others closely associated with the case that the actual bomb was thrown by Rudolph Schnaubelt, who fled to Europe, lived on anonymously and died quietly in his sleep.

The bomb throwing had one important aftereffect. To the members of the Commercial Club, the Haymarket episode was not an isolated phenomenon but a threat of revolution. They were aware no federal troops had been close enough to protect their interests if the anarchist strategy had been successful. To correct what they felt was a serious hazard, they offered to give the government six hundred acres of land along the shore of Lake Michigan, twenty-six miles north of the center of the city, if the government would establish a military base there. On March 3, 1887 the government accepted the offer and Fort Sheridan was founded. It was to remain long after it had fulfilled its original purpose of reassuring the newly wealthy Chicagoans that their property would not be subject to violent expropriation or destruction. More than a fort, however, was to be needed to bring tranquillity to turbulent Chicago.

"BRIDGED"—A FAMILIAR CHI-
CAGO EXPERIENCE, *by Charles
Graham*

14

Chicago Builds Its Parthenon

THE LOSS of Crosby's Opera House and the other concert halls in the great
fire made it necessary for musicians and actors to use any setting available.
The musicians made their most frequent appearances at the dedications of
new buildings, ceremonies that were repeated with a kind of grandiose
monotony as the skyline of a new city began to appear. One of the more
spectacular of these concerts was presented at the opening of the depot of
the Chicago, Rock Island and Pacific Railroad. The director was the ubiquitous P. G. Gilmore, fresh from a quantitative musical triumph in Boston
where he had conducted an orchestra of more than one thousand pieces as
part of the Boston Peace Jubilee. His performance at the Rock Island Depot,
if less formidable, was still of a proportion to quell the timid. He augmented
his own band with more than one hundred local musicians and supple-
mented these with a locally organized chorus of more than a thousand
voices. This massive combination of musical talent presented a program
ranging from "Anthem to Peace" to the "Anvil Chorus," the latter sung
to the accompaniment of a collection of red-shirted firemen pounding
rhythmically with sledge hammers on a row of blacksmiths' anvils. A local
historian reserved his opinion about the musical merits of the performance
but took sensible consolation in the fact that "The affair served its purpose

in furnishing a harmless diversion and in advertising the fact that Chicago had any amount of spirit left, subject to call."

The most congenial home for good music during these years was under the domes and towers of the crystal palace erected for the Interstate Industrial Exposition. Chicago had always had a fondness for fairs and expositions. Shortly after the fire, Potter Palmer, Richard T. Crane and a group of business leaders were already planning an exposition to advertise the greatness of the partially rebuilt city. The exhibits at the exposition were intended to cover the entire field of human knowledge, but the emphasis was quite naturally on the subjects about which the founders knew most—industry and commerce. The plan of the exposition, which opened its doors in the summer of 1873, was a reflection of the culture and interests of Chicago. The main divisions listed displays of Food, Drinks and Tobacco, Products of Farm and Orchard, Instruments and Machinery of Useful Arts, Raw Materials, Minerals, Objects Used in Dwellings and for Personal Wear, Natural History and Fine Arts. The Fine Arts classification presented a unique definition of this hallowed phrase. It included, in addition to the usual subjects of painting, sculpture, architecture and stained glass, a further subdivision of the Liberal Arts classified by the catalogue as "publishing and instruments, surgical, musical and telegraphical." For those who wished to add to the horrendous collections which were a feature of every fashionable living room, there was an exhibit of bric-à-brac.

The exposition itself was open for only a few weeks each fall, when the interior of the building took on the appearance of a gargantuan general store in which it was possible to find anything from groceries to steam engines. Four years after the exposition's first show, the building was rented by the forerunner of the Chicago Symphony Orchestra as a temporary home for a series of concerts under the direction of Theodore Thomas. At the end of the long hall used for the concerts an attempt had been made to alleviate the barrenness with a semblance of a German garden decorated with evergreen trees sprouting from big wooden tubs. Around the periphery were small tables where good Milwaukee brew and other refreshments were served during the concert as well as at intermissions. The conditions in the temporary hall with its long rows of hard and noisy wooden chairs were far from ideal. The sound of a passing train on an adjoining lake-front railroad track would often obliterate the music. The residual fragrance of an exhibit of a vinegar manufacturer lingered in the building, leaving some Chicagoans with a permanent identification of good music and the smell of vinegar. Under such difficulties, Theodore Thomas introduced the city to fine music gently, filling his program with good standard works, providing at least one special "composer's program" and one full symphony (still a

INTERSTATE INDUSTRIAL EXPOSITION, 1884

novelty in Chicago) in every week's series of concerts. After a few years of this, he had the boldness to stage a Wagnerian festival which, possibly through the influence of the Teutonic scenery or refreshments, was given a more appreciative reception than Wagner received in more sophisticated musical capitals.

Another leader in the efforts to elevate Chicago's music was Dr. Florenz Ziegfeld, who with George F. Root had founded the Chicago Musical College. One of his apt students was his own son Florenz, though the boy often seemed to be more interested in showmanship than musicianship. When Florenz was thirteen he went to see Buffalo Bill's Wild West Show, then incongruously housed in the Academy of Music on Halsted Street. After a demonstration of marksmanship by Buffalo Bill, the plains scout challenged any member of the audience to try his skill. Young Flo Ziegfeld accepted the challenge, stepped on the stage and hit the bull's eye. Buffalo Bill, impressed as much by the young man's nerve as his shooting ability, offered him a job; when the company left Chicago on a three weeks' tour, Flo Ziegfeld had his first taste of show business.

Buffalo Bill, or Colonel William F. Cody, as he called himself on more dignified occasions, made his own stage debut in Chicago under the sponsorship of Ned Buntline, the famous dime novelist. In addition to acting as Buffalo Bill's manager, Buntline provided Cody with a plagiarized play under the title *Scouts of the Prairie*. It called for Cody to be supported by about twenty actors smeared with grease paint and billed as Indian warriors. On opening night Buffalo Bill had stage fright so badly he couldn't speak a line. The inventive Buntline stepped onto the stage and began questioning the star about his life on the plains—a subject of far greater interest to the audience than the pilfered drama. Under Buntline's questioning the frontier hero was more at ease. When the manager felt the audience had enough of talk, he signaled for the twenty actors; they came rushing on stage shouting for the scalps of Cody and his companion, "Texas Jack" Omonundro, who had been a scout with Jeb Stuart's cavalry. This cue was one to which the two scouts reacted easily and they swung into action, disposing of the supposed redskins with a ferocity that made their first night's efforts a popular triumph.

The arrival of Sarah Bernhardt on her first American tour presented more of a problem to Chicagoans than the simple heroics of Buffalo Bill. French art and literature were still suspect. From many of the city's pulpits came denunciations of the star and her art when it was announced that she was to appear at the McVicker's Theater. The annual reception given by N. K. Fairbank, the president of the Chicago Club and his wife, was scheduled for the night of her opening, but it would have been considered a scandal to invite anyone from the stage to so sedate a gathering. One man, however, was determined that Madame Bernhardt should have the finest reception possible. He was Potter Palmer, the proprietor of the Palmer House. There is no evidence that his wife made any effort to entertain the actress but Palmer himself could not have made more elegant preparations. A suite of rooms along an entire side of the hotel was set aside for her. A new "five glass landau" was placed at her command with Henry Wentsel, a "handsomely bearded veteran of the 197th Pennsylvania infantry," as its driver. All her meals were individually prepared in her rooms and only the French dishes for which she had a fondness were served.

A grotesque annoyance of her Chicago appearance, as it had been of every city in which she had appeared on tour, was the presence of a Yankee promoter named Henry Smith whom Bernhardt described with disgust as "the whale man." When she had arrived in Boston, Smith persuaded her to pay a visit to the harbor to see a whale which one of his fishing boats had harpooned. There he arranged for her to pull a small bone, of the kind from which women's corsets were made, from the whale. Smith lost no time in exploiting the connection of the petite Sarah and the mammoth whale. He immediately arranged for a tour that would coincide with her; when she arrived in a town, Smith and his whale would follow closely behind. In anticipation of the whale's arrival the city was plastered with signs which read:

Come and See
THE ENORMOUS CETACEAN
which Sarah Bernhardt killed
by tearing out its whalebone for her corsets

Other signs advised that the whale "is just as flourishing as when it was alive" and added that it had $400 worth of salt in its stomach and every day the ice upon which it was resting was renewed at a cost of $100. When Sarah Bernhardt stepped from her private railroad car at the station, her eyes fell upon Smith, who was there to greet her along with the French consul and a deputation of Chicagoans. Sweeping along in a light green coat trimmed with tawny fur and wearing a fur hat trimmed with plumes and a bird's head with glittering eyes, she mustered all her French invective to the task of driving him away. However, as few witnesses understood the cause of the clash, it served to advertise the whale further and increase the stature of the canny Smith.

At Bernhardt's opening performance an extra squad of police was required to handle the crowd outside the theater. There was not an equivalent rush at the box office, unfortunately, and there were empty seats in the rear when the curtain went up on *Adrienne Lecouvreur*, the first night's play. The distraction which the audience felt at hearing a play in French must have been matched by that of the actress at the peculiar sounds from the pit. A critic, in recording his reservations about Bernhardt's acting, admitted part of the effect might have been lost because so many members of the audience brought English copies of the play and kept ruffling the pages as they followed the plot. The *Daily News* critic found himself listening only half to the performance on the stage and giving the balance of his attention to the star's sister, Jeanne, and other members of the Bernhardt party who sat in the empty seats in the rear making uncomplimentary remarks about the audience as the play progressed. Another, more provincial critic, complained: "There are people who suppose Bernhardt is giving her performance in English. Whether any of them have paid $5 a seat to see it is not known, but the deep disgust of such an individual may be imagined. To give up an exorbitant sum for the sake of sitting four hours through an incomprehensible entertainment because the greatest actress in the world figures in it is one thing; to expend the same amount with the idea that the same result is to be obtained plus an understanding of what is spoken is something different."

As one play followed another at the McVicker's, the critic of the *Daily News* grew more enthusiastic about Bernhardt and that of the *Tribune* increased his reservations. This lack of approbation from the morning paper critic led to an editorial in the *News* commenting that "if the young men who 'do the dramatic' on the Chicago morning papers knew their business as well as Bernhardt knew hers, ah! then one might read 'criticisms' which appear daily and not be struck with apprehension that in many instances the plow has been forsaken for the pen by young men who would have made excellent agriculturists."

In order "not to meet the sandwich-men advertising the whale," Bern-

REPUBLICAN NATIONAL CONVENTION OF 1884. A Parade on Michigan Avenue hardt permitted herself to be taken on a series of sight-seeing trips, including one to the stockyards. The evening of her excursion to the slaughterhouses she was to play *Phèdre*; but at curtain time she still found herself "trying to do everything to get rid of the horrible vision of the stockyards" and the "dreadful and magnificent sight" than which nothing could have been "more Hoffmannesque." So ardently did she throw herself into her role that at the play's conclusion she fainted and had to be carried from the stage.

The talented Bernhardt was an amateur painter and sculptress and an exhibit of her work was arranged for O'Brien's art gallery to promote her stage appearance. Hundreds of invitations were sent out. Although Chicago society had decided it would not receive her, the social ban did not extend to being received by her. The social predicament was noticed by at least one of the reporters on hand to watch Bernhardt, dressed in a clinging black gown, receive her guests. "There had not been time," he explained, "for social bread-and-butterdom to meet and formally resolve on a course. The result was that, each acting on her own impulse, hundreds of ladies decided with truly feminine curiosity to 'take it in' . . . There was no small room for amusement in watching the effect upon the ladies who came when they found themselves actually **in the same room with The Naughty Sara** against whose skirts they were liable to be swept at any moment by the almost resistless human eddy which surged around the room . . . For the most part . . . the women visitors seemed to regard [Sarah] somewhat in the light of an interesting but highly dangerous beast. They stood about her in rows four or five deep and watched the play of her features and her every movement, with mingled curiosity, admiration and fear, the last predominating and giving an expression which seemed to say 'Have a care! An accident is liable to happen any minute.'" The only person of consequence to have the courage and good manners to spend some time with Bernhardt was Amy Fay, a musician who had lived both in France and Germany and had been a pupil of Franz Liszt.

But if society shunned "the divine Sarah," there were others of possibly less status and more interests who did not. In her memoirs, Bernhardt was to look back on her Chicago visit as "the most agreeable days I had had since my arrival in America." She also gave evidence that she had observed Chicago as closely as the city had scrutinized her:

"First of all," she wrote later, "there was the vitality of the city in which men pass each other without even stopping, with knitted brows with one thought in mind, 'the end to attain.' They move on and on, never turning for a cry or a prudent warning. What takes place behind them matters little. They do not wish to know why a cry is raised and they have no time to be prudent: 'the end to attain' awaits them . . . Women, here, as everywhere else in America do not work, but they do not stroll about the streets as in other cities: they walk quickly: they also are in a hurry to seek amusement." Nor was this affection one-sided; when it was the time for parting, Bernhardt received from the "Ladies of Chicago" a collar of camellias made of diamonds.

The final chapter of this incongruous romance between the actress and the city she would not allow to reject her was written after she left town. To the bishop who had denounced her before she arrived came a note from her manager:

> Your Grace:
> Whenever I visit your city I am accustomed to spend $400 in advertising. But as you have done the advertising for me, I send you $200 for your poor.
>
> Henry Abbey

The year after the visit from Bernhardt, Chicago prepared to receive another celebrity in the person of Oscar Wilde. The poet was on a lecture tour arranged by Richard D'Oyly Carte to exploit the notoriety associated with Wilde's name as a result of the phenomenal success of Gilbert and Sullivan's *Patience*. Wilde was unquestionably the original of the operetta's esthetic hero, Bunthorne. The announcement of Wilde's visit created irresistible opportunities for provincial humorists. One cartoon showed a tailor's advertisement of "Wilde Oscar" labeled "Balaam, the Ass-thete." A *Daily News* writer turned to verse:

> He comes! The simpering Oscar comes.
> The West awaits with wonder
> As bullfrogs list to beating drums
> Or hearken to the thunder.
>
> The women pause with bated breath,
> With wild and wistful faces,
> And silent as the halls of death
> Seem all our public places.
>
> Here in the energetic West,
> We have no vacant niches
> For clowns with pansies in the vest
> Or dadoes on the breeches,
>
> We do not live by form or rule,
> We love our wives and lassies;
> We like to look at Western mules
> But not aesthetic asses.

The best that may be said of such humor is that it was no worse than Wilde had met in the other cities he visited.

OSCAR WILDE. A caricature by E. Jump from the Chapin and Gore Restaurant

The poet's first impression of Chicago after his arrival was a good one. He was taken directly to the Grand Pacific Hotel where John B. Drake had perfected a technique for receiving celebrities and where every clerk carried himself with the demeanor of a Lorenzo the Magnificent. After a dinner of brook trout, boiled quail, steak, sweets and champagne, Wilde confessed his amazement that "such good wine could be obtained so far west." He spoiled his host's triumph, however, by requesting Turkish cigarettes which were not available in Chicago. After dinner, Wilde received the press. When the reporters arrived he was lying on a large sofa pulled up before the fire and covered by a wolfskin and tigerskin. His head was resting on a gold-colored silk shawl. To the *Inter-Ocean* reporter he offered a handclasp that was "like the clinging of a vine." The *Tribune* interviewer was more impressed. He admitted that he "went to scoff" but "remained an hour" to hear such Wilde pronouncements as "life without industry is barren and industry without art is barbarism."

Wilde was faced with the necessity of being in top form. He was competing for public attention with John L. Sullivan, who had just returned to Chicago after hammering the world heavyweight title away from Paddy Ryan. While Wilde held court at the Grand Pacific, Sullivan received the plaudits of the crowd at Chapin & Gore's. It was a contrast which the *Tribune* found significant:

"Mr. Wilde represents a soulful past when military knights rode to the fray picking mandolins," the editorialist observed, "but Mr. Sullivan belongs to the rude present and fights in twenty-four foot tournaments unaccompanied by lutes . . . Mr. Wilde's school recognizes the ugliest flowers and birds, fills houses with uncouth jugs and bottles, covers wallpaper with geometrical impossibilities, covers floors with hideously figured, faded, colorless rugs. It destroys every curve, the lines of beauty, and substitutes an angle or a straight line. It clothes lean, lank women in draperies without a fold or curve, dishevels their hair and suggests uncleanliness. It changes the Venus de Milo into a clothes pole. Whatever is hideous, grotesque, bizarre and unreal and false it substitutes for the beautiful in aesthetics and from every art eliminates repose, which is the soul of art. As between the two schools it may at least be said for Mr. Sullivan's that it cultivates the muscle and develops a high type of physical manhood, however much we may be disgusted with the method of its use." The author of this artistic lament was probably a victim in his own home of the new vogue for the "esthetic" which had swept Chicago in the wake of the success of *Patience*. The sniffing of a rose or a lily "for bodily refreshment" was a matter taken seriously by many Chicagoans.

Literary notoriety being rated as less objectionable than that of the stage, Wilde was entertained by the same society which had avoided the lovely Sarah Bernhardt. Mrs. Horatio O. Stone gave a dinner at which he was the guest of honor. There was a large reception at the mansion of Mr. and Mrs. Franklin MacVeagh. It was at this reception that a departing guest gave a word of reassurance to a reporter by saying Wilde had talked "very pleasantly and sensible." Wilde was quoted as having expressed the view that artificial flowers should never be worn and that only an Oriental beauty should wear a sunflower. This latter advice was a hard blow to feminine Chicago, for sunflowers were at the moment the ultimate in fashion—a fact which may not have escaped the quick-witted visitor when he issued his dictum. The MacVeagh reception had an indecorous dénouement. A group of boy hecklers outside the house waved sunflowers and lilies and made it necessary to smuggle Wilde out through the stable and down the alley.

The lecture with which the poet was to enlighten Chicago was a discourse on the decorative arts. Wilde said much of the lecture had been written after his arrival and an audience of 2,500 packed Central Music Hall to hear his views. Their attitude, observed the *Times*, was the same as if they had paid "to see a two-headed Australian 'what-is-it' who would talk Greek or Choctaw." Wilde did not disappoint those who had come to look rather than listen. He appeared on the platform wearing black breeches tied at the knee with a black bow and black silk stockings and pumps. A fitted dress coat revealed a low-cut white vest and an expanse of white shirt front. His hands were encased in white gloves.

As might have been expected, what he had to say gave little excuse for ridicule. The audience tittered over his pronunciation of telephone; but his comment that "the value of the telephone is the value of what two people have to say" was worth the effort of remembering. His audience forgot his strange costume when he remarked that after the fire "the pouring out of the generous treasures of the world [for Chicago] was as noble and beautiful as the work of any troop of angels who ever clothed the naked." But a few minutes later the same audience was stirring in resentment as, after paying tribute to the waterworks as "simple, grand and natural," he went on to express his shock at the tower as "a castellated monstrosity with pepper boxes stuck all over it." He was amazed, he said, "that any people could so abuse Gothic art." Despite a vigorous attack by the newspapers, Wilde refused to recant his heresy about the city's beloved water tower that had survived as an ironic symbol of its own failure. He did consent to swell the city's pride with a departing interview in which he said that there was no "tinsel or shabbiness" about Chicago, that its women were handsome and well dressed and that it had been hospitable. To this a newspaper could only add as its au revoir, "Go, Mr. Wilde, and may the sunflower wither at your gaze."

Another celebrated visitor was Mme Helena Modjeska, whose conquest of at least one Chicagoan—a young columnist for the *Daily News* named Eugene Field—was complete. When Modjeska appeared in *Camille*, Field sat in the front row or a box during every performance. Wherever he sat, his large solemn visage had a fascination for Modjeska and she involuntarily played at him. It soon became a game between the two; Field attempted to adopt a facial expression exactly contrary to the sentiment the actress was portraying. After the theater, Modjeska would reproach him, "Ah, Meester Field, why will you seet in the box and talk with your overcoat on the chair to make poor Camille laugh, who is dying on the stage. You are a very bad man—but I lof you." It was a "lof" which was reciprocated appropriately in a verse:

> Nor will revolve, since rising sons are we,
> Round any orb, save, dear Modjeska, thee
> Who are our Pole Star, and will ever be.

The visits of Theodore Thomas and his orchestra, Sarah Bernhardt, Oscar Wilde and Modjeska were attractions which any provincial city might expect to have. Their performances emphasized to a small group of thoughtful Chicagoans that the time was near when Chicago should have its own culture with native artists, musicians and writers. One of those who dreamed of a more sophisticated Chicago was Ferdinand Wythe Peck, the son of a pioneer who had been a founder of the city's fire department. Peck envisioned one building that would be the home of opera and the arts, a Parthenon of modern civilization. To make his vision practical, he proposed

INTERIOR OF THE AUDITORIUM, 1889

the new home for opera be constructed in connection with a hotel and office building. He intended to make it self-supporting as Crosby had intended his opera house should be; profit was as important to Chicagoans as esthetic principle. Out of Peck's planning came the Auditorium. Its erection symbolized to Chicagoans the beginning of an era when they might add to the pleasures of accumulating a fortune the satisfaction of indulging in the pleasures it could buy.

Peck, after first presenting his idea to the increasingly important Commercial Club, had no difficulty in raising the money through the sale of stock. For his architects he engaged Dankmar Adler and Louis Sullivan, partners who were beginning to lay down basic principles for a new American architecture. The building which Adler and Sullivan designed could only have been erected in an opulent city expansive with new fortunes. The most expensive marble obtainable was used for the floors and thousands of manhours were spent in forming it into intricate mosaics. The theater auditorium was based on a radically different principle; it was designed according to acoustical principles rather than sight lines. The floor rose much more sharply than was necessary for the audience to see; this arch, combined with the vault of the ceiling, provided nearly echoproof acoustical perfection. The equipment of the stage was as highly mechanized as any in the world. To permit the banking of the stage for concerts the floor was in sections which could be lifted separately by hydraulic lifts beneath the stage. Laid flat with an overlay of hardwood, it could be extended to a ballroom floor that would accommodate several thousand. The boxes were another departure from tradition and were only forty in number. It was Peck's idea that there was no place in Chicago for privileged classes; he said the city "regards the Metropolitan Opera House of New York where the whole structure is sacrificed to boxes with infinite scorn and patriotic dislike." Peck regarded boxes as a reflection of effete European ideas. If there was one thing he impressed upon the architects it was that he wanted the Auditorium to represent "the future and not the corrupted past." The hotel was also in a new tradition. Among the innovations was the location of the kitchens and dining rooms on the top floors. This, it was explained, enabled the wind to take away the cooking odors without offending the guests.

There were social questions as well as cultural problems to be solved when the Auditorium was erected. It was obvious that only the most formal wear would be appropriate for the members of society who appeared in the elegant surroundings of the Auditorium. To the ladies this meant the décolleté gown, still regarded as daring in Chicago and not suitable for public entertainment. To establish a standard in the matter for readers of the *Tribune*, a reporter made a survey among the city's social arbiters, who were ready to reveal their opinions if nothing more.

Mrs. William B. Howard expressed the majority opinion. "I think it would be too bad to do away with it," she said, "now that we have such a magnificent building to display it in. The luster of any evening is undoubtedly increased by the appearance of women in low-necked dresses." Mrs. Marshall Field felt the subject "one which every woman must decide for herself. I never wear a low-necked gown myself and hold that a slender woman's appearance is vastly improved by the Bernhardt style of dress. Of course it is all right for women who have handsome necklaces to cut the dress low enough to display them. But as I never wear jewelry of that kind myself I always have the necks of my dresses cut high. I really think that quite as dressy an effect can be produced by omitting the sleeves." Mrs. Carter Harrison said she felt that the low-necked gowns might be all right but that by the time a woman became a grandmother, she should no longer wear them. To this view Mrs. H. O. Stone, "the grandmother of a sweet little baby myself," took exception. She told the reporter her late husband had always wanted her to wear such gowns and she had no intention of abandoning the practice which she did not find at all immodest.

Economy and health also entered into the discussion. To Mrs. Fernando Jones the décolleté dress was "less expensive than the high-necked one, for it takes elegant material and a good deal of decoration to make the latter dressy enough." Mrs. Reginald De Koven, the wife of the composer of "O Promise Me," was another who gave her approval to the low-cut dress, disdaining charges that it was unhealthy. "Not in the least," she retorted.

"I have always worn low-cut bodices for evening since my coming out and I always shall wear them. I have a sensitive throat and take cold easily but have never been able to trace a single illness to the wearing of a low-necked dress." Mrs. John W. Jewett was also concerned with the issue of health. "For the years between sixteen and twenty-eight when the neck is plump and full and the skin like satin a dress cut modestly low is not in my opinion inappropriate provided the wearer has exceptionally robust health, but after that . . ." Here the reporter discreetly remarked that "an expressive gesture with the hands completes the sentence."

The question of ladies' dress having been aired if not finally settled, Chicago began to prepare for the dedication of the Auditorium. The event was considered worthy of the presence of the President of the United States and the Pecks rushed work on their new mansion in order to have it ready to entertain President and Mrs. Harrison as their house guests. But though the Auditorium was finished, the Peck house at 1826 South Michigan was not. With only three days remaining before the dedication, Mrs. Peck called upon Marshall Field and a few other business leaders to come to her rescue. Within an hour, contractors, painters and decorators began arriving at the house, which was finished and completely furnished in time to receive the Harrisons. The city took an immense interest in the Harrisons' entertainment. For breakfast, the newspapers reported, the President had eaten a parsley omelet, porterhouse steak, mutton chops, breakfast bacon, hothouse tomatoes and a baked potato—"No frills but good eating." By lunch the Chief Executive was at least moderately hungry as he sat down to a repast at the Union League of Blue Points, Schloss Vollrader, Crème de Terrapin, Sherry Solero, Fillet of White Fish, Roman Punch, Chicken Wings, Champagne, Larded Quail, Chateau Pichon, Cheese and Crackers, Fruit and Cake and Coffee. In response to a question, the President said he had been informed his coming to Chicago had been criticized in the East because the Auditorium was a private enterprise. "Such criticism," he said, "springs from those who have never seen your great buildings. It marks a period in the development of our country. Altogether exceptional itself, my presence at its opening can set no precedent." If there were those who did not agree with the President, they were not to be heard in Chicago.

The crowd that began to gather on the night of the opening had grown to about twenty thousand persons by curtain time. Attorney Wirt Dexter described it as "a well dressed mob and with wit enough to become exasperating." Its comments were loud and to the point. The *Tribune* reported the following morning that "whether the cream of society or only its boiled milk, all had to pass through the serried ranks of upturned, swaying, laughing, gibing, hooting faces." But if it was a noisy mob it was not unfriendly; every one felt that this was the greatest night in the history of Chicago.

The mob outside was as proud of the new symbol of the city's success as any of the select group which picked its way across the street through the lines of carriages while the rain dripped upon high-piled coiffures and made little furrows in brilliant complexions.

Once inside the Auditorium the members of the audience sat proudly through speeches by the governor, the mayor, the President and an address of dedication by John S. Runnells. They listened attentively as a "Triumphal Fantasie" was played and a chorus sang "America" and a cantata written for the occasion by young Harriet Monroe. But their great affection was reserved for Chicago's favorite singer, Adelina Patti, who had returned to sing "Home, Sweet Home" and the "Swiss Echo Song."

Patti, so the readers of the newspapers learned, had bleached her hair "red-gold" because her own dark tresses had "cast a depressing effect" on her feelings while she was in mourning for her sister, Carlotta, who had died six months before. She added in the same interview that she was to wear "half-mourning" in her appearance at the Auditorium—"a white brocade dress with black slashings and steel beads." That the feminine members of her audience took note of her appearance and particularly of her hair was indicated by an item in the newspapers several days later: "A State Street hairdresser says that many women of Chicago with black hair have called upon him recently and talked to him in a confidential manner which he is bound to respect." Chicago, no longer the young girl in gingham, was ready for a few frills.

PART THREE
The Spirit of Democracy

1890=1910

MRS. EDWARD TYLER BLAIR,
1883, *by George P. A. Healy*

15

Why Do We Need a Genealogy?

EVEN WITH the development of great fortunes there was no leisure class in Chicago. An air of continued striving and aggressiveness was still the chief Chicago characteristic. There was a general consciousness that the city lacked some sense of form or elegance of refinement not to be found in "her corn and railways, her hogs and by-products and dollars." Typically, or so it seemed to most visitors, the city was now striving to add this refinement with the same purposeful determination which had always marked its pursuit of wealth. And, as an English observer was quick to remark, although the city did not quite know what it lacked, it was determined to have it, "cost what it may." A *Harper's* correspondent in the nineties was more severe. He found that local conditions were "Arcadian"—or, as he expanded his theme, "part and parcel of the kinship that permits Chicagoans to bring their rugs out and to sit on the stoops in the evening."

The local press was not entirely in disagreement. The *Saturday Evening Herald*, which sought to chronicle the first movements of the embryonic society, lamented that "it has always been said of Chicago that it was impossible to conduct a grand fete or hold a grand function year after year (be it a charity ball, a Derby or a fete of any kind) without making it common inside of a few years." Even the Assembly Balls, which for a long period were the city's most fashionable affairs, originated as a protest against the more exclusive invitation list of the Entre Nous Club. The Entre Nous members had excluded most of the younger married couples from the list of those invited to their affairs. Rather than accept the principle of exclusion, the offended group banded together as the Assembly Association, inviting only enough of the Entre Nous members to split that organization's loyalties. The invitations to the Assembly Ball then became the most eagerly sought social honor, with a packing-company executive, Arthur Meeker, and his wife acting as final arbiters in dispensing them. Within a short time, the Assembly Balls had grown from a restricted four hundred to nearly eight hundred. The Charity Balls sponsored by Mrs. Palmer had far outgrown their original dimensions and were open to all who had the resources to contribute to charity. After the 1909 charity ball, where music was provided by the incongruous alternates of Johnny Hand's society orchestra and the First Regiment Band, the *Record-Herald* reported triumphantly that "all stiffness of formality was absent. It breathed the spirit of democracy, the spirit of the most democratic city of the most democratic nation of the world. There was no one who couldn't belong." Mrs. Walter Brewster, one of the leaders of society, was to sigh somewhat wearily that "if you are anybody at all, you are it. You are invited to every ball, wedding, debut, charitable entertainment and opening."

Not everyone was satisfied with the emphasis on democracy which had been characteristic of society from the earliest parties at Beaubien's Sauganash Hotel. The exclusive Fortnightly Club, distressed by the city's reputation, scheduled a discussion to determine "Is Chicago Provincial?" A society columnist suggested that the city needed a new club—one in which members could enjoy themselves "without thought of any useful occupation." But Joseph K. C. Forrest, who wrote a column in the *Daily News* which he signed "Old Timer," said he doubted "if those who have made business their chief end in life could transpose the order of their existence and make a business of pleasure." He was not sanguine about the chance of "even your retired, much less your active banker, your bloated speculator, your pork packer" developing into society leaders as long as they carried "the spirit of the store, the bank, the packing house and the mart of trade into society with them." A suggestion that ancestral blood lines and genealogies be referred to as a criterion of social standing met with a rebuff from Marshall Field. To a prospective genealogist who wished to prepare a chart showing the merchant's forebears back to the time in 1630 when they landed in Massachusetts, Field had a quick answer. "I have nothing to give you," he said. "Why do we need a genealogy?"

A catalogue of the standards of social acceptance more generally recog-

nized than any kind of social register or genealogical bluebook was that found
in the *Tribune* when the excitement over the Klondike gold rush was at its
height. "Chicago is still the best Klondike," the *Tribune* proclaimed. "Today there live in Chicago over two hundred men whose fortunes reach and
pass the million mark. Every large fortune was made here. What you need
is an outfit of good sense, sobriety, industry, economy and stick-to-it-iveness.
Without an exception, so far as can be ascertained, these millionaires started
in without capital." Typical, the paper indicated, was Silas B. Cobb, who
had arrived in the city without enough money to pay his fare to the captain
of the schooner which brought him. Cobb went to work for John Kinzie,
who had bought his release from the captain, and at fifty-five had been one
of the richest men in Chicago. This model citizen, according to the account,
"never kept a clerk or a bookkeeper, never asked any man to go on his note,
never went to law in his life, never paid a lawyer or a doctor a cent. He had
no extravagances and no dissipations." On the list of millionaires which
accompanied the article, the paper listed Cobb's wealth at fifteen million
dollars or as much as that of Potter Palmer. The richest man on the list was
Marshall Field, whose wealth was estimated at seventy-five million dollars
and whose firm was credited with making more men millionaires than any
other one concern in the United States. Philip D. Armour, who was not
only the world's largest packer but whose firm handled more wheat than
any other single company in the world, was credited with forty million
dollars. Calling attention to the fact that so many men on the list were
Chicago pioneers, the *Tribune* explained that they "had survived the wear
and tear of time so well" because they "led frugal and abstemious lives in
their youth."

Though the city was young and its leaders durable, there were many names
on the *Tribune's* list that reflected a changing leadership. The name of Montgomery Ward appeared on the list as having made his first one million
dollars. William Deering, who had competed with Cyrus McCormick, had
accumulated ten million dollars. But the new order was most readily seen
in the growth of the stockyards which had been founded in 1848 and in
the expansion of the packing houses which surrounded the yards. The third
richest man in Chicago, according to the *Tribune*, was Samuel W. Allerton,
who had operated his packing business on the credo that "nobody can
succeed unless he can build up character and credit." At one time, Allerton
had possessed enough of both these virtues to buy up all the hogs in
Chicago and hold them until the price rose enough to satisfy him. Allerton,
whose worth was listed as twenty million dollars, was less active in business.
Allerton's contemporary, Nelson W. Morris, was also a less dominant figure.
It was Morris who was credited with knowing more about buying cattle
than anyone else in the United States. It was said he could tell from which

MONTGOMERY WARD & CO., *about 1900*. Lithograph published under the title "A Busy Beehive"

section of the country a steer had come by the taste of a steak after the animal had been butchered. Philip Armour still dominated the yards, but more was being heard of John and Michael Cudahy, who had formerly been Armour partners but had established their own chain of packing houses and accumulated a combined fortune of five million dollars. The real challenger to Armour, however, was Gustavus Swift, whose thrifty practices were reflected in a quickly accumulated fortune of ten million dollars.

THE SPIRIT OF DEMOCRACY   184

Gustavus Swift found Chicago a comfortable city in which to live. "A man can get wholesome food in Chicago more cheaply than he can in the East," he explained, "and he can live as well on a smaller amount of money. I can spend my money fast enough here." He thought Chicago "was the finest city in the world for the moderate, natural average man of affairs." Swift's idea of being moderate was firmly expressed in his personal life. For many years after he accumulated a fortune, he kept his family in a modest house near the stockyards on the ground that it was convenient to his work. When he finally permitted a move into a garish and monstrous yellow brick house at 4848 South Ellis, he saw no need of adorning it with such frills as draperies or lace tablecloths. He told his wife, Ann, who had been living without curtains for thirty years, that he would not permit them and yielded only after she threatened to leave him. But he still would not permit any curtains to be purchased for his own bedroom.

Swift, who told an interviewer that "no young man is rich enough to smoke 25-cent cigars" and that "no man, however, rich, has enough money to waste in putting on style," was under continuing pressure at home to add a bit of style. In the new house he discovered there were social rules to be obeyed as well as such fripperies as curtains and draperies to be tolerated. He was in the habit of sending for the cook to give her instructions about his food, but was prohibited from such informality by his wife. "We are doing things differently in the new house," she informed him. Stringent as were the prohibitions imposed by the family's social status, they did not

MASONIC TEMPLE, 1895

approach the business rebuke Gustavus Swift received from his brother, Noble. Swift & Company was preparing to bring out a new issue of stock and Gustavus wrote Noble to tell him that he might have some of the shares. "Brother Gustavus," Noble wrote in a tone of exasperation, "I do not care for any more Swift & Co. stock. Do you remember when we were boys, that everybody on the coast fished? What has become of the fish now? Fished out! Where will Swift & Co. be when the cattle are killed off? I don't want any more stock. Perhaps I have too much already."

There was some significance in the fact that Noble Swift did not live in Chicago. As novelist Henry B. Fuller observed, it was "the only great city in the world to which all its citizens have come for the avowed purpose of making money. There you have its genesis, its growth, its object; and there are but few of us who are not attending to that object very strictly." Philip D. Armour expressed the same Chicago philosophy in a slightly different way when it was suggested that he might retire. He explained he could not give up his business activities "because I have no other interest in life but my business. I do not want more money; as you say, I have more than I want. I do not love the money; what I do love is the getting of it, the making it. All these years of my life I have put into this work and now it is my life and I cannot give it up. . . . I do not read, I do not take any part in politics, what can I do? But in my counting house I am in my element; there I live and the struggle is the very breath of life to me." Armour was above worrying about criticism. "I can stand a lot," he said, "for my hide is thick. . . . That is the result of my early habits. I was raised like a farmer and I still have a pitcher of water in the center of the table as we used to at home."

The Reverend Dr. Frank Gunsaulus, the minister of the Plymouth Congregational Church which Armour attended, thought he might be able to persuade Armour to develop new interests. He announced as his sermon topic "If I Had a Million Dollars." When he mounted the pulpit to preach he saw that Armour, his richest parishioner, was in his regular place in the church. The minister's plan, as it was expounded in the sermon, was to establish a school to help young people help themselves. It would be an outgrowth of the educational plan developing in the Armour Mission. The mission had been founded with a $100,000 bequest in the will of Philip's brother, Joseph, and its operations had been continued with an equivalent grant from Philip. Julia Beveridge, the mission's librarian, was using the facilities of the building—constructed for a Sunday school—to teach wood-carving, drawing, designing and other manual arts to more than four hundred boys; an equal number of girls were learning dress-cutting and millinery work. Armour listened carefully as the Reverend Gunsaulus described the need for technical training on a higher level. After the sermon, he had a question for the minister. "Would you carry out those ideas if you had the means?" he asked. When the minister expressed his willingness to put his sermon into practice, Armour offered a million dollars if the minister would give "five years of your time." The bargain was sealed with a handclasp. Out of this Sunday morning colloquy came the Armour Institute of Technology, later merged with Lewis Institute to form the Illinois Institute of Technology.

Philanthropies such as that of Armour were remarkable because of their rarity. Rudyard Kipling, after a disapproving visit to Chicago, found nothing in it but an expression of materialism:

> I know thy cunning and thy greed
> Thy hard high lust and willful deed
> And all th' glory loves to tell
> Of specious gifts material.

There was much that Kipling missed. Had he been less prejudiced against what he called the "most American" of American cities, he would have seen the evidence of an esthetic revolution in architecture which had its origins in the materialism he deplored.

The preparations for the revolution had been going on for a generation. The first of the innovators was George H. Johnson, who had adapted an abandoned art of the Egyptians to create a process for making fireproof hollow tile. Another of the early arrivals was Louis Sullivan, who was to become the philosophic spokesman of the Chicago school of architecture. Sullivan, who had created the Auditorium in collaboration with Dankmar Adler, had an intense dislike of the classical style. During the 1880's he had become an advocate of the Romanesque, believing that its horizontal, low lines best harmonized with the prairie city and were best adapted to masonry construction. It was as a philosopher, however, that he had his greatest influence. He based his architectural ideas on two general principles. One was that architecture had no significance unless it reflected the life of the people. The other was that the form of a building should be an expression of its function. Out of these twin principles came the American skyscraper and modern functional design.

The function of a building in the business district was obviously that of multiplying as many offices as possible on valuable ground whose price had risen to several million dollars an acre. Multiplying offices required high buildings, but Chicago's swampy base provided a poor foundation for such structures. Once again Chicago had to conquer its notorious mud. The solution came from a new architectural firm formed by John Wellborn Root and Daniel H. Burnham. Root had the idea of floating "rafts" of crisscrossed steel rails and concrete in the subterranean gumbo and erecting the high structures on these. On a series of these rafts Burnham and Root put

NATATORIUM AT THE CORNER OF JACKSON AND MICHIGAN AVENUE

up the sixteen-story Monadnock Building, the highest masonry structure ever erected. The final step in the creation of the modern skyscraper was taken in 1884 by William Le Baron Jenney, a former army engineer. His design for the Home Insurance Building was aptly described by Carl Condit in *The Rise of the Skyscraper* as the step of evolution which "converted a building from a crustacean with its armor of stone to a vertebrate clothed only in light skin." The Monadnock Building had been based on stones six feet in thickness. The strength of the Home Insurance Building came not from such mass but from a skeleton of steel beams erected on floating foundations of the kind designed by Root. These were the first steel beams ever used in a building in America. Burnham and Root were quick to add Jenney's ideas to their own and in 1891 they erected at Randolph and State Street a twenty-two-story Masonic Temple, then the highest building in the world.

Paul Bourget of France was more perceptive than Kipling in noticing the changes that were taking place in Chicago. At first, he wrote, "you have around you only buildings. They scale the sky with their eighteen or twenty stories. The architect who has built them, or rather who has plotted them, has accepted the condition imposed by the speculator, multiplying the planned offices. It is a problem of interest only to an engineer, one would suppose. Nothing of the kind. The simple force of such a need is such a principle of beauty, and these buildings so conspicuously manifest that need that in contemplating them you experience a singular emotion. The sketch appears here of a new kind of art, an art of democracy made by the crowd, and for the crowd, an art of science in which the certainty of natural laws gives to audacities, in appearance the most unbridled, the tranquillity of geometrical figures."

It was not possible to rebuild the city in the nineties as completely as had been done in the seventies. Around the trim figures of the new skyscrapers were grouped a collection of buildings four and five stories high, dull in color and with no particular distinction of architecture. The pavement was of cedar blocks or cobblestones, the sidewalks mainly of stone with a few remnants of wooden walks which frequently gave way beneath pedestrians and formed a substantial source of income for lawyers adept at collecting damages from the city. A principal quality of the streets was noise—compounded from cable cars and street-level railroad tracks from which there was an "incessant tinkle of locomotive bells that seem to be sounding in advance the knell of those they are about to crush."

Horseless carriages were beginning to appear on the streets. In 1900, there were ninety permits for electric cars, fifty-five for gasoline vehicles and forty-four for steam cars. Among the licenses were ten issued to women who were bold enough to defy convention and to face the hazards of breakdowns from the capricious new carriages. There was already talk of a motorized bus line, a plan which the Tribune conceded might sound "chimerical, were it not for the fact that exactly the same thing, according to the Scientific American, is now being done in New York . . . Chicago, so the experts say, offers a much more inviting field [for horseless carriages] because of its level topography and long stretches of asphalt paved boulevards."

The South Park Board took a disapproving view of the new contraptions. In 1902 it banned from Michigan Avenue and Jackson and Washington Parks all automobiles which emit "spurts of vapor" (steam cars), "offensive odors" (gasoline cars) or cars with "a speed of more than eight miles per hour." All horns and whistles were prohibited.

The most popular form of transportation remained the bicycle. The Chicago Post reported in May of 1897 that all society was awheel and the boulevards and parkways gay with the latest model cycles. "The fashionable girl no longer lolls about in tea gowns and darkened rooms," the paper said, "but stands beside you in short skirts, sailor hat, low shoes and leggings, ready for a spin on the wheel." Every afternoon and evening cycling parties might be found at the Saddle and Cycle Club north of the city. A popular rendezvous for less fashionable cyclers was Fisher's Beer Garden at the north end of Lincoln Park. The Auditorium Hotel was another cycling

TOURING BY BICYCLE, 1896

center. Neighborhood clubs met at their own clubhouse, took a preliminary spin and then converged on the Auditorium for dinner. In the evening, there might be a spontaneous parade on Michigan Avenue, with the clubs moving in column down the street and then breaking ranks to move off toward their homes.

Cycling guides were best sellers. The books included such traffic information as a list of regulations prohibiting cyclers from riding at a speed exceeding eight miles per hour or riding more than two abreast, and requiring them to carry lighted lamps at night. Ambitious wheelmen could choose their objective from a distance table which indicated it was twenty-seven miles to Wheaton or Highland Park and seventeen miles to Western Springs. The ride to Aurora or Elgin and back was a hundred miles; those who made it in a day over the dirt roads were awarded a well-merited gold medal.

Cycling was not without hazards. A story by Poliuto, a popular newspaper columnist, told of a romance between one of the town's best cyclists and the daughter of a prominent family. The attachment had been suddenly terminated by the girl, who refused to give any reason for her action. The suitor was baffled until he found a newspaper clipping in a plain envelope among the letters and presents which, as propriety demanded, the girl had returned to him. The clipping explained his broken romance. It read: "Competent medical authorities have decided that serious results are caused by riding the velocipede. Among these, not the least is giving to Malthusian doctrines a practical and eminently undesired effect." Even a sheltered girl of the nineties could understand that this was reason enough to beware a young man on a velocipede.

Munsey's Magazine, looking at Chicago about this time, called it the "City of the Big Idea"—of the skyscraper, the refrigerator car, the mail-order store, the Pullman car and the packing house. At twenty-seven, Chicagoans would tell you, their city was as large as Athens or Damascus; at forty-three she had caught up to Rome; and at fifty she had surpassed Vienna, Constantinople and St. Petersburg, three of the empire centers of the world. The most remarkable portrait of the city, however, and one which rivaled anything ever produced by its native poets was the work of an English tourist, G. W. Steevens. "Chicago," he wrote:

> Queen and guttersnipe of cities, cynosure and cesspool of the world: Not if I had a hundred tongues, everyone shouting a different language in a different key, could I do justice to her splendid chaos. The most beautiful and the most squalid, girdled with a twofold zone of parks and slums; where the keen air from lake and prairie is ever in the nostrils and the stench of foul smoke is never out of the throat; the great port a thousand miles from the sea; the great mart which gathers up with one hand the corn and cattle of the West and deals out with the other the merchandise of the East; widely and generously planned with streets of twenty miles [in length], where it is not safe to walk at night; where women ride straddlewise and millionaires dine at midday on the Sabbath; the chosen seat of cutthroat commerce and munificent patronage of art; the most American of American cities and yet the most mongrel; the

"BEAUTY ON A BIKE," 1889

second American city of the globe, the fifth German city, the third Swedish, the second Polish, the first and only veritable Babel of the age; all of which twenty-five years ago next Friday was a heap of smoking ashes. Where in all the world can words be found for this miracle of paradox and incongruity?

To celebrate this "miracle" which had occurred in the quarter of a century since the great fire, it was inevitable there should be a parade. The plans for the parade were appropriate to a city where, as Steevens also noted, "if it is not the biggest thing of its kind that has ever been done, why then Chicago has lost a day." There was a practical end to be served by the mammoth demonstration. A national election was to be held in 1896. The candidate of the Republicans was William McKinley, who stood for the sound-money principles which were part of the basic inventory of the Chicago philosophy. The candidate of the Democrats was William Jennings Bryan, who had been nominated in Chicago a few months before after his famous speech in which he proclaimed "You shall not press down upon the brow of labor this crown of thorns, you shall not crucify mankind upon a cross of gold." The connection was obvious to the leaders of the business community; the parade would pay tribute to the principles of sound money from which the city's business prosperity stemmed and simultaneously advance the cause of McKinley. The Democratic city authorities were not hospitable to the idea of the parade and refused to proclaim an official holiday. The businessmen who formed Chicago's unofficial government declared a holiday on their own authority by closing the Board of Trade, the stockyards, the banks, the stock exchange, and most of the stores, offices and factories. When the day for the parade arrived, the theme of the fire anniversary was only an echo of the cries for sound money.

The parade began at 10 o'clock in the morning and lasted for five hours. The cable cars, horsecars and elevated trains reported they carried a total of two million passengers during the crowded day. The crush in the parade district was so great that twenty-four hours later there were still eight unclaimed children at police headquarters who had been lost during the day. The parade column was composed of more than 68,000 men and stretched out for thirteen miles. The Chicago Hussars led the groups and were followed by mounted police, floats, and charter members of the Lincoln Wide-Awakes walking with gold-painted canes rather than their oilcloth capes and torches. All the men in the parade wore some kind of gold decoration, either gold cords on their hats or colored sashes around their waists. A long section of Civil War veterans was followed by battalions of marchers regimented according to political clubs or business houses. Marshall Field, his partner, Harlow Higinbotham, and four other company executives rode abreast in the fore of an army of employes representing the firm's floorwalkers, salesmen, cashiers, porters and office boys. Just behind came the Carson Pirie Scott & Co. Sound Money Club, the first of several hundred such clubs to proclaim its identity in the parade. Following the business houses came the representatives of the stockyards and the packers—ten thousand men led by a brigade of stockyards cowboys sitting easily astride their mounts beneath capes of gold cloth and splitting the air with bugle calls. Megaphones appeared for the first time in Chicago, many of them mounted on the handlebars of bicycles, and increased the multiplication of noise. At the Chicago Telephone Building a huge telephone speaker was suspended from the building and into it the paraders shouted their cheers to be carried to William McKinley at Canton, Ohio, where the candidate was conducting his famous front-porch campaign. The parade over, the local papers counted up the marchers and the crowd; by their reckoning it was not only a record-breaker in politics, but the largest civil demonstration in the history of the world.

The Democrats celebrated the anniversary with a silver-metal parade the same night but could muster only a diminutive force of about fifteen thousand. The Democrats charged that many of their party members had been forced to march in the day's parade or be faced with the loss of their jobs. At night the darkness masked the marchers' identities while torches outlined a row of white-clad "ghosts" carrying placards reading "Murdered in Pennsylvania by Carnegie." There were other issues to be considered in addition to that of sound money.

Labor unrest was but one of the new currents flowing in society which

THE SLEIGH RIDE, Samuel W. Allerton and his son, *by Henry H. Cross*, 1879 were only partly understood by the titans who ruled the city. Another revolt came from the second generation, victims for the most part of their parents' success. Philip Armour's son, Ogden, returning home from a trip to England, told his father he did not much like the idea of going to work in the stockyards. The father, who prided himself on setting an example for the younger men coming up around him, did not share Ogden's enthusiasm that "so many Englishmen had a leisurely life on a small income." As the elder Armour put it, "Ogden thought there would be something he would like to do instead of grubbing for money. He thinks I should retire. I told him to be at the yards in his working clothes at seven on Monday morning."

Frazier Jelke, whose father made a fortune from oleomargarine, wrote in his autobiography that "this must be said of the Chicago tradition: it was hard on the second generation. . . . It is a matter of record that few sons of men of outstanding success made names for themselves or kept pace with their sires." The explanation lay in the fact that the fathers, who had little formal education, sought to give their sons the softening cultural advantages of college, art, travel and luxury. Then, on graduation, the sons were expected to go to work at jobs for which their training had not fitted them; they had been taught to live like gentlemen of leisure and unexpectedly found themselves put in the position of laborers or clerks or factory hands, as their fathers had been in their youth. As Jelke was to testify, "It didn't work."

Joseph Leiter, whose father had been the first partner of Marshall Field, was so brash as to challenge Philip Armour on the Board of Trade. Leiter attempted to corner the world supply of wheat by buying against Armour. When the chances appeared best that Leiter might succeed in his coup, Armour learned of seven million bushels of wheat in Duluth that had been passed over on the assumption it could not be shipped until spring. Armour, who assumed nothing, hired a fleet of ice-breakers and tugs to bring the shiploads of wheat to Chicago where he dumped it on the market. The price plummeted and Joseph Leiter had to take a loss on his buying of two and a half million dollars. To make good the debt, his father, Levi Leiter, returned to Chicago and sold some of his downtown real estate; for a Chicago businessman it was an act of desperation.

Leiter's sisters fared better by pioneering in a new area—that of marrying titled foreigners. After Marshall Field bought out Leiter's interest in the store, the Leiters took their three daughters to Washington, where Mrs. Leiter began an extensive campaign of elegant entertainments so that her daughters might meet titled suitors. Her average of success was high. Two of her daughters married English noblemen and the third married a cousin of the Duke of Argyll. Mary Leiter became the wife of the eldest son of the Fourth Baron Scarsdale, a bright young man who was to become Lord

Curzon, Viceroy of India. Daisy, whose baptismal cognomen was Marguerite, became the wife of Henry Molyneux Page Howard, who was twice an earl, being both the nineteenth Earl of Suffolk and the twelfth Earl of Berkshire. Nancy, the youngest daughter, married Major Colin Campbell, who overcame reported objections of his future mother-in-law against his lack of rank by proving a link to an Irish king. These marriages were proudly claimed by Chicago. Photographs of the Leiter girls were on sale in many of the stores which had not, as yet, Hollywood film queens to offer as models for young girls with the dual endowments of beauty and an ambitious mother. Mrs. Evelyn Clayton, a young Chicago widow, became a princess of Imperial Russia after her marriage to Prince Nicholas Engalitcheff, a Russian envoy. The union drew an added bit of attention when the new princess announced she was taking up cigarettes as the prince "loved to see a woman smoking."

There were other signs of sophistication. Rose Farwell, the youngest daughter of United States Senator Charles B. Farwell and a niece of John V. Farwell, in whose firm Marshall Field had once been a young clerk, wrote her graduating essay at Lake Forest College on "The Decay of Puritanism." This was strong language for a community still dedicated to the Yankee virtues. But even more indicative of a change was a newspaper's description of Rose Farwell on her wedding day. "Her father says she can ride any horse which she can mount," the *Journal* boasted, "and her latest acquisition in that line is a thoroughbred racer brought for her special use from Kentucky and which she handles with consummate ease. Add to that her proficiency in lawn tennis, her skill in handling the ribbons and she is a perfect specimen of a beautiful and accomplished daughter, the result of an education thoroughly American. And all this triumph of civilization has most fittingly chosen to adorn the home of the groom of today, Mr. Hobart Chatfield-Taylor, a young man whose wealth is counted among the millions and which he inherits from his father." The time of the pioneer was at an end.

Lake Shore Drive, 1889

A YOUNG STUDENT AT BOURNI-
QUE'S DANCING ACADEMY, 1881.
By Edward H. Hart

The Cultivated Class is
Comparatively Small

THEODORE THOMAS, after moving west to establish the Chicago orchestra
in 1890, indicated that he was thinking in terms of a combination of practicality and esthetics which was pleasing to Chicago. One of his objectives,
he said, was to demonstrate the soothing qualities of fine music on the
perpetually fatigued American business executive. "One reason I came to
Chicago," he wrote in his autobiography, "was that I understood the excitement and nervous strain that everyone, more or less, suffered who lived
there, and realized the consequent need of establishing a permanent musical institution in such a community."

Thomas, who had accepted the Chicago offer with the tart comment that
"I would go to hell if they would give me a permanent orchestra," found
quickly that he had not arrived in paradise. His first season was not a success. The programs were on a higher level than those of the summer concerts, for which he had offered music of a lighter character, with symphonies

administered in very small doses. Although Chicago had the boldness to establish a permanent orchestra, it was still so uneducated in its tastes that it generally regarded symphonies as too severe. For this reason, Thomas arranged to give a large proportion of programs without a symphony in the second year and work the audience up to the symphonic standard a little more slowly. The conductor, conscious that most of his potential audience belonged "to the class employed in mills, factories and at all kinds of manual labor, while the cultivated class is comparatively small," arranged a series of special concerts for workingmen. Various schemes were adopted to raise money among them a benefit concert at which Thomas conducted the symphony orchestra for dancing at the conclusion of the concert. The orchestra protested this indignity but consented to play when Thomas threatened to mount the podium and conduct before the rows of empty chairs.

The Chicago music critics were another hazard. Thomas had once written George Upton, the *Tribune* critic (and later Thomas' biographer), that "I have no need to cultivate the critics for I know my work." Yet the critical onslaught against the orchestra's program was so intense that Thomas finally offered his resignation. He was persuaded to stay after a vote of confidence from the orchestra board, which indicated its faith in him by renewing his tenure without a written contract so that he would be free to do as he pleased. There were other difficulties. The members of the orchestra had to be assembled from all over the world, as there were few local musicians qualified to play symphonic music. Violinist Frederick Stock, hoping for a position with the new orchestra, had to switch to the viola because viola players were harder to come by than violinists. Many players were reluctant to come to Chicago because they thought there were so few families with an interest in music that the opportunities for earning extra money from teaching were too limited. Even the climate expressed its hostility to culture. "In many cases," Thomas wrote, "the men imported were unused to such a rigorous climate as that of Chicago and were driven away again by sickness and had to be replaced."

Meanwhile, Thomas resumed patiently his task of accomplishing the musical education of a city of almost two million people. A prerequisite of success was a concert hall; when the orchestra played in the vast Auditorium it was impossible to sell season tickets as audiences knew there were always seats available. A drive for a new building produced the first dividends from the efforts of Thomas to democratize the appeal of the orchestra. Contributions of scrubwomen and mill hands were listed next to those of the members of the Chicago Club. The total subscriptions surpassed the $750,000 it was expected to cost to erect the new building on Michigan Avenue with its twin stones bearing the name of Theodore Thomas. The impatient

THE WATER TANK LIBRARY,
established in an abandoned water
tank in 1871

conductor gave his first concert before the plaster was dry on the walls. The dampness, plus his exertion in readying the building, caused complications which resulted in his death within a month after the completion of the hall which was to be his monument. Cultural maturity, like wealth, appeared to have come rapidly to the young city. The successor to Thomas was found in the ranks of his infant orchestra; he was Frederick Stock, who after putting down his viola to take up the conductor's baton, became the symbol of the proudest moments of Chicago's musical history.

Two years after the founding of the symphony, a brilliant professor from Yale, William Rainey Harper, agreed to accept the presidency of the new University of Chicago. The city had known an earlier Chicago University which had been founded on ten acres of land donated by Stephen A. Douglas in 1856, but the recurrence of financial panics led to its closing in 1886. Thomas W. Goodspeed, then secretary of the Baptist Theological Seminary in Morgan Park and one of the university's alumni, immediately started to seek a means of re-establishing the school on a larger scale. The man to whom he turned for help was John D. Rockefeller, already an important contributor to the seminary. Rockefeller listened patiently to Goodspeed's ideas but took no action until Frederick Gates, secretary of the new American Baptist Education Society, added his pleas to those of Goodspeed for the establishment of a new denominational school at Chicago.

Rockefeller agreed to give $600,000 if another $400,000 could be raised by the Baptist churches of Chicago. It required long months of effort to raise the additional money and it was produced only after ardent solicitations to every church of the denomination throughout the Midwest. Marshall Field then aided the cause with a gift of ten acres of property just north of the proposed site for the World's Columbian Exposition and this was chosen as the location for the school.

The choice of the new president had been expected. Goodspeed had been urging the trustees to name Harper, who had the additional recommendation of being on friendly terms with Rockefeller. Both Harper and Rockefeller enjoyed cycling. When the Harpers visited the Rockefellers in Cleveland the cycling often took the form of a game of follow the leader with the entire Harper and Rockefeller clans pedaling through the countryside until dusk made it necessary for the leader to identify himself with a white scarf trailing behind. On these visits Harper would tell Rockefeller of his plans for a new college as he had outlined them in detail in his notebooks. Sometimes he would show the oil magnate the section of the book in which he had laid down additional plans for a great university which might be the outgrowth of such a college. As plans went forward for the first buildings of the new school, Rockefeller surprised the thirty-three-year-old president with a gift of an additional million dollars in bonds "as a gift to the Almighty God for returning health."

The extra million dollars made Harper turn from his plans for a college to those he had outlined for a university. He had written out in precise language the distinction. "A college," the notebook explained, "teaches; but a university teaches—and also learns." The principal effort of his university was to be directed toward graduate work and the training of students to push out along new lines of investigation. Many of Harper's ideas were new to education, among them the establishment of a junior college, a university extension course which provided home study and adult education, the creation of a university press and a special division of laboratories and museums which foreshadowed the university's emphasis on scientific research. All these plans were written out in detail before the university enrolled its first student. Not in the notebooks, but doubly welcome, were the victories of the University of Chicago football teams under Amos Alonzo Stagg. Harper was the team's most ardent fan; if he could not attend a game he would have the score phoned to him at the end of every quarter.

Harper applied the Chicago techniques of aggressiveness and "stick-to-itiveness" to higher education. He persuaded nine college presidents to leave their schools and be among the 120 faculty members who greeted the nearly six hundred students who entered the university on October 1, 1892. He used his persuasive abilities to instruct the newly rich Chicagoans in the practices of philanthropy; the endowment of the new school mushroomed beyond the reach of any financial panic. Harper was an amateur cornetist and when he practiced always insisted on every window in the house being shut, explaining "This is going to be noisy." He was just as noisy about his school but played with all the windows open. So much money poured in from John D. Rockefeller that the Standard Oil founder made a collection of cartoons showing Harper pursuing him for another grant. Rockefeller liked best those showing him "fleeing across rivers on cakes of ice with Dr. Harper in hot pursuit or perhaps he would be following close on my trail, like the wolf in the Russian story, in inaccessible country retreats, while I escaped only by the delay I occasioned him now and then by dropping a million-dollar bill which he would be obliged to stop and pick up." The university's chief benefactor visited it only twice, on one of his visits being so dismayed by the absence of enough clocks in the president's house that he slipped Mrs. Harper a check for a thousand dollars with instructions to "buy some more."

The cultural awakening extended to art as well. Martin A. Ryerson, seeking paintings for the new Art Institute Building under construction on the lake front, went about his task with "Chicago hustle" hardly to be expected of so soft-spoken and gentle a man. Chicagoans, it seemed, could find the same bargains in art as they did in wheat or corn or hogs. Ryerson studied art and the new catalogues as conscientiously as any member of the Board of Trade followed the weather and grain reports to determine the prospects for winter wheat. He secured a series of four art panels for the Institute,

THE PAVILION, JACKSON PARK, 1890, *by Charles Graham*

ardently desired by a European museum, by getting to the dealer's before European competitors were up and about in the morning; it was the same technique Gustavus Swift and Nelson Morris had used in outsmarting cattle buyers in the Chicago stockyards. Ryerson's companion on many of his buying trips was the president of the Institute, Charles L. Hutchinson, whose father had been a Board of Trade pioneer. Hutchinson did not have the educated taste of Ryerson, but by his enthusiasm and ability to raise funds for the paintings eased Ryerson's task. When Prince Demidoff was offering a group of Dutch masters for sale, Ryerson and Hutchinson rushed to the prince's villa near Florence and bid $200,000 for the cream of the collection. By this bold gesture they acquired fifteen prize paintings, including such names as Ter Borch, Hals, Hobbema, Van Ostade, Rembrandt, Ruisdael and Jan Steen. Among the treasures were Ostade's "Golden Wedding" and Rembrandt's "Young Girl at an Open Half-Door." Returning to this country after the purchase of the Demidoff collection, Hutchinson brusquely dismissed the questions of the New York ship reporters about the paintings. "They are corkers, every one of them," was all he would say, explaining that the details were too bothersome for a busy man. The New York Press of July 4, 1890 commented sarcastically:

> The hypercritical New York spirit that is tempted to revile Brother Hutchinson for not remembering what the Rubenses, Rembrandts and the Van Dykes were about deserves a stern and uncompromising rebuke. For our part, we have no doubt whatever these corkers are the largest specimens of the schools of Rubens, Rembrandt and Van Dyke that Mr. Hutchinson could find in Europe. He probably paid $1000 a foot for them and we presume the citizens of Chicago will give him a triumphal procession along the lake front when they arrive, carrying them and him in huge floats, drawn by a team of milk-white Berkshire hogs that have been newly washed with a ten-inch hose jet of water until their pink flesh shows under the clean bristles.

The ridicule was wasted. Ryerson augmented his coup with a trip to Spain where he bought El Greco's "Assumption of the Virgin"; he was the first American collector to recognize El Greco's genius.

The opening of the University of Chicago and the increasing interest in art among all classes of Chicagoans—some of whom collected French paintings when they went abroad much as they collected French clothes—encouraged Chicago's literary magazine The Dial to claim proudly that the city was "passing to a higher and maturer stage of civic existence." In an article on "Chicago's Higher Evolution" it cited such developments as the founding of a permanent orchestra, the establishment of the university, the founding of the Newberry and John Crerar libraries and the erection of the new building for the Art Institute. William Morton Payne, associate editor of *The Dial,* was less sanguine in an article written for the *New England Magazine.* "A chapter upon the books of native Chicagoans would be little less barren than the famous chapter upon the snakes in Ireland," he observed. It was his view that Chicago had but recently passed from the stage in which literature was regarded with "indifference or even positive contempt" to a level where there was a first awakening of interest in literary matters. As evidence of what he regarded as cultural barbarity, he alluded unhappily to the visit of James Russell Lowell, a recollection that made "most intelligent Chicagoans blush for their city [and] is too humiliating to be dwelt upon."

Lowell, whose expansive abilities embraced careers as poet, essayist and novelist as well as terms as minister to both England and Spain, had been invited by the Union League Club to give a public lecture on American politics as part of the observance of Washington's birthday. Chicagoans anticipated the event would be at a minimum historic; the *Morning News* reported that the audience which overflowed Central Music Hall represented the best of the "brains, fashion and wealth of Chicago society." To the great surprise of everyone Lowell announced he would not speak on politics but on literature. Specifically, he told his stunned listeners, he would discuss the principles of literary criticism as illustrated by Shakespeare's *Richard III,* a paper he had once delivered to the Edinburgh Philosophical Association. At this, said the *Times,* his audience "settled back into a fixity of intentness which only such a theme could inspire." The paper added that among the dignitaries on the platform there were some who "endeavored but ineffectually to refrain from a gentle but grateful slumber."

Lowell explained his change of topic by saying he wished to avoid controversy because he was a guest of the Union League Club. He hardly could have caused a greater furor than by his talk on what the *Tribune* described as "a singularly uninteresting subject." Many Chicagoans, always sensitive to the British influence, suspected that the speaker's associations with the English were responsible for his conduct. The *Morning News* reported that the organ had played "Yankee Doodle" because the organist "feared Mr. Lowell had forgotten it during his long sojourn abroad." An anonymous member of the Union League told the press that perhaps "Mr. Lowell prepared a speech in which he recognized our indebtedness to the English government—he is quite an Anglomaniac you know—and was advised or concluded that it would offend the Irish who have just had Justin McCarthy, the famous Irish editor, here, so he changed the subject." The Reverend Frank Briston, disappointed that Lowell's eloquence failed to keep its appointment with destiny, was of the opinion "he threw away the opportunity to make himself famous throughout the annals of American political history." The *Morning News* expressed the consensus of Chicagoans when it said "it was well for . . . the audience . . . that it went out to see James Russell Lowell rather than to hear him."

The unfortunate speaker, embarrassed and bewildered by the uproar, attempted to repair the damage by delivering his speech on politics at a banquet that evening in the Union League Club. In a room decorated by numerous flags and banners—"every one of them the Stars and Stripes of America; not a Union Jack was to be seen," noted a reporter—the poet spoke forthrightly on the need for independence in politics. The talk did not increase his popularity, as the club had recently expelled Lowell's Chicago host, Wirt Dexter, for rebelling against the dominant Blaine wing of the Republican Party. The *Tribune* dismissed the evening's talk more curtly than that of the afternoon, describing it as "a postprandial speech before a few college graduates." The other papers were as caustic.

The degree of anger at Lowell was a measure of the city's sensitivity over its own lack of men of letters and its resentment of a continuing dependency on eastern communities for intellectual leadership. The city was still too busy making money to have a literature of its own. George Horace Lorimer spoke for many in his *Letters of a Merchant Prince* when he had one of his characters say, "We don't have much use for poetry in Chicago, except in streetcar ads." It was a comment which gave some meaning to a later generation's discovery that the conductor of a West Side horsecar in 1889 was a young man who aspired to be a writer; his name was Knut Hamsun. The only Chicago novel to achieve any recognition before the 1880's had been Mrs. John Kinzie's *Waubun*, a fictionalized account of life in early Fort Dearborn and of the experiences of her father-in-law and family during their escape from the massacre. Stone & Kimball, Chicago's outstanding publishing firm, had no local authors of importance on its list, though it showed real literary awareness through such discriminating endeavors as the publication of the plays of Henrik Ibsen, the authorized American translations of the plays of Maurice Maeterlinck and the issuance of George Santayana's first book, *Sonnets and Other Verses*. Joseph Kirkland, an early midwest realist, was first published in 1888 and Mary Hartwell Catherwood was only at the threshold of her writing career. Most of the literary talent was expressed through the columns of the newspapers or magazines rather than in books.

The most widely quoted of the literary journalists was Eugene Field, whose "Sharps and Flats" column in the *Daily News* was the outstanding newspaper feature in Chicago. A favorite retreat of Field's was McClurg's bookstore, located in an old-fashioned red brick building at the corner of Monroe and Wabash. Field was to be found at McClurg's almost every noon, usually in a corner of the rare-book department where a verse of his was pasted on the bookcase:

Swete friend for Jesus sake forbeare
To buy ye boke thou findest here
For when I do get ye pelf
I mean to buy ye boke myself.

A small coterie met in the store regularly and the witty exchanges provided much of the material for Field's column. Among the members of the circle was the Reverend Frank Gunsaulus, whose varied accomplishments included the writing of a novel *Monk and Knight*, and whose presence among the free-spoken writers and reporters led Field to dub the meeting place the "Saints and Sinners Corner."

McClurg's took its name from General Alexander C. McClurg, a soldier-scholar who had had a remarkable career in the Civil War. He had been elected captain of a volunteer infantry company and after serving through a series of battles and marching with Sherman to the sea had been discharged as a colonel. He was devoted to literature and carried with him throughout the war a copy of *A Golden Treasury of English Verse*. Though he had his horse shot out from under him twice at Mission Ridge, the book was as spotless after four years in the field as if it had been kept under the glass of a museum. His wife was Eleanor Wheeler, a niece of William B. Ogden, whom McClurg met when she was acting as hostess for her bachelor uncle during a visit to Chicago. Her family in the East was so disapproving of her marriage to a midwesterner that they refused to enter her married name on the family plaque in the village church. After the war, McClurg had been promoted to general for organizing Dandy First, the state's first national guard regiment; he continued to maintain his literary interests by contributing articles to the *Atlantic Monthly* and the *Forum*.

The general believed that a classical education was the only proper one. He disapproved of the midwestern public-school system and imported two teachers from the Roxbury Latin school in Massachusetts to tutor his son, Ogden, and a few children of friends. When Ogden was old enough to be taken on a trip to Europe, McClurg thought it would be unfair to discharge the tutors. Feeling responsible for bringing them to Chicago, he arranged to finance them in setting up a Chicago Latin School for boys and a comparable school for girls. A man of strong opinions, McClurg welcomed the members of the "Saints and Sinners Corner" to the store but disapproved of the publicity the store received through Field's column, feeling that such notices were an "offense against the dignity of literature."

In the evenings Field liked to linger over a meal with other newspapermen at Billy Boyle's English Chophouse, a favorite rendezvous for gamblers. This diversion was spoiled when the intensity of the newspapers' attacks on the gambling houses led Boyle's patrons from Gambler's Alley to view the reporters as intruders and perhaps as spies and they were no longer wel-

SAINTS' AND SINNERS' CORNER AT McCLURG'S BOOKSTORE

comed. Another rendezvous of the literary journalists was the Press Club, founded two decades before by a group of newspapermen headed by Melville E. Stone of the *Daily News*. Impromptu entertainment or all-night poker games were the usual diversions at the Press Club. Among those to be found there regularly was George Ade, whose *Stories of the Streets and the Town* were running in the Chicago *Record* and whose books *Artie* and *Fables in Slang* were popular successes. Opie Read, who published his humorous weekly, *The Arkansaw Traveler* in Chicago, was an inveterate performer, always willing to stretch up to his six feet of height and drawl out a tale of Arkansas life. He was also one of the most prosperous of the writers. His novel, *The Jucklins*, was a favorite at railway newsstands and sold more than a million copies. Another of the Press Club group was Finley Peter Dunne, creator of Mr. Dooley, the loquacious saloon philosopher of Archey Road. Among the Dooleyisms were: "Trust ivirybody—but cut the cards . . . I care not who makes th' laws iv a nation if I can get out an injunction . . . Manny people'd rather be kilt at Newport thin at Bunker Hill . . . and Th' modhren idee iv governmint is 'Snub th' people, buy th' people, jaw th' people!' "

A successor to the Press Club was the Whitechapel Club, a dimly lit refuge existing in one room opening on an alley back of the *Daily News* office. It had neither janitor nor key. Its center table was a large coffin which had once served to carry a dead Indian to the Indiana dunes, where the

Whitechapel members cremated him with what they considered appropriate rites. The walls contained grisly relics of famous murders. Lamps had been fashioned from human skulls; in a place of honor was a skull claimed to be that of Waterford Jack, the millionaire streetwalker of early Chicago. When the club was in need of funds, the members put up Hobart Chatfield-Taylor, one of their number, for mayor. They raised $900 in campaign contributions but the money went directly into the club treasury. Chatfield-Taylor was given nearly as much space in the papers by his colleagues in the club as the legitimate candidates received. Running on a platform of "No gas, no water, no police," he polled about a thousand votes.

A more consciously literary group was that which met Friday afternoons after the symphony and went by the name of the Little Room. It was made up for the most part of professional writers and artists who hoped to develop interest in the genteel tradition of the East; it was self-conscious about its cultural standards and some midwesterners complained that it excluded more literary people than it admitted. Its name was taken from a short story in the *Atlantic Monthly* about a room which vanished and reappeared, reflecting the fact that the group originally had no special meeting place but gathered in the studio of any one of a number of artists. Among those who came regularly to the Little Room were Harriet Monroe, the young poet whose odes were a feature of every civic dedication; George Barr Mc-Cutcheon, whose melodramatic adventure novel, *Graustark*, was a best seller; novelists Edith Wyatt and Henry Kitchell Webster, critic Floyd Dell, cartoonist John McCutcheon, sculptor Lorado Taft, concert pianist Fannie Bloomfield Ziesler (Chicago's first virtuoso) and the poets Wallace Rice and William Vaughn Moody. Hamlin Garland, whose novels of the poverty and frustrations of midwestern farm life were setting the pattern for a new American realism, was a frequent visitor, but the dominating figure—and the one who best expressed the group's admiration for the literary standards of the East—was Henry Blake Fuller.

Fuller had been a precocious youth; at fifteen he published two controversial articles on "The Marriage Question" in the *Tribune* and found himself locally famous. His personal delicacy bordered on the effete. Hamlin Garland said Fuller regarded the chirp of a robin as a "yelp" and when at Garland's country home "carried wads of cotton with him so that he could stuff his ears against the 'drone of the katydids and the crowing of the roosters.'" Fuller's most successful novel, which won him the recognition he coveted from the critics in the East, was *The Cliff Dwellers*. In the phrase of its title, the book gave a name to the new society developing around the Chicago skyscrapers. But with this initial success, Fuller lost interest in the themes of Chicago and what he considered the crudities of midwestern living. Like Henry James, he sought the subject matter for his books in

Europe; he returned to Chicago only to accept the acclaim and tribute of his circle in the Little Room.

A group originally as peripatetic as the Little Room was the Attic Club, which in 1909 moved into its own clubrooms on the top floors of Orchestra Hall and changed its name to the Cliff Dwellers. The club was organized by Hamlin Garland, Henry Fuller, Lorado Taft, Charles Francis Browne and Ralph Clarkson as a counterpart in Chicago of the Players Club in New York. It did not, as is popularly supposed, take its name from Fuller's novel but directly from the cliff-dwelling Indians of the Southwest.

In later years the Little Room met in the Fine Arts Building, a center for the awakening literary and artistic interests of the young city. It was here Arthur W. D. Denslow had his studio and where, in collaboration with Frank Baum, he created probably the most immortal of Chicago books—*The Wizard of Oz*. Hobart Chatfield-Taylor and his wife, who were members of the Little Room, both had studios in the building as well. Chatfield-Taylor was the epitome of the sophisticated Chicagoan and for two decades there was scarcely a literary or social function of importance with which he did not have a connection. He had ambitions to write and had published a novel of merit called *With Edge Tools*, though his later books were to be in the form of personal memoirs. With a friend, Slason Thompson, he founded a short-lived literary magazine called *America*, which forever established its identity by publishing for the first time Eugene

THE CLIFF DWELLERS. An illustration for Henry Blake Fuller's novel

Field's "Little Boy Blue." Chatfield-Taylor after the turn of the century founded the Society of Midland Authors, still Chicago's most active literary group. Mrs. Chatfield-Taylor, the *Journal's* "perfect specimen of a beautiful and accomplished daughter," operated a craft bindery for fine books. Another tenant was Ralph Fletcher Seymour, who published illustrated books in the manner of a medieval craftsman.

The vitality of the activity in the Fine Arts Building had its origins in the interests and energies of the Browne family and the publishing activities which had grown out of *The Dial* magazine. Francis Fisher Browne was another of the transplanted New Englanders. For many years he had been an editor of the publishing division of McClurg's and in 1880 had persuaded General McClurg to finance a literary magazine which would stand "preeminently for objective and scientific criticism." Later, to avoid suspicions that McClurg books were given preferential treatment, Browne arranged for McClurg to withdraw and established *The Dial* as an independent magazine. Though *The Dial* was published in Chicago it was not in any way a regional magazine. Among the writers to whom it provided early encouragement were Frederick Jackson Turner, Woodrow Wilson, Norman Foerster and Henry Seidel Canby. Turner called it "part of my education" and Barrett Wendell was to describe it as the "most unbiased, good-humored and sensible organ of American criticism." Like the musicians of Theodore Thomas, Francis Fisher Browne found Chicago winters too rigorous and spent much of the winter in California when the active management of the magazine was taken over by various of his four sons. The consistency of *The Dial's* viewpoint was the work of the associate editor, William Morton Payne, who wrote most of the reviews of fiction and poetry. A self-educated man, Payne spoke four languages, had translated a number of books from the Scandinavian languages and later was to be elected a member of the National Institute of Arts and Letters. *The Dial* was the most durable of American literary magazines, surviving for thirty-eight years before expiring after its transfer to New York. Another of Browne's ventures was the establishment of a bookstore in the Fine Arts Building for which he had the foresight to engage a young Oak Park architect, Frank Lloyd Wright, to design the interior. Architecturally, and perhaps intellectually as well, the store was a generation ahead of its times. The walls were of a light oak plywood and dominated by the straight functional lines Wright was to make famous. In connection with the store was a reception room with a huge fireplace where visiting literary celebrities gave occasional talks. Although the store was located in the center of a nest of studios of Chicago's painters, architects, sculptors, cartoonists and musicians, and in the same building as the clubrooms of the Chicago Literary Club, the Fortnightly Club and the Caxton Club, which had been founded in 1895 for ". . . literary study and the promotion of arts pertaining to the production of books" the venture was not a success. On its closing, Jenkin Lloyd Jones said he feared its failure had been one of "an excess of excellence . . . Chicago has a way of killing things that are too good to be true."

One of the most important ventures in the Fine Arts Building was the Little Theater conducted by Maurice Browne (not a member of Francis Fisher Browne's family) and Maurice's wife, Ellen Van Volkenburg. This was the first little theater in America. It had only ninety-one seats in the miniature Grecian temple which served as an auditorium and its credo was "create your own theater with the talent at hand." It was primarily a theater for participation. On a stage not much bigger than a large dining-room table, the Brownes presented the plays of Shaw, Strindberg and Schnitzler and tested the acting theories of Stanislavsky and Reinhardt. The Little Theater of the Brownes had only an ephemeral existence but led to one important consequence for the commercial theater. Lawrence Langner, visiting Chicago on business as a patent attorney, attended a play staged by the Brownes; from their theater group he took the idea for the Washington Square Players that evolved into the American Theater Guild.

Yet it was not from the ferment of the Fine Arts Building but from the mind of a lonely figure walking the streets as an installment collector for an easy-payment furniture company that the most durable literary achievement was to come. Theodore Dreiser, after reading the column of Eugene Field faithfully for two years, was "beginning to suspect, vaguely at first, that I wanted to write, possibly something like that." To Dreiser, nothing else that he had so far read gave him quite the same feeling for "constructive thought" as Field's daily notes, poems and aphorisms. Dreiser noted particularly that they were mostly about Chicago, "whereas nearly all others dealt with foreign scenes and people."

To Dreiser there was no more romantic topic than the young city. "It is given to some cities and to some lands to suggest romance and to me Chicago did that hourly," he wrote in *Newspaper Days*. "It sang, I thought, and in spite of what I deemed my various troubles, I was singing with it. . . . Chicago was so young, so blithe, so new, I thought. Florence in its best days must have been something like this to young Florentines or Venice to young Venetians." Later, as a reporter for the Chicago *Globe*, Dreiser continued to store up impressions of his "metropolis of men and streets." Out of these observations he drew the material for *Sister Carrie*, a novel which shocked Victorian readers because Carrie, her virtue gone, did not meet the traditional tragic end but rather pursued her life of amoral independence "with as much success as attended any other human proceeding." There was little reason for Chicagoans to be shocked; in their papers they could read daily of the success of their own Mrs. Leslie Carter. It was a career of which Carrie might have been envious.

An Ardent Temperament Rather Than a Weak Will

THERE WAS only one subject for Chicagoans in April of 1889—the marital difficulties of the Leslie Carters. Leslie Carter was a leading member of Chicago society, president of the Chicago Dock Company, and had been president of both the Chamber of Commerce and fashionable St. Luke's Hospital. Mrs. Carter was born Caroline Louise Dudley in Kentucky, the child of a British businessman and a daughter of the southern aristocracy. The father later took the family to Dayton, Ohio, where he held a position with the Standard Oil Company until his death. The Dudleys lived in the grand manner with tutors and maids, but Mr. Dudley left Caroline and her mother only the shadow of an estate. To maintain their social position a fashionable marriage was clearly necessary. When Caroline met Leslie Carter at a party in Chicago, it was not long before that fashionable marriage was arranged.

From the time of the marriage, the Carters spent much time apart. A son, Dudley, was born, but Mrs. Carter preferred a summer home in Cooperstown, New York, or traveling in Europe to domestic life in Chicago. The couple's friends, aware that Mrs. Carter's extravagances were a continual worry to Carter and that he had mortgaged his property to meet her bills, were astounded when it was announced he was the object of a divorce suit. As the legal maneuvering proceeded, the newspapers reported that Mrs. Carter's charges were too sensational to be printed. Before the case could be brought to trial, Mr. Carter brought a countersuit, asking the divorce be granted him and charging adultery, a prosaic accusation by the standard of Mrs. Carter's suit.

If, as was rumored, Mrs. Carter planned a stage career, her press notices on the first day of the trial were a favorable omen. The *Times* reporter noted as she came into the courtroom that "her hair was the color of an August stubble field and her lips red and inviting." The *Morning News* readers were told she was "a decidedly attractive woman of the blonde type" and that "her poses have a languorous sentimental air and her face suggests an ardent temperament rather than a weak will." The quality of her hair caused all the newspapermen to strain for hyperbole. To the man from the *Morning News* her hair was "a breath of autumn sunset, neither yellow nor red but pale auburn." His colleague on the afternoon editions, after noting that "from her swelling bosom" hung an oxidized silver scent bottle for use in case she should be compelled to faint, rhapsodized over her hair as "golden as the dandelions which dot the meadows on a fine spring day. It was not blonde under which come all colors from bright orange—falsely called 'red hair'—to the hue of dried hay. It was yellow,—yellow as a sunflower, yellow as a buttercup, yellow as yellow." The *Tribune's* fashion-conscious correspondent reported that Mrs. Carter was "fashionably attired in a rich, tight-fitting walking suit of black that showed her mature figure to excellent advantage. . . . Through a flimsy black veil her complexion seemed matchless. . . . One feature alone," he said with less gallantry than his colleagues had shown, "detracted from the beauty of the fair complainant—the mouth with its red, strawberry-like lips looked too coarse for the fairer emotions."

When the jury was selected, Mr. Carter's lawyers announced they would name five men as co-respondents in his countersuit for divorce. They added that it was only necessary to prove one case of infidelity, explaining with a show of magnanimity that while "propositions had been made to take the depositions of a number of gentlemen in Europe," Mr. Carter had preferred "to avail himself of proofs of her infidelity on this side of the ocean which were ample."

The first of the men in Mrs. Carter's life had been a D. S. Gregory. The attorneys charged that he had been "kissing in the roses" with Mrs. Carter outside a Cooperstown hotel when a chambermaid had interrupted the tryst with a well-aimed pitcher of cold water. The second man was State Senator James F. Pierce of New York, who, it was said, had sent Mrs. Carter love poems and had been found seeking inspiration for his muse near her room at Cooper House at three o'clock in the morning. The third name on the list was a doctor, J. B. Gilbert. The lawyers said they would produce witnesses from the room next to Mrs. Carter's who would testify in detail as to the noises and conversation which emerged from her room when Dr. Gilbert made a late-at-night call. ("He treated me like a gentleman," was Mrs. Carter's comment.) The fourth man named by the attorneys was Kyrle Bellew, the actor. It was charged that he had dined frequently with Mrs. Carter at Delmonico's and had found it convenient to have an adjoining room at the Colonnade Hotel in New York while giving her dramatic lessons at $25 each. The fifth name on the list was that of a mystery man, William K. Constable, who for reasons of his own had sent Mrs. Carter $45,000 for a trip to Europe.

Among those in the courtroom as these extended charges were presented was Edward Gilmore, a New York theatrical manager. He was believed to be ready to offer Mrs. Carter a stage contract. "I should be delighted to engage Mrs. Carter," he told reporters as he left the courtroom. "But if the trial moves as it moved today I shall have retired from the theatrical business long before she could make her debut."

Mrs. Carter was to require all her potential talents as an actress when she took the witness stand to match wits with her husband's lawyers. It was a drama, as the *Tribune's* reporter saw it, to determine only one question: "Was the woman lying?" The climax came during her fourth day on the stand, when her husband's lawyers brought up the charge she had made against him. The accusation was too infamous for Victorian readers and the reporter could only hint that "after hovering awhile around the edge of the cesspool which furnishes Mrs. Carter's cause of complaint, Mr. Carter's lawyer made a dive into it, dragging the witness with him, and for a while there was in the room the oppressive atmosphere of Phallic rites and other bestialities." For hours the witness and the lawyer parried question and answer as he attempted to get her either to confess or deny that her husband had been successful in forcing her to participate in the unnatural act with which she charged him. The inquiry was one which might have defeated her; if she had admitted the participation, she would have appeared in the wrong for not bringing the charge before she did; if she denied it, her case would collapse.

When the cross-examination turned to other subjects, Mrs. Carter continued to evade skillfully the queries she did not wish to answer. One clue to her character emerged when she was forced to confess that she had signed her letters of credit in Europe as Louise Dudley rather than as Caroline Carter. "Caroline was simple, homely, American and therefore thoroughly objectionable," a reporter noted. "Louise was foreign, theatrical, operatic.

There was a dressmaker of the name in London. Queens had been called Louise. So Caroline Carter bought her letters of credit in the name of Louise." They had been impressive letters of credit, one of them having been used in buying a $10,000 cloak which, Mrs. Carter explained, had not been an extravagance but had been purchased in anticipation of taking up a career on the stage.

By the end of the week, the trial had become the outstanding theatrical performance in Chicago and the papers were running sketches of fictional billboards outside the courtroom. On Mrs. Carter's last day on the stand, a small program was handed about the courtroom which read:

Positively Last Performance
of
Mrs. Leslie Carter
The Beautiful and Accomplished Society Belle
Accompanied by
Mr. Kyrle Bellew
And an Efficient Cast of Co-respondents
Regular Prices

The *Morning News* reported the trial was such an attraction to "flashy young men known in common parlance as dudes" that the bailiffs were compelled to bar the doors against the crowd. Judge Egbert Jamieson, who was presiding, announced a minimum age limit of thirty-five for the courtroom audience—thereby, said the *Tribune*, "excluding most of the ladies." The age rule proved to be impracticable. As the trial entered its second week the judge was forced to take cognizance of the "number of graybeards and baldheads among the spectators." As the *Tribune* quoted him, "We have no desire to take the place of the departed Gayety Burlesque Company. An old curiosity monger is quite as reprehensible as a young curiosity monger." To this the chief bailiff added his own moral opinion. "We must check," he said, "the spread of immorality among the old and decrepit."

It required five weeks of daily court sessions for the lawyers to trace the travels and adventures of the peripatetic Mrs. Carter. Four of the five men named by the lawyers appeared to deny the charges. The fifth, Mr. Constable, was reported ill in New York; the case against him collapsed when his wife sent a statement saying it had been she who had given Mrs. Carter the $45,000—for what purposes she did not explain. Kyrle Bellew was the last of the co-respondents to appear. He combined an appearance in court with a professional performance at McVicker's where he had the role of Antony in Shakespeare's *Antony and Cleopatra*. In court he said "Mrs. Carter had some talent for a comedienne and I did not see why with some development she should not show talent for high comedy." In Shakespeare's play that night he was hissed—six times, according to the critic—despite his insistence that his attentions to Mrs. Carter, like those of Dr. Gilbert, had been professional.

The jurors were more critical of Bellew's performance than the McVicker's audience. After twelve hours of deliberation, they found Mrs. Carter guilty of the charges made against her and Bellew; they acquitted Carter of the accusations against him and granted him the divorce. Mrs. Carter wept in her hotel room when the jury's verdict was brought to her. A few days later she was sufficiently composed to set out for New York and a stage career in which she hoped to put the name of Mrs. Leslie Carter on every "billboard and fencepost in the country." Through the impatient Gilmore, then manager of the New York Academy of Music, she secured a letter of introduction to David Belasco.

Though Mrs. Carter had appeared in amateur theatricals, she had no professional dramatic training other than the few lessons from Kyrle Bellew. Her most valuable attribute was self-confidence. When Belasco asked whether she wished to appear in comedy or tragedy, she replied: "I am a horsewoman and wish to make my first entrance on a horse, leaping over a hurdle." This interview with the young producer-playwright was a failure. Hearing that Belasco had gone to a small country hotel for a rest, Mrs. Carter sought him out to plead her case a second time. Belasco granted her another interview, chiefly, he confessed later, because of the memory of her "bizarre and alluring appearance" and the "copious and resplendent hair" which had fascinated the Chicago reporters. At the second meeting, Mrs. Carter poured out the story of her life while Belasco, saying nothing, began to see "possibilities in her—if only she could act, on the stage, with the same force and pathos she used in telling her story." Though Belasco was already a successful director and playwright, he had ambitions of becoming an independent producer. To do this he needed a star; by making a star of Mrs. Carter he could establish himself without obligation to anyone.

The task was not easy. Mrs. Carter's training began with such funda-

MRS. LESLIE CARTER IN *Zaza*

mentals as physical exercises to increase the grace of her motions on the stage. Within the period of a year Belasco required her to learn more than forty roles and rehearsed her in every one. There was very little money; lunches at Delmonico's gave way to "25-cent table d'hôte on Fourth Avenue." There were also strong prejudices against Mrs. Carter because of the divorce trial. Charles Frohman wrote Belasco that "The stockholders request me not to have Mrs. Carter use our stage any more." When the producer sought to arrange for his star's first appearance in Chicago, he was turned down by the manager at Hooley's Theatre who wrote him: "This is the most fashionable theatre in Chicago; Mrs. Carter is not wanted here and we cannot afford to make enemies."

Financial help came surprisingly from N. K. Fairbank, who a little more than ten years before had been unwilling to receive Sarah Bernhardt at a reception in the Chicago Club. Both Fairbank and his wife had taken Mrs. Carter's side during the divorce dispute and he invested $40,000 in one of her plays before his lawyers persuaded him to withdraw the backing after the play had a disastrous tour. It was five years after her first interview with Belasco before success finally came to Mrs. Carter and the producer who had worked so patiently to make her a star. Her indebtedness to Belasco was measured by the fact she achieved stardom in *The Heart of Maryland*, a

Civil War romantic drama which he had written particularly for her. Even a Chicago critic conceded that there was not "the same amount of artificiality in her performance which would naturally suggest itself to those who were familiar with her more uncouth endeavors." *The Heart of Maryland* was followed by triumphs in *Zaza* and *Du Barry*. To those who suggested that these latter roles were much in character, Mrs. Carter replied, "I delight in such roles—especially when the tour takes us to Chicago." It was a tremendous triumph for the "fair defendant" whose face suggested "an ardent temperament rather than a weak will."

There are but two more chapters essential to the story. In 1906, Mrs. Carter broke with Belasco and said she would never have another thing to do with him. And while she won the world's acclaim for the name of Mrs. Leslie Carter, the man whose name it was—proclaimed innocent by the jury, but his fortune gone and mind slipping—turned on the gas in a kitchen stove and quietly left the world behind. Chicagoans read the news and thought of Sister Carrie.

It was difficult to keep the theater out of the courtroom. A decade after Mrs. Carter established her reputation as an actress on a local witness stand, Samuel Eberly Gross, a Chicago real-estate man, came before the bar of justice to claim authorship of Edmond Rostand's *Cyrano de Bergerac*. Gross's basis for his suit was that he had written a play much like Cyrano, called *The Merchant Prince of Cornville*, which he had sent to the Porte St. Martin Theater in Paris, where it was held a short time before being returned. He charged that Constant Coquelin, the actor-manager and a close friend of Rostand's, had allowed the French playwright to purloin the essentials of the play. As evidence he cited the circumstances that both *The Merchant Prince* and *Cyrano* featured a character with a large nose who stood under a balcony impersonating a much duller but handsomer lover.

Gross asked for an injunction against any American performance of the play and sent a Chicago detective, W. J. Sutherland, to France for additional evidence of the alleged plagiarism. Sutherland returned with an affidavit from an English-speaking servant of Rostand's who contradicted the playwright's assertion that *Cyrano* had been written before *The Merchant Prince* was copyrighted in 1896. Sutherland had not obtained his affidavit without difficulty, for Rostand was then living in a chateau surrounded by a twelve-foot fence and well guarded by dogs and watchmen. That Sutherland, who spoke no French, was able to return with an affidavit on a literary dispute was hailed by the *Tribune* as a case of "Chicago hustle against French police, bodyguards, dogs, iron fences, and interpreters and Chicago won."

When an American tour was announced for *Cyrano* with Sarah Bernhardt and the same Coquelin in the principal roles, it was not known whether Chicagoans would get to see the play. This was but one of many difficulties confronting Bernhardt, who had sent ahead a white cabriolet with yellow wheels for her stay in Chicago only to have the rail car on which it was traveling attached to the wrong train in Washington and the coach temporarily unavailable to greet her with its similarly imported French driver on the box. Bernhardt, it was explained, had particularly wanted the carriage for use in Chicago because "the reports telegraphed East of the state of Chicago's health have troubled her. Of smallpox she has a horror and the grip she regards as an archfiend. Both maladies she thinks are more apt to attack her in this city of chilly winds than elsewhere." Ultimately the cabriolet arrived, as did word from Gross that he would not seek an immediate injunction against the performance of *Cyrano*. Part of his mellowness may have been the result of a visit Coquelin paid to the city's Art Institute. As the *Tribune* reported it, the actor spent the afternoon "unobstrusively flattening out the stigmas Henry B. Fuller has been throwing at Chicago." Coquelin's enthusiasm was difficult to resist. "Never outside my own France have I seen French art more nobly represented than in this Art Museum of yours," he told a reporter.

For his part, Gross assured the press that he did not desire "to interrupt the pleasures of the citizens of Chicago so I will not do anything which might prevent the play's being given. Besides I want to see the French version of the play to be performed here by M. Coquelin." He reiterated his

SARAH BERNHARDT

claim to the play, however, and promised that as soon as it was through being shown he would "carry the fight to the finish in true Chicago style." The finish was to be delayed for fourteen months while a master in chancery took a number of depositions, among them an indignant protest from Rostand that "there are big noses everywhere in the world." Finally, in May of 1902, Judge Christian C. Kohlsaat in United States District Court ruled that Gross was in fact "the author of Cyrano's being." An injunction was issued preventing Richard Mansfield from producing Cyrano and Gross was awarded nominal damages of $1, which he accepted as vindication and waived all rights to royalties.

In Paris, Bernhardt and Rostand laughed at the verdict, Bernhardt asserting that it must have been the first of April in Chicago. Mansfield suggested that the decision might result in the "great American and European artists overwhelming Mr. Gross with orders for plays and Chicago may in the future be the center of another new industry." The legal rights had been settled; but the question remained of whether, as the master in chancery asserted, it had been a case of "clear and unmistakable piracy" and that "the greatest dramatists have been the most persistent purloiners of literary property of those less gifted." George Jean Nathan, a friend of Gross, had his own views, which added artistic judgment to legal right. "I thoroughly believe Rostand swiped my friend's play," he said. "But Rostand made it into a beautiful thing, didn't he, so what's the odds?"

There always seemed to be something not in the script for a Chicago theater. When Jean de Reszke and Nellie Melba were singing Romeo and Juliet at the Auditorium, a psychopath rushed onto the sage and began threatening de Reszke who drew his sword and pinned the maniac in the corner while the rest of the singers on the stage retreated until the stagehands could come out to remove him. Melba was less calm, shouting for the manager to ring down the curtain because her voice was gone. De Reszke paused again to call up "For God's sake, keep quiet, Melba. Open the window and come out." The startled Melba, her fear gone, meekly complied and the pair ended the evening in triumph.

There was another unscheduled drama with no humor. On December 30, 1903, Eddie Foy was playing in Mr. Bluebeard to an overflow crowd of more than sixteen hundred at a special holiday matinee in the Iroquois Theater, a showplace of marble, plush and mahogany with an ornate lobby suggestive of an old-world palace. As a double quartet appeared on the stage for a number titled "In the Pale Moonlight," a flash of flame spurted from an overloaded electrical circuit and touched fire to a flimsy drapery at the side of the stage. The mishap was a repetition of an accident in Cleveland two weeks before, but the show's management had not dropped the dangerous practice of overloading the floodlight circuits for the number.

Chicago was not to be so lucky as Cleveland, where the fire was quickly extinguished. The flames skimmed over the flimsy stage decorations and within a minute were out of control. No adequate fire-fighting apparatus was on the stage and one box of fire powder—out of only two available—had no effect on the flames. A stagehand tried to lower the asbestos curtain but it snagged when only partially closed; the tunnel formed between the curtain and the front of the stage acted like a tremendous suction tube and swept a jetlike blast of fire out into the auditorium and up toward the galleries and balconies. The theater was in a panic. Except for a few unfortunate victims killed by hysterical spectators leaping from the galleries above, those on the main floor were able to escape. In the galleries and balcony there was a holocaust of fire and panic. Fire doors were locked and exits opened inward; before these inflexible barriers victims were piled five and six feet in depth. Others were still in their seats and sat glassy-eyed in death where they had been scorched to lifelessness by the jets of flame from the stage. The fire was out within half an hour; some firemen said it had been only ten minutes before the blaze was subdued. Yet the counting of the dead and the injured dragged on for a day and a night; there were so many that the toll was never exactly known. The newspapers said that 575 had been killed; the coroner insisted there were 601 bodies, only one of them unidentified. Most were women and children, trapped on a holiday adventure.

The managers of the theater and play and several public officials were indicted for the criminal negligence which caused the catastrophe but there were no convictions. Not a person was punished, although the fire did lead to the adoption of a new set of safety regulations for American theaters. Buildings were required to have ventilators covering 20 per cent of the roof over the stage to prevent a recurrence of the draft which swept the flame outward over the Iroquois auditorium, and automatic sprinklers were added as a second safety precaution. The safety innovations were commendable; but they obscured the fact that if the Iroquois had observed the minimum regulations in effect before the fire there would have been no tragedy to mar that Wednesday holiday in 1903.

A footnote to the history of the Iroquois: The archway which formed the stone front of the theater was a counterpart, except in minor details, of a monument that had been erected in Paris to commemorate the death of 150 victims in a flash fire at a charity bazaar there in 1857. It had been a prophetic design.

CARTER HARRISON. A caricature by William H. Schmedtgen from the Chapin and Gore Restaurant

18

The Glories of the White City

"GENIUS is but audacity," Mayor Carter Harrison told a gathering of mayors during the Columbian Exposition summer of 1893. "Chicago has chosen a star and, looking upward to it, knows nothing it cannot accomplish." The mayor chose an appropriate setting for his boast. The genius—or audacity—of Chicago was never more remarkably illustrated than by the World's Columbian Exposition, a bold scheme to bring to the attention of the world the accomplishments of the city by the lake.

The ostensible purpose of the exposition was to celebrate the four-hundredth anniversary of the discovery of America by Christopher Columbus. Chicago's claim was put forward first by the directors of the old Interstate Industrial Exposition. Nowhere, they argued, had American enterprise and ingenuity been better demonstrated than in the phenomenal growth of Chicago, which in sixty years had been transformed from a village by a swamp into a city of a million and a half people. A company was organized to raise five million dollars to underwrite the costs of the exposition and Senator Shelby M. Cullom of Illinois agreed to introduce a bill which would make the exposition an official project of the United States Government. It was at this moment that Chicago's aspirations were most seriously endangered. Cullom, in a moment of senatorial absent-mindedness, neglected to specify that the fair be held in Chicago. A vigorous competition immediately arose among New York, Washington and St. Louis, each of which wanted to take the honor of the fair away from Chicago. It was during the bitter exchanges over the site for the exposition that Chicago's sobriquet as the "Windy City" was popularized. Charles A. Dana, arguing the cause of his city in the pages of the New York Sun, admonished his readers daily to pay no attention "to the nonsensical claims of that windy city. Its people could not build a World's Fair even if they won it." When New York made a matching offer of five million dollars for the fair, Chicago offered to double that sum. At last the city had its prize. On April 25, 1890, President Benjamin Harrison approved an Act of Congress providing for an "international exhibit of arts, industries, manufactures, and the products of the soil, mine and sea, in the city of Chicago" and invited the nations of the world to take part. A national commission was appointed to supervise plans for the fair. Harlow Higinbotham, a self-made Chicagoan who had seen the city for the first time from the top of a load of hay being brought into market, was named president of the exposition and the architect Daniel Burnham was designated chief of construction.

Two years before the fair was to open, a group of architects met in Chicago to plan its buildings. Among them were Frederick Law Olmsted, the landscape architect who had laid out New York's Central Park and the Chicago suburb of Riverside; Richard Morris Hunt, Charles McKim, George B. Post, Henry Ives Cobb, Louis Sullivan and such sculptors as Augustus St. Gaudens and Lorado Taft. When the group met for luncheon at Kinsley's, St. Gaudens called it "the greatest meeting of artists since the fifteenth century." There was artistic disagreement at the luncheon. The Chicago architects wanted to express their functional ideas in the fair buildings; the eastern group insisted upon a classical theme. Burnham, anxious to secure the greatest possible participation in the exposition, prevailed upon his Chicago colleagues to accept a compromise. Louis Sullivan grumpily predicted that the harm done by the influence of the exposition would set native American architecture back by half a century. With the responsibility for designing the major buildings assigned, the work began of transforming a bleak South Side beach broken only by ridges of sand and wild oak into a landscaped park. It was soon evident that the grandiose plans of the architects could not be carried out in time for the fair to be held in the summer of 1892 and the date was advanced to 1893.

To pay proper tribute to the anniversary of the discovery of America, a special dedication was planned for October 20, 1892, within twenty-four hours of the time historians were agreed that Columbus set foot in the New World four centuries before. More than 150,000 curious Chicagoans—twenty-five acres of people according to official reports—tramped through the mud of the partially completed grounds to hear a series of dedicatory speeches and a concert by a chorus reputed to contain five thousand singers. The speeches were hardly audible beyond the platform, but this detracted little from the enthusiasm of the crowd, some seven thousand of whom jammed into the half-finished Manufacturers Building to partake of a free lunch.

There were other preparations to be made for the fair. It was time for a municipal election and the choice of a mayor to represent Chicago before the world. The Democrats named Carter H. Harrison—"Our Carter"—to run for a fifth term. The Republican candidate was packer Samuel W. Allerton, who promised to make Chicago a respectable city for the visitors to the exposition. The campaign was one of the bitterest ever staged in a city where unscrupulous political maneuvering was the norm. The press was almost unanimously against Harrison because of his outspoken sympathy for the men accused of the Haymarket bombing and his tolerance of gambling and segregated prostitution. To state his own case, he was forced to purchase the Times which, becoming a political organ, did not long survive the campaign. Harrison was elected by a narrow margin and his victory was taken as a sign that Chicago would be a wide-open town during his administration (except for those gamblers who had been so unwise as to oppose his candidacy). Down in Marion, Indiana, Otto McFeely heard two residents of the Hoosier State discussing Harrison's election. "I'm a goin' to Chicago to the fair," said one, "but I'm goin' to wear nothin' but tights and carry a knife between my teeth and a pistol in each hand." In Chicago the demand for roulette wheels became so great that the ordinary source of supply was inadequate and a new factory was started. At George Hawkins' gambling place a doorkeeper assured a reporter that there was no danger of a raid from the authorities: "We's the people," he explained. "We're all right." Mayor Harrison was quick to assure prospective visitors from over the country a genuine Chicago welcome. He promised the latchstring would always be out at the mayor's house. The city's hospitality might be rough, he said, but it would be genuine. He announced that he had purchased a supply of two hundred barrels of whiskey for official entertaining—adding a discretionary warning that Chicago whiskey could kill "at the distance of a mile."

In New York, Ward McAllister, counselor and chamberlain to Mrs. William Astor, whose edicts were the supreme law of New York society, was alarmed at the prospect of New Yorkers being treated with such boisterous informality. Through the columns of the New York *World*, he suggested to Mayor Harrison that "it is not quantity but quality that the society people here want. Hospitality which includes the whole human race is not desirable." He also conveyed some suggestions to Chicago hostesses. In New York, he explained, it was the custom to keep abreast of the times when entertaining. He recommended that Chicago women follow the practice of the East where "society supplies itself with a résumé of everything that is going on" before attending a dinner party. This, he said, explains the fact that "when you go into fashionable houses you will find a good deal of intellect."

Dining, McAllister explained, was a matter of great importance. "I would suggest that Chicago society import a number of fine French chefs," he said. "I should also advise that they do not frappé their wine too much. Let them put the bottle in the tub and be careful to keep the neck free from ice. For, the quantity of wine in the neck of the bottle being small, it will be acted upon by the ice first. In twenty-five minutes from the time of being placed in the tub it will be in a perfect condition to be served immediately.

AGRICULTURAL BUILDING, WORLD'S COLUMBIAN EXPOSITION, 1893

What I mean by a perfect condition is that when the wine is poured from the bottle it should contain little flakes of ice. That is a real frappé." The *Journal*, reporting a dinner which the mayor was giving for sixty foreign naval officers, assured McAllister that "the mayor will not frappé his wine too much. He will frappé it just enough so the guests can blow the foam off the tops of the glasses without a vulgar exhibition of lung and lip power. His ham sandwiches, sinkers and Irish quail, better known in the Bridgeport vernacular as pigs' feet, will be triumphs of the gastronomic art."

Not wishing New Yorkers to become excessively alarmed, McAllister assured them that "the women of Chicago are well-dressed and cultivated. They will do their best to entertain New York society and they will have plenty of money to do it with." He disclosed that "a number of our young men are already beginning to make their investigations as to the wealth and beauty of Chicago women with the result that they are now more anxious to go to the fair than ever." These matrimonial investigations were somewhat aided by the *Journal* which ran a story of "Eligible Maidens [who] Abound in This Fair City"; but, the paper warned, though many of the girls have wealth, "fortune hunters find them possessed of a keen instinct and plenty of common sense."

Chicago's replies to McAllister's views were rapid in coming. He was addressed by the local papers in such terms of disaffection as Singular Personage, Head Butler, New York Flunky, A Mouse Colored Ass, A Popinjay, A Delightful Duffer and by the *Times*, traditionally supreme in epithetical exchange, as The Premier of Cadsville. Gussie Gander, a columnist for the *Times*, submitted a list of questions which she thought applicants for high social position might be required to answer. One of them was: "Do you consider Ward McAllister a great man, a simple poseur, or an ordinary every day matter-of-fact damn fool?" To this McAllister replied haughtily, "I require no Chicago indorsement."

The uproar over McAllister's etiquette suggestions offended the New York *World*, which tried to explain with more condescension than good will that McAllister had only spoken "in a kindly spirit as one who is anxious to see the society of the West elevate itself by observing the society of the East." McAllister was almost pedantic in his detachment. "I never intended to convey the impression that any New Yorker as a man is necessarily superior to a native of Chicago," he said. "We in New York are familiar with the sharp character of Chicago magnates and many of us have learned to our cost that the Almighty Dollar is the trail they are following." But he did not think "these Chicagoans should pretend to rival the East and Old World in matters of refinement. Their growth has been too rapid for them to acquire both wealth and culture. . . . The leaders of society are the successful Stock Yards magnates, cottolene manufacturers, soapmakers, Chicago gas trust speculators and dry goods princes. These gentlemen are undoubtedly great in business but perhaps in some cases unfamiliar with the niceties of life and difficult points of etiquette which constitute the society man or woman. For several years, for example, society persons have always hired a man to lead their Germans. He gets $25. That, to a New Yorker, appears extraordinary. It is a little out of the line. Again, Chicago's most famous millionaires have a ballroom in the attic which is approached by an elevator. This seems to be an incongruity. Here, in the East, the opinion is that the approach should be as artistically effective as the ballroom itself."

Chicago was particularly vulnerable to the thrust about third-floor ballrooms. Putting these seldom-used party rooms on the third floor was the accepted practice in almost every Chicago mansion. The city's press defended its finest houses and their unusual features only to incur more of McAllister's disapprobation. Denying that he had ever said anything unfavorable about "ladies sitting on the doorsteps in summer," he repeated that his sole criticism had been about "the novel idea of putting a ballroom in a man's attic. In this city we don't go to balls in private houses by climbing a ladder or going up in an elevator. . . . A bowling alley," he added for the benefit of those who had cited these appointments as an indication of the luxurious quality of the dwellings of Chicago millionaires, "is also an objectionable feature in any house. Why not have a shooting gallery?" In hopes of terminating the dispute, he turned to a philosophical approach. "It takes nearly a lifetime to educate a man how to live," he said. "Therefore Chicagoans can't expect to attain social knowledge without experience and contact with those who have made such things the study of their lives. In these modern days, society cannot get along without French chefs. The man who has been accustomed to delicate fillets of beef, terrapin, pâté de foie gras, truffled turkey and things of that sort would not care to sit down to a boiled leg of mutton dinner with turnips. . . . One paper says it is evidently my opinion that cultivated society is one in which the entertainment of the stomach is perfectly understood. That is a sound maxim."

McAllister was more tolerant of the Duke and Duchess of Veragua, when they arrived in New York en route to Chicago for the opening ceremonies of the exposition. The Duke was the only living descendant of Christopher Columbus, and as such McAllister conceded the Duke should be recognized. "The line of descent from Columbus is rather remote but still it is the only link we have to cling to and we should therefore extend to him every courtesy," McAllister explained. He went on to say that Columbus himself "in a social way was an ordinary man, being born in a humble station in life. But he was born with genius. He discovered the New World."

Having been passed by McAllister, the Duke and Duchess arrived in Chicago where they were greeted at the station and escorted to their hotel

GRAND COURT AT NIGHT, WORLD'S COLUMBIAN EXPOSITION, 1893

by the yellow-plumed cavalry and blue-coated infantry of the United States Army. President Cleveland had also come to Chicago for the opening. On May 1, 1893, with a chilly spring haze still on the ground, a parade of twenty-three carriages carrying the President, Harlow Higinbotham, the Duke and Duchess and other dignitaries made its way southward to the White City which had been created on what had once been a wasteland and deserted beach. A crowd of 620,000 people followed the parade southward, jammed through the exposition gates and crushed toward the speaker's platform for the opening ceremonies, meanwhile battering each other with umbrellas and lunch boxes. Eighteen tightly corseted women fainted and a company of United States troops had to be called to bring an end to the pandemonium. The speeches once again poured unheard into the uproar; President Cleveland pressed a golden switch and the World's Columbian Exposition was officially under way. The only dissenting view in the jubilation over the opening was that of Red Cloud, appearing nearby in an arena with Buffalo Bill. "This big show all about pale face who found red men over here," he was quoted as saying. "Ugh! Bad medicine."

Chicago society competed for the privilege of entertaining the Duke and Duchess of Veragua. The Duke, given the place of honor at every dinner table and overwhelmed by the excess of attention he was receiving, showed an understandable reluctance to fix the date of his departure. The committee of the national commission responsible for paying his expenses was growing restive. The *Times*, in discussing the delicate problem of persuading the Duke he should make way for other expected celebrities, suggested that the visiting nobleman felt "it would be undignified in a guest of the United States Government to be in a hurry about making his departure." The Duke, who was in fact a farmer who raised prize bulls for the Madrid fighting ring, was unaccustomed to such public acclaim and found it difficult to comprehend the rapidity with which the American public tired of celebrities. After a month the commission felt it necessary to tell him his welcome, or at least the expenses-paid portion of it, was at an end. The blow to the courtly gentleman was made worse when a tactless officialdom made no provision to escort him to the station in a manner similar to that in which he had been received. Hobart Chatfield-Taylor, who seemed to be everywhere at one and the same time, took it upon himself to assuage the royal couple's feelings. When the time came for the Duke and Duchess to depart, Chatfield-Taylor appeared at their hotel with a group of amateur hussars mounted on shining black chargers and carrying polished sabers at their belts. The troopers were entirely without official status but to the uninformed Duke they represented the majesty of the United States Government and he departed as ceremoniously and gratefully as he had arrived.

The energies of much of Chicago society were taken up by the activities at the Woman's Building, the domain of Mrs. Potter Palmer and the Board of Lady Managers made up of feminine representatives from every state. The appointment of a woman to an executive position had been regarded as a radical innovation and Mrs. Palmer was determined that it should not be regretted. During the previous year she had toured Europe soliciting exhibits. The list of those upon whom she called read like the pages of Burke's Peerage and she persuaded many of the families of the European nobility to lend precious heirlooms for the exposition. From Italy, Queen Margherita sent laces from among the crown property which dated back to Roman expeditions hundreds of years before Christ; the laces had not been out of Italy since they had been brought back by Roman armies from Egyptian tombs.

The Woman's Building, designed by a feminine architect, Sophia G. Hayden, was more than an exhibit hall. It was, in the days before home-making magazines and food columns in the daily newspapers, a demonstration laboratory to teach American women how to live. There was a model kindergarten, then still an innovation in education, and a kitchen in which ten girls in white caps and aprons—among them Alice Higinbotham, whose father was president of the fair—spent two hours every day demonstrating cooking methods and the most efficient ways of tidying up a kitchen. Exhibits on child care provided the first instruction on the subject that many women ever had. There were, of course, exhibits of what women had accomplished in the arts, sciences and professions. Concerts in the auditorium featured the works of women composers. And, at a series of "Congresses," women met to discuss the political issues of the day nearly thirty years before they were to be granted the vote.

The Woman's Building was opened in a special ceremony on the second day of the fair with Mrs. Adlai Stevenson, the wife of the vice-president, driving the silver nail which marked its symbolic completion. The address was given by Mrs. Palmer, who said bluntly that she did not have any use for the "chivalric type" of man who raised objections to a woman's finding a job. Perhaps, she said, "they might possibly consent to forgive the offense of widows with dependent children and of the wives of drunkards and criminals who so far forget the high standard established for them as to attempt to earn for themselves daily bread, lacking which they must perish. The necessity for their work under present conditions is too evident and too urgent to be questioned. They must work or they must starve."

Quite unexpectedly, on the fourth day of the exposition, the Woman's Building was the scene for an unscheduled exhibition of feminine temperament. A group on the Board attempted to rebel against the leadership of Mrs. Palmer in a meeting marked by "tears, flushed cheeks and excited speech." The discontent had been stirring since the opening ceremonies when some members of the board felt they had been given insufficient opportunity to meet the Duchess of Veragua, Lady Aberdeen and other distinguished guests. Another cause of dissension was Mrs. Palmer's plan to put the affairs of the building in the hands of a more manageable subcommittee once the exposition opened. The leader of the opposition was Miss Phoebe Couzins of St. Louis. After Miss Couzins stated her objections, Mrs. Palmer rose to reply. She was upset and spoke slowly so as to be sure her emotions were in restraint. "I presume that all this discontent cannot have existed without some reproach upon me," she said, "and I refer to that matter with the greatest reluctance and humiliation. I do not wish to make any defense or plea. Good intentions count for nothing. . . . Congress was paying these ladies a per diem for their subsistence and I felt that for us to send a bill to Congress for a luncheon provided for this board . . . would savor of junketing and we had no right to do it. . . . We have thought we were working together as a band of women for something fine, for representing the interests of women . . . that we mark an epoch. . . . If I am mistaken in that estimate and we are all torn up and pulling hair over an introduction to a Duchess, I have nothing to say to this board except that I feel deeply humiliated." By this time Mrs. Palmer's excitement had communicated itself to the audience and there was an unparliamentary rush of weeping delegates toward the speaker's stand. Katherine Minor, a delegate from Louisiana, cried out above the hubbub: "I boldly say for the state of

Louisiana that Mrs. Palmer is the only woman in the United States that can lead me and I bow to her . . . as our American queen." When the tears were wiped away and the women once more in their seats, a vote of confidence was moved and passed: only Miss Couzins and four colleagues expressed their dissent by not voting. The *Record* spoke proudly of Mrs. Palmer's victory as "a brilliant, sensational and bloodless coup d'état."

A series of similar minor explosions marked almost every week of the exposition. There was a demand that the fair be closed on Sundays, an issue which had to be fought through both Congress and the courts before the gates were finally opened. The French, who like the other nations, had a special exhibit, negotiated with Harlow Higinbotham throughout the summer in pressing a claim for additional funds to support their display. The greatest single *cause célèbre* was that of Paderewski's piano. The products of the Steinway Company and several other eastern music firms had been banned from the exposition after they refused to exhibit their products. The order caused little difficulty with the assorted musical organizations which were daily pouring out a "Columbian cyclone of harmony" with Columbus marches, Columbus galops, Columbus fantasies and Columbus nocturnes as well as more substantial music. Paderewski, who had been engaged to play a concert with Theodore Thomas and the official exposition orchestra, refused to play on anything but a Steinway. The issue was finally referred to the national commission which held there could be no exceptions to its ruling. Thomas, angered by the commercial aspects of the quarrel, smuggled a Steinway into the hall by night and gave the concert with Paderewski in defiance of commission orders. For his disregard of the ban, the high-principled Thomas was pilloried as an agent of the Steinway Company, a charge which ultimately led to his resignation as musical director for the exposition. The effect of the squabble on Paderewski was more enervating. He canceled a performance in New York with an emphatic declaration that "I'll shoot myself before I'll play tomorrow. Tell them to take all the money I've got but I won't play." When his secretary attempted to remonstrate with the soloist, Paderewski threw his unfortunate aid bodily out of the room, an episode which a reporter redundantly attributed to the circumstance that "great excitement was telling upon his mental faculties in a degree."

More subtle difficulties arose with the arrival of Her Royal Highness, the Infanta Eulalia of Spain, and her husband, Prince Antoine. All that Chicagoans knew of the princess was that the Duke of Veragua had said her name should be pronounced E-oo-la-li-a. There was a long debate in the newspapers over the propriety of shaking hands with a princess, which was firmly resolved by Mrs. Palmer, who said, "If she does not want her hand shaken like a pump handle . . . we [will] comply therewith." The Infanta

arrived in George M. Pullman's private car, after a trip in which she had
ordered the train stopped in Pennsylvania while she sent out for a fresh
supply of Spanish cigarettes. The carriage of Mrs. Palmer, drawn by four
chestnut horses, was waiting for the Infanta at the station, as well as a
reception committee of Mayor Harrison, Allison Armour and Hobart Chatfield-Taylor, who, among other functions, was serving as Spanish consul.
The mayor had discarded his slouch hat for a silk topper, "the most sincere
compliment he could pay the lady." Cavalry troops presented arms as the
princess made her way to the carriage, but she was not at all pleased. She
told Chatfield-Taylor that she wished only "to see the World's Fair in
peace and comfort without an official in sight." She made one official visit
to the grounds (when thirty thousand pansies were strewn in her path), but
during most of her stay she made her trips to the exposition via the lake in
Allison Armour's small steam yacht and disembarked away from the public
piers. She usually avoided public recognition for an hour or two but the
reporters were adept at learning of her whereabouts and the deception was
only temporarily successful. Meanwhile the prince visited the stockyards,
went shopping, had most of his beard trimmed off to look more like an
American and spent such time as he could, according to Chatfield-Taylor,
"roaming incognito through the streets of the city by night, like the caliphs
of old."

The visit of the willful young Infanta might have attracted no more
than an average amount of attention if it had not been for the social scandal
she created by daring to arrive late and leave early at a reception given for

her by Mrs. Potter Palmer. The story has persisted that the Infanta snubbed Mrs. Palmer after discovering that she was the wife of the proprietor of the Palmer House where the princess had her suite. As Chicagoans told the story the next morning, the princess had asked if Mrs. Palmer were "the wife of my innkeeper." Upon being informed that she was, the princess had at first refused to attend the reception and had only agreed to go later under duress. A review of the evening indicates the princess may have been guilty of capriciousness, but does not bear out the theory she was adamant about being received by the wife of her innkeeper. Her suite at the Palmer House was fitted out with furnishings more suggestive of an old-world castle than a modern American hotel. Massive antique furniture filled the suite; the Infanta slept in an oversized mahogany bed inlaid with pearl and covered with heavy draperies of gold cloth. Ornate vases decorated every corner of the apartment. The princess and Mrs. Palmer had met several times before the reception. So far as is known, Mrs. Palmer never referred to the episode and it is possible that the impatient guests—and the crowd of several thousand outside the brightly lighted Palmer mansion which was driven away by a torrential rain before the princess arrived—might have been seeking explanations for her tardiness.

One cause of her being late was that she was visiting with Adlai Stevenson, the vice-president, who had only arrived in the city at 8 o'clock. According to the newspapers, Stevenson was told that the princess wished to see him and he arrived at her apartment shortly before 9, the time at which Mrs. Palmer's reception was scheduled to begin. The princess' carriage left the Palmer House at about a quarter to 10, not excessively late for a guest of honor—at least by royal standards. The length of time the princess stayed at the Palmer mansion is in dispute. All are agreed that she arrived about 10:15, "blazing with jewels and radiating graciousness." Both Mr. and Mrs. Palmer came down from the front steps to greet her and escort her to the French room, where a small dais had been arranged for her to meet the guests. Some accounts say she stayed only an hour, others that she stayed until 1 in the morning. The time may have been short to Chicagoans, but it was at least sufficient for the Infanta to meet four hundred people, partake of a Spanish supper, listen to a short concert and watch the guests dancing in the ballroom, where the orchestras of Johnny Hand and the increasingly celebrated band of John Philip Sousa alternated in providing music. One account says the princess received the guests in "sullen, unbending silence" but the Times quoted the princess as telling one of the guests she looked exactly like the Infanta's favorite sister, hardly the remark of a rigidly formal guest.

The Infanta's popularity was not great. When she was presented with a featherweight dress of spun glass, the general hope seemed to be that she would wear it, fall and cut her throat. When the Infanta was invited to the Higinbothams' for dinner, she insisted on passing on the guest list, in advance. She did not object to the presence of Mrs. Palmer on the list, but did say she would sit only with the governor rather than the mayor. The governor at the time was John Peter Altgeld, however, and he avoided the social whirlpool of the exposition summer rather than embarrass those to whom he would have been an unwelcome guest.

Whether the story of the Infanta's snub of Mrs. Palmer was true or false, it could hardly have been comforting to the dignity of Chicago's society queen to hear it so often repeated. The opportunity to repay the Infanta in kind did not come until six years after the exposition when the United States was at war with Spain. Mrs. Palmer was invited to a reception in Paris which Sebastian Schlesinger of Boston and his daughter, Baroness de Reibnitz, were giving for the Infanta. The intensely patriotic Mrs. Palmer declined and there was much chuckling in Chicago where the *Tribune* quoted her as replying curtly that "I cannot meet this bibulous representative of a degenerate monarch."

Another royal visitor in the summer of 1893 was the Archduke Ferdinand, the heir to the Austro-Hungarian throne. He was so genuinely incognito that few Chicagoans knew he was in their midst. The Archduke's Chicago escort, unhappy that his titled visitor would not even visit the Old Vienna café, summed him up as "half-boor" and "half tightwad," unaware that the unsocial visitor was later to be considered worthy of a major war.

Meanwhile, as the exposition months passed by, more than twenty-eight million people strolled through the six hundred acres of classical white buildings, gazed at exhibits which told them how their life could be made better or easier or sought adventure among the international entertainments of the Midway Plaisance. Many of the visitors came to the fair on the new South Side elevated road with its steam "dummie engines." Others piled into the "cattle cars" which the Illinois Central had fashioned from boxcars and fitted up with wooden benches. Once the passengers were located in these cars, the conductor twisted shut a wooden gate, giving stockyards-conscious Chicagoans a feeling of kinship with the cattle who were penned in railroad cars in much the same fashion. Others came by the lake, disembarking at the eastern end of the fair grounds after a trip from the special piers erected opposite the Auditorium Hotel.

At the fair grounds, visitors saw an extended panorama of mammoth buildings that suggested a multiplication of the glories of the Acropolis. To the west the dome of the administration building rose higher than that of the Capitol in Washington. Immediately in front of the administration building was the spectacular MacMonnies fountain with its graceful rowing maidens, a work acclaimed by St. Gaudens as the masterpiece of masterpieces. Along the sides of the lagoons lay the showplaces of the exposition—the buildings for Agriculture, Fine Arts, Electricity and the Hall of Mines and Mining. The Manufacturers Building, designed by George B. Post, was not only the giant of the exposition but the largest building in the world. Visitors were told that "if the great pyramid of Cheops could be removed to Chicago it could be piled up in this building with the galleries left from which to view the stone." Statistics were awesome. Seven million feet of lumber were used in the floor and it required five carloads of nails just to fasten it down. There were eleven acres of skylights and forty carloads of glass in the roof. The iron and steel used in the frame would have provided two structures the size of the Brooklyn Bridge and the individual trusses in the ceiling were double the size of any that had been constructed before. All this, Chicagoans would remind you, was an exposition, a show, a flexing of the muscles to demonstrate what Chicago might accomplish if it had a mind for it. A gem in miniature was the Merchants and Tailors Building, which S. S. Beman had designed and which he was to adapt for the First Church of Christ, Scientist, in Chicago and make a model for such churches over the country. At night the white buildings were lighted by the greatest electrical display the world had seen, a spectacle with a special attraction for a young English immigrant named Samuel Insull, who had left a post with inventor Thomas Edison to become the new president of the Chicago Edison Company. In the shadows and waterways of the lagoons, visitors with more ordinary ideas

MIDWAY, WORLD'S COLUM-
BIAN EXPOSITION, 1893

of romance drifted along and talked of the newest sensation among the shows of the Midway.

The Midway Plaisance, a long stretch of land connecting Washington and Jackson Parks, was the playground of the fair. Here the tourists walked down the streets of a German or Austrian village, gazed curiously at a group of Dahomey huts with sixty native warriors, traded for knickknacks in a Chinese market or Japanese bazaar, listened to the chatter of the thousand parrots in the Hagenbeck animal show that had been imported from Hamburg or craned their heads for a better look at the captive balloon which carried twenty people to a height of six hundred feet. They stood in line for a ride on the newly invented Ferris Wheel, a monster "bridge on an axle" which George Ferris had invented to match the structural glories of the Eiffel Tower which dominated the Paris Exposition of 1889. The Ferris Wheel, like the Manufacturers Building, was a behemoth. It carried forty persons in each of its thirty-six cars; during the summer more than 1,750,000 people took the ride in the big circle. At the top of the ride they could look north to the outlines of first skyscrapers or peer downward, as did young Harold Swift, at the first buildings of the new University of Chicago.

Eugene Field sang the praises of the Midway in a short rondel.

> Come boys, let's away to the Midway Plaisance
> There are visions of loveliness there to behold
> Oh, the lithe Moorish maidens with bangles of gold
> And eyes that will set you afire at a glance.

> And the houris from Germany, Italy, France,
> And the Javanese maidens of minikin mold!
> Come boys, let's away to the Midway Plaisance.

> They discount the marvelous yarns of romance
> Ingeniously spun by the authors of old:
> Why the half of the charms of that place can't be told
> And hush, we will see that Algerian dance—
> Come boys, let's away to the Midway Plaisance.

The most famous attraction was not the Algerian torture dancer but a sleek Egyptian, Fahreda Mahzar, who had come to America with a troupe of Syrian dancers engaged for the Streets of Cairo and who was billed as Little Egypt. Although Little Egypt wore a full skirt, only semi-transparent, and an unrevealing brassiere, there were thousands willing to swear with a Chicago policeman that when she danced "you could see every muscle in her body at the same time." Her dance, which was exotic enough to reveal the diamonds on her garters, was the Midway's most talked-of attraction. Seeing Little Egypt became synonymous with going to the fair. (That the dancer did not share the public's opinion of her performance was evident a generation later when she sued a motion picture company for using "naked girls" in connection with a film portrayal of her dance.)

Passing through an Irish market town or perhaps stopping for a cup of coffee in a Tunisian café, the adventurer might then make his choice among one of the sideshows where models were grouped in "artistic poses" on the stage. For the gullible there was a "nudist colony," where a spectator peered through a small hole in the wall—and saw only his own reflection mirrored over an unrevealing painting of a nude body. There were occasional shows not on the exposition list—such as that which occurred when someone gave the dwarf elephant several buckets of beer and the intoxicated pachyderm escaped for a romp through the grounds. James J. Corbett was the star of his own show, *Gentleman Jim*, though his thespian efforts consisted mostly of punching the bag. Corbett was enchanted with the food at the Viennese café and spent so much time there—where the public could view him without buying a ticket to his show—that his manager threatened him first with "a Smith & Wesson" and finally with a lawsuit if he did not spend more time in the exhibition room of the theater. Nearby a young professor in white tights who gave his name as Bernarr Macfadden was flexing his lithe muscles and demonstrating a new exercising machine invented by his sponsor, Alexander Whiteley.

Florenz Ziegfeld, Jr., who had been assigned to procure military bands from the different countries of Europe for the fair, had brought back as an extra attraction Sandow, the European strong man, and was acting as Sandow's sponsor and manager. Amy Leslie, the drama critic for the *News*, described Sandow as a fascinating mixture of brute force and poetic sentimentality. On a walk through the Wooded Island (carefully arranged by the shrewd Ziegfeld), Sandow snipped a tiny cup from a stock of snapdragon. "Now, when we were little in Germany," Sandow told the astonished Miss Leslie, "we took these blossoms and pressed them so, and if the flower mouth opened, why that was a sign they were calling us at home." As Amy reported it, "he touched the tinted bud and its rosy lips parted in a perfumed smile." Just as Sandow finished his sentence, a Columbian guard shouted that he had violated the rule against picking flowers. To emphasize the reprimand, the guard seized Sandow by the elbow and attempted to push him away. At this effrontery Sandow lifted the surprised guard off the ground and held him at arm's length, examining him as though he were a curious discovery. Miss Leslie, more conscious of the dignity of the law, persuaded Sandow to put the guard down, which the strong man did with an outburst of German expletives and an explanation (in English) to Miss Leslie that he did not think much of humans as guards. "I prefer nice, well-bred dogs," he said.

Throughout the exposition summer the theaters downtown and on the Midway offered all-star bills. At the Columbia Theater was a former Chicago singer christened Helen Louise Leonard but more easily recognized as Lillian Russell. Lillian's father was an unsuccessful Chicago publisher who issued the works of Robert Ingersoll and other agnostic literature. Her mother had been an early and ardent feminist, who liked to discuss social issues at women's meetings which she usually called in an ice-cream parlor. After the Chicago fire Lillian's mother had founded the Good Samaritan Society to alleviate the suffering of shelterless prostitutes. Mrs. Leonard had aspirations toward authorship as well, one of her works being entitled *Failing Footsteps, or The Last of the Iroquois*. Helen Leonard gave her first concert at fourteen in Chicago's Kimball Music Hall but shortly afterward her mother found Chicago too limited for suffragist ambitions and moved to New York to join the ranks of the crusaders around Susan B. Anthony, taking Helen Louise with her.

In 1893, Helen Louise, now Lillian, was back in Chicago for a sixteen-week engagement at the Columbia Theater. One of those who followed her from New York was James Buchanan Brady, a wealthy salesman of railroad equipment who was better known as Diamond Jim. Brady, who was Lillian Russell's faithful, if platonic, admirer, divided his time between the theater, the Fine Arts palace at the fair and several restaurants where he could get an abundance of his favorite dish, sweet corn. The café owners competed to please Brady's gourmand's palate and the sight of Diamond Jim dining with Lillian became one of the most widely sought, if unofficial, attractions of the fair.

Derby Day at Washington Park was to be more festive than usual that summer and Lillian had changed her matinee day from Saturday to Thursday so that she might attend. According to her biographer, Parker Morell, her appearance in the Washington Park clubhouse caused consternation among the women and a few self-conscious members objected to her presence. The president refused to listen to the outraged ladies until the wives and daughters of the club officers were persuaded to join in the protest. Then the unhappy gentleman had to ask Lillian if she would accept a box in the grandstand. Lillian did occupy a box for the races but the *Tribune* described it as "one of the best in the grandstand." There was, however some evidence that Chicago society was too puritanical in its attitudes to receive actresses. The *Record*, in reporting the race, said Miss Russell held a levee between races and "all sorts greeted her" but chiefly members "of the profession which Miss Russell adorns." If society did snub her, its satisfaction must have been spoiled the next day when the democratic reporters put her name at the top of their lists of women at the races.

Despite this apparent show of morality at the race track, the city was

PRENDERGAST,
the Assassin,
From a Sketch from Life.

like Monte Carlo. Carriages full of merrymakers rode up and down the boulevards through the late hours of the night singing "After the Ball." Roulette, chuck-a-luck and piquet flourished in the parlors of such gambling kings as Harry Varnell. Brothel rents were tripled and paid without complaint or hardship. The city, with every theater and café crowded, had never known such a spectacular night life; the carnival spirit was everywhere.

On Chicago Day more than three-quarters of a million Chicagoans—over half the population of the city—jammed, pushed and shoved their way into the exposition grounds. By October 28th, when Mayor Carter Harrison received the plaudits of his colleagues on Mayor's Day, the fair was a success by every standard, including the fundamental Chicago measure of showing a profit. That night, after Carter Harrison returned home, a psychopath took advantage of the latchstring that was always out; he called Carter Harrison to the door and killed him because of a hallucinatory grievance over not being appointed corporation counsel. The city grieved, but consoled itself with the knowledge that the world now knew of the greatness of Chicago. The work of "Our Carter" was done. There was good reason to believe he was satisfied.

19

From Pullman City to Hull House

FIVE DAYS after the gates of the World's Columbian Exposition were opened; the stock market crashed, throwing the country into one of its recurring financial panics. Henry Adams wrote that "men died like flies under the strain and Boston grew suddenly old, haggard and thin." Chicago, bolstered by the influx of funds from exposition visitors, did not immediately feel the full effects of the economic recession. Philip D. Armour and Marshall Field told alarmed depositors standing in line for their money when a run started on the Illinois Trust and Savings Bank that all deposits would be personally guaranteed by the two richest men in Chicago. Harlow Higinbotham took time from his duties as president of the exposition to reassure the depositors further: when one woman would not be dissuaded from taking her savings out of the bank, he held her baby while she waited for the money. But the effects of the fair and the personal courage of the city's leaders could not offer permanent immunity to the blight of a nation-wide depression. The winter of 1893–1894 saw a widening of unemployment and poverty; starvation was averted in many instances only by the food on the free-lunch counters in the saloons of Democratic politicians.

The effects of the depression were most severely felt in Pullman City, the manufacturing town ten miles south of Chicago's business district where George M. Pullman had planned a community from which he had hoped to eliminate "all that was ugly, discordant and demoralizing." The nation's railroads, hardest hit of any industry by the panic, canceled a large part of their orders with Pullman. Because Pullman City was a one-industry town, the workers had to make railroad cars or starve. By 1894 they were starving.

Pullman City, which had been in existence for little more than a decade, was erected on a bold and original plan. After the fire, when Cyrus McCormick had moved his reaper works away from the business district to a sprawling plant on the West Side, George Pullman was seeking a similar location for his main car works. St. Louis, anxious for the factory to be located there, sought to lure Pullman with an offer of free land for the plant's erection. Pullman declined this immediate economic bonus for a long-term advantage; he preferred Chicago because he thought a man could do at least 10 per cent more work in the summertime where the lake breeze would serve as a natural form of air-conditioning. With this in mind, he purchased a tract of about three thousand acres on the shores of Lake Calumet, an area where Stephen A. Douglas had once made such extensive investments the lake had been called derisively "Douglas's Frog Pond."

With the site selected, Pullman engaged S. S. Beman to design a self-contained industrial city. The physical planning of Beman was elaborate and foresighted. The houses were built around a central arcade for the city's shops, theater and library, a design which anticipated other American suburban planning by half a century. All the buildings were of brick, which in turn was fabricated in the town's own brick kilns from clay taken from the bottom of Lake Calumet. Considerable care was taken in landscaping the community's small park. An elegant hotel was erected and given the name of the inventor's daughter, Florence. The streets took their names from such modern inventors as Stephenson, Watt, Fulton, Morse and Pullman himself.

It was Pullman's objective to demonstrate "that such advantages and surroundings made better workmen by removing from them the feeling of discontent and desire for change which so generally characterize the American workman, thus protecting the employer from the loss of time and money consequent upon intemperance, labor strikes and dissatisfaction which generally result from poverty and uncongenial home surroundings." He did not regard his five-million dollar investment as an altruistic venture. A separate Pullman Land Association was formed to handle the affairs of the model town. It was expected to show the same profit as the Pullman Palace Car Company, whose main manufacturing plant, dominated by a high clock tower that became the landmark of the town, was allotted five hundred acres of community property. "I have not contributed 50 cents to all that you see here," Pullman proudly told French economist Paul de Rousiers. "I have never had any idea of giving alms to my men and every dwelling pays the rent it ought to do to give the company a sufficient revenue for the money sank [sic] in building Pullman City." The industrialist did not understate his case. Gas and water bought from Chicago by the company were resold to the householders at a profit. Rents were high, investigators later establishing that the equivalent of a $15 a month cottage in Chicago rented for $18 a month in Pullman City. Even the sewage from the town's houses was collected in a reservoir to be pumped to a Pullman farm several miles away and used as fertilizer.

Pullman called his city self-governing; its critics called it feudal. As one resident put it, the citizens "paid rent to the Pullman Company, bought gas of the Pullman Company, walked on streets owned in fee simple by Pullman [and] paid water tax to Pullman. Indeed, even when they bought gingham for their wives or sugar for their tables at the arcade or market house it seemed dealing with Pullman. They sent their children to Pullman's school, attended Pullman's church, looked at but dared not enter Pullman's hotel with its private bar, for that was the limit. Pullman did not sell them their grog." All saloons and drinking resorts had been banned by Pullman on the ground he wanted to do all he could "to develop the better nature of our workmen." The man who wanted a glass of beer or nip of whiskey had to walk nearly a mile to a group of low-class saloons which had been thrown up at the edge of nearby Kensington to cater to the thirst of the frustrated Pullman workers.

Pullman was particularly proud of the town's theater and library, which he anticipated would improve his workers' "better nature." Special trains brought his Prairie Avenue neighbors to the opening of the theater in 1883. The entertainment was not a frivolous drama but a lecture by Stewart L. Woodford. The speaker found it easy to praise the munificence of Pullman but added a warning that "I do not dream that the millennium is about to dawn, even at Pullman. It will be strange," he told his audience of multimillionaires and carefully screened Pullman executives, "if the serpent does not hiss, even under the rose leaves of this Eden." The Reverend David Swing of Chicago's Central Church was more lyrical when he dedicated the library a few months later. It was his hope, he said, that "the rich men of the West will always prefer libraries, and parks and music temples and even good theaters to the perishable display of the ballroom. A library is almost as sacred as a sanctuary." To the Pullman workers the library was an expensive sanctuary. Only two hundred and fifty out of about five thousand families could afford the annual fee of $3 for adults and $1 for children which Pullman assessed those who wanted to use its facilities. Even the local church was expected to show a profit. A minister who hoped to lease the church for less than the established rent was firmly turned away. "When the church was built," Pullman told the astonished clergyman, "it was not intended so much for the moral and spiritual welfare of the people as it was for the artistic effect of the scene." For many years the parsonage stood vacant because its rent was more than a clergyman could afford.

When Pullman cut his workers' wages and hours after a falling-off in business, he refused to lower their rents. He insisted the rental of houses was a separate business from the manufacture of Pullman cars and there was no connection between the town's employer and its landlord. No one was allowed to fall behind in his bills; all charges against the workers were deducted by the company from the pay checks. Some workers in 1894 were getting as little as 7 cents a week in cash; others were in debt to the company and receiving no money for their work. Exasperated, and in many cases physically weak from hunger, the workers sent a delegation of forty-three representatives to discuss their plight with Pullman. He refused to meet the appointed committee, fired every one of its members and dispossessed them from their homes the following day. Fearful of more such reprisals, the workers turned to the American Railway Union in which many of them had taken out secret memberships since it had been founded a short time before by Eugene Debs. On May 11th, without consulting Debs or the union, the Pullman unit voted to go out on strike. The attitude of the workers as the walkout began was summarized by the strike chairman, Thomas Heathcote: "We do not expect the company to concede our demands. We do not know what the outcome will be, and in fact we do not care much. We do know that we are working for less wages than will maintain ourselves and families in the necessaries of life and on that proposition we absolutely refuse to work any longer."

When the strike was called, three thousand workers left their jobs and an additional group of several hundred was promptly laid off by the company. Debs, who had urged caution after being informed of the possibility of the walkout, hurried to Pullman City to see if a compromise could be found. He knew his young union was in no way strong enough to win a strike against Pullman and the forces which might be aligned with him. There was great pressure on Pullman to arbitrate the issues. The newly formed Civic Federation, through such spokesmen as banker Lyman Gage and Mrs. Potter Palmer, urged him to meet with the workers. The mayors of fifty-six American cities wired to urge arbitration. Pullman's stubbornness in the face of such appeals was so monumental it caused even Mark Hanna to explode in Cleveland's Union League Club that "a man who won't meet his own men halfway is a goddamn fool!" The stalemate dragged on. Pickets patrolled the gates of the Pullman Company but there was so little prospect of violence that the company did not ask for additional police protection. This was the situation when the American Railway Union opened its first convention in Chicago on June 12th.

The delegates demanded action against Pullman. Debs urged caution. When a motion was made that all Pullman cars be boycotted, Debs refused to allow it to be put to a vote. He insisted that another committee be sent to meet with Pullman, a move which failed when Pullman refused to talk with the group. A second committee, this time made up only of Pullman workers, was also refused an audience; the members were told they were "in the same position as the man on the sidewalk"—that is, no longer employes. There was no alternative but to ask for a plan of action. A committee recommended a boycott of all Pullman cars; the union voted unanimously to start the boycott on June 26th unless the Pullman Company expressed a willingness to arbitrate.

As Debs had foreseen, the boycott brought the union into conflict not only with Pullman but with all the nation's railroads, which uniformly refused to move trains without the Pullman cars. The General Managers' Association, a group of twenty-four railroads, saw in the strike an opportunity to break Debs's union in its infancy. On the sidelines were the comparatively young brotherhoods of conductors, switchmen, trainmen and engineers, craft unions which disapproved of Debs's attempt to unite all rail workers in one organization.

Clashes were inevitable as the railroad workers sought to cut the Pullman cars out of the trains. On June 30th, there was a minor disturbance at Cairo, Illinois, and, after an appeal from the local mayor and sheriff, Governor Altgeld sent three companies of militia to keep order. In Chicago, Mayor John P. Hopkins saw no need for troops, though the local United States Attorney was persuaded to wire Washington for authority to hire more deputies. The strategy of the railroads was to bring the federal government into the dispute; to do this they attached unnecessary Pullman cars to mail trains in order to provoke an interference with the United States mail.

In Washington, the situation was being watched closely by Attorney General Richard Olney, one of the founders of the General Managers' Association. He was not long in finding a pretext for action. On July 2nd, he secured an injunction to prevent the strikers from interfering with the mails or interstate commerce. Simultaneously, he recommended to President Cleveland that troops from Fort Sheridan be sent into Chicago to keep order. This idea was opposed by General Nelson A. Miles and Secretary of War Daniel S. Lamont and vetoed by the President. The following day, however, Olney produced a telegram predicting there would be disorders in Chicago on the Fourth of July and persuaded the President to send the troops into the city. Governor Altgeld was circumvented just as Governor Palmer had been by-passed after the Chicago fire. The fact that Alt-

THE FIRST MEAT TRAIN LEAVING THE STOCKYARDS UNDER ESCORT
OF THE U. S. CAVALRY, 1894

geld had sent troops to Cairo when there was a necessity for it counted for
nothing in the eyes of his political enemies; they insisted that because of
his advanced social views he could not be trusted. To Altgeld's protests,
Cleveland replied, "We are confronted with a condition, not a theory."

Olney was being much more solicitous about the railroads than he had
been about the coal-mine owners a few weeks earlier. At that time, there
had been widespread coal strikes in both Ohio, where William McKinley
was governor, and Illinois. Twice Altgeld had sent state troops to keep
order during the coal-mine disturbances. When a federal judge in Springfield applied for federal troops, Olney had wired: "Understand State of
Illinois is willing to protect property against lawless violence with military
force if necessary. . . . If such protection proves inadequate, the governor
should be applied to for military assistance." The date of Olney's wire was
June 16th; less than a month later he was willing to persuade Cleveland to
call out federal troops not only in Illinois, but in Kansas, Colorado, Texas
and Oregon—where the governors protested the disregard of their consti-
tutional rights with equal futility.

Violence was at a minimum, although there were a hundred thousand
men idle between New York and San Francisco. Without the intervention
of the federal government, Pullman might have been compelled to arbitrate.
But with the widespread hiring of deputy marshals recruited from the worst
elements of every city—termed by the governor of Colorado a group of

"desperadoes" hired "without any regard for their qualifications"—violence increased. Mayor Hopkins, Governor Altgeld and the Civic Federation denounced the turning of law enforcement over to toughs recruited in the Levee district. At Pullman City a bystander was killed by one of the temporary deputies. Chief of Police John Brennan charged that the deputies were shooting "innocent men and women" and said his men had arrested several deputies for stealing from the railroad cars they had been assigned to protect.

The test of strength moved rapidly toward a climax as the troops from Fort Sheridan pitched their tents around the public buildings and on the lake front. A major clash occurred when the soldiers tried to move a train out of the stockyards, shut down because the railroads could not deliver hogs and cattle. As the first train started to move out of the yards, the strikers overturned boxcars in its path and spiked the switches. The heavily guarded train was able to move only six blocks. Violence erupted all over the city. Executives trying to man switchtowers or locomotives were dragged from their posts and beaten by howling, brick-throwing mobs. The night sky was aglow with the flare of burning boxcars (some of which, according to Chief Brennan, had been fired by gangs in the employ of the railroads to rouse public opinion against the strikers). The carnage of war littered fashionable Grand Boulevard as an artillery caisson exploded, killing three soldiers and hurling fragments of metal into the drawing rooms of the mansions along the street. Suburban trains ran only irregularly. On one of the trains running the gauntlet of violence out of the city, young Cyrus Adams was warned to lie on the floor to escape the bullets and stones which the strikers were firing through the windows of the coaches and Pullman cars. After several days of rioting, President Cleveland warned that he would send in as many additional federal troops as were necessary to move the trains. On July 9th, realizing that his union stood alone against the federal government, Debs conceded defeat and the strike was broken without a single concession from Pullman. The defense of his citadel had brought death to more than a dozen men and caused property damage far in excess of half a million dollars. Debs and several others were sent to jail for violating Olney's injunction, despite the shrewd defense presented by Clarence Darrow, who had only recently left a position with the Chicago and North Western Railway, and D. S. Gregory, who was later to be president of the American Bar Association.

The Pullman plant reopened on August 2nd. Almost a quarter of the workers were new employes; all were required to sign pledges they would not join a union. Governor Altgeld appealed to Pullman to help more than a thousand men from the model city who were jobless and destitute; Pullman refused to accept the message until it was officially forced on him by a National Guard officer in full uniform. At last, despairing of dealing with Pullman, Chicago accepted the responsibility for the relief of the outcasts from the community where its founder had hoped to eliminate "all that was ugly, discordant and demoralizing."

Three years after the strike George Pullman died. His achievements in helping Chicago to raise itself out of its own mud, in founding one of its great industries, in planning a model community a generation ahead of its time in its physical conception and in leading Chicago to second rank among American cities merited a statue such as that to Stephen A. Douglas which scaled the skyline along the city's lake shore. His monument was to be of a far different kind, reflecting not affection but terror and fear. The funeral services for Pullman were held privately in his mansion on Prairie Avenue late in the afternoon. The funeral cortege pulled away from the house just at dusk. It was night when the procession arrived at Graceland Cemetery where elaborate preparations had been made to assure that Pullman was "more secure from the encroachment of the living world" than any of "the Egyptian monarchs supposedly resting under the ponderous weight of the pyramids." A pit as large as an average room had been dug on the family lot and lined across its base and walls with reinforced concrete eighteen inches thick. Into this the lead-lined mahogany casket was lowered,

UNITED STATES TROOPS ENCAMPED IN FRONT OF THE POST OFFICE, 1894

covered with a wrapping of tar paper and covered with a quick-drying coat of asphalt which would exclude all air from the casket. The balance of the pit was filled to the level of the casket with solid concrete, on top of which a series of heavy steel rails were laid at right angles to each other and bolted together. The steel rails were then imbedded in another layer of concrete. The work of filling in the grave required two days. Then "the sod was replaced, the myrtle planted" and the grave "differed in no outward respect from the thousands of others under the shadow of the trees of Graceland." Such was the price of victory in the Pullman strike. Pullman's will showed his estate to be about seventeen million dollars, of which more than a million was set aside for a manual-training school where boys might learn the skills of the hands. That George M. Pullman had never mastered the more difficult skills of the heart was evident from a further provision of the will. To his twin sons he left a pittance of $3,000 a year, explaining that neither had developed a sense of responsibility "requisite for the wise use of large properties and considerable sums of money." The regimen which pressed down upon the workers of Pullman City extended even to Prairie Avenue.

The Pullman strike emphasized the need for a boldness in social thinking which would match the originality in enterprise which had been a principal quality in Chicago's phenomenal growth. A pioneer in this more modern field was Lyman Gage, president of the First National Bank and founder of the Civic Federation, who had tried unsuccessfully to arrange for arbitration of the Pullman dispute. Gage had also urged clemency for the men accused of the Haymarket bombing, arguing that free speech and adequate discussion were better weapons than prejudiced courts in the defense of liberty. To implement his theory, he organized discussion groups in which speakers were allowed to express every variety of idea. The first meetings were held in his home but interest grew until it was necessary to transfer them to the recital hall of the Auditorium. At these forums everyone was allowed his time to be heard—speculators, clergymen, Republicans, Democrats, the few surviving anarchists and the Henry George single-taxers. Gage noted only one element absent at the meetings. "I am sorry to say," he confessed, "they are attended but feebly by the well-to-do people," adding an expressive comment that "higher classes" was not the best term for this group; he felt "self-satisfied is nearer." There was nothing self-satisfied about Gage. He persuaded Mrs. Palmer to take the post of first vice-president of his Civic Federation and as second vice-president he enlisted a union official, J. J. McGrath. On his various committees appeared the names of Marshall Field, Harlow Higinbotham, Cyrus McCormick, Jr., and Jane Addams, who had established America's first settlement house in the building once occupied as a home by Charles J. Hull and which more recently had been used by the Washingtonian home as an institution for "female inebriates."

To Jane Addams the Pullman strike was not an isolated phenomenon for which one man was responsible but a symbol of the growing demand for "a more democratic administration of industry." At Hull House, which she and Ellen Gates Starr had founded in 1889, she insisted that the real enemy of social progress was not so much deliberate aggression as brutal confusion and neglect. The area around Hull House afforded many illustrations of her thesis. The settlement was located in the vortex of the whirlpool of new immigration, an area of little wooden houses grimy with soot and often falling to pieces. The pathways were of rickety and worm-eaten planks and the streets quagmires of black mud. When the crown prince of Belgium paid a visit to Hull House he insisted that "such a street—no, not one," existed in all Belgium.

When Jane Addams began her work at Hull House, the feminist movement was growing rapidly. But the feminist movement in Chicago was to take on the individual characteristics of the city which had grown in the shadow of such giants as William B. Ogden, Long John Wentworth, Joseph Medill, Marshall Field, Philip D. Armour—yes, and George M. Pullman. Self-reliance was a cardinal virtue; the best way to get things done was not to wait until others were persuaded to do it but to do it yourself. This was a tradition suited to the temperament of Jane Addams. When a survey disclosed nineteen thousand people in one area of the city without any bathing facilities except those furnished in the warm months by the lake and river, her ire was so great that more than half of the city's sanitation-inspection bureau was discharged. When she saw that garbage collections were inadequate, she had herself appointed the ward's garbage inspector, taking a fat political plum away from the party bosses. Her supervision was more than nominal; after a few months her buggy became known as the garbage phaeton. She felt that education in esthetics was as important as cleaning up the streets and alleys. John Galsworthy's play *Justice* was given its American premiere on the stage at Hull House with Theodore Roosevelt mingling with the first-night audience of workingmen and their families.

An ally of Jane Addams in the war on brutal confusion and neglect was Louise de Koven Bowen, a third-generation member of one of Chicago's first families. Mrs. Bowen's grandmother had come to Chicago in a covered wagon with a rifle across her knee. Mrs. Bowen's mother had been the third white child born in the reconstructed Fort Dearborn. The family was fashionable and among the first in the city to have a uniformed driver and coachman on the box of its carriage. Although young Louise de Koven liked such shows of style, she had a strong social conscience. When only eight, she had seen a girl injured by a runaway horse in front of her home at Wabash and Monroe. Following the men who carried the victim home,

LINCOLN PARK, 1887, by *Charles Graham*

Louise de Koven found a miserable shack, with nothing but rags upon the girl's bed. She quickly returned to her own neighborhood, pounded on the doors of the big mansions and demanded contributions. Within an hour she had accumulated $57 which she gave to the injured girl. At sixteen, she had volunteered to teach a Sunday School class of boys with a reputation for being "bad." When one of her new pupils challenged her instructions she threw him bodily out of the room. Her authority established, she opened a boys' club in the basement of her parents' mansion and invited the class, most of whom were from poor homes, to spend their free time in the club. When Louise de Koven, then Mrs. Joseph T. Bowen, met Jane Addams, she was already practicing a philosophy of direct action. "When one of us became aware of the existence of a wrong," she was to recall, "we took down our bonnets, we put them on, we tied the strings under our chins, we got out a horse and buggy—if we had them—we put in a hitching strap with a weight on the end and we started off for the scene of the trouble."

Another of the women who joined the Hull House group was Dr. Alice Hamilton, who had been dissatisfied with the finishing-school education she received at Farmington, New York, and gone on to a study of medicine. Dr. Hamilton found time for elaborate medical investigations in the Hull House neighborhood. Her discovery during a typhoid epidemic in the 1890's that the common fly was a carrier of the disease was an important contribution to the ultimate control of typhoid.

Not everyone was as sympathetic with Miss Addams as Mrs. Bowen or Dr. Hamilton. The outspoken opinions of these three, plus the views of Florence Kelley on factory legislation and Julia Lathrop in the field of social welfare, gave the Hull House group what Jane Addams called "an early reputation for radicalism." Backers frequently withdrew their pledges because of the controversies this little group of individualists initiated; yet with Mrs. Bowen as treasurer some means were always found of carrying on. An honorary membership which the Daughters of the American Revolution had given Jane Addams was withdrawn after one such quarrel. "I thought it had been given for life," remarked Miss Addams, "but apparently it was only for good behavior." The Fortnightly Club, of which Mrs. Bowen was a member, withdrew an invitation for Miss Addams to speak because of alleged radicalism. Mrs. Bowen would tolerate no such nonsense and called a special meeting of the Fortnightly, more or less dragging Jane Addams to the platform so the speech could be given as scheduled.

It was Mrs. Bowen who acted as field marshal for much of the war on the political front. She supported Florence Kelley's efforts to secure the first factory-inspection law. She fought for and secured the establishment of the first juvenile court in Chicago and soon persuaded the county and city to co-operate in erecting a juvenile court building and detention home. In effect, she dictated the judges who were to be permitted to sit in the court as well. She organized the Juvenile Protective Association for the reduction of delinquency and it was at her insistence that policewomen and matrons were hired for the first time by the Chicago police department. She was practical enough in her sympathies to be among the first to hire a relief investigator to see that charity money was being properly spent. No subject was too indelicate for her consideration. As her agents brought in reports, Mrs. Bowen bombarded the city with pamphlets on "The Department Store Girl," "The Straight Girl on the Crooked Path," "Equal Suffrage," "A Study of Bastardy Cases," "Five and Ten Cent Theaters," "A Study of Public Dance Halls" and other such topics. Through it all, she bowed to no one in her fidelity to the Republican Party. When Presidents Theodore Roosevelt and William Howard Taft visited Chicago, it was Mrs. Bowen who introduced them.

The measure of Mrs. Bowen's influence was best illustrated when she came into conflict with the Pullman Company, almost as intransigent thirteen years after its founder's death as it had been during his life. At the time, Dr. Hamilton was making an investigation of industrial diseases for the federal government. She reported to Mrs. Bowen that conditions at the Pullman plant were substandard. Painters frequently contracted lead poisoning. Men who were hit in the eye by steel fragments or suffered any type of accident were all treated by an elderly doctor. Those with eye injuries frequently lost their sight as the result of such superficial treatment. Mrs. Bowen, a large stockholder of the Pullman Company, augmented Dr. Hamilton's findings with a private report of her own. Both reports were sent to the president of the company, who refused to acknowledge them. Then Mrs. Bowen wrote again, suggesting that the company take action or she would publicly refuse to take her dividends because of the poor working conditions at the plant. This threat brought action; the Board of Directors agreed to meet with Mrs. Bowen. The outcome of the meeting was an agreement by the board to invest $75,000 in new hospital facilities and the hiring of a competent medical staff. Special precautions were introduced to prevent lead poisoning and other safety recommendations adopted. This was only one in a series of victories which Mrs. Bowen scored as an individual arrayed against the power of the corporation. With Charles Cabot of Boston, she led an assault on the twelve-hour day which was then standard for workers of the U. S. Steel Corporation. Another time, a letter to her friend, Cyrus McCormick, Jr., brought an end to the practice of hiring women to work in the Harvester Company's twine mill at night and the establishment of a minimum wage for women in the company plants.

Throughout these social battles Mrs. Bowen held her place in society. Through the pattern set by her work at Hull House and the initiative shown by Mrs. Potter Palmer in the Civic Federation and at the Columbian Exposition, a new standard of social acceptance was established for Chicago women. A writer for *McCall's* found that while "the men busy themselves with speeches and the rebuilding of Chicago . . . and the making of more money, the women tend the poor and search out talent that should be encouraged and run baby clinics—all with a furious energy." Julian Ralph, writing in *Harper's*, confirmed this impression. "I do not believe," he wrote, "that in any older American city we shall find fashionable women . . . so forward in works of public improvement and governmental reform as well as of charity. Indeed, this seems to be quite a new character for the woman of fashion." No longer was it enough to contribute funds or lend one's name to the letterheads of genteel charity benefits. Social success was now subject to the same tests as economic success had been a generation earlier. Hard work and the Yankee virtues were still the criteria. There was no time to develop a café society; there was still too much to be done.

Life Along the Levee

"CHICAGO presents more splendid attractions and more hideous repulsions close together than any place known to me," a correspondent wrote the London *Daily Mail* about the turn of the century. "It takes elaborate care to present its worst side first to the stranger. It makes a more amazingly open display of evil than any other city known to me. Other places hide their blackness out of sight; Chicago treasures it in the heart of the business quarter and gives it a veneer." Even the locally published Rand McNally guide suggested "entrusting your valuables with the clerk of your hotel" before venturing into the Levee district where an extraordinarily thin veneer covered the city's "worst side first."

The Levee, whose name was a heritage of the early influx of southern gamblers, was, of all the city, the area most careless of its morals. No one was quite certain of the exact borders of the Levee and equal doubt prevailed about the limits of Levee entertainment. It was always carnival time on the Levee. There were gambling houses, barrelhouse saloons, dance halls, pawnshops, tintype galleries, voodoo doctors, penny arcades, fake auctions and a few legitimate livery stables, blacksmith shops and oyster bays. Within the borders of a few blocks were located more than two hundred brothels. They ranged from low dives and panel houses, where robbers worked in collaboration with prostitutes, to elegantly furnished mansions governed by a strict code of conduct. A visitor who headed for the Levee usually said he was "going down the line"; he was lucky if he returned with his bait.

Exotic entertainment ranged from that at the French Elm, where the walls were covered with mirrors, to the attractions of John Williams' Opium Den or the House of All Nations where girls of a dozen nationalities—most of them born in Chicago—worked interchangeably between a five-dollar side and a two-dollar side, as economic conditions on any particular night dictated. At the Park Theater, boxes were available in which the actresses might be entertained between numbers and private wine rooms were provided for those who wished to enjoy a champagne tête-à-tête. Nearby was the California, a wide-open place which boasted of fifty girls and operated on a simple principle—keep moving. Frankie Wright also kept her house in the Levee, adding a collection of books and calling it the Library. Vina Fields, the exceptionally high-principled madame, was another who kept open house. She maintained decorum with a set of rules more strict, according to legend, than those of an exclusive girls' boarding school. A police matron testified that Vina Fields was a good woman. Vina herself had no illusions. It was misery that brought her girls to her, she said, "always misery."

The social center of the Levee was Freiberg's dance hall, the most notorious saloon in the city. Its manager was Ike Bloom, who insisted on only two things—decorous dancing and a prompt cut of his girls' earnings. Beyond that, anything went and often did. Bloom loved publicity and tried·to make his dance hall a popular slumming spot such as the Moulin Rouge of Paris. He liked to recall the night Walter Shafter's horse had won the American Derby. Bloom, told that Shafter might pay him a visit, had decorated a box with the Shafter colors. The proud winner, out to make the rounds, tarried only to drink his glass of champagne. Then, according to Bloom, Shafter said: "Ring this up . . . and hands me 2500 iron men." An unexpected visitor at Freiberg's was Arthur Burrage Farwell, a cousin of the city's successful Farwell clan who, as president of the Chicago Law and Order League, devoted his energies to reform. Bloom received Farwell and the group with him courteously. "I tell 'em to go as far as they like," he told Ashton Stevens later. "I give them the freedom of the tables; I order the drinks all around—lemonade; and when they ask for the center of the dance floor to kneel down and pray and sing 'Washed in the Blood of the Lamb' I give it to 'em. I give 'em my jazz band too, which plays their accompaniment and plays it mighty damned well. One of the papers carried a story next day that was all straight except where it says I knelt and sang with 'em. That was an error, I don't sing."

The pride of the Levee and its showplace was the Everleigh Club, an elegant mansion under the direction of Ada and Minna Everleigh. The

Everleighs were two upper-class Kentucky girls with ambitions to go on the stage and a remarkable precocity for the profession of a madame. When the Everleigh Club opened its doors, Ada was twenty-three and Minna just twenty-one. Their scale of prices began at $50, unheard of even on the free-spending Levee. "I've heard of southern hospitality," one of their competitors sneered, "but not at these prices." Minna set the tone of the club. Girls were given daily instructions in etiquette and told to use the library which had been installed. "Be polite and forget what you are here for," Minna told them without conscious irony. "Stay respectable by all means; I want you girls to be proud you are in the Everleigh Club." She explained bluntly that the sisters had no time for the "rough element, the clerk on a holiday or a man without a checkbook."

Ada did the hiring. "I talk with each applicant myself," she said. "She must have worked somewhere else before coming here. We do not like amateurs. To get in a girl must have a pretty face and figure, must be in perfect health, must look well in evening clothes and must understand what it is to act like a lady." To this Minna added, 'Don't forget—entertaining most men at dinner is more tiring than what the girls lose their social standing over." Minna regarded her girls as members of a professional class. They accepted fees for services rendered, she explained, and did not sell themselves "as these eggheads keep shouting."

Patrons of the Everleigh Club were entertained genteelly in one of a number of elegant parlors bearing such names as the Moorish, Japanese, Egyptian or Chinese and decorated appropriately. There were Silver and Copper parlors for the mining kings who came to call and a famous Gold Room which was refinished each year in gold leaf and polished industriously

THE LEVEE AT NIGHT, 1898, by H. G. Maratta

every day. The sisters established these parlors on the theory that "the contemplation of deviltry" was more satisfactory than its performance. Dinners were sumptuous affairs and always accompanied by champagne. Although banjos were the favored instrument for music in many Levee houses, the Everleighs preferred a small ensemble of a violin, cello, piano and occasionally a harp. The piano player received sizable sums from music publishers for popularizing new songs with the select crowd which visited the Everleighs. Both sisters had a fondness for reporters. Newspapermen had the freedom of the house. The sisters let it be known that they preferred the reporters avoid the upper floors but there was no absolute rule even about this. On Christmas Eve there was always a party for the press with much champagne, dancing and small but valuable gifts for the guests.

The Everleighs were both sentimental. Their name was a pseudonym fashioned from their grandmother's letters which concluded "Everly yours" and Minna's fondness for the poems of Sir Walter Raleigh. The sisters were offended when no one praised them for "such noble gestures" as donating Sunday nights to old-fashioned romance. Sunday was Beau Night and the girls were permitted to entertain their sweethearts as if they had been receiving them in more conventional surroundings. Every Sunday evening a parade of swains bearing candy, perfume and flowers would file into the Everleigh Club, where the evening would be spent in the manner of much less sophisticated sweethearts.

The genteel approach of the Everleighs had its hazards. One of these was gambling. Realistic Minna thought that any man would rather gamble than spend his time with women. "Admitting that women are a risk," she told Charles Washburn, her biographer, "I still say that men prefer dice, cards or a wheel of fortune to a frolic with a charmer. I have watched men, embraced in the arms of the most bewitching sirens in our club, dump their feminine flesh from their laps for a roll of the dice." With such experiences in mind, Minna placed a half-hour limit on gambling. Besides, she said, it was illegal.

The sisters prospered. "If it weren't for the married men we couldn't have carried on at all and if it weren't for the cheating married women we could have made another million," they said when they balanced the books on their efforts. After ten years they had accumulated nearly a million dollars in cash, diamonds estimated to be worth $200,000 and books, paintings and tapestries worth $150,000 more. Even royalty came to the doors of the twin buildings at 2131–33 South Dearborn Street. When Prince Henry of Prussia came to Chicago he asked to be taken to the Everleigh Club and a special party was arranged in his honor. Minna, who had a professional interest in mythological revelry, had dressed all the girls in fawn skins and planned an orgy she considered worthy of the Roman gods. She had hoped to have her nymphs carrying torches but the flames smoked up the room in rehearsal and she compromised by dimming the lights. She taught the girls a ritualistic dance, the climax of which was the tearing to pieces of a bull (made of wood and cloth) in a frenzy of sexual excitement. After the dance, the girls went to their rooms and donned evening gowns, returning as fashionably dressed courtesans for a feast of steaks and champagne with the prince and his party. At first the dinner had all the formality of a royal banquet, with toasts to the prince and his brother, the Kaiser. When the table was cleared, a former dancer was lifted up for a schottische. During her dance a slipper flew off and hit a glass of champagne, spilling some of the drink into the dancing pump. "Boot liquor," said a quick-witted guest who deserves more than the anonymity which surrounds the incident. "The darling mustn't get her feet wet." He lifted the slipper to his lips and drank the champagne. The toast was imitated on the instant by almost every man in the room, who seized his partner's slipper, filled it with champagne and—according to the Everleighs—drank toasts "to the prince—to the Kaiser—and to beautiful women the world over." The episode at the Everleigh Club popularized in America, if it did not actually originate, a toast which was to be repeated a thousand times by gallant libertines.

The sisters had only one narrow brush with scandal. That they were not directly involved was attributable to their high standards and the loyalty inspired by their determination to make their girls "proud you are in the Everleigh Club." Nathaniel Ford Moore, the son of a Rock Island Railroad executive, was a frequent visitor to the Levee and a lavish entertainer. But

MUSIC ROOM AT THE EVERLEIGH CLUB (From Minna Everleigh's brochure)

when a narcotics peddler came to the door of the Everleigh Club after Moore arrived one Saturday night, he was politely asked to leave. The Everleighs banned drugs because narcotics mixed with champagne, the only drink they served, sometimes slowed the heart to the point of death. The sisters were less polite with the girl who had been entertaining Moore and who had violated the rules by making contact with a dope peddler. As a result of the quarrel, the girl quit and transferred her few belongings and talents to Vic Shaw's, a popular resort for young society men.

The incident was not considered serious until the following afternoon when Minna received a telephone call. "They're framing you," the caller told Minna. "They've got a dead man at Shaw's and they're going to plant it in your furnace. It's Nat Moore."

Minna quickly sent an emissary to Vic Shaw's. He forced his way in and found a group of madames and saloon owners meeting in one of the parlors. All were known to be hostile to the Everleighs. Minna's envoy, charging them with murder, threatened to call the police if they did not report the dead man. Vic Shaw first denied Moore was in the house but finally capitulated and asked Roy Jones, a saloon keeper who was also her liaison man with the police, to call and tell them Nat Moore was dead. The suspicion of murder did not prevail long. It was revealed that Moore had been treated in the house by a doctor that Sunday morning after a heart seizure and had died from a heart attack while sleeping in the afternoon. The police refused to become excited about a mysterious broken window in the front of Vic Shaw's. It had nothing to do with the case they said; Moore's death was "a plain case of going to the limit in the gay pace that kills." The surprising twist to the case was that Minna's caller had been the girl expelled the previous night; but she was loyal in her own way to the trademark of quality which the Everleigh Club had become in her sordid profession.

There were other hazards facing the Everleighs and the Levee district. A strong reform movement was taking shape. The man who first aroused the reform forces was not a Chicagoan but William T. Stead, English reformer and editor of the *Review of Reviews*. Stead had been among the millions attracted to Chicago by the World's Columbian Exposition. His methods were dramatic. When he was invited to give a lecture at the young University of Chicago, he sighted a pitcher of ice water near the speaker's lectern. He plunged his hand into the pitcher, seized the ice and flung it to the floor. "You Americans overheat your houses and freeze your drinking water abominably," he shouted at his startled audience. He was to be shocked by more than ice water. After a few months he called a conference of civic and religious leaders at Central Music Hall to discuss the flagrant vice, crime and political corruption. Knowing the city's traditional lack of interest in doing anything about such matters, he wakened its curiosity by promising a recital of what might happen "if Christ came to Chicago." The meeting was held without important results, but a year later when Stead published a detailed extension of his findings in a book called *If Christ Came to Chicago*, sentiment began to solidify behind a genuine effort toward reform.

Stead's principal target was political corruption which, because of a general indifference, allowed vice to flourish. He was in full agreement with another English tourist, G. W. Steevens, who found that "everybody is fighting to be rich, is then straining to be refined and nobody can attend to making the city fit to live in." Gambling was so widely tolerated that *Harper's* commented "the man with the slightest drop of sporting blood in his veins never descends to the depths where he buys his cigars. He shakes dice for them with the proprietor of his store." The Reverend Hugh F. Given of the Second Presbyterian Church thought it necessary to warn a new pastor at a public installation that "Chicago people are money and pleasure mad. In other cities the question is 'Does reform help the community?' In Chicago it is 'Does it pay?' " To this Stead added that "Here we have asserted in its baldest and plainest form the working principle on which the smart man of Chicago acts. Everything that is not illegal is assumed by him to be right . . . so long as it is permitted by law or so long as they can evade the law by any subterfuge, they consider they are doing perfectly all right. They believe in the state; they have ceased to believe in God."

The religion of the church, Stead found, had been replaced by that of the Democratic Party. It was a faith, he said, "built upon bribery, intimidation, bulldozing of every kind, knifing, shooting and the whole swimming in whiskey." Stead, who was the shrewdest kind of reformer, was aware that such political power did not survive without a better side. He found the basis for that power in talking with Democratic precinct workers. "I attained a clearer view and a surer hope for the redemption of Chicago than anything I had gained from any other conversation," he said of these talks with the party rank-and-file. "Here even in this nethermost depth was the principle of human service, there was the recognition of human obligation, set in motion, no doubt, for party reasons, and from a desire to control votes rather than to save souls. But whatever might be the motive, the result was unmistakable. Rough and rude though it might be, the Democratic Party organization and of course the Republican Party organization to a lesser extent are . . . setting in motion an agency for molding into one the heterogeneous elements of various races, nationalities and religions which are gathered together in Chicago."

The instruments of this unifying process were described by Carter Harrison II, Chicago's first native-born mayor, as a "motley crew." Looking over the Council of Aldermen with which he was supposed to administer the affairs of the city, he described it in his autobiography as a collection of "saloon keepers, proprietors of gambling houses and undertakers." As he saw the council, it was "a rare conglomeration of city fathers [that] ruled Chicago in the nineties, a great growing energetic community, whose citizens for years from lack of interest, supineness, from absolute stupidity had permitted the control of public affairs to be the exclusive appendage of a low-browed, dull-witted, base-minded gang of plug-uglies with no outstanding characteristic beyond an unquenchable lust for money, with but a single virtue, and that not possessed by all, a certain physical courage which enabled each to dominate his individual barnyard." The *Herald*, a Democratic newspaper, wrote that "the average Democratic representative is a tramp if not worse."

Not the least remarkable feature of the council was that it could still be sensitive of its honor in the face of such testimonials. In 1902, Alderman Nathan T. Brenner of the Ninth Ward asserted in the heat of an argument that there were only three aldermen in the entire group of sixty-eight who were not able and willing to steal a red-hot stove. The aldermen, who were quick to realize the futility of stealing a red-hot stove (as it would not serve as a container for currency) demanded a retraction. Otherwise, they said, they would appoint a committee to investigate Brenner. One alderman suggested however, that "if a red-hot stove has been passed around and he [Brenner] did not get a piece of it, let him speak out and tell us about it." It was necessary for Brenner to submit a written denial of the statement— which had been heard by every member of the council and a gallery of witnesses—before the bruised honor of the aldermen could be assuaged.

Subterfuge was the normal procedure for doing business in the council, one such instance providing Chicago with a subway it was unwilling to construct by legitimate methods. An ordinance had been passed permitting an independent telephone company to bore holes beneath the streets to install cables and wires for automatic telephones. The dirt was to be used in filling in more of the lake between the Illinois Central tracks and Michigan Avenue. As caravans of wagons made their way steadily toward the lake front, it was evident the quantity of dirt they were removing was far in excess of that required for the laying of a telephone cable. An investigation revealed the ordinance permitting the boring was altered after it left the council chambers and before it was legally recorded. The modified statute permitted a group of eastern speculators to dig a tunnel twelve feet wide, fourteen feet high and many miles in extent. The telephone company had served as a façade for a group planning to establish an underground freight railway on which downtown stores would be dependent for the delivery of much of their merchandise. A roar of protest was raised and charges filed against the officials responsible. As was expected, the proceedings against those accused of duplicity in the case failed and the defendants "went free and enjoyed a good lunch at Vogelsang's." The earth kept coming up until there were sixty miles of tunnel under the business district which connected the freight terminals with the principal stores.

It was generally believed that the first digging for the tunnel was done in the rear of an emporium owned by Alderman John Powers, better known as Johnny de Pow. Alderman Powers, who represented the Irish-Italian Nineteenth Ward, had an inordinate fondness for funerals and was proud to be known as Prince of the Boodlers. Boodle, or graft, had been developed to a high level of artistry at City Hall. The Civic Federation, slightly more generous than Alderman Brenner, estimated that fifty-seven out of the sixty-eight aldermen representing the city's thirty-four wards were grafters. The boodle value of an alderman's job was variously estimated at between $15,000 and $25,000 a year. For one important ordinance, a group of leading aldermen were said to have been paid $25,000 each while a larger group received a minimum of $8,000 each. On unimportant matters, an alderman cast his tally for as little as $300 or $400. Utility companies using the city's streets and alleys were the largest sources for graft. When the rights to the streets had been sold, the inventive Powers devised a method of setting up dummy competing corporations which were granted franchises. The operating companies were then forced to buy up these dummy corporations—owned in large part by the aldermen—in order to protect their established investment. Another device of the rapacious "gray wolves" of the council was to force the transit companies to "buy" new franchises when the method of operation was changed from horsecars to cable cars or electric trolleys. Powers' only difficulty in handling these matters was that of keeping the boodlers in line; some of them could only be persuaded with difficulty that it was unethical to sell out to two competing interests simultaneously. Powers' authority stemmed not only from his intellectual ingenuity but from the fact he was the representative in the council of Charles T. Yerkes, the city's traction magnate and most generous contributor of boodle. "You can't get elected to the council unless Mr. Yerkes says so," Johnny de Pow once told his constituents and there was every reason to believe it was true.

Yerkes was from Philadelphia but had more than an ordinary connection with Chicago. As a young man he had made a fortune as a flour commission merchant. When Philadelphia issued bonds which could find no purchasers at the legally established price, the city treasurer asked Yerkes to sell the bonds. Yerkes agreed, forcing the price up with his own purchases and disposing of eleven million dollars worth of the bonds in a year. The flaw in his technique was that he had been forced to buy back five million dollars worth of these same bonds to keep the price up. He might have been successful if the Chicago fire had not caused such heavy losses in the East that his loans were called sooner than he had expected and he was unable to pay. He was convicted for misappropriation of funds but pardoned upon the petition of the businessmen of Philadelphia. To his credit, he later repaid all his obligations though freed by the City Council of any legal obligations to do so. It was perhaps natural that Yerkes should think of Chicago when planning a new start.

Shortly after his arrival, he began a series of investments in street railways. After a succession of financial manipulations, he assumed control of the city's transit system and was again a multimillionaire. Operating in the council through Powers, he received his franchises at a fraction of their value. When no more revenue was to be obtained from the streets he began the construction of the elevated railway that was to form a circle around the business district and give the downtown area its characteristic name of the Loop.

Yerkes built his fortune by inflating the value of his companies' stocks rather than by service to the public. "Buy old junk, fix it up a little, unload it on the other fellow" was his expressed standard of operation. To a suggestion that he run more cars on his lines, he replied, "Why should I? It's the straphangers who pay the dividends." These and other practices met cold disapproval among the established members of the community. "He shocked me," Marshall Field told a friend after a business conference with Yerkes: "He is not safe." Such disapproval would have carried enough weight to put Yerkes out of business if the transit speculator had been dependent on local capital. But as the midwestern representative of an eastern traction ring with unlimited resources he was able to disregard public opinion with impunity in gaining control of the local transit lines. Keeping control was another matter.

To protect the value of inflated stock holdings by assuring themselves continuing franchises, Yerkes and his backers put through the state legislature a group of "Eternal Monopoly" bills which would have given Yerkes unquestioned rights to the streets for ninety-nine years. After turning down a bribe of half a million dollars from Yerkes, Governor Altgeld vetoed the bill. At the next session of the legislature, Yerkes had a new plan which would have extended his franchise for fifty years without additional compensation to the city. This bill failed in the legislature but Yerkes did succeed in putting through another bill, the Allen Law, permitting the City Council to give him the rights which the legislature had refused. Even this gesture cost him several hundred thousand dollars in bribes.

The battle shifted to Chicago, where Carter Harrison II promised to eat his brown fedora if Yerkes could pass the ordinance over the mayor's veto. The struggle was fierce and expensive. Harrison spoke in every neighborhood of the city, campaigning harder against the ordinance than if he had been

BATHHOUSE JOHN, *by John Mc-Cutcheon*

running for office. Yerkes bought a newspaper, the *Inter-Ocean*, and imported an editorial writer from New York to attack Harrison and the other newspapers. After a long tussle, the ordinance was defeated and the power of Yerkes broken. In Harrison, who, like his father, was considered a man of the people, Yerkes had met an opponent whom no amount of money could defeat.

The traction king acted quickly to sell his inflated holdings before they should collapse. He left the city for the four-million-dollar brownstone mansion he had built in New York with profits from his Chicago enterprises. There he could contemplate his collection of paintings in the largest private art gallery in the country or stroll over fine Persian rugs purchased at a cost of a million dollars to gaze at a $30,000 portrait of himself.

It was one of the recurring anomalies of Chicago politics that the defeat of Yerkes had been as much due to the efforts of two representatives from the lawless Levee district as to the forces of reform. John "The Bath" Coughlin and Michael "Hinky Dink" Kenna, the two aldermen from the First Ward, which included the Levee, were both skilled practitioners of the art of boodle. But when Yerkes came to them with an offer of $150,000 as well as other inducements for their votes, they turned him down. They had explained their reasons to Mayor Harrison at a conference a few days earlier. "Mr. Mayor," said The Bath, "I was talkin' a while back with Senator Billy Mason and he told me, 'Keep clear of th' big stuff, John, it's dangerous. You and Mike stick to th' small stuff; there's little risk and in the long run it pays a damned sight more.' . . . Mr. Maar, we're with you. An' we'll do what we can to swing some of the other boys over."

What the pair could do was considerable. Their ward was the most solidly Democratic in the city. Hinky Dink tended to the details of political organization, dealt with the police, devised strategy and worked out improved systems of chain voting. The Bath, who derived his nickname from the bathhouses of which he was proprietor, was the spokesman for the two, arguing the cause of "the people" in florid language in the council chamber and troubleshooting when collections went awry in the Levee vice district. "I formed my philosophy," The Bath soliloquized, "while watching and studying the types who patronized the bathhouses. I met 'em all, big an' little, from LaSalle Street to Armour Avenue. You could learn from everyone. Ain't much difference between the big man and the little man. One's lucky, that's all."

When The Bath and Hinky Dink attended the special convention called by Governor Altgeld in Springfield to put the state Democratic Party behind the free-silver boom, an eastern reporter wrote "These Chicago Democrats are for 16 to 1—sixteen parts whiskey and one part water." The sentimental oratory of William Jennings Bryan made a great impression on The Bath, who returned to Chicago and opened a saloon called The Silver Dollar. The walls and ceiling were adorned with gargantuan replicas of silver coins. The opening of The Bath's saloon attracted every politician in the city. As the guests arrived, they were welcomed by one-eyed Jimmy Connelly, already famed as a gate crasher. Connelly translated the E Pluribus Unum on the painted dollars as meaning "He brews us new rum" and assured anyone who would listen that "Dis is de proudest moment dat me an' de city of Chicago ever witnessed."

Hinky Dink customarily remained in the background, though he did consent to be interviewed after a trip to Europe. "Rome?—Most everybody in Rome has been dead for 2,000 years. . . . Monte Carlo?—Great place. I spent two days there an' broke even. I didn't play. That song about the man who broke the bank is just a bedtime story. The bunkerino. . . . Paris?—You sure get a run for your money in that man's town. There is no lid on that burg. Even th' stoves don't have lids in Paris."

The Bath was flamboyant enough for both men. He pretended to be a poet and frequently amused the council with his non-scanning verses, composed for him on dull news days by a newspaper reporter. The climax of his vicarious career came when he claimed authorship of a song called "Dear Midnight of Love" and arranged a special concert at the opera house where it was sung by May de Sousa, whose father was then a detective on the Levee beat. The only time The Bath was known to be reticent was when Theodore Roosevelt condescendingly remarked that the selection of Chicago for the site of a Republican convention was more a question of bathtubs (i.e., hotel rooms) than politics. "I ain't going to be unethicult for nobody," The Bath told a Record-Herald reporter who asked his views on the Republican feud over bathtubs. "It wouldn't be professional for me to butt in."

The Bath's wardrobe was even more expressive than his vocabulary. For his first appearance in the council he donned a coat of gray with matching trousers set off by a dark green waistcoat checked with white—his racing colors, he explained. His shoes were a yellow-hued tan and his shirt of brown silk. For a trip to Saratoga, he took a mountain green dress coat "cut in conservative fashion," a striped Prince Albert coat with plaid vest and plaid trousers. He augmented this basic wardrobe with a red vest with white buttons and six double-breasted white vests and a four-button cutaway. Notable among his collections of shoes were a pair of patent leather pumps with dark green tops and a pair of russet shoes with bulldog toes. Giving the press the details of his sartorial plans as he set forth for Saratoga, he explained, "I'll show them a thing or two in dress reform for the masculine gender. I want to be strictly original. I think the Prince of Wales is a lobster in his tastes. He may be all right playing baccarat and putting his coins on the right horses at the races, but when it comes to mapping out style for well-dressed America, he's simply a faded two-spot in the big deck of fashion. People have been following his lead because no other guy has the nerve to challenge him for the championship. But I'm out now for first place and you'll see his percentage drop."

The social careers of The Bath and Hinky Dink reached their apex with the First Ward Balls, annual masquerades to raise funds for the ward Democratic organization. The idea for the balls came from the annual benefit party for Lame Jimmy, the violin player at Carrie Watson's. For fifteen years Jimmy had been honored with an annual benefit, where, in the words of Carrie Watson, "joy reigned unrefined." But in 1892 when a member of the police force offended Levee proprieties by critically wounding another officer in a dispute over the attentions of a charmer, an edict went out to Lame Jimmy that he could stage no more parties. The Bath, pondering the loss of Jimmy's convivial entertainment, thought perhaps he was the man to sponsor a function to replace it. He was not thinking in terms of a party for three or four hundred people such as Jimmy had held; he thought the Seventh Regiment Armory was about right to hold the crowd he intended to invite. When the invitations were issued, saloon keepers and madames were apt in realizing it would be wise to accept and buy tickets; most freely welcomed the opportunity to renew their annual frolic. Brewers, wine merchants, distillers and other merchants dependent upon the good favor of the council were quick to volunteer supplies of liquor at special prices and buy large blocks of tickets. Waiters stood in line to pay $5 for the privilege of serving a party where tips were expected to be plentiful and large. The armory was subdivided with boxes which The Bath sold with the same enterprise he might have shown in disposing of real estate.

The ball was set for 8 o'clock but it was after midnight before the consci-

entious ladies of the Levee began to arrive. They found a large crowd jammed
around the doors to the armory but The Bath had thoughtfully arranged for
a police escort. All the girls wore costumes, most of them preferring the
scanty garb of Egyptian dancers, Indian maidens, geisha girls, gypsies and
other guises which would justify wearing an abbreviated skirt. The *Tribune*
reporter, noting a certain similarity in the costumes, reported that only a
few of the dancers were hampered by long skirts, "it being considered bad
form to wear anything that would collect germs from the floor." The Bath
had banned *Black Crook* tights of the kind worn in America's first musical
comedy, however, with the explanation that they were "too indecent."

The First Ward Ball was such a success that it had to be transferred in
subsequent years from the armory to the larger quarters of the Coliseum.
At the 1907 ball, a statistically minded reporter counted two bands, two
hundred waiters, one hundred policemen, thirty-five thousand quarts of
beer and ten thousand quarts of champagne "before they sent for reinforcements." The Bath reported that every alderman was there except those "who
are sick abed." In the boxes, champagne was a favored trouble chaser while
at three bars in the annex a battalion of bartenders was emptying seventy-
five mammoth kegs of beer. Over a hundred square-shouldered ushers with
greased hair and full dress suits were kept busy punching guests in the ribs to
keep them in line. On the dance floor, a solid jam of merrymakers danced
to a program of tunes that skipped the musical gamut from "Tipperary" to
the "Teddy Bear's Picnic" and Franz Lehar's "Merry Widow Waltz."
Hinky Dink was moved to hyperbole. "It is far ahead of anything I saw in

Paris," he said. "There is nothing like it in the world." The Bath promised that in 1908 the ball would be even more grandiose.

There were others who had plans for 1908 which did not include another First Ward Ball. One of these was Arthur Burrage Farwell, who presented a description of the 1907 affair to Mayor Fred Busse with a demand that the mayor refuse to issue a liquor license for the 1908 ball. One of the sections in the Farwell report was a *Tribune* story which said that "if a great disaster had befallen the Coliseum, there would not have been a second story worker, a dip or plug ugly, porch climber, dope fiend or scarlet woman remaining in Chicago." When the mayor told Farwell the liquor license had already been issued, the reform groups sought to get the Coliseum management to refuse The Bath and Hinky Dink the use of the auditorium. This failing, an injunction against the holding of the ball was asked. It was not granted, the judge holding that the contract with the Coliseum was sacred and inviolable. Despite the victory in the courts, the pressure was building up on The Bath to tone down his celebration. "All right, we'll compromise," he shouted at a reporter. "We won't let parents bring their children. There!"

Meanwhile, both aldermen increased their efforts to make the 1908 ball a success. Extra precautions were taken to see that nothing happened which might be considered disorderly, at least by Levee standards. (One precautionary measure was the establishment of a squad of pickpockets to mingle with the crowd and spot troublemakers.) The Bath even produced a poem for the occasion, the most pertinent portion of which read as follows:

On with the dance
Let the orgy be perfectly proper
Don't drink, smoke or spit on the floor
And say keep your eye on the copper.

More than fifteen thousand people tried to force their way into the Coliseum on the night of the ball. Traffic was at a stop in the surrounding streets and alleys. The crowd swarmed into all the bars, pushed into the annex and overflowed into the basement where an additional source of supply for beer quaffers had been established. "So close was the press," recorded the *Record-Herald*, "that even those already drunk were forced to stand erect." The ball degenerated into a riot. Tables were upset, glasses smashed and chairs broken as the more timid climbed the iron girders of the Coliseum in an effort to get out of the way. The doors and exits were firmly locked to prevent gate crashers but the pressure on one of them was so terrific that when it gave way more than fifty celebrants were dumped into the alley. The mêlée continued until midnight when it was temporarily stilled by the flourish of trumpets for the grand march. The Bath and Hinky Dink, each with an Everleigh sister on his arm, started down the floor followed by the members of the First Ward Democratic Club twenty-six abreast—the pride of Levee society and its shame. Outside, those who had not been able to get in charged the police and slugged and scratched each other until hats, bracelets, scarf pins and furs were scattered over the sidewalk. Inside, the revelry resumed after the grand march. "It's a lollapalooza," said Hinky Dink. "There are more here than ever before. All the business houses are here, all the big people. Chicago ain't no sissy town."

In an obscure box, escorted by a detective from the city's dance hall and amusement detachment, sat a spectator who was less approving of what he saw. He was Dean Walter Sumner of the Espiscopalian Cathedral of SS. Peter and Paul, newly designated chairman of the vice commission appointed by Mayor Busse. Sumner spoke affably to the Levee celebrities who greeted him and they found him "a decent fella," but he reported angrily to the mayor the next day that "The ball is a disgrace." He conceded that the demi-monde in large cities almost invariably had a yearly celebration but found "Chicago is unique in holding this revel of the underworld in a downtown building of great capacity and wide reputation." Sumner's report, plus a threat of the Roman Catholic archbishop to order a denunciation of the ball from every pulpit of his faith in the ward, forced Mayor Busse to order the balls stopped. "I'm an optimist," said The Bath, when he heard his $20,000-a-year privilege had been canceled, but his optimism ignored a growing number of omens which foreshadowed the end of the Levee and its pattern of segregated vice.

The groundwork for reform had been carefully laid by the Civic Federation under the direction of Lyman Gage. It had maintained a steady attack upon public gambling, payroll stuffing, fraudulent street paving and sweeping, registration and voting frauds, crooked assessors and collectors, opium dens and many other municipal evils. Police raids on gamblers were such a farce that the Civic Federation staged its own raid upon Harry Varnell's gambling parlors where twenty-four faro dealers, twelve croupiers and sixty other employes catered to a never-ending stream of customers. The outcome of the raid was not surprising to experienced Chicagoans—the raiders were the ones taken to jail. The law also intervened to thwart a Civic Federation raid on Condon's gambling rooms, known as the House of David. Big Jim O'Leary, whose mother's cow had started the great fire, was the proprietor of a palatial gambling temple and saloon on South Halsted Street. He boasted that "I been raided a thousand times but I've never had a real raid." After operating a gambling house all his life, Big Jim was finally subjected to a real arrest at fifty-three; he was convicted of gambling and fined $100 as a first offender. He died three years later, never having been caught in a second offense.

In addition to a frontal assault upon gambling and related evils, the Civic

THE FIRST WARD BALL, by John McCutcheon. "Led by Bathhouse John, Ten Thousand Joyless Reveling Pickpockets, Bartenders, Prostitutes and Police Captains Celebrate the Reign of Graft, While Grief-Stricken Hinky Dink Sways in the Corner."

Federation organized a division known as the Municipal Voters League to try to interest public-spirited citizens in accepting public office. The attitude of most Chicagoans was expressed by Joseph Medill when he resigned shortly before the end of his term as mayor. "Politics and office-seeking are pretty good things to let alone for a man who has intellect and individuality," Medill said. "Generally, he will get more happiness out of life, I am sure, tending his business, respecting God, his conscience and the grand jury and doing only what those powers will let him."

The man who accepted the responsibility for persuading like-minded Chicagoans to change their views and enter the fray of politics was George E. Cole, a stationer who described himself to Lincoln Steffens as a "second-rate businessman" but who looked to Steffens more "like a sea captain and he worked and talked like one. He picked a crew of nine and shouted that he was going to beat the crooks up for re-election." Cole didn't quite do all of that, but he did succeed in getting a number of young men with independent financial resources to enter public life; among them were a grandson of Joseph Medill, Robert Rutherford McCormick, who won election as alderman from the Twenty-first Ward and William E. Dever, afterward mayor. The league also secured the election of other reform candidates; if it did not change the nature of Chicago politics at least it provided a temporary leavening which made it possible to do away with the worst abuses of the past.

There were other evidences of a revolt against lawlessness, not all of them of equal significance. Carrie Nation visited the First Ward saloon of Hinky Dink and announced she had come "to pray not to smash." Virginia Brooks, who had led a chopping expedition against the red-light district of Hammond, Indiana, transferred her energies to Chicago. She organized an anti-vice parade in which five thousand people marched despite a downpour of rain. Lucy Page Gaston carried her anti-tobacco crusade through the doors of the Everleigh Club. "There is something you must do," she told Minna. "You alone can stop your girls from going straight to the devil. You must make them stop smoking cigarettes."

Evangelist Gypsy Smith led a crowd of several thousand into the Levee and held a series of prayer meetings in the street, one of them in front of the Everleigh Club. All the brothels were shuttered and dark while the evangelist and his followers held their meeting but as soon as they left the lights went up and the Levee was as wide open as ever. Many sightseers who had come in the wake of the reformers entered the portals of the Levee houses. "I was sorry to see so many young men coming down here for the first time," Minna Everleigh said the following morning.

The most effective ammunition against the Levee was that provided by Dean Walter Sumner and the Vice Commission which Mayor Busse had appointed. The commission's 311-page report was so specific and sensational that it was barred from the mails. The commission found that the profits of the red-light traffic amounted to more than fifteen million dollars per year. For the benefit of the practically minded city, the commission computed the capitalized value of a prostitute at $26,000. This compared with the $6,000 value of a girl clerking in a store, computed on the same basis. Madames in the brothels could count on an income of from $100 to $500 a week. At the Everleigh Club, the commission estimated the sisters cleared about $100,000 a year. Minna confirmed that it was a good guess, saying the figure was actually $120,000.

Although the Everleighs were the most powerful madames of the Levee, their house was the first to be closed. The immediate cause of their downfall was the desire of Minna to be an author. Not content with the generous publicity given the club by the newspapers, Minna prepared an illustrated brochure describing the attractions of the Everleigh Club and including pictures of its many parlors. (The second edition added a suggestion that the visitors might like to see the stockyards, another great Chicago attraction.) The brochure was so widely distributed that Mayor Carter Harrison II, who succeeded Busse, found himself chided about it by every visitor. Like his father, Harrison had believed that segregated vice was inevitable, but after a narrow victory over the reform candidate, Charles E. Merriam, whose campaign was shrewdly run by Harold Ickes, Harrison saw that new forces were at work. He ordered all vice flats off Michigan Avenue and followed this with an order closing the Everleigh Club because of the flagrant publicizing of the city's evil through Minna's brochure.

The police hesitated to enforce the closing order, even though it had come from the mayor himself; that night the Everleigh Club was still open. The sisters had been tipped off, however, and there was a desperate gaiety animating the celebrations as lights blazed in every parlor, music rang through the tapestried halls and wine corks popped in every room. Shortly after midnight a police lieutenant and a squad of patrolmen knocked at the door. "From downtown," explained the lieutenant. "Nothing we can do about it." Minna was not perturbed. "If the mayor says we must close, that settles it," she said. "I'm not going to be sore about it either. I never was a knocker and nothing the police of this town can do to me will change my disposition. I'll close up my shop and walk out of the place with a smile on my face."

There was no excitement. The patrons had been forewarned and they left quietly. A line of carriages and cabs, their drivers informed of the potential closing through their own sources of information, waited in line much as they might have before the curtain was to be rung down on a play. At the door, well-dressed gentlemen lingered over their farewells; optimists like The Bath, they did not believe the order was irrevocable. But the Everleighs themselves made no effort to reopen. They lived quietly on the West Side of Chicago, coming downtown only for trips to the theater or to McClurg's bookstore, where Minna was a frequent visitor, her literary bent still unsatisfied.

With the passing of the Everleigh Club, such glamour as had affixed itself to the shoddy traffic of the Levee vanished. The following year the State's Attorney, John E. Wayman, caught in the crossfire of the city's war over reform, issued 135 vice warrants for houses in the Levee. When the city's police served only twenty of the warrants, Wayman ordered his own men into the city with instructions to raid all the brothels and gambling parlors they found open and to keep raiding them until they remained closed. With Wayman's action, segregated vice in Chicago came to an end.

PART FOUR *The Inheritance*

1910=1930

One Ecstasy After Another

AFTER THE turn of the century a new kind of commerce animated Chicago. From the prairie states that produced the grain and livestock which funneled through Chicago for the East came a sudden outpouring of writers, all of them attracted by the vigor and promise of the young city by the lake. These new arrivals traded as voraciously and as greedily in ideas as any early speculator dickered in real estate. They found in Chicago an eager if often uninformed audience, willing to tolerate artistic experiment and to give an unprejudiced acceptance to artistic forms which represented a break with the traditions of older communities. The period of their activity was brief. Like the hundreds of trains which daily snaked into Chicago's rail terminals, many paused only long enough to refuel—or perhaps to switch tracks or change to another line. But no one was to forget they had passed by.

There was always to be a transient quality about Chicago's relations with the arts. A few years earlier young George Spoor and E. H. Ahmet had been among the pioneer experimenters with a new kind of drama which could be represented by moving figures on film. In their Essanay (S and A) studios on the North Side, they had formed the nucleus of a film colony that brought to the screen Wallace Beery, Gloria Swanson, Lewis Stone, Colleen

Moore, Edward Arnold and Tom Mix. By 1910 one-fifth of all the movies in the world were being made in Chicago. Carl Laemmle, hearing of the opportunities in the young film industry, sold his clothing business in Oshkosh, Wisconsin, to open a Chicago movie theater. Adolph Zukor gave up the fur business he established in Chicago after the World's Columbian Exposition to investigate the possibilities of these new films. But as soon as the industry prospered it fled its North and West Side studios for California. There, the owners explained, it was possible to make motion pictures outdoors without the expense of artificial lighting—an economy necessary to pay the salaries of such stars as Francis X. Bushman who demanded and received $125 a week. Bushman was so popular that the department stores discouraged his visits—they were afraid he would distract their girl clerks and shoplifters would have a holiday. The hostile Chicago climate was another factor in the move. In the winter, the actors, like the musicians of Theodore Thomas, suffered too much from colds and coughs. Even the growth of the city militated against the screen pioneers. The prairies used in the western films which formed most of the industry's product were vanishing in the ever accelerating expansion of the city itself.

The literary journalists, who as in earlier years formed the center of the new writing ferment, were a hardier strain. They brought to bear on the problems of writing a fresh view, based on the reporter's traditional disrespect for authority and a skill in dealing with the raw materials of the drama to be found in ordinary daily life. They worked individually, but because there was a fundamental similarity in their approach they came to be known as the Chicago school. Together they formed an academy from whose writings the best authors of the twentieth century were to acquire their precepts and maxims.

Because it was a time for muckraking, there was a strong tone of social protest in much of the writing. Frank Norris, famous as a war correspondent, was drawn back to the city of his birth to write *The Pit*, a fictional account of the gargantuan manipulations in grain and dollars on the Board of Trade that was intended to be part of an epic trilogy on wheat. Theodore Dreiser, gone on to New York but remembering his Chicago newspaper days, drew on Chicago's Charles T. Yerkes to create the character of Frank Cowperwood, hero of his novels *The Financier* and *The Titan*. The stockyards were the magnet for the young social rebel, Upton Sinclair, who wrote with sociological meticulousness and called his novel of stockyards life *The Jungle*. No sociological tract was ever so effective in dramatizing the need for reform as his novel. Robert Herrick, a professor at the new University of Chicago who claimed the city as his permanent home, took a skeptical look at politics in *The Memoirs of an American Citizen*. In the novel, he told of the accepted devices by which a poor Indiana boy might rise to the heights of the

United States Senate. Some readers called it cynical; others saw in it an effort to unmask some of the hypocrisy of politics.

The revolt against the old order in society extended to a rebellion against traditional forms in expression. It was here that the Chicago influence was to be greatest. The first prophet of this revolution in language was Harriet Monroe. Bored with composing odes for civic dedications and teaching elocution to the children of wealthy families, she announced a new magazine, called with a poet's economy of words, *Poetry*. It was to be centered entirely around poets and their work. There were many reasons why poets could look to Harriet Monroe for leadership. One which was basic was her unique ability to make poetry pay in the best Chicago business manner. When she was asked to write a Columbian Ode for the exposition of 1893, she demanded twice the sum the national commission offered her and held out until the committee of businessmen met her terms. When the New York *World* published the ode prematurely, she sued that publication and collected an additional $5,000 for her efforts. She did not compromise easily. A portion of her ode was a tribute to her brother-in-law, architect John Wellborn Root, who before his death had sketched out the ground design for the Columbian Exposition. The national commission did not think it should subsidize eulogies to relatives, however distinguished, and asked to have the lines deleted. Miss Monroe refused, fighting her cause with such fervor that the commission finally conceded defeat and voted to let the verses remain. It was not surprising that when Harriet Monroe founded *Poetry*, she specified that it would pay its poets.

The disrespect for established precedents, a Chicago trait, was important to *Poetry's* success. "The old prosody is a medieval left-over," Harriet Monroe proclaimed. "It is as completely out of relation with the modern scientific spirit as astrology would be if solemnly enunciated from the summit of Mount Wilson. All the old terms should be scrapped and a modern science of speech rhythms should be built up." Fortunately for Miss Monroe's aspirations, there were in Chicago two young writers with the ability to express in poetic form the substance of her editorial theories. They were Carl Sandburg, soon to be a movie critic and later an editorial writer on the *Daily News*, and Edgar Lee Masters, a law partner of Clarence Darrow who was experimenting with a number of free verse styles that he was to merge into the form of his *Spoon River Anthology*, published in 1915.

Sandburg's *Chicago Poems* were the signal of a break as defiant as Dreiser's *Sister Carrie* had been. William Morton Payne, defending the old order in *The Dial*, read Sandburg's verses with horror. Most of Sandburg's lines, he said indignantly, "were nothing less than an impudent affront to the poetry loving public." Payne refused to recognize the *Chicago Poems* by the name of poetry, calling them only a "collocation of words descriptive of Chicago."

To those who questioned his ideas about poetry, Sandburg replied: "Here's the difference between us and Dante: He wrote a lot about Hell and never saw the place. We're writing about Chicago after looking the town over."

Sandburg, going his independent wanderer's way, insisted that the spoken language of the people was the only proper language for poetry. The artist, he said, should express his sympathy for people by speaking with their tongues and out of their hearts. "Unless we keep on the lookout," he warned, "we write book language and employ the verbiage of dead men instead of using the speech of people alive today, people whose tools, games and sacrifices are wearing out an old language and making a new one." Of style, in his *Chicago Poems*, he said this:

> Style—go ahead talking about style.
> You can tell where a man got his style just
>   as you can tell where Pavlowa got her legs
>   or Ty Cobb his batting eye.
>
> Go on talking.
> Only don't take my style away
> It's my face.
> Maybe no good
> but anyway, my face.
> I talk with it, I sing with it, I see, taste and
>   feel with it, I know why I want to keep it.

Sandburg was a radical in the American tradition of Thomas Paine (one of his early jobs had been as secretary to the socialist mayor of Milwaukee). His poems were filled with protests against social injustices and he defied all those who called them propaganda. Because of his Whitmanesque style, his liberal social ideas and his solid Scandinavian stubbornness, he became the foremost target of traditional critics attacking the new free verse ideas being expressed by the contributors to *Poetry*. But as Sandburg stood almost alone, he was less alone; more and more writers sent along their own experimental ideas to Harriet Monroe. T. S. Eliot, Robert Frost, Ezra Pound, John Masefield and Edna St. Vincent Millay were among those who forwarded contributions. A new language was in the making in the crude commercial city of Chicago; out of this new kind of melting pot was to pour the bright, fresh metal of a modern American literature.

It was a time for individualists. Vachel Lindsay, a friend of Edgar Lee Masters who chanted poems aloud for a free meal or a night's lodging, was another of the experimenters. Lindsay was an odd combination of poet, evangelist and troubadour. He dressed carelessly and his hair was usually tousled; but his face was keen and there was the aura of an inner peace that gave him dignity, even when he chose to address audiences on such a topic as the Anti-Saloon League. Abraham Lincoln, whose mark and memorials were everywhere in Springfield where Lindsay was born, was the poet's idol, an emotion which was to find its artistic expression in "Abraham Lincoln Walks at Midnight." Lindsay's poetry was written to be read aloud and he did not stir up the intellectual controversy which Sandburg evoked. But as Lindsay spoke the lines of "General William Booth Enters into Heaven" or "The Congo" he echoed the ideas of the literary rebels.

The Dial stood disdainfully apart from this clangorous new literature. A new critical magazine soon erupted, however, whose mood was suited to the bold and often wild experimentation of the Chicago school. It was The Little Review, founded by Margaret Anderson—just turned twenty-one years of age and feeling "it was time to confer upon life that inspiration without which life is meaningless." The Little Review, she announced, would be a new kind of critical journal and "the most interesting magazine that had ever been launched." She tossed out the "objective and scientific criticism" which had been the goal of The Dial's editors. She accepted or rejected manuscripts on only one basis: art as the person. "An artist is an exceptional person," she wrote. "Such a person has something exceptional to say. Exceptional matter makes an exceptional manner. This is 'style!' In an old but expressive phrase, 'style is the man.' "

The first issue of The Little Review had only a slight relation to Chicago. Its most notable contribution was a letter from John Galsworthy. "It seems you are setting out to watch the street of life from a high balcony where at all events the air should be fresh and sunrise sometimes visible," he wrote. "I hope you will decide to sleep out there under the stars, for what kills

MARGARET ANDERSON'S CAMP AT BRAESIDE

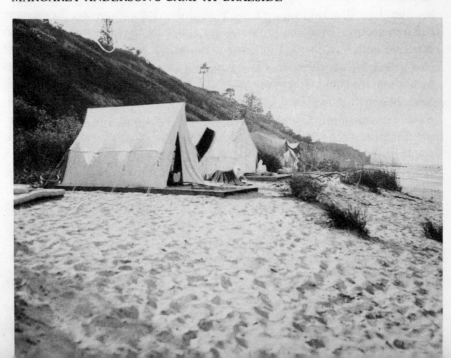

most literary effort is the hothouse air of temples, clubs and coteries." Margaret Anderson, with no source of funds for her magazine, was to be taken literally out under the stars of which Galsworthy wrote. All the money which she and Jane Heap, her chief collaborator on the magazine, could raise went into assuring its publication. When there was no money remaining to pay rent for the home which she occupied with her sister and two little boys, Margaret Anderson, "feeling that inspiration was demanded of me and that it was about to descend," followed Chicago custom by seeking a better place to live along the lake shore north of the city. At Ravinia, she walked east to the lake near Braeside, where she found a wide strip of beach that had not been claimed by any summer colony. Returning home, she loaded her few possessions, her family, and the oriental rugs which were her particular delight into a wagon and headed for the lake shore. En route, she acquired some tents and a few dollars worth of lumber for floors on which to unroll the expensive oriental rugs. In this sandy atmosphere the little group spent the entire summer, living like gypsies and roasting corn over the campfire and baking potatoes in its ashes. Each tent was equipped only with a soldier's cot, a deck chair and an oriental rug. After an early-morning swim by moonlight, Margaret Anderson commuted to Chicago to work on *The Little Review*. Her wardrobe consisted of a blouse that did not need to be ironed, one hat and one blue suit. The blouse was washed at night and donned again in the morning after being dried over the open fire. The campers stayed on the beach until the middle of November when, after a final cold swim, they moved to an empty and furnitureless apartment in the city.

The Little Review was as unorthodox financially as artistically. A luncheon date with a stranger might produce a check for enough to publish one issue. The next issue would be published the same way. Eunice Tietjens, the poet, came bearing a diamond ring. "I don't want this any more," she told Margaret Anderson. "Sell it and bring out an issue." Frank Lloyd Wright gave a hundred dollars. Contributors went without pay; Margaret Anderson believed magazines which paid writers could not afford to publish the material which went into *The Little Review*. She assumed in her confident and exuberant way that writers agreed it was better to be published without pay than to remain unprinted. Her contributors were the measure of her foresight. They included Sherwood Anderson, Malcolm Cowley, Gertrude Stein, Wyndham Lewis, Hart Crane, T. S. Eliot, Aldous Huxley, Marianne Moore and Ernest Hemingway. Sinclair Lewis was not completely happy with her ideas. He wrote that her theories of art for art's sake were too remote from the common herd and urged her to become interested in the psychology of the average person as well as that of the exceptional person. Upton Sinclair was more disapproving. "Please cease sending me *The Little Review*," he wrote. "I no longer understand anything in it, so it no longer interests me."

To this Margaret Anderson replied: "Please cease sending me your socialist paper. I understand everything in it, therefore it no longer interests me."

Margaret Anderson and Jane Heap were never at a loss for a means of getting attention. When there was nothing of interest to publish, they produced an issue of sixty-four empty pages, stating that since no art was being produced they could not publish any. Only the two center pages of the magazine contained some sketches of their activities—the Mason and Hamlin piano Margaret played, anarchist meetings (she was a disciple of Emma Goldman), horseback riding, fudge breakfasts and intellectual combats. "Life," said Margaret Anderson about this time, "is just one ecstasy after another."

Sherwood Anderson, restless in his job as an advertising copywriter, used *The Little Review* to set out his goals as a writer. "What I quarrel with is writers who look outside themselves for their material," he wrote. "It is the most unbelievably difficult task to catch, understand and record your own mood." His statement was a reiteration of the right to personal judgment characteristic of the Chicago school. "In the trade of writing the so-called new note is as old as the world," he wrote another time. "Simply stated, it is a cry for the re-injection of truth and honesty into the craft . . . In all the world there is no such thing as an old sunrise, an old wind upon the cheeks or an old kiss from the lips of your beloved; and in the craft of writing there can be no such thing as age in the souls of the young poets and novelists who demand for themselves the right to stand up and be counted among the soldiers of the new."

Anderson was less agile than Dreiser or Sandburg in finding his place among the soldiers of the new. He wrote of ordinary men in average situations within a framework of form so loose as to be in some cases unrecognizable. Publishers for his books were found with difficulty, and then only after the insistent recommendations of Dreiser and the Chicago critics. Anderson tried to break away from his advertising job but was forced to return to it. Then suddenly, stimulated by the experimentation of the other writers in Chicago, he burst forth with the luminous *Winesburg, Ohio*, a book conceived in a form so distinctively individual there was never to be a name for it. *Winesburg* had been written out of the conflict between materialism and the creative instinct which Anderson recognized in his dual personal life as an advertising writer and novelist; it was a conflict accurately mirrored in the city around him. Yet with the establishment of his reputation as a writer Anderson lost interest in the struggle which had produced *Winesburg* and sought to escape it. "Great projects arise within me," he wrote. "I have a brain and it is cunning and shrewd. I want leisure to become beautiful and there is no leisure." Like many others, he left Chicago in search of beauty unmarred by paradoxes. It was too late for

Anderson to be persuaded that the material out of which he created beauty lay all about him in Chicago—the "grotesques," as he called them, of *Winesburg*, were the same awkward mortals who formed the throngs of Chicago's streets.

Margaret Anderson, too, was ready to move on to New York. "I found my reasons for wanting to go," she wrote in *My Thirty Years War*. "Chicago had all it wanted from me and we had all that it could give. It was time to touch the greatest city of America. It would then be time for Europe. We hadn't as yet met all the interesting people of the world." In New York there remained only one final, glorious chapter for *The Little Review*. Month after month for a period of three years, the magazine published the first installments of James Joyce's *Ulysses*, and four times the post office seized and burned the copies as obscene. Margaret Anderson called it "a burning at the stake." Brought into court by the Society for the Suppression of Vice for having published Joyce's Episode XIII, Margaret Anderson was as irreverent as the pages of her magazine. She was found guilty and given a light fine, thereby establishing indisputably her claim to having introduced America to the most influential novel of modern times. *The Little Review* finally faltered and failed, joining the many magazines of which Keith Preston wrote:

> Among our literary scenes
> Saddest this sight to me;
> The graves of little magazines
> That died to make verse free.

The emigrants to New York were many. They had been touched by Chicago and having, as Margaret Anderson said, all that it could give, went on to touch the greatest city of America; some of them went on with the editor of *The Little Review* to Paris. First had gone Dreiser, then Francis Hackett, the brilliant literary editor of the Chicago *Evening Post*. Ring Lardner, who had given up conducting his column "In the Wake of the News" for the *Tribune*, was writing his baseball stories in New York. The diamond-sharp Percy Hammond, drama critic on the *Tribune*, had been hired away to New York, to be followed in less style by the incisive Burton Rascoe after he was fired from the *Tribune* for a slighting reference to Mary Baker Eddy, but taking with him a reputation made by his perceptive discovery and popularizing of James Branch Cabell and from his literary feuds with Ben Hecht and Henry Blackman Sell, then literary editor of the *Daily News*. Edna Ferber, walking miles and miles along the lake and "finding it exhilarating," had taken the typewriter she pounded in an isolated South Side room and moved to the East; but not without a note of affection for one of the "most vital, unformed, fascinating, horrible, brutal, civilized and beautiful cities in the world." Floyd Dell, the protégé of Francis Hackett on the *Post*, was gone, too. It was Dell who planted the seed of *The Little Review's* flowering with his instruction to Margaret Anderson, then one of his apprentice reviewers: "Here is a book about China," he said. "Now don't send me an article about China but about yourself." The departure of Dell left a void in the Bohemian colony which had grown up in the group of low red buildings which clustered around the corner of Fifty-seventh Street and Stony Island as dilapidated reminders of the World's Columbian Exposition for which they had been erected. To the colony of which Dell and his wife, Margery Currey, were the central figures came Sherwood Anderson, Sandburg, poet Eunice Tietjens with her oriental dances and Thorstein Veblen and Robert Morss Lovett from the nearby University of Chicago. It was here that those free spirits, Maxwell Bodenheim, universally known as "Bogie," and Ben Hecht, indulged their whims and fantasies as well as their fondness for obscene poetry and practical jokes.

Hecht and Bodenheim, drifting between the city's bohemian clubs and the bookstore of Pascal Covici and Billy McGee on Washington Street served as a rear guard for the army of writers which conquered Chicago and then moved on toward the citadel of New York. Remaining in Chicago were only the deep-rooted Sandburg, Vincent Starrett, who penned shocking lyrics for relaxation, made scholarly investigations of Sherlock Holmes and wrote detective stories, poet Lew Sarrett, young Harry Hansen, the precocious war correspondent who patrolled the borders of new literature for the *Daily News*; and the two Bohemians, Bodenheim and Hecht.

Hecht, a child prodigy who had given his first violin concert at the age of ten, was a columnist on the *Daily News*. An irrepressible prankster, he dominated the gatherings at Covici and McGee's bookstore that were reminiscent of the crowd at the Saints and Sinners Corner of McClurg's a generation earlier. In 1923, Hecht persuaded Pascal Covici to underwrite a publication which he called the *Chicago Literary Times* but which was chiefly an outlet for Hecht's Rabelaisian humor. The first issue offered this salutation: "Chicago, the jazz baby—the reeking, cinder ridden, joyous Baptist stronghold, Chicago the chewing gum center of the world, the bleating, slant-headed rendezvous of sociopaths and pants makers—in the name of the seven Holy Imperishable Arts, Chicago salutes you." It was a tenet of the paper that headlines should be unconnected with the stories which followed them. Neither Hecht nor Bodenheim had the talent to make purposeful use of their ardent iconoclasm; when they tired of their efforts to shock Chicago they moved on to New York as the other writers had done.

There were traces of earlier glories. A few writers, most of them from the *Daily News* where Sandburg, Henry Justin Smith, Keith Preston, Lloyd Lewis and Harry Hansen still held forth, met for luncheons at Schlogl's and

LUNCH AT SCHLOGL'S, 1925. Seated, left to right: Philip Davis, Alfred MacArthur, Ashton Stevens, William F. McGee, Charles Collins, Harry Hansen, Leroy T. Goble, John Gunther, Peter Hecht, Dr. Morris Fishbein, J. U. Nicholson, Lloyd Lewis. Standing: Richard Schneider, Dwight Haven, Keith Preston, Pascal Covici, Ben Hecht, Vincent Starrett, Henry Justin Smith

exchanged wisecracks with visiting authors, Clarence Darrow, Senator J. Hamilton Lewis or other celebrities who had a tolerance for artistic eccentricities.

Jack Jones, a member of the International Workers of the World, or Wobblies, organized the Dill Pickle Club in a "deverminized garret" at 18 Tooker Street near the city's Gold Coast area of elegant apartments. Here speakers were invited to be insulted and wit more rude than original was poured out in a loud stream. A more sedate literary center, a favorite with such visitors as Rabindranath Tagore and John Masefield as well as many local poets, was the home of Harriet Moody, the widow of William Vaughn Moody. In a large brick home in a section of Chicago no longer fashionable, Mrs. Moody entertained genteelly with butlers and maids, winning such a reputation as a hostess that she was able to expand her income by founding a catering service.

By the early 1920's, most of this literary activity had receded. When H. L. Mencken bestowed the accolade of literary capital of the United States on

Chicago, most of those who had been the legislators of the new rules of literature were gone. Among the leaders, only Sandburg and Anderson remained. Yet Mencken's words, if read more closely than Chicagoans eager for honors were inclined to read them, took cognizance of this, too. "In Chicago," he wrote in an effort to explain the city to English readers of *The Nation* of London, "there is the mysterious something that makes for individuality, personality and charm. In Chicago a spirit broods upon the face of the waters. Find a writer who is indubitably an American in every pulse-beat, snort and adenoid, an American who has something new and peculiarly American to say and who says it in an unmistakable American way and nine times out of ten you will find that he has some sort of connection with the gargantuan and inordinate abbattoir by Lake Michigan— that he was bred there, or got his start there or passed through there in the days when he was young and tender." It was a city, Mencken said, which offered "free play for prairie energy . . . some imaginative equivalent for the stupendous activity they were bred to."

Although Mencken was to repudiate this tribute in a few years, his initial instinct had been right. Not all the writers he praised were Chicagoans, to be sure, but it took very little to put the mark of Chicago on a man or woman who had once been part of the teeming city. The entire literary upheaval that was in later years to be called a renaissance was concentrated in less than ten years; the founding of *Poetry*, *The Little Review*, and the publication of Sandburg's *Chicago Poems* had been concentrated in less than five.

When the writers left, the jazz musicians came. Their stay was equally brief. Louis Armstrong, following King Oliver from New Orleans to the Lincoln Gardens in Chicago, knew "it was just an accident that swing and I were born and brought up side by side in New Orleans, traveled up the Mississippi together and in 1922 . . . were there in Chicago getting acquainted with the North and the North getting acquainted with us." It wasn't Chicago jazz that Louis Armstrong played but New Orleans jazz— and yet it was Chicago that put his name in lights for the first time. It was in Chicago too that young Muggsy Spanier, Frank Teschmaker, Jess Stacy and George Wettling sneaked in to hear Armstrong play. It was in Chicago that young Bix Beiderbecke skipped his classes to play the cornet in prohibition dives. And it was in Chicago that five kids from Austin High School—Jim Lannigan, Jimmy McPartland, his brother, Dick, Frank Teschmaker and Bud Freeman—took New Orleans jazz and gave it the beat that was recognizably Chicago jazz. It was a town where Benny Goodman learned to play the clarinet—but a town that wouldn't listen to what he had to say about how it ought to be played.

For movie-makers, writers or musicians Chicago was a town where somebody was always coming or going—going down to the shadows of those skyscrapers that were a tribute to the imagination of Chicagoans of nearly half a century before. It was a city that had ideas too big for any but the largest city in the land; and it wasn't quite that big yet.

AL CAPONE

22

Nobody's on the Legit

THERE WAS always an irony about Chicago's efforts at reform. The Municipal Voters League, seeking a nominee for alderman in the Second Ward in 1902, had accepted the recommendations put forward for the son of a prominent citizen. The league was told the young man was able to finance his own campaign and could do no harm. "The worst that you can say of him is that he's stupid," the league was advised. The young man, who won a place in the council with the league's backing, was William Hale Thompson.

Bill Thompson had shown very little aptitude for education as a youth and was sent west to a ranch where he substituted the uninhibited pleasures of cowboy life for more arduous intellectual pursuits. Back in Chicago, he found the rough-and-tumble of Chicago politics a congenial activity. Forming an alliance with the least desirable faction of the Republican Party, he was able to emerge as the Republican candidate for mayor in the election of 1915. His Democratic opponent was Robert Sweitzer, who with the support of the German communities had wrested the Democratic nomination from Carter Harrison II. The campaign, in a city in which nearly a third of the population was foreign-born, carried bitter echoes of the fighting which had broken out in Europe after the assassination at Sarajevo. As anti-German sentiment increased, Sweitzer's German associations were transformed from an asset to a liability. Thompson, with the aid of disgruntled Harrison forces, was able to win the mayoralty.

The mayor soon established a reputation for unpredictability. First, he opened the door for unrestricted gambling and then, to satisfy the reform element, he ordered the saloons closed on Sunday. One of the persons to profit from this abortive reform effort was George Wellington Streeter, a soldier of fortune who had staked out a claim to Chicago's lake front and who for thirty years was able to defy a city grown to two and a half million people. Streeter, a former Mississippi River steamboat pilot and circus proprietor, had run aground on a sandbar off the shoreline in 1886 while testing, more or less soberly, a craft named *The Reutan* with which he hoped to make a fortune running guns for South American revolutions. Unable to dislodge his ship and separated from land by only a shallow strip of water, Streeter decided to make his home on the *Reutan*. Through the years the water separating him from the shore filled with sediment until the *Reutan* rested on the mainland. This suggested to Streeter that he might claim the land as an annexation of the island where the *Reutan* was lodged, basing his assertion on an 1821 survey which showed the shores of Lake Michigan to be much farther to the west. Christening his land the District of Lake Michigan, he announced he owed allegiance only to the federal government and named a crony, William Niles, as military governor of the district. With a battered top hat perched on the back of his head and wearing a stained frock coat, he opened offices in the Tremont House and spent his days exhibiting to gullible purchasers the documents on which he founded his right to the valuable lake front property.

In 1889, five constables sought to evict Streeter, but he drove them away from the "deestrict," as he called it, at the point of a rifle. Ten years later, after extended litigation in which Streeter challenged such formidable opponents as Potter Palmer and N. K. Fairbank, a group of policemen managed to capture the squatter but were routed by a kettleful of boiling water thrown by his loyal wife, Maria. On another occasion, Streeter sent two bullets crashing through the buggy of a police captain and a force of five hundred police was sent to the shore to capture him. Learning of the prospective attack, Streeter moved in an army of hoboes and squatters who dug in behind a series of driftwood barricades. The arsenal of Streeter's defense force consisted principally of rocks, stones and clubs with just enough rifles to make an attack dangerous. When the police charged, a volley of rifle fire caused the attackers to fall back for further orders. The delay in the battle worked to their advantage; by nightfall a large part of Streeter's unstable army had been demoralized by rumors and deserted. Cap Streeter was taken the next day, but the police found they had no specific charge on which to hold him—firing at a Chicago police officer not being considered a crime at the time. When Streeter later shot an intruder in his district with a load of buckshot he made such an eloquent defense as his own attorney that the jury acquitted him. But when he killed a night watchman whom he accused of being a trespasser, Streeter was finally sent to the penitentiary. His term was a light one and he returned to re-establish his claim to the district. The ludicrous spectacle of a squatter defying the entire city continued until the advent of Thompson. Then Streeter incurred the mayor's wrath by doing a lively Sunday business in beer and whiskey after the saloons were ordered closed. The District of Lake Michigan became a favorite resort for thirsty Chicagoans. The mayor ordered the liquor sale stopped and erected a fence to keep Streeter out of his lake-shore shack, but Streeter hacked it down. Finally, exasperated, the police dispossessed him and burned his shack and all its trimmings. The farce was over—though Streeter continued to press his ludicrous claim in the courts.

Thompson's eviction of Streeter and his closing of the saloons on Sunday—which was soon dropped—were about his only gestures in the direction of law enforcement. Slot machines appeared in such numbers that the saloons took on a frontier aspect. Gambling houses were running wide open. Graft piled into City Hall just as it had in the worst days of the gray wolves.

Meanwhile, there were formidable problems to be faced. The United States entered the war in 1917 and the large foreign and German population of·Chicago was watched closely for any signs of disaffection such as had occurred during the Civil War. Frederick Stock, the city's beloved symphony conductor, resigned because he had not taken out his naturalization papers. Technically an alien, he did not wish to embarrass his sponsors (who rehired him immediately after the armistice). Thompson was so openly hostile to the war effort his opponents called him "Kaiser Bill." He spoke out against the national draft law and opposed supplying food to America's allies. When Marshal Joffre of France visited America, Thompson refused to invite the French hero to Chicago. "Are these foreign visitors coming here to encourage the doing of things to make our people suffer further or have they some other purpose?" he asked rhetorically. The City Council, not yet powerless, rebuked him by issuing a unanimous invitation to Joffre to come to Chicago. The war was to cause no harm to Thompson's political fortunes, however. When the draft took thousands of men from Chicago industries, Thompson was quick to exploit the new voters from the South who arrived to take the empty places in Chicago industries. The southern Negro, a free man for nearly sixty years but never recognized as an equal by his former masters, rushed to Chicago in such numbers that the Negro population quadrupled in only two years. Thompson, sensing the voting power of this largely uneducated group, established himself as its political champion.

Thompson counted heavily on these new voters when he ran for re-election in 1919. To get the city's mind off such troubles as a treasury in which a three-million-dollar surplus had been dissipated and turned to a four-and-a-half-million-dollar deficit, Thompson organized the Chicago Boosters Club. Businessmen were asked, under the threat of facing difficulty in having their licenses renewed, to contribute a million dollars to help "publicize Chicago." The cry was, "Throw away your hammer and get a horn." Big posters went up all over town. "A booster is better than a knocker!" Others said "All hats off to our mayor, Big Bill, the Builder."

A report on Big Bill's term of office had this to say: "Caesar Augustus found Rome a village of wood and brick; he left it a marvelous city of stone and marble. William Hale Thompson found Chicago with many unsightly spots, congested streets and a lack of recreation facilities; he is making it a city beautiful with wider thoroughfares, monumental buildings and all modern conveniences." The achievements of which Thompson boasted were in reality those of Daniel Burnham's Chicago Plan; they had been accomplished in spite of the fact he was in the mayor's chair rather than because of it. Chicago must have sensed this truth beneath the propaganda; though Thompson won his second term, his margin of victory was measured in his plurality in the poverty-burdened wards of the South Side where Chicago's new workers had been forced to settle in a black ghetto.

Thompson's interest in the new arrivals was only political, and he made little effort to ameliorate their conditions. On a July Sunday in 1919, a Negro boy who crossed an invisible line at a bathing beach used by both Negroes and whites was stoned and drowned. A policeman was called but he passed by the white man accused of starting the stone throwing and arrested a Negro. Trouble signals went out. The Negroes, fearing a recurrence of the terror under which they lived in the South, rushed to the beach. Police reinforcements arrived simultaneously. A Negro fired at the police and was shot down. The following day there were riots on the crowded streetcars; before the disturbances were quelled, thirty Negroes were injured and four Negroes and one white man were killed. At midnight, the streetcar workers went out on strike (over issues unrelated to the riots). With the public vehicles gone from the streets, automobiles filled with young hoodlums and race-crazed fanatics sped through the Negro area, shooting capriciously at anyone in sight. Two Negroes were murdered on downtown streets. Mayor Thompson, their champion, consented to ask Governor Frank O. Lowden for state troops only after a series of delaying actions. The arrival of five thousand state troops, most of them only half-trained recruits, was a sufficient show of force to stop the riots.

It was an era for madness. In 1924, two University of Chicago students, Richard Loeb, seventeen, and Nathan Leopold, eighteen, committed the purposeless thrill murder of fourteen-year-old Robert Franks. Trapped through an unusual pair of eyeglasses dropped by Leopold, the two young murderers were brought to court for trial. Defending them was Clarence Darrow—"sixty-eight years old and very weary . . . tired of standing in the lean, lonely front line and facing the greatest enemy that ever confronted man—public opinion." Darrow, champion of the workingman, was moved to take the case because of the same sympathies which had led him to identify his own cause with that of the poor. "In a terrible crisis, there is only one element more helpless than the poor," he wrote. "And that is the rich." His skillful defense enabled Loeb and Leopold to escape execution in the electric chair and they were given life sentences. Darrow thought the verdict just; he was convinced that except for the wealth of the families, a plea of guilty and a life sentence would have been accepted without contest.

From the time of Mike McDonald, there had been a close link between Chicago's criminals and politicians. But with the amoral Thompson in the mayor's chair, the alliance flourished as never before; its operations were marked by a new brazenness and by a new ruthlessness and efficiency. The era of the gangster in Chicago is often attributed to prohibition. It is true that the sale of illegal liquor constituted a sizable proportion of the gangsters' activities. But the genesis of their power could be traced back along before the advent of the Eighteenth Amendment.

The successor to Mike McDonald as kingpin of the underworld and the founder of the criminal dynasty which ruled Chicago during the Thompson regimes and much of the 1930's was Big Jim Colosimo. Big Jim's was a Levee success story. He made his first appearance in Chicago carrying a water pail to quench the thirst of section hands working on the railroad.

Later, he ascended the social scale to a job as a street sweeper, showing such political aptitude in organizing the sweepers that he won the sponsorship of The Bath and Hinky Dink. He also came to the attention of Victoria de Moresco, owner of a series of Levee brothels who admired his way with the politicians as much as his ability to break open a locked door with a shove of his huge shoulders. Thinking he might be a handy man to have around the house, she married him, elevating him to a position of money and power. As a gesture of his appreciation, he sentimentally named one of their brothels the Hotel Victoria. Soon he ranked second only to Ike Bloom in his influence in the district. Big Jim continued to prosper, not only operating Victoria's resorts, but taking over the Italian national lottery and the illegal wine industry, farming out carloads of grapes to Sicilian families and then selling the wine they made without paying the government tax. He assumed control of many of the Italian immigrant laborers, hiring them out for a fee to railroads or other industries in need of unskilled labor. All these activities brought him into frequent contact with the Unione Siciliane and the Mafia. Neither organization was easy to do business with and frequent extortion demands prompted him to import a bodyguard in 1910. The gunman he chose to protect him was John Torrio, member of a notorious New York gang.

Big Jim displayed other evidences of success. His dress became flashier. Diamonds were his trademark. He wore diamonds on his fingers, diamond studs on his shirt, a diamond horseshoe on his vest, diamonds on his belt and suspender buckles; even his garters were studded with diamonds. After the closing of the Levee resorts, Big Jim opened a café on Wabash Avenue; it soon was drawing a fashionable trade because of its exceptional food. Colosimo was a restaurateur at heart. Even when running a Levee resort, he prided himself upon the quality of his food and the discriminating choice of wine he offered his patrons. Though Colosimo's Café was only a front for Big Jim's more extensive illegal business activities, its standards were high and it became a favorite rendezvous of theater and opera personalities. Colosimo was a regular attendant at the opera and opera music was a frequent feature of the café entertainment, attracting such stars as Galli-Curci, Tetrazzini, Caruso and the opera's maestro, Campanini. George M. Cohan was a regular patron when a show of his was in Chicago.

The power of Colosimo reached its peak with the coming of prohibition. As a man who knew how to do business with Mayor Thompson at City Hall, Big Jim took control of the bootleg industry. He might have ruled it for a dozen years if it had not been for his fondness for opera—a fatal indulgence, as matters turned out. It was a desire to offer the patrons of Colosimo's the best in singing which led Big Jim to hire Dale Winter to sing in his café. Dale Winter was not a cabaret entertainer and didn't like to be called one—

she was a former vaudeville singer whom a Chicago reporter had found singing in a church choir and recommended to Jim. She was another diamond for Jim and a polished one; her qualities, by the testimony of all who heard her sing, were those of a fine, gentle-bred girl. Morris Gest traveled to Colosimo's to sign her to a Broadway contract and Ziegfeld also came with an offer. But by the time Dale Winter's reputation was made, she was in love with Big Jim and refused to leave. Every night she pitted her voice against the cabaret racket of noisy merrymakers; during the day she took singing lessons from Big Jim's friends at the opera. Colosimo asked Victoria for a divorce. "I raised one husband for another woman and there is nothing in it," Victoria said sadly and gave him the divorce without protest. When Big Jim and Dale were married, the groom promised his bride she could resume her singing career without the strain of the nightly appearance in the café. "You don't have to earn a living now," Jim said. "You can rest and study and rest and sing and rest and perform roles in the Auditorium." Dale Winter said "That was the thing we were silliest about—my being a great singer some day."

John Torrio, busy managing many of Colosimo's enterprises and establishing his own control over the city's gambling, had no time for silliness. Worried that Colosimo's marriage to the high-principled Dale Winter might result in the weakening of the empire that had been established, Torrio decided to eliminate Colosimo from the top spot, a feat only possible through murdering him. Although a professional killer, Torrio imported a special gunman from New York to take care of Big Jim. Setting a time for the assassination, Torrio told Colosimo that two truckloads of whiskey from Jim O'Leary's would be arriving at the café at that time. When Colosimo arrived to check the shipment, he was dropped to the floor with a bullet behind the ear and the way was clear for Torrio to take over.

Colosimo's funeral was a gaudy event which paraded the intimate relationship between the city's criminals and its political leaders. The honorary pallbearers included three judges, an assistant state's attorney, two congressmen, state representative Michael L. Igoe, who later became a federal judge, and numerous aldermen, including James P. Bowler, later a wheelhorse for the Kelly-Nash machine. The Roman Catholic Church refused Colosimo its rites because of his divorce; a Protestant clergyman conducted the service—after which Alderman John "The Bath" Coughlin knelt at the bier and recited the Catholic prayer for the dead. The assassination of Colosimo was believed to have cost $150,000, of which $20,000 went to the killer and the balance into the treasury of the Mafia. The friendship of the leading politicians for Colosimo did not prevent their being realists; with their acquiescence, Torrio succeeded to the command of the army of the underworld.

As chief of staff in maintaining discipline among the various forces involved in liquor traffic, prostitution and the gambling rackets, Torrio picked a twenty-three-year-old killer named Al Capone, a quick man with a gun who had been trained as a member of New York's tough Five Points gang. Torrio established his headquarters in the Four Deuces at 2222 Wabash Avenue, a combination saloon and brothel. The Four Deuces was never visited by the fashionable slumming parties which had found amusement at Colosimo's; a dozen murders were said to have been committed there and Chicagoans were already finding it unhealthy to be a witness to a killing. Though Torrio was not hesitant to order a murder, he avoided open clashes with a combination of compromise and threats as astutely employed as the diplomatic maneuverings of a European statesman. His authority was so complete he walked the streets alone. He carried a gun only infrequently; some people said he never carried one.

The gang chief with whom Torrio was most careful to maintain a delicate balance of power was Dion O'Banion, who bossed a North Side gang from his flower shop near Holy Name Cathedral. O'Banion, a former altar boy, was the son of an indigent plasterer and had been reared in poverty. In his youth he peddled papers on the Loop streetcars; an accident in a fall from one of the cars had left him with one leg shorter than the other. He graduated to employment as a terrorist during a newspaper circulation war and then to bootlegging and killing for a fee. He had killed two men in the entrance to the LaSalle Theater and had not been prosecuted for the crime. He carried three revolvers in specially constructed pockets of his tailor-made clothes and could shoot with either his right hand or his left. He was surrounded by a bunch of humorless thugs. When Samuel J. "Nails" Morton, a member of the gang, was thrown and kicked to death by a horse in Lincoln Park, the gunmen vowed vengeance. They kidnapped the unfortunate horse, led it to the spot where Morton's body had been found and solemnly "rubbed it out" in gangland fashion. O'Banion was also a political power, controlling the vote in the area of the Gold Coast and the slums behind it just north of the Loop.

The truce was broken when O'Banion became involved in a feud with the six Genna brothers, who amassed a five-million-dollar fortune by hiring hundreds of Sicilians and Italians to cook alcohol for them in West Side apartments. The Gennas—Angelo, Sam, Jim, Pete, Tony and Mike—had five police captains and four hundred patrolmen regularly on their payroll. When Angelo Genna married, he ordered a wedding cake which required four days to bake; it contained four hundred pounds of sugar, four hundred pounds of flour and seven cases of eggs. The opulent Angelo had dropped $30,000 gambling at The Ship, a Cicero gambling establishment in which O'Banion shared an interest with Torrio. Torrio wanted to cancel the debt, but O'Banion refused and issued a telephone ultimatum to Angelo to pay up within a week. Angelo, a powerful leader in the Unione Siciliane, did not like such treatment; he was also smoldering with resentment over the hijacking of a truckload of his whiskey by O'Banion's gang.

O'Banion's assassination had been planned several times with the full assent of Torrio, but was always stopped by Mike Merlo, the first president of the Unione Siciliane. Then, in May of 1924, O'Banion knowingly let Torrio get caught with thirteen truckloads of beer in a raid which was turned over to the federal government for prosecution. Torrio's fix did not extend that high and he was indicted for bootlegging with thirty-seven other defendants. It was a humiliating experience for the powerful gang boss. A short time later, Mike Merlo died and Torrio gave Genna the go-signal for the murder of O'Banion. While his death was being plotted, O'Banion was doing a rush business in flowers for Merlo's funeral. A hundred thousand dollars' worth of flowers were sent to Merlo's home and overflowed onto the lawn outside; one floral tribute contained a life-size wax effigy of Merlo. Torrio sent a $10,000 floral piece from O'Banion's and Capone ordered an $8,000 tribute from the shop. Even one of the Gennas called for a floral piece.

On the morning of November 10, 1924, while O'Banion was busy with

THE ELEVATED AT NIGHT, *by Aaron Bohrod*

the flowers for Merlo's funeral, three men stepped out of a car and went into his shop. O'Banion came out of the back room; apparently recognizing the visitors, he stepped to the front of the shop with a carnation in one hand and scissors in the other. One of the visitors grabbed his arm and pulled him forward, another held him and the third pumped five bullets into him, including a coup de grace to the head. O'Banion's funeral exceeded the splendor of Merlo's. He was buried in a $10,000 casket, bought in Philadelphia and shipped to Chicago in a special car. At his funeral there were so many flowers it required twenty-six trucks to transport them to the cemetery. Among the mourners at the funeral were Torrio and Capone, both conscious they were being blamed for the killing which could hardly have been done without their approval. The actual killer was believed to have been one of the Gennas, who had been looking at more than flowers when he ordered Merlo's wreath.

Hymie Weiss, a Polish boy who had shortened his name from Wajcie-chowski, took over the O'Banion gang and promptly ordered the murder of Torrio. The gang boss fled the city, with Weiss and his gunmen in pursuit; the chase led to several southern resorts and then across the Florida keys to Cuba and back again to Chicago. Torrio's pursuers caught up with him at the entrance to his Chicago home just before he was to start his sentence in the Lake County jail for bootlegging. He was severely wounded and lay for a long time near death in Jackson Park Hospital, guarded by a dual watch of police officers and personal bodyguards. A witness identified the man who fired on Torrio as Bugs Moran, a Weiss ally, but Moran was not indicted. Slowly recovering his health, Torrio went from the hospital to the Lake County jail where he had the sheriff install bullet-proof shutters on his cell windows and hired three extra deputies to guard him during the period of his incarceration. A free man at last, he decided to leave Chicago for reasons of health; he had an estimated ten to thirty million dollars in banks in New York and Europe. As far as was known, he never returned to Chicago, but rose to a new eminence in the more gun-free rackets of New York. In Chicago, his chief of staff, Al Capone, assumed Torrio's place as ruler of the underworld.

Capone, without the imagination or the keen business mind of Torrio, ruled by the bludgeon and the gun rather than by the arts of diplomatic strategy. Finding that Angelo Genna had installed himself as new president of the Unione Siciliane without Capone's permission, the gang chief moved quickly to show his anger. On May 26, 1925, Angelo Genna was killed; a month later Mike Genna was shot down and in July Anthony was trapped and killed. The remaining Gennas departed for Sicily.

The empire which Capone inherited was organized with the businesslike efficiency of a legitimate corporation. The Better Government Association wired the United States Senate that "Chicago politicians are in league with gangsters and the city is overrun with a combination of lawless politics and protected vice." Capone lacked the executive ability to keep this alliance running smoothly, however, and had to enforce his edicts by indiscriminate murder. The corruption of the police had been pushed to the point of saturation under the two terms of Mayor Thompson and the city was paralyzed. In an aldermanic election in one ward—the Nineteenth—a candidate for alderman and three of his aides were killed while two captains of the perennial alderman "Johnny de Pow" Powers were mowed down. Massacre was the only word for the Capone rule. During the first four months of 1926 there were twenty-nine gang killings in Chicago; the total for four years was more than two hundred—and all without a single conviction for murder.

When Mayor Thompson conceded he could not win a third consecutive term and withdrew from the race for mayor, Capone sought a stronghold outside the city as protection against any reforms introduced by Mayor William Dever, who was trying to beat down the criminals with a demoralized police force and courts riddled by Thompson appointments. The location Capone chose was Cicero, where the syndicate already had made sizable inroads. His first move was to take over the city government. He secured the nomination on the Democratic ticket of a group of subservient politicians and on election day moved his army of ex-convicts and aliens into Cicero in the manner of a latter-day European dictator.

The Illinois Crime Survey recorded in a matter-of-fact way that "automobiles filled with gunmen paraded the streets, slugging and kidnapping election workers. Polling places were raided by armed thugs and ballots taken at the point of the gun from the hands of voters waiting to drop them in the box. Voters and workers were kidnapped, taken to Chicago and held prisoner until the polls closed." Three men were killed, another had his throat slashed and a Cicero policeman was blackjacked. Late in the afternoon an appeal for help was sent to County Judge Edmund K. Jarecki, who swore in seventy policemen as special deputies and sent them to Cicero. When a police squad came upon Al Capone, his brother, Frank, and Charles Fischetti standing in front of a polling place, Frank Capone opened fire and was shot dead by a patrolman. Al fled down Cicero Avenue, fighting off another squad of police with a pistol blazing in each hand, and finally escaping. The rescue attempt had come too late. Cicero was taken.

Capone ruled the town of fifty thousand as firmly as he had bossed Chicago under the acquiescent Thompson. When an alderman opposed one of Capone's projects, the gangster waited for him and beat him up outside the council chambers. Another time Capone knocked down and kicked his hand-picked mayor while a Cicero policeman stood by, afraid to intervene. The federal constitution said there could be no sale of alcoholic liquors in the United States; but in the Capone-run town of Cicero there were 161 bars open day and night. At the Hawthorne Smoke Shop, a hand-book for bets, the play totaled $50,000 a day. Capone himself was the heaviest bettor. He estimated that he lost nearly a million dollars a year to the bookies. Incongruously, he had never invested a dollar in the stock market. "It's a racket," he said.

Open warfare existed between Capone and the Hymie Weiss gang on the North Side. At noon on September 20, 1926, eleven cars of Weiss gunmen roared down the main street of Cicero. As the cars approached a restaurant where Capone was having lunch, a fusillade from machine guns, pistols and shotguns poured into the restaurant and nearby Hawthorne Inn, Capone's Cicero headquarters. Capone dropped to the floor and escaped unhurt but thirty-five cars parked along the street were raked with bullets. A woman sitting in a car with a baby in her arms was grazed over the eyes, damaging her sight. Capone made the headlines by paying all the hospital expenses of the woman—the first innocent bystander to be hurt in the wars (not counting the police heroes who paid with their lives). Capone ordered an immediate revenge. On October 11th, Hymie Weiss and a beer peddler were killed by a spray of machine-gun bullets as they stepped from their car near O'Banion's former flower shop; the assassin's bullets ricocheted and chipped the stones on Holy Name Cathedral. Chief of Police Morgan Collins did not arrest Capone. "It's a waste of time to arrest him," Collins said. "He's been in before on other murder charges. He has his alibi. He was in Cicero when the shooting occurred." A short time later, Antonio Lombardo, who had been placed at the head of the Unione Siciliane by Capone, was shot down and killed as he was walking with two bodyguards near State and Madison—famed as the busiest corner in the United States. The killers disappeared in the crowd.

In 1927, the voters of Chicago returned Big Bill Thompson to the mayor's seat for a third term. Al Capone, who had underwritten the mayor's campaign expenses and provided an army of hoodlums to "guard" the West Side polls on election day, moved back to Chicago. Thompson by this time had a new tactic to divert attention from his alliance with criminals; he declared war on England. He uttered his notorious threat to "punch King George in the snoot" and issued scholarly ukases about the alleged pro-English bias of the textbooks in the Chicago schools. He pushed through the state legislature a bill which said "The official language of the State of Illinois shall be known hereafter as the American language." A wit said later, "Mayor Thompson was for America First and Capone was for America's Thirst. Maybe they weren't so far apart at that." The Reverend John Thompson of the Chicago Methodist Temple found nothing humorous in the city's tawdry reputation; at a service he offered up this prayer:

THE FUNERAL OF ANTONIO LOMBARDO

"O, Thou that didst care for Nineveh and didst spare it, and Thou that didst weep over Jerusalem, dost Thou still brood over these great modern cities? We pray Thee to rule over Chicago, this young and strong, good and bad, city—and out of man's worst to bring Thine own."

Capone was difficult to reach, even by prayer. After Mayor Thompson's return to power, the gang chief set up a Chicago headquarters in the Metropole Hotel, 2300 South Michigan. His entourage occupied fifty rooms on two heavily guarded floors. They had their own service bars and operated their private elevators. The hallway outside Capone's suite was patrolled by gunmen as alert as military sentinels. In a large office, calculated to awe visitors, Capone sat beneath photographs of three men he considered great Americans: George Washington, Abraham Lincoln—and Big Bill Thompson. The offices of the Capone bootleg syndicate, methodically organized by Jacob "Jack" Guzik, whose brother was in charge of the white-slave traffic, were located in a nearby doctor's office whose pharmacopoeia of bottles and vials was composed of stock samples of the liquors handled by the syndicate. In the office files were the names of several hundred prominent Chicagoans who were customers, the list of police officers and prohibition agents who were receiving pay-offs and a record of the channels through which liquor was brought from New York, New Orleans and Miami. A special looseleaf ledger was set up to show the cost-accounting procedures followed in the brothels under Capone control.

Incredibly, while Capone terrorized the city—there were sixty-two bomb-ings in 1928, many directed against reform leaders—he was being painted as a kind of public hero. When Commander Francesco de Pinedo, the round-the-world flyer, landed in Chicago in May of 1927, Al Capone was among the official greeting party. The police explained that his presence was requested to prevent possible anti-Fascist demonstrations against Pine-do's sponsor, Mussolini. The law could not preserve order—but Al Capone could. When the depression hit, Capone was the first to establish soup kitchens; hungry men murmured "Good Old Al" as they waited in line for their handout. Meanwhile, John Gunther in an article in *Harper's* was estimating that the sixty or more rackets then in operation in Chicago were costing its citizens thirty-six million dollars a year—enough to feed a good many more hungry men than those who stood in line waiting for Capone's charity.

The gangster boss lived lavishly. He was childish in his emotions, quick to anger and had to seek frequent stimulation in betting huge sums on the races or rolling dice for nothing less than a thousand dollars a pass. He had a flat nose, thick lips, the short neck of a night-club bouncer and a scar on his left cheek which he claimed was a war memento but was actually the reminder of a brawl in a Brooklyn dance hall. When he attended a play in the Loop, he went in the company of eighteen bodyguards, all in tuxedos, who were seated at strategic points around the theater. When he left his headquarters, he rode in a seven-ton bullet-proof car with fenders of steel it was nearly impossible to dent. Machine-gun bullets would have splattered harmlessly off its surface. Its doors were equipped with special combination locks so his enemies could not jimmy the doors and plant a bomb under the seat. Even so, he was not careless. When he drove, a small scout car always preceded him and a touring car of bodyguards protected him from the rear. When Capone entered one of the city's seven thousand speakeasies his hoodlums took up posts at the doors and no one was allowed to enter or leave while he was there. As compensation, he frequently bought drinks for the house.

The Fish Fans Club, a schooner clubhouse in Belmont Harbor owned by Big Bill Thompson, was a favorite speakeasy for politicians. It was organ-ized supposedly to encourage the propagation of fish in American waters, but was in fact a part of the Thompson promotion machine. The club was padlocked by federal agents, but reopened; it came to a humiliating end when so many people crammed aboard to celebrate Big Bill's election to a third term that it became overloaded and sank. Fred Mann's Rainbo Gardens was another big speakeasy. Mann was a friend of the Mayor's and when federal agents padlocked his place he made a personal appeal to Secretary of the Treasury Andrew Mellon, in charge of the revenue agents, to be permitted to reopen. Mellon, however, did not intervene. In all the speakeasies, shootings were frequent; but as Eddie Condon was to recall later, "in all the joints the bands kept playing no matter what happened." He said the gangsters liked jazz. "It's got guts and it don't make you slobber," one of the gunmen said. The favorite speakeasy of the musicians was the Three Deuces (not to be confused with the Four Deuces) at 222 North State Street. It was here that Mezz Mezzrow says the nation's first jam session was staged, with Bix Beiderbecke and Bing Crosby, both appearing at the Chicago Theater nearby, as its principal participants. Entertainers had to bow to the wishes of their gangster bosses. When Joe E. Lewis notified the Green Mills Gardens he was leaving to play the Rendezvous, he was slashed on the face, throat and tongue by Machine Gun Jack McGurn.

McGurn was later arrested but never prosecuted for the greatest blood-bath of the Capone era. It occurred just a year before the gang wars sputtered to an end with Capone in complete control of the city. On St. Valentine's Day of 1929, a squad of four killers disguised as policemen and detectives ambushed with machine guns seven members of the Bugs Moran gang, successors to the interests of Dion O'Banion and Hymie Weiss. But while the gang wars were proceeding without letup in Chicago, Philadelphia nabbed Capone on a gun-carrying charge and sent him to the penitentiary. Even in Pennsylvania, Capone's influence was sufficient to procure a transfer from the strictly disciplined Holmesburg jail to Eastern Penitentiary where he was given his own cell, permitted to make long-distance telephone calls and allowed the use of the warden's office for running his illegal enterprises.

Always, he protested he didn't want to be in the rackets. "You fear death every moment," he said in one of the hundreds of interviews which were glamorizing his shoddy murders. "Worse than death you fear the rats of the game who would run and tell the police if you didn't constantly satisfy them with favors." He forgot easily about his murders. "All I ever did was to sell beer and whiskey to our best people," he said with a total disregard of facts. "All I ever did was supply a demand that was pretty popular. . . . They talk about me not being on the legitimate. Nobody's on the legit. You know that and so do they. Your brother or your father gets in a jam. What do you do? Do you sit back and let him go over the road without trying to help him? You'd be a yellow dog if you did. Nobody's really on the legit when it comes down to cases."

It sounded noble but it was wrong. A few people were "on the legit," even if they didn't count for much in local politics. The federal government put an investigator to work on Capone's tax returns. The investigator narrowly missed being assassinated at least twice, but finally found what he was seeking. Capone was brought to trial for income-tax evasion. The witnesses against him had to be hidden and shifted from place to place;

Capone was not beneath threatening the Government of the United States. But in 1931, after a long presentation of evidence, Capone was found guilty and sentenced to ten years in prison, a year in jail and $50,000 in fines.

The organization survived Capone just as it survived Mike McDonald, Big Jim Colosimo and John Torrio. In 1950, James M. Ragen, Sr., proprietor of a racing-news service which provided race results for handbooks, said, "The Capone syndicate is just as strong as it ever was." Three weeks later Ragen was shot to death on the streets of Chicago; the murder weapon, once found, vanished from the custody of the Chicago police department.

Grand Opera — A Libretto for Romance

THERE WERE great plans for the future. Daniel Burnham, buoyed by his triumph at the Columbian Exposition, urged the powerful Commercial Club and the Merchants Club to form plans for Chicago as great as those that had been made for the temporary white city on the South Side. His arguments were practical. "Beauty has always paid better than any other commodity and always will," he said. "We have been running away to Cairo, Athens, the Riviera, Paris and Vienna because life at home is not so pleasant as in those fashionable centers. . . . No one has estimated the millions of money made here in Chicago and expended elsewhere but the sum must be a large one. What would be the effect upon our retail business at home if this money were circulated here?" Burnham had other words which matched his dream. "Make no little plans," he urged the city. "They have no magic to stir men's blood and probably themselves will not be realized. Make big plans; aim high in hope and work, remembering that a noble, logical diagram once recorded will never die but long after we are gone will be a living thing, asserting itself with growing intensity."

Mayor Fred Busse, a crude and rough product of professional politics, heard Burnham's words, shared his vision and appointed a Chicago Plan Commission to lay out the objectives of the city of the future. Busse was not a reform mayor; but it was under Busse that the two greatest reforms of twentieth-century Chicago politics were originated—the Chicago Plan and the Vice Commission, which laid the groundwork for the destruction of segregated vice. Inexplicable? Just Chicago, people said.

A new pattern of cosmopolitan living was emerging too. The pattern of homes with wide lawns—a heritage of "The Garden City"—was giving way reluctantly to the new apartment houses. Ogden McClurg, nurtured on a classical education but grown to be a bold promoter and planner, built his first apartment house at the far end of a sandy strip reaching eastward to the lake from the Harold McCormick mansion. McClurg numbered the building 999 Lake Shore Drive, indulging the same superstition which led him to locate McClurg's wholesale store at 333 East Ontario because of a belief that nine was his lucky number. When 999's ornate walls towered lonely against the lake sky, the area was considered desolate; maids refused to cross the windy stretch to go to work. But in a few years there was a row of buildings in the area, numbered 179, 199, 209 and 219, carrying out the theme of nines and confusing Chicago taxi drivers for all time.

On the night of November 3, 1910, the city felt it had actually achieved the cosmopolitanism and sophistication which had so long escaped it. "Everybody's happy," Harold McCormick, the son of the reaper king, told the reporters. "We could not ask for more." There was much to be festive about. At the Auditorium the new Chicago Opera Company was presenting *Aida* to a brilliantly dressed first-night audience. The nucleus of the company was an inheritance from Oscar Hammerstein's Manhattan Opera, which had gone bankrupt in its war with the Metropolitan; yet Chicagoans were already claiming the opera company as part of their own cultural garland. "The success of Chicago opera means the success of all culture in this city [and] the establishment of a finer standard of art than has ever been known here before," music critic Felix Borowski wrote in the *Record-Herald* the following day. There were few to disagree with his prediction. Arthur Meeker, the governor of the Assembly Association, pronounced the evening's performance a triumph. "I never saw the opulence of the East better staged than right here," he said. There was a democratic note about the opening night's crowd as well. Clarence MacKay, president of the Postal Telegraph Company, had come out from New York and given one hundred of his messenger boys opening-night tickets. Every Chicago employe, he announced, would be given a pair of tickets for at least one opera performance.

The impetus for bringing opera to Chicago had come for the most part from Harold McCormick and his wife, the former Edith Rockefeller, who was rapidly assuming the social power which Mrs. Potter Palmer relinquished through her long absences from the city. Two of Rockefeller's daughters had married Chicagoans. Alta Rockefeller had married Ezra Parmelee Prentice, a brilliant young lawyer, but the couple moved to New York shortly after their marriage. Edith and Harold settled in Chicago in 1897 in a turreted mansion at 1000 Lake Shore Drive which had been erected in the 1880's by S. S. Beman for Nathaniel Jones, a wealthy member of the Board of Trade. Surrounding the house was a high iron fence which had been designed to match a pair of gates purchased from the German exhibit at the Columbian Exposition.

From this gray stone palace on the lake shore, the McCormicks dominated Chicago society. Mrs. McCormick carried out her social program in a regal manner; no queen or ruler of a court could have been more rigid in attention to protocol. Even her children, when they were grown, could see her only by appointment. She required that printed menus in French be provided for every meal; at formal dinners there were menus and place cards engraved in gold. A butler stood behind every two chairs at dinner. Four men were required to serve a luncheon for two. Her large household staff included a first and second butler, two parlor maids, a coachman, footman, houseman and six detectives. Her personal maid had a helper, a sewing woman, who in turn had an assistant, described as a mending woman. In the kitchen were a chief cook and a second cook in addition to more menial help. The cooks had a coal stove; they were not permitted to cook with gas. Mrs. McCormick allowed herself to speak to only two servants—the chief steward and her personal secretary. Through these she ruled her entire household. When she called for her carriage (and later for a car) the coachman was given detailed instructions for the trip before he left the house. He was never addressed directly during the trip; the time at which he was to return for his passenger was set before he left, eliminating the need for Mrs. McCormick to speak to him.

The furnishings of 1000 Lake Shore Drive were in fact those of a ruler's palace. Most were selected because of Mrs. McCormick's belief she was descended from the La Rochefoucauld nobility of France. (Actually the Rockefeller family was German in its origins.) One or her rugs, purchased for $185,000, had been sent by the Shah of Persia as a present to the Winter Palace of the Czars at St. Petersburg during the reign of Peter the Great. Subsequently, before finding its way to a London auction, it was given to the Emperor of Austria in gratitude for Austrian aid to destitute Russians. In a huge chamber called the Empire Room, Mrs. McCormick installed four of Napoleon's royal chairs, two marked with the crest initial N and two with a B for the family name of Bonaparte. On the fourth floor was a fifteen-thousand volume library with such collector's treasures as the *Night of the Swan* valued at $30,000; *Histoire Héliodore*, worth $6,000; a *Patissier François dated* 1655 and a Byzantine manuscript of the New Testament in Greek valued at $14,000. In her bedroom, Edith Rockefeller Mc-Cormick slept in an enormous Louis XVI gilded bedstead and walked to a directoire loveseat across an ornate Aubusson carpet. On her dressing table was a small oblong box in gold with the diamond-encrusted initials "M.L.," believed to have been a gift from Napoleon to the Empress Marie Louise. In the halls and parlors were Buddhas from Chinese temples, tapestries from Brussels and English silver dating back to the time of Oliver Cromwell. For her large dinners, which might have an invitation list as large as two hundred, Mrs. McCormick served the guests on a golden service which Napoleon had given his sister, Pauline. It consisted of one thousand pieces and contained more than eleven thousand ounces of precious metals.

Mrs. McCormick's jewel collection, though not as extensive as that of Mrs. Palmer, contained single pieces of such great value they could never be sold. An emerald necklace, formed from jewels collected by Cartier at a cost of nearly $600,000, came to be valued at more than a million dollars. Ten large emeralds were the central features of the necklace and were spaced on a rope fabricated of 1,657 small diamonds. Another necklace was believed to be made in part of Russian crown jewels. It was made up of twenty-three large pearls, twenty-one large diamonds of various shapes and one hundred lesser diamonds. A slip of a woman with exquisite feet and ankles, Mrs. McCormick frequently wore a tiny golden anklet. Her formal dinners were so much like affairs of state that it was often said "she taught Chicago how to wear and to own a dress suit." The formality, however, never called for champagne. She was a "dry" and never permitted cocktails or liquor in her home. In later years she said that her father had made her promise that she would never serve a drink of liquor in her home. Recalling her first formal dinner, she said "my party was not very well under way before I noticed a certain lack of spontaneity that had marked the other dinners I had attended. The gaiety seemed forced and formal . . ." When the young bride asked her husband the cause of it, he replied, "My dear, don't you realize that these red-blooded young Chicagoans are used to having their liquor? They simply must have their cocktails, their wine, their highballs and cordials." The pledge, if it existed, was never broken, and no alcoholic liquors were ever served at 1000 Lake Shore Drive.

Mrs. McCormick, who hated hymns because her pious father had made her sing them so much as a girl, had a great devotion for the opera which was shared by her husband, Harold. The pair entertained frequently on opera nights. Mrs. McCormick sat at the end of the table with a jeweled clock beside her and insisted that a strict schedule be kept so that no one would be late for the performance. Those who did not eat quickly might expect to have their plates snatched away when Mrs. McCormick signaled the end of the time allotted for a particular course.

It was at such a fabulous dinner party that tragedy struck close to the heart of Edith Rockefeller McCormick. Her first-born son, John Rockefeller McCormick, was ill with scarlet fever at the family home in Lake Forest. During dinner, Mrs. McCormick's secretary received a call from the McCormick country home. The message was of such importance that the imperious rule against interruptions during dinner had to be broken. The secretary whispered to Mrs. McCormick that her son was dead. The shock was one from which most Chicagoans believed Edith Rockefeller McCormick found it hard to recover. It was also the beginning of an era which found both Edith and her husband playing roles as baroque as any in the repertoire of their beloved Chicago Opera Company.

The opera itself was to lead a tempestuous career. Three weeks after its opening it incurred the wrath of the moralists with a presentation of *Salome* with Mary Garden in the leading role. Mary Garden had been one of Hammerstein's stars at the Manhattan Opera but it was to Chicago that she owed her opportunity to sing. As a young girl she had been discovered singing in an afternoon recital by Mrs. David Mayer, wife of a partner in the Schlesinger and Mayer clothing store and a patroness of the arts. Mrs. Mayer, attracted by Mary's personality and voice, took Mary into the family, where the young singer served as nurse for the Mayers' boy, David, Jr., and continued her vocal training under professional instructors provided by Mrs. Mayer. Subsequently, Mrs. Mayer agreed to finance Mary's studies for two years in Paris. The relationship of sponsor and protégée was abruptly terminated before Mary returned to Chicago for an engagement with the new opera company. Mary charged that Mrs. Mayer had withdrawn her support because of a rumor that Mary had borne an illegitimate child in Paris. Mrs. Mayer, explaining frankly she had had the rumor investigated but did not give it any credence, pointed out that she had extended her support of Mary from two years to three. The break came, she said, when Mary, tasting intoxicating success at the Manhattan, had refused to recognize the woman who made her career possible. Because of this, Mrs. Mayer asked Mary to return the $20,000 advanced for the Paris training. Mary complied and Mrs. Mayer immediately turned the money over to charity.

This mild controversy was obliterated by the furor over *Salome*. Miss Garden always made it clear that it was not "Come and hear Mary Garden" but "Come and see Mary Garden." She insisted she was a "singing actress and not a singer." Percy Hammond, after watching her in *Salome*, was in full agreement. He called her "the feminine colossus who doth bestride our operatic world" and found her performance a "florid, excessive, unhampered tour de force, lawless and inhuman."

MRS. HAROLD McCORMICK
(Edith Rockefeller) *From a painting
by Frederic August Von Kaulbach*

Chief of Police LeRoy T. Steward, who was also in the audience for *Salome*, was of a different opinion. "It was disgusting," he said. "Miss Garden wallowed around like a cat in a bed of catnip. There was no art in her dance that I could see. If the same show were produced on Halsted Street the people would call it cheap but over at the Auditorium they say it is art. Black art, if art at all. I would not call it immoral. I would say it was disgusting."

Miss Garden, who made a special study of the dance because, as she said, "I want the dance of the Seven Veils to be drama and not Folies Bergère," was astounded—but not so much she was at a loss for a reply. She dismissed the police chief by saying, "I always bow down to the ignorant and try to make them understand, but I ignore the illiterate."

To the second performance the police chief sent his chief censor, Detective Sergeant Charles O'Donnell, who wore "a black suit he usually reserved for funerals." Arthur Burrage Farwell, who had been denouncing the opera but had not seen it, was given a ticket but refused to go, terming Mary Garden a "great degenerator" of public morals. "I am a normal man," he said, "but I would not trust myself to see a performance of *Salome*." The *News* commented that if "curiosity caused the fall of man, it also led to the progress of the race and it continues a duality of service . . . it also produced the best crowd of the season." In New York, Oscar Hammerstein facetiously suggested that Mary wear some flannel petticoats in her veil dance

THE INHERITANCE 306

because "when she worked for me she had a deadly fear when singing *Salome* of getting cold feet."

The second performance intensified the moral outcry, aided by an adverse report from Sergeant O'Donnell. Chief Steward offered to compromise if Mary would "tone down the head business" when she danced with the severed head of the prophet. Mary would have none of it. "If there is any more of this twaddle about immorality I shall leave Chicago and go to Philadelphia or some place where art is appreciated and viewed as art," she said. The Board of Directors, motivated by a desire to shelter their infant opera company, suddenly terminated the quarrel by withdrawing the third performance. In her autobiography, Mary Garden was to charge that the cancellation was ordered by Edith Rockefeller McCormick. According to Mary, Mrs. McCormick sent for her and said, "The truth came to me after your third [sic] performance . . . I said to myself, Edith, your vibrations are all wrong." As there were only two performances of *Salome*, there is at least one inaccuracy in this account; it seems more probable the cancellation was due to a recurrence of Chicago's unpredictable puritanism—which tolerated the nation's largest vice area on the edge of its business district but rose up in horror over a sensuous work of art.

It was apparent to Chicagoans that a mutual interest in the opera was about the only one shared by the McCormicks. In 1911, hopeful that a house in the country might provide a happier atmosphere, they built Villa Turicum, a forty-four room mansion in Lake Forest, but the housewarming was abruptly called off without explanation. Several barrels of French china stood unpacked for thirty years; two massive chairs from the Italian renaissance period, purchased for the marble-walled drawing room, were set in place but never uncrated. An unusual feature of the mansion was that the thirteen master bedrooms were identical and furnished in the same way, varying only in the color of the walls. Villa Turicum was seldom visited and never for an overnight stay; the McCormicks were reminded of it only by a purple truck with "Villa Turicum" on its panels which brought fresh flowers to the house in town every day. Harold McCormick developed an enthusiasm for flying and sponsored the first international aeronautical show in Chicago. Planes were paid $2 for every minute they could remain in the air and some of the builder-owners were able to make as much as $8 or $9. McCormick also established the nation's first aeronautical research laboratory at Cicero and built a field for a flying club there. In 1913, he made news by flying to work and landing on the waters off Grant Park in his aeroyacht.

It was in 1913 that Mrs. McCormick confirmed the rift in her marriage by leaving Chicago for Switzerland where she planned to study psychology— then called "synthetic psychology"—with Dr. Carl Jung. She did not return for eight years. Meanwhile Harold McCormick continued to bolster the tottering Chicago Opera Company with new transfusions of funds. Through his interest in opera he was to be led to the greatest romantic adventure of his life.

The opera company, under Cleofonte Campanini, scored a series of brilliant triumphs but was unable to avoid overshadowing headlines of an entirely different kind. When the company presented *The Secret of Suzanne*, an inconsequential farce, Lucy Page Gaston stalked out after the third cigarette lighted by one of the singers. "Horrible," she said. "Horrible. One after another. I saw her with my own eyes. It is enough to turn one forever against grand opera. An artful embellishment of a pernicious vice which should receive the stamp of disapproval from every true American woman."

Carolina White, the soprano who replaced Mary Garden when the latter was on tour, made the front pages by going on strike, adding that general manager Andreas Dippel was a slave driver. To this, Dippel replied, "The prima donnas do not work too much; they eat too much. It is terrible the way they have been entertained by society here in Chicago. Too many dinners and too many late hours. I eat too much—we all eat too much—but I don't complain."

There were many exciting moments of a better kind. There was the time, for example, when Chicago first heard Maggie Teyte, the mite of a soprano who talked with a touch of a Cockney accent. There was the memorable Saturday matinee in 1916 when an unheralded singer named Galli-Curci made her local debut in *Rigoletto*. Her triumph was so great that the audience would not go home but shouted, cheered and stamped its feet while Campanini hurried backstage to sign up the new star for more appearances before other managers should hear of the ovation. Galli-Curci was involved in a more disturbing drama when she was singing *Dinorah* on the opening night of the season in 1917. She had just left the stage when the sound of a hissing flame and a sudden stench startled the audience in the Auditorium. Campanini ordered the orchestra to strike up "The Star Spangled Banner"; Galli-Curci, who did not know a word of the anthem, rushed to the front of the stage to send its notes ringing through the hall and still the threat of a panic. Meanwhile, Battalion Chief Michael J. Corrigan of the fire department (later the city's fire commissioner) rushed to the bomb, wrapped it up in his coat and ran with it to the street where it sputtered out. The bomb was the work of a crank, later apprehended and found to have the operatically appropriate name of Faust. It was wartime, however, and there was little comfort in thinking of what might have occurred if the maniac had been slightly more skilled in devising his contraption.

The success and prestige of the Chicago Opera Company, which for a time neared that of the Metropolitan in New York, was largely the work of Cleofonte Campanini. A measure of his thoroughness was the time he called for twenty-seven full rehearsals of an opera before he considered it ready to be presented. When he died in 1919, his funeral was held in the Auditorium which had been his own temple. The stage was set for the transformation scene from *Parsifal*. In the center of the stage lay the body of Campanini, with a lone candle at either side and his baton and an opera score resting on his conductor's stand nearby. Rosa Raisa sang the "Inflammatus" from Rossini's *Stabat Mater* and the orchestra played the final movement from Tchaikovsky's *Symphonie Pathétique*. It was an impressive farewell.

With the passing of the brilliant Campanini, Harold McCormick lost hope that he would be able to establish a native opera company on a paying basis. By 1921, he was confiding to Mary Garden that it was going to be his last season and he asked her to become the director. "We want to go out in a blaze of glory," she remembered his saying, "and we need your name." Mary accepted, stipulating that she be known as "directa," which she considered the feminine of director, and that "you don't give me a business manager with whiskers."

Blazing was the appropriate adjective for the season; but it applied more to tempers than to glories. Conductor Giorgio Polacco tossed the score of *Louise*, Miss Garden's favorite opera, into her lap and shouted, "Lead your own orchestra. You don't sing with me." The feud was carried to the dressing rooms and ended with the petite Mary pushing Polacco bodily out of the room. Another day, when the French conductor, Henri Morin, was conducting a rehearsal of *Aphrodite*, Mary grabbed the baton, twisted it from his grasp and, when she had finished tussling with him on the podium, denounced him for knowing nothing about music. Lucien Muratore, one of the company's leading singers, said "it was impossible to come back under the management of Mary Garden." Miss Garden, unperturbed by either the charge or the fact she herself had kept her British citizenship and was not an American citizen, filed a counter blast asserting, "Foreign dictation is a thing of the past. We are to have a little American dictation for a while and see how that will work out. It is a great pity to see an artist of the value of Signor Muratore so badly counseled"—the last comment a slap at Muratore's wife, Lina Cavalieri. Muratore and Mary were reconciled in Paris the following season; by the time Mary wrote her autobiography she remembered the fuss as just a feud in the newspapers.

The "directa" signed up so many artists there were not enough nights in the season for all of them to perform. As she said of herself, "There never was anything tentative about Mary Garden. She was always out in the front of the picture." (Or as the *Tribune* remarked, "Somebody is always running Miss Mary through a printing press.") She had an instinct for publicity. When Emile Coué, the French exponent of "Every day in every way I am getting better and better," came to this country, Mary announced that his formula had cured her of bronchial pneumonia, buzzing in the head, little colds, irritability and depression. Such loquaciousness had its hazards. When she appeared at the Stock Exchange to auction off boxes for a charity affair, a revolver fell at her feet and the police seized an awkward assassin who had been determined to shoot her. After he had been locked up, a friend of Mary's visited the man in his cell to ask him why he wanted to kill the opera star. All that could be gotten out of the demented man was one statement: "She talks too much."

Mary's artistic standards were high. Among her accomplishments was the staging of the American premiere of Prokofiev's *The Love for Three Oranges*. But by the end of the season her temperamental outbursts had resulted in the resignations of her business executive, artistic director and many of her important singers. She left by mutual consent, saying "I am an artist and my place is with the artists." Her own estimate of the season, in *Mary Garden's Story*, is this: "The newspapers said that the company lost one million dollars during the season I was director. I don't know because I had nothing to do with the business end of it. It was news to me. It may very well have happened, but I didn't know. I do know we finished the way Mr. McCormick wanted us to finish—in a blaze of glory. That's what he asked for and that's what he got. If it cost a million dollars, I'm sure it was worth it."

By the time Mary Garden finished her term as "directa," Harold McCormick was thinking more of a Polish diva than of the Chicago Opera Company. He had become enamored of Ganna Walska, a singer of little ability with an astonishing predilection for extraordinarily wealthy husbands. She had taken up singing, she said, because the first man to attract her (whom she conscientiously described as the "second richest man in Russia") had been given an honorary appointment to the Maryinski Imperial Opera House and she wished to impress him by appearing on that stage. She first married the Baron Arcadie d'Engor, but he was killed in World War I. She came to New York, where she was engaged to sing at the Century, a French-language theater subsidized by Otto H. Kahn. She told Kahn she was having trouble with her throat and he sent her to Dr. Joseph Fraenkel. Dr. Fraenkel, a man much older than she, was so interested by her resemblance to Frau Gustav Mahler, for whom he bore an unrequited love, that he proposed on their second meeting and was immediately accepted. When Dr. Fraenkel died a few years later, he left Ganna Walska an estate of half a million dollars.

Ganna Walska met Harold McCormick while still married to Dr. Fraenkel. Her own account is that when she was sitting in her "regular front-row seat" at the opera, she observed a gentleman who seemed to be looking at her persistently throughout the performance. The next day she learned, or thought she did, that it had been Harold McCormick. Because he was identified with the Chicago Opera Company, Walska was eager to meet him. She called him at the Plaza Hotel. He said he was catching a train and could not meet her, but the determined Walska intercepted him in the lobby. To her "amazement" he was not the man who stared at her, she said. She was not too abashed to notice his "wonderful boyish blue eyes," however, and to confide to him her ambition to sing with the Chicago Opera Company. At the next meeting, Harold McCormick brought his son Fowler, a precaution he might have been wise to follow on subsequent occasions. Gradually, Walska won his confidence and when she sailed for Europe after Dr. Fraenkel's death, Harold McCormick was on the *Aquitania* with her.

Another passenger on the *Aquitania* was Alexander Smith Cochran, whom the papers of the day described as the "world's richest bachelor." When Ganna Walska met Cochran, whose wealth was estimated at eighty million dollars, she thought she recognized him as a man "who had made me aware of himself" at a wedding reception several years before. Cochran proposed to her the night he met her. Later he gave her a pearl ring, saying, "If in January you still do not want to marry me, send me back this ring. I will understand that Harold McCormick is too much on your mind." As the days passed, Cochran was less noble. While Harold McCormick was in Switzerland seeking his freedom from his wife, Cochran and Ganna Walska were married in Paris. Though Mrs. McCormick reluctantly agreed to a divorce, Harold arrived in Paris with her consent only to learn of Ganna Walska's marriage to Cochran.

For the events of the next few days, the historian has only the remarkable testimony of the new bride. "While Mr. Cochran was still sleeping in the next room in his first day of married life," she wrote later, "I was pouring coffee for Mr. McCormick." Apparently the unhappy suitor needed a cup of coffee. "After my sudden marriage I was more preoccupied with Mr. McCormick's helpless state than with my own thoughts," she said. Her distraction was such that she "did not react at all" when at breakfast Cochran told her he was giving her a house on the Rue de Lubeck, formerly the home of James Gordon Bennett, and invited her to pick out anything she wanted at Cartier's for a wedding present. Even his "businesslike announcement" that she would receive $100,000 a year for "pin money"— "All that went by me without actually touching my inner being," the bride wrote in her autobiography, *Always Room at the Top*. Life with Cochran was to be a great trial for the sensitive Walska. Immediately, she says, she was "so crushed by cruel reality" that she was unable to preserve the "image my illusion had created." An excruciating experience, according to Walska, was that when Cochran gave her a present done up in "ugly looking rubber bands." To her "great surprise," she found that "eight or nine" bracelets she had seen at Cartier's fell onto her desk and her heart "stood still in disgust." When Cochran went hunting, he offended her with the gift of "a beautiful Rolls Royce; forced me to accept a sable coat worth a million francs and so big, so heavy it made me look old and fat; reserved almost an entire floor at the Carlton Hotel in Cannes and sent me there alone with half a dozen servants to enjoy the grand season on the Riviera." He was so insensitive, she complained, that he failed to realize Walska did not want to cover the "natural beauty of [her] delicate wrists with artificial beauty of rubies, diamonds and emeralds."

Walska did not permit the indignities of her marriage to Cochran to interfere with her plans for a debut with the Chicago Opera Company, scheduled for December 21, 1920. She was to appear in the title role of Leoncavallo's Zaza. The house was sold out and she was to come out in triumph. Then, without explanation, a few days before the performance, she fled the city for Europe. Opera director Herbert Johnson would say only that the opera was not ready, that they could not get it ready and so the

GANNA WALSKA AND HAROLD
McCORMICK, 1929

performance had been postponed. Those who had been present at Mme Walska's final rehearsal were able to provide more details, though few found their way into print. At the first rehearsals, Gino Marinuzzi, who had succeeded Campanini as musical director, pleaded unsuccessfully with Walska to raise her voice so it could be heard beyond the orchestra pit. Seeing the cause was hopeless, he absented himself from rehearsals and turned the responsibility for the opera over to Pietro Cimini, who for four years had been conductor of the Warsaw opera. The singers were still using their books and were sitting in a small circle on the stage. Cimini, after stopping Walska several times, finally implored her, "Madame, please sing in your natural voice." She looked into the deep vaults of the balconies, then down at the grim conductor. Crying out, "Pig, you would ruin my performance," she rushed from the stage. Later she found Johnson and Marinuzzi together in the opera office. "Gentlemen," she announced, "I am packing my bags. At the end of this season you will be packing yours."

With that she was gone. Publicly she blamed her failure to appear on Cochran, saying he had reneged on a promise to let her have a stage career because he had heard reports of scanty costumes and long stage kisses.

Cochran, at the time of the canceled debut, fled Chicago in a huff just a few hours ahead of his wife. He was angry because he found her registered at the Blackstone as Mme Walska rather than Mrs. Cochran. Later he obtained a divorce. Walska had planned a counter suit but dropped it and allowed Cochran to give her a cash settlement of $200,000. (There is no record that she complained about this insensitive gesture.)

In the meantime, Harold McCormick had been granted his divorce and was free to marry the diva. For her birthday, he sent to her chateau near Versailles one of every kind of machine which International Harvester produced. When she arose on the morning of her birthday she saw "to my great surprise . . . a whole regiment of robot soldiers." But if Harold was free to marry, he did not feel ready for the step. In the summer of 1922, he entered Wesley Memorial Hospital for a secret operation by Dr. Victor D. Lespinasse, a widely known specialist in gland transplantation and the author of the aphorism that "a man is as old as his glands." The surgeon refused to confirm the exact nature of the operation but the newspapers speculated that the glands of a young man were transplanted to McCormick. It was rumored a cable had been sent to Ganna Walska notifying her of the success of the operation about a week after it was performed. McCormick then asked to have the records of his divorce settlement brought to his hospital room, indicating he was interested in determining if he was free to marry.

Harold had been interested in the operation by a European doctor. The doctor, informed of the strict regimen of exercise and diet through which Harold hoped to keep young—he claimed to be able to do fifteen handsprings in succession—had advised him it was too strenuous for a man over forty. The doctor recommended instead a gland transplantation from a younger man, an operation it was believed would prolong life as much as ten to fifteen years. While Harold looked hopefully forward to his recuperation, the newspapers sought ways to describe the operation and evade the penalties for invasion of privacy. The *Journal* suggested that McCormick, who was fifty-one, was "a leader in the Boy Scouts and wants to be a boy as long as possible." In society's drawing rooms, a paraphrase of Longfellow was making the rounds:

> Under the spreading chestnut tree,
> The village smithy stands;
> The smith a gloomy man is he;
> McCormick has his glands.

Harold McCormick married Ganna Walska in Paris, calling for her at the house Cochran had given her and riding to the mayor's office for the ceremony in the limousine which had been a present from Cochran. Floyd Gibbons, in reporting the wedding for the *Tribune*, wrote that there was some doubt about the legality of the marriage as Harold was not supposed to marry until a year after his divorce; his lawyers assured him, however, that the law meant only that he could not marry in Illinois until a year had elapsed.

The final disappointment was still ahead for the rejuvenated bridegroom. Ganna Walska, writing of the marriage later, said, "When still very young, Harold's pockets were already filled with pills of every kind. In later years his blind submission to the disciples of Aesculapius became absolute to the point of hypochondria. Unfortunately, the same idiosyncrasy led him to idolize the physical expression of love. Nature in her wisdom having fulfilled him by giving him four children had chosen for his second wife an idealist who was able to put so much value on the richness of his soul that she could not even imagine the possibility of his preferring to seek further for a gross and limited pleasure rather than being satisfied with the divine companionship of the spiritual love she was willing to share with him."

While Harold McCormick pursued Ganna Walska to Europe, Edith Rockefeller McCormick returned from Switzerland, bringing with her Edwin Krenn, a young architect she met at the psychological clinic where she studied. "It was pointed out to me that psychologically Chicago will be the greatest center in the world," she said on her arrival. "That is why I have come back here to live. That is why I have planted my roots in the soil, hoping they will grow deeper and deeper. I am vitally interested in psychology."

With Krenn, Mrs. McCormick developed a new social pattern. At 9:15

each morning, she would phone Krenn at the Drake Hotel, across the street from her home. With Krenn she mapped out the day's routine. Shortly after 1 o'clock in the afternoon, Krenn appeared in one of the two hundred suits he was acquiring and the pair had luncheon, speaking German if no other guests were present. The early afternoon was usually devoted to language tutors. At four o'clock Krenn reappeared and he and Mrs. McCormick usually had tea and then went to the movies, sometimes taking in two or three in an evening. A car with a chauffeur and footman always waited outside even if it were only a low-priced neighborhood theater. She seldom went south of the river, however, except to go to the symphony or opera. After the theater, the car took Mrs. McCormick home; unless it was unusually early Krenn did not enter the house. Two butlers always had to be on duty at the door. Usually it was only necessary to bow Mrs. McCormick in, but some evenings she would decide to rearrange the furniture, joining in with the two men at the door in moving it around, an informality she would never have permitted before her trip abroad.

Mrs. McCormick became a student of the occult and once paid $25,000 for a horoscope. She also developed interests in philosophy and poetry. "My object in the world is to think new thoughts," she told an interviewer. Occasionally she entertained on a scale approaching that of her early years in Chicago. One such occasion was the visit of Queen Marie of Rumania when Mrs. McCormick was hostess to eighty for luncheon.

One of her unfortunate ambitions was to prove to her father that she was his equal in business acumen. She formed the Edith Rockefeller McCormick Trust and installed Krenn and Edward Dato, Krenn's prep-school classmate who had followed him to Chicago, as managers. To finance the operations of the trust she pledged five million dollars of Standard Oil stocks. She sent a copy of the trust prospectus to her father, who wrote in reply: "While you are a brilliant and mature woman of great mental capacity, I cannot forget you are my own flesh and blood. Therefore, it seems to be my duty to warn you of the pitfalls and vagaries of life. I would urge you to select an honest, courageous and capable man to advise you in these affairs."

His daughter thought she had such a man in Edwin Krenn, but she refused to allow him to leave the city to inspect any of her properties. When he suggested he give her a receipt for several million dollars in bonds, she said it was not necessary, that the business would be successful only if it were built on mutual trust. She never entered the office of the trust or looked at its books. Her supervision went only far enough for her to walk past the office one day and tell Krenn to stop the salesmen from smoking. One of her plans was the creation of a dream city of millionaires on the shores of Lake Michigan which she would call Edithton. As the site for the city, she purchased more than fifteen hundred acres of land south of Kenosha,

Wisconsin, for more than a thousand dollars an acre. Four million dollars were spent in landscaping and building a yacht harbor. The town was to be designed by Krenn in the style of Atlantic City and Palm Beach with homes like the castles of Spain. To prevent deviation from the Spanish style no building could be erected without approval from Krenn. The project was stopped by the stock-market crash of 1929 which brought an abrupt end to the Edith Rockefeller McCormick Trust. After the failure of the trust, Mrs. McCormick's brother salvaged what he could of the estate, arranging for her to move to a suite at the Drake where she was given a generous annuity of $1,000 a day.

Harold McCormick and Ganna Walska, who had spent only a slight amount of time in Chicago, separated in 1931. The cost to Harold was six million dollars—one fourth of his Harvester holdings. Having given up his professional sponsorship of opera to Samuel Insull, Harold took up whistling and became proficient enough to offer a whistling recital over the radio. His name was linked with a protégée, Betty Noble, and with a motion-picture actress, Pola Negri. He was also a good friend of Baroness Violet Beatrice von Wenner, a portrait painter and harpist, who frequently accompanied him on the harp when he gave a whistling concert.

In 1932 Edith Rockefeller McCormick died in her suite at the Drake Hotel. Her former husband, who had sent her a single rose every year on her birthday, rushed from California to be at her bedside. Then it was revealed that for years Mrs. McCormick had kept a room for him at 1000 Lake Shore Drive in the hope he might return. It was a story worthy of the opera they both loved so well.

24

Insull Builds His Empire

By 1910 the giants were gone. Before the turn of the century William B. Ogden, John Wentworth, Cyrus McCormick and George M. Pullman had yielded to the exigencies of time. Then, after 1900, with a kind of mournful regularity, had come the deaths of Philip D. Armour in 1901, of Potter Palmer in 1902 and of Gustavus Swift in 1903. Prairie Avenue, once the dwelling place of power and wealth, became a shadow street of widows and widowers. In 1906, President William Rainey Harper of the University of Chicago and Marshall Field I, the city's patriarch after the departure of Ogden, were taken by death.

During the hours when the death of Marshall Field was expected, a Chicago business executive was dictating a letter to a friend in France. "I expect from hour to hour to hear of the death of Mr. Marshall Field," he wrote. "Long before you get this letter you will know the result of the attack of pneumonia from which Mr. Field is suffering. It seems to me very deplorable that Mr. Field's life should not be spared for years to come as he certainly is the most prominent citizen of the western country and represents the very best element of American business life." If the writer of this letter was aware that Marshall Field I was the largest taxpayer in the United States, he gave no indication of his knowledge. "I do not suppose," he continued, "his death will hardly make a ripple in business affairs. It certainly will not bring securities on the market as he is not considered in any way a great leader in financial affairs. While he is a great leader in his own business, in corporative affairs I look upon him as just an investor." The letter was signed "Samuel Insull." A postscript added that Insull had not seen "a single statement to change the idea that Marshall Field's career is a great example to all those who desire to become successful by legitimate business methods."

Insull's own career had been a remarkable success story. He was born in England, where his father was a moderately successful manufacturer's agent (salesman). Both his parents were temperance crusaders and for many years his mother conducted a temperance shelter. At fourteen, young Sam Insull had gone to work as an office boy; at nights he learned the Pitman shorthand system. When Insull's employer replaced him with a rich man's son who was willing to work without pay for the experience, Insull advertised in the paper and had a new job within two days. His new employer was Colonel George E. Goraud, English representative of the Thomas A. Edison Company, who was at the time in the middle of a campaign to install Edison telephones in England. When Goraud set up his first telephone exchange, Samuel Insull sat at the switchboard and thus became the first telephone operator on the eastern side of the Atlantic. (Taking care of the batteries for him was a bright, irascible youth named George Bernard Shaw.) Insull's progress in the London office was rapid; soon he was sent to America to serve as Edison's confidential secretary. A year later he was directing the inventor's business affairs, keeping his bank account, signing his checks and exercising Edison's authority through a power of attorney. When the Edison manufacturing plant was erected at Schenectady, it was Insull who supervised the construction. But when the firm was merged with the Thomas Houston Company to form General Electric, Insull's precociousness placed him under suspicion from the other partners and members of Edison's family. He was relegated to the position of second vice-president in charge of manufacturing and sales.

Insull's demotion had hardly been accomplished when he received a letter from banker Byron Smith and investment broker Edward Brewster asking him to recommend a president for the Chicago Edison Company. The Chicago Edison Company was only one of a number of firms selling electricity in the Chicago area, as four blocks was the extent of economical power transmission for the early generators. But Samuel Insull, remembering a remark of Edison's that Chicago was "one of the best centers in the country for our line of business," recommended himself for the post and was accepted.

Soon after his arrival Insull took steps to revolutionize the distribution of electric power. From General Electric he ordered the largest power generator ever built; when the factory suggested a generator with a one-thousand-kilowatt capacity, he instructed them to construct one with a five-thousand-kilowatt output. The new unit was the first in the world entirely dependent on steam turbines. When the untested generators were installed, the engineer, Frederick Sargent, tried to dissuade Insull from standing by for the tests. There was a loud scraping on the casings and Sargent was afraid of an explosion. "That's all right," Insull said. "If this thing doesn't work, I'm dead anyway." The plant did not explode; and from the moment it started to produce power, the wheels of Chicago industry were dependent on one man—Samuel Insull. At once Insull made it clear he not only wanted to sell electricity in the Chicago area; he wanted to sell all of Chicago's electricity—and more of it than any man had dreamed.

He did not hesitate to express his ambitions of establishing a monopoly although monopoly was politically unpopular. "Ours is a business that is a natural monopoly," he said with some foresight. "It matters not what the legislation of the moment may be, what the opinions of the politicians may be, what our own opinions may be; eventually all the electrical energy for a given area must be produced by one concern." He was not worried about government regulation. "If there is anything wrong with my business I want to know it," he said. "And the best way for me to know is to have a public official who has the right to look into my affairs in a position so he can employ the highest class of talent to help him." He conceded that "regulation interferes with arbitrary action, and that is very unpleasant to a man of positive character. . . . On the other hand I think it is very good discipline. One of the great disadvantages the world over is that the human being when he is working for a little larger corporation or business than the average man in the community works for gets very much 'sot up.' I often think I have to take that criticism myself." And he added, "If public regulation fails, public ownership ought to come."

There was no reason during the first quarter of the twentieth century to think that private ownership under Samuel Insull was going to fail. His plans went beyond the city limits of Chicago. In 1902 he took over a group of struggling companies which provided sporadic electric service to the communities along the North Shore; many of the towns had service only from dusk to twilight and were forced to burn candles or lamps during frequently recurring power failures. Insull joined these companies together in the Public Service Company of Northern Illinois, extended his power lines to small communities in nearby Lake County, which had previously been without any service, and in two years was providing the entire area with dependable electrical power twenty-four hours a day. In Chicago, he persuaded the street railway companies and elevated railroads that it was cheaper to buy power from him than to manufacture it themselves. To convince the streetcar lines they would be saving money, he had an analysis made of their power costs and his own; he then laid it on the president's desk without a word of comment or salesmanship. All the transit systems were operating on temporary franchises, but Insull was bold enough to spend eleven million dollars for plants to supply them power. He had no guarantee they would be permanent customers except his own conviction he could sell them electricity cheaper than they could make it themselves.

It was soon an accepted tenet of Chicago business life that Samuel Insull was the man to get things done. When the Chicago, Aurora and Elgin suburban railroad went into bankruptcy, Insull took it over; he converted it to electrical power and soon was running it at a profit. He did the same for the Chicago North Shore and Milwaukee Railway and the Chicago, South Shore and South Bend Railroad when those lines collapsed into bankruptcy. To the North Shore he added a special Skokie Valley Route which cut the time of a trip to Milwaukee and provided a close link to the city for the new suburbs which grew up along the right of way. The transportation industry gave him two of its prized Coffin medals for the most efficiently operated electric lines in the United States. Like William B. Ogden, who built his first rail lines to the West away from the centers of population, Insull was building his power and rail lines to serve the cities of the future. It was this far-sightedness that led John T. Flynn to call Samuel Insull the commercial pioneer of electric power just as Thomas Alva Edison was its scientific pioneer.

The gains were not won easily. Insull, boasting that he had never touched a drop of liquor, found little time for social life. His seeming infallibility gave determination the quality of ruthlessness; he was arbitrary and expected to be obeyed rather than consulted. His days began nearly as early as those of the meat packers who rushed to the stockyards to buy cattle before the less ambitious merchants were awake. Insull's secretary was under orders to pick up the mail at the post office shortly after 6 o'clock in the morning; Insull himself arrived at 7:10 A.M. He expected to find waiting on his desk an operating report of the previous night for each of his power plants with an account and explanation of any power failures. The banker, the investment broker, or the stockholder who called up to inquire why his lights had failed was always able to get a detailed explanation from Insull himself; it was the shrewdest kind of salesmanship. By 8:45 Insull expected all the mail to be sorted and on his desk. He read first any clippings about himself from the newspapers. Though he was never friendly with the reporters, hated to have his picture taken and was curt with photographers, he was conscious that his customers formed their impression of him through what they read in the newspapers. For this reason he always took care to inform himself as to what the papers were saying about him—though he never admitted the fact. Any gifts in the mail were returned unopened. "Don't accept anything from anybody," he told his aides. Even a box of cigars was not acceptable.

The day was usually filled with meetings and conferences at which Insull kept his own notes by scribbling in his Pitman shorthand. Later these notes would be given to his secretary for transcription, one of the secretary's qualifications being an ability to transcribe the uncommon Pitman script. On Sundays Insull climbed into his electric car—later a Buick—and headed for the country to inspect new routes for power lines or possible sites for electrical generating plants. He had to see the physical expression of his plans in order to comprehend them. Though his ability to show a profit on all his ventures had given him a reputation as a financier, he had little interest in balance sheets or columns of figures. When he spoke it was not in terms of costs but with a map on the table where he could trace the physical growth of his expanding power and transportation companies.

It was a lonely life and not entirely satisfactory. Insull was self-conscious about his lack of a family and patiently looked forward to the day he would find a woman who could provide him with a son and heir for the industrial empire he was creating. When asked about his antecedents, he would only say, "My family tree is so short I can't tell. All that I know is that my parents were good Presbyterians." Typical of the prejudices of the day was a widely held opinion that Insull's tremendous successes were due to his "Jewish blood." To this Insull replied, "If I have some Jewish blood, I should not be ashamed. Some of England's greatest men were Jews." Then he met Gladys Wallis, a dark-eyed, white-skinned actress known as the "Pocket Venus" because of her exquisite features. This was the kind of perfection he had been seeking. When Gladys Wallis came to Chicago in *The Squire of Dames* with John Drew and Maude Adams and young Ethel Barrymore, Insull began a persistent stage-door courtship. He wooed the actress with the same intensity that characterized all his business dealings, even following her to New York, where she lived at Helen Windsor's theatrical boarding house with Maude Adams, Ethel Barrymore, Minnie Dupré, Edna Wallace (Hopper) and other promising young actresses. While Insull was proposing marriage, Gladys Wallis was made the star of her own stock company, but the power magnate persuaded her to relinquish her theatrical ambitions to share the unofficial throne from which he ruled Chicago. About a year after their marriage, a son, Samuel, Jr., was born and Insull turned with renewed fervor to the establishment of a durable inheritance for his family.

Chicago continued to regard Insull as the man to rely upon when there were big tasks to be done. In 1917, when the United States entered World War I, Insull was named by Governor Frank O. Lowden as chairman of the Illinois State Council of Defense. His performance was unique. The defense groups in other states spent sums of from $100,000 to $500,000 in carrying out their duties. Insull, given only a modest appropriation of $50,000, spent none of it and returned the state a profit of $300,000. He issued a patriotic cookbook which became the envy of publishers by selling 300,000 copies and showing a profit of $15,000. He made $150,000 by selling seed corn. People said that if he had been running the war he could have made it pay a dividend. A contemporary biographer wrote that Insull displayed "financial ability of a high order and inspired the confidence of bankers and investors. As a result, his securities are becoming widely known and are sought after in all parts of the investing world."

No additional assignment was too large for Insull to accept, although he was already the most powerful man in Chicago. After the war, the People's Gas Light & Coke Company was completely disorganized. Hundreds of thousands of Chicagoans were getting the wrong gas bills every month and only a fraction of the bills were being collected. The directors asked Samuel Insull to take over; he accepted the presidency, subjected the company to a drastic reorganization, straightened out the billing department and launched a typical Insull program to replace the antiquated gas plants with modern equipment. In a short time the company was prosperous.

The size of Insull's accomplishments was to be measured in the circumstance that Chicago, a city of two million people, was in many ways as much of a one-man town as the community erected by George M. Pullman. Samuel Insull provided it with its gas, furnished its electricity and ran the elevated system and suburban railroads which carried a high proportion of its commuters to and from their work. As Edgar Lee Masters dramatically pointed out, "with a flick of his hand he could plunge the city into darkness or in cold." Still Insull was not satisfied. He continued to be, as he had expressed himself nearly a quarter of a century before, "a great bull on Chicago." In 1926, two decades before the city was willing to take on the job, Insull was pressing for permission to build a passenger subway. He was not interested in owning the new transit facilities as Yerkes might have been; all he asked was a permit to build and operate it. "If the city is unable to [build it] and will give me an ordinance on which I can finance it, I will undertake the job," he told the City Council. The aldermen turned him down.

By the end of the war, Insull's horizons had expanded far beyond Chicago. His companies were operating in eleven states and furnishing power to 385 cities of which little more than half were in Illinois. He was always looking for new customers and wise enough to see that eventually women would be the greatest users of his electrical power. He outlined and put into effect a broad public-relations program, furnished speakers and literature to women's clubs on electrical living and in two years distributed more than five million pamphlets and broadsides.

Because of his visual approach to a problem, Insull's greatest interest was in the firms which served the Chicago area. The other businesses and the holding company of Middle West Utilities, which served to combine them into a single operation, were entrusted in large part to his brother, Martin. To Martin was also left most of the responsibility for arranging the financing with the bond houses which made possible the acquisition of these properties in distant states. Martin, who was often photographed in English riding clothes and who raised fine horses on his farm near Highland Park, was not popular with Chicagoans. Most of them distrusted him because of his pronounced preference for the English way of doing things; it was frequently pointed out that Samuel Insull had become an American citizen in 1896 but Martin never took the step. There was no one who dared criticize Martin to his brother, for Samuel resented a slur on Martin more than any attack upon himself. Yet one reason for Martin's rapid expansion of Middle West Utilities was to escape the shadows thrown by the reflected glory of Samuel Insull's name. It was this jealousy, of which Samuel Insull was unaware, that provided the flaw in his plans for a family dynasty.

When the personal direction of Samuel Insull was absent there was a tendency for trouble to develop. He was in Europe in 1926 when Frank Smith was running against William McKinley, a downstate utility owner, for the Republican nomination to the United States Senate. Insull's subordinates and Martin were eager to defeat McKinley because of a personal feud between the McKinley and Insull families. A cable was sent to Insull asking for a decision on how to defeat McKinley; Insull sent a reply giving Martin and the others carte blanche. Under the delusion that money was all-powerful, the aides dumped $125,000 into Smith's campaign. He won the nomination but his victory in the fall elections was nullified when he was turned back at the Senate door because of the excessive amount of money spent in his behalf. The incident gave Illinois the besmirched distinction of having two senators turned down because their victories were bought; Senator William Lorimer had been expelled from the Senate on much the same grounds a little more than ten years earlier.

Much has been written of the dealings of Insull with the Chicago politicians on whom he bestowed great quantities of money. Like many of the Chicago businessmen who preceded him, he erroneously considered a politician an item for sale on the same terms as any other commodity. There is a legend that Insull was contemptuous of politicians. It would be nearer the truth to say they were among his few friends. He dined often with the family of Roger Sullivan, the Democratic boss. Dinners with politicians provided an important part of his social life. Most of the time he came alone.

That ambitious men do not always make satisfactory husbands had been represented theatrically so often that Gladys Wallis must have been aware of her risk when she married Chicago's fast-rising young utility executive. By 1926, there were signs she felt the risk had been a poor one. She lived on a five-thousand-acre estate in a $125,000 Italian villa near Libertyville. A sliding roof which rolled back to reveal the canopy of stars on summer nights was little consolation as she read of the rise to theatrical stardom of her companions at Helen Windsor's theatrical boarding house. Walking through the baronial grounds of the estate with its artificial lagoons, monstrous goldfish, or pinning up the ribbons of Insull's prize Brown Swiss cattle or Suffolk Punch draft horses soon palled. Margaret Bird Insull (Gladys Wallis was her stage name) dreamed of hot, crowded dressing rooms and the discomfort of grease paint and quick changes in the wings. She told her husband she wanted to return to the stage. She had faithfully kept her bargain to relinquish her career. Her only stage appearances had been in 1905 in an amateur performance of Edmond Rostand's *Les Romanesques* in Winnetka and in 1908 when she gave a reading of Maeterlinck's *Pélléas* and *Mélisande*—to the accompaniment of what the papers called soulful music—to the Friday Club.

When Mrs. Insull announced her return to the stage, it was twenty-five years after Samuel, Jr., had been born; Chicagoans, reading of the role Mrs. Insull had selected, wondered if she had forgotten to count them. She would play, she said, Lady Teazle, the lively, innocent country maiden in Sheridan's *The School for Scandal* who marries a man old enough to be her grandfather. Insull, disapproving of his wife's plans, nonetheless consented to them, hoping that the magic of a stage success might restore some of the warmth which had disappeared from his relationship with his wife. Always

MRS. SAMUEL INSULL IN *The School for Scandal*

one to guard against failure, Insull suggested that his wife appear first in a series of charity performances for St. Luke's Hospital. He guaranteed the hospital $125,000 from a two weeks' run at the Illinois Theater. On opening night boxes went for $500 to $1,000 and no seat sold for less than $5. In two weeks the play netted the hospital $140,000, a sum which probably caused several other theater managers to be hospitalized with envy.

The local success of the play prompted Mrs. Insull to take it to Broadway where it had a short run. It then returned to the Selwyn in Chicago for another four weeks. Tasting triumph, Mrs. Insull leased the Studebaker Theater for five years and announced plans for the establishment of a repertory company in Chicago. After appearing in *The Runaway Road*, she retired to the role of director and producer, presenting *Heartbreak House* and *Mr. Pim Passes By* before she was forced to announce the closing of the theater. Her remarks on terminating her plans for the Studebaker were more familiar to theatrical managers than her two weeks' profit of $140,000. "I have reluctantly reached the belief that my ambition was misdirected, my plan a mistake and my money wasted," she said with commendable directness. "I'm not crying; indeed, I feel proud that I'm quitting with a laugh! I've learned that Chicago is not a marketplace for the raw materials of a repertoire theater such as I hoped to make of the Studebaker. I can easily have scenery painted here and properties manufactured here. But dramatists do not send their plays here to be read and actors do not walk Michigan Boulevard looking for Chicago engagements." Yet there was a trace of permanence even in this Insull failure; it was Mrs. Insull who persuaded the Theater Guild to start its touring subscription series with a Chicago engagement that opened with Alfred Lunt and Lynn Fontanne in *Arms and the Man*. Insull, who underwrote the costs of the engagement, made a profit on it, a token of success from the battery boy named Shaw who had proved so inefficient at the Edison Company switchboard in London he had been discharged.

During the twenties, Insull no longer had to sell securities in his companies. Customers fought for the privilege of sharing in his money-making magic. He continued to concentrate upon his Chicago interests. Mornings he spent at the People's Gas Light & Coke Company and afternoons in his offices at the Commonwealth Edison Building. The stock market, buoyant about every issue, could not be restrained in its enthusiasm for Insull. In 1922, when the country was still recovering from the post-World War I slump, Commonwealth Edison shot up to $122 a share. Royal Munger, then a financial reporter on the *Daily News*, called on Insull to ask what favorable factors Insull believed were responsible for the advance: "I will not say one word that will send that stock a point higher," Insull snapped. "It is too high now. That is more than the stock is worth." One of the privileges of owning Insull stock was that it carried rights to buy more Insull stock whenever additional shares were issued. Insull also had a preferred list of sixteen hundred Chicagoans who were permitted to buy new issues of stocks below the market price. To those who objected to this favoritism, Insull had a blunt answer: "It is not worth more." Even when it was known that those on the preferred list were getting stock for $12, the same shares were bringing $30 on the market. The plush carpet to Insull's office was being worn thin by people of every kind, all seeking market tips to make a clean-up.

Perhaps Insull's most audacious act was to accept the responsibility for making a paying proposition of Chicago opera after the "blaze of glory" season directed by Mary Garden. Before giving up the opera, Harold McCormick had generously paid all its bills and made it a gift of scenery and other properties worth approximately a million dollars. When Insull was given control he formed a committee willing to pledge $500,000 a year for five years to support opera. He also issued a statement that "no contract will be signed by any general director or business manager or any other individual from this day on. Every contract in the future must bear the signature of the chairman of the finance committee and one member of the Board of Directors. We will spend our own money." There were some objections to such a businesslike approach. Many of those who had a professional connection with the opera subscribed to the view of Oscar Hammerstein that opera should be run not as a business "but as a disease." Insull did not think opera stars would object to dealing with him. If the singers "want to stay at home and receive stage money," he said, "they may do so, but they'll have to come here to get real money. . . . One cannot ignore the dollar without getting into trouble." It was recognizably the Chicago approach.

Then, in a curious way, history began to repeat itself. Insull, like Uranus H. Crosby and Ferdinand Wythe Peck, conceived the idea of combining an opera house with an office building, convinced that office rents would pay for the opera. Insull attributed the fact Peck's scheme was not working at the Auditorium to the antiquated building. He made up his mind to erect a new home for opera on the banks of the river at the western edge of the business district, an area which the Chicago Plan Commission had designated as the site of a great Chicago civic center. The fact that not a single building rose in the area to confirm the Plan Commission's hopes did not deter Insull; he liked to be a generation ahead. He dispatched a group of architects to Europe to study the opera houses there. After they returned, he announced plans for a forty-five-story, twenty-million-dollar office building, opera house and theater on Madison Street near the river. The financing had that clarity and boldness typical of all Insull enterprises.

GRAND FOYER AT THE CIVIC
OPERA HOUSE

He sold ten million dollars' worth of stock among the "music lovers of the city" and gave the Metropolitan Life Insurance Company a mortgage on the remainder. If the entire income of the building had gone to wipe out the debt, the property would have been fully owned by the opera in about twenty-five years. Eventually, Insull envisioned a twenty- to thirty-million-dollar property, debt free, with its income supporting the opera. To make the task easier, he made a gift of the $300,000 in stock he had purchased to the opera company. All that was necessary, he told audiences throughout Chicago, was "reasonable foresight and management such as you would give to any other business." Opera was also to be democratic. It was one of the few points on which he agreed with Mary Garden, who said that the supporters of opera ought to be found in the telephone directory rather than the social register. In the new opera house, Insull said, boxes would be only at the rear. Society people who wished to wear their diamond tiaras and fine clothes would not be allowed to detract from the spectacle on the stage. It was his opportunity to put Chicago society in what he considered its proper place.

The building went up with amazing speed. The first ground was dug in February of 1928; by November 4, 1929, the opera house was ready for its grand opening—despite such a touch of local color as the theft of a large tapestry worth $4,000 from the stage. The opening night, with Rosa Raisa singing the traditional *Aida* was one that "disarmed criticism," according to a helpless critic. Samuel Insull stood in the foyer and greeted as many of the opening-night crowd as he could. The *Times* said Insull and Stanley Field had done everything that day to get the opera house in order but "dust off the seats," adding that "rich and poor mingled in the milling mob before the doors of opera gone democratic." James O'Donnell Bennett of the *Tribune* called the cavernous auditorium a "jewel casket"; he then switched metaphors to describe the hydraulic mechanism necessary to lift the enormous curtain as on the scale of machinery in the locks of the Panama Canal. Even a city which worshipped big figures found it hard to visualize an elevator seventy-five feet high which carried the scenery to storerooms beneath the stage. Mary Garden was not to be as impressed. She said "it wasn't like an opera house but more like a convention hall" and complained there was absolutely no communication with the public.

The opening of the opera house, just a few days before Insull's seventieth birthday, was the climax of his career. He was not as rich as either John D. Rockefeller or Henry Ford, but through his subsidiary companies he was the most powerful businessman in America. He sat on the boards of eighty-five companies, was chairman of the board for sixty-five, president of eleven and through his holding companies controlled six thousand power units in thirty-two states. With investments worth only twenty million dollars, he controlled a group of properties worth four hundred million. And still bankers competed for the privilege of extending him credit.

Insull had hoped that the opening of the new opera house would serve as the closing chapter of the forty years in which he had dominated the Chicago scene. There were many signs that he planned to abdicate his power, give much of it over to his son and play the role of elder statesman and patron of the arts. This plan was knocked askew less than a month before the grand opening by the crash of the stock market on Black Friday. Insull decided to stay on until economic conditions were more stable.

Insull's principal concern was to keep the price of Middle West and his holding companies high enough to cover the loans at the banks which had been necessary to finance Martin's extensive acquisitions. A few years before, Insull had been so seriously ill that he had gone to Arizona for a long vacation to recuperate. Returning, he found Middle West in such a groggy condition that he reorganized it, arranged new financing and left it with ten million dollars in the bank. He left soon afterward for a trip to Europe; when his boat docked a cable came from Martin asking for authority to raise fifty million dollars more which he asserted Middle West needed. Insull did not answer his brother, but sent a cable to his son, whom he had named vice-chairman of Middle West. "If you and Uncle Martin want to fail, do what you want," he wrote. "I am only an old man." In a few years he was to be fighting desperately to prevent that failure.

The Insull properties weathered the early years of the depression better than most companies. The banks still had money to lend Insull, although they refused to take a chance on the tax warrants of the city of Chicago. "Do you mean to tell me that the credit of the city of Chicago is not as good as that of Samuel Insull?" an alderman demanded at a public hearing. "Exactly that," replied Silas Strawn, who was on the witness stand. Like William B. Ogden, Samuel Insull was a big man to Chicagoans.

There were those outside Chicago who saw the weaknesses in Samuel Insull's position. One of these was Cyrus Eaton, the Cleveland financier, who had learned Insull was borrowing and buying heavily to keep up the values of his stocks. Eaton knew the stock-market game and Insull didn't. Slowly Eaton accumulated a large holding of Insull stocks, buying them when the stock fell and throwing just enough of the shares back on the market when the price rose to test Insull's strength. When he saw that Insull was committed to keeping up the price of his stocks, he showed his hand: unless Insull took over his holdings at a price far above that of the market, Eaton would dump the stocks, force the price down and put Insull in a position where the banks would call his loans and force him into bankruptcy. Insull was trapped; he had to pay Eaton forty million dollars for the stocks to keep them off the market. The move was that of a man playing desperately for time in the hope that normal conditions would return; but, as he was to learn, normal conditions as he understood them would never return.

Despite Insull's purchases, the values of the stocks continued to slip past the point where they would cover the bank loans. The banks, in their cautious but ruthless way, stepped in to take control, intending to leave Insull as their administrator. But there was one more revelation to come; it brought the Insull dream of empire and dynasty crashing to the ground. Martin Insull had taken more than half a million dollars of company funds to cover the margin on his personal brokerage account; and the man who had signed the check to give him that money was Samuel Insull.

On July 5, 1932, Samuel Insull sat in his paneled office in the Commonwealth Edison Building waiting to receive the directors of corporations who for years had done no more than nod assent to his every idea. There was a long directors' table in the room and from early in the morning until late in the afternoon groups formed, dispersed and formed again around the table. Secretaries carrying the bulky minute books of the various corporations hurried in and out of the room. At the head of the table sat Samuel Insull; near him was his son, his head erect and face taut, struggling to control his emotions over the collapse of his father's world. In an outer room the newspapers kept a death watch, the reporters noting that some of the directors had tears in their eyes as they left the room. As the meetings progressed, Samuel Insull resigned from every one of his positions and turned all his assets and those of his family over to the directors.

After the last directors' meeting, Insull asked his secretary to get his wife on the phone, adding "Do not disturb her if she is resting." When the call was put through, he said, "Well, it is all over. . . . It was a very tiring day. After dinner we will take a drive. Good-bye." At the table an office aide blurted, "You will be back in six months, Mr. Insull. Your stockholders will demand it." But the white-haired man at the phone could be ruthless with himself as well. "No," he said, "I will not come back. I am through." On the way out, he stopped to say a word to the newspapermen, his traditional enemies. "Here I go, gentlemen," he said, "after fifty years a man without a job."

The crash of the Insull stocks closed a Chicago bank and brought ruin to hundreds of small stock owners, many of whom had been pressured into buying stocks during the final days when Insull was using gas and electrical repairmen, clerks and even janitors as salesmen of his stocks in order to keep their value high. His opera stars suffered with the rest. Augusta Lenska, a retired contralto, attempted to commit suicide by throwing herself in front of a streetcar. Only shrewd Mary Garden lost no money. "I never accepted favors from Mr. Insull, which turned out to be rather fortunate, didn't it?" she said. Those who had doubled their fortunes with Insull stocks were often most bitter at the man they considered infallible.

SAMUEL INSULL AT THE
HEIGHT OF HIS POWER

There were many explanations for the Insull crash. Royal Munger, in the most dispassionate analysis, said that if Martin Insull "had spent less time on Pullman trains [that is, in expanding into all parts of the country] and more studying figures he would still be on top." As it was, Munger said, Martin's lack of sound business principles produced results "for both himself and his stockholders [that] can only be called ghastly." Much of the blame was of course Samuel Insull's, who was probably not familiar with Lord Acton's comments on the corruptive possibilities of absolute power but was just as much a victim of that corruption.

More than three hundred thousand stockholders could not be deprived of their savings without a demand for retribution. A series of charges were brought against Samuel Insull, Martin Insull, Samuel Insull, Jr., and a group of executives for various alleged illegal manipulations. In addition, Cook County charged the brothers with embezzlement because of the use of the money for Martin's private stock accounts. In the midst of the investigations which preceded the filing of the charges, Samuel Insull slipped quietly out of the country for Europe and Martin fled to Canada. The flight was the least creditable act of Insull's life. It would have been better, a newspaper editorialist reminded him, to remember the words of Plato: It is better for the wrong-doer to be punished than to escape punishment. It is less evil to suffer wrong than to do wrong.

The story strays then from Chicago to Paris and Greece. After many legal maneuvers, Insull lost his asylum in that country and fled ignominiously in disguise, being finally apprehended in a ship off the port of Istanbul. He was brought back to trial on a series of charges and in every case acquitted. The jurors at the final trial told reporters they had known what their verdict would be six weeks earlier, even before Insull took the stand. The Chicago *Times*, exuberant over the promise of President Franklin D. Roosevelt's New Deal, summed the verdict up: "Insull and his fellow defendants—not guilty; the old order—guilty. That was the Insull defense and the jury agreed with it." Mrs. Insull, reunited with her husband in his moment of tribulation, paid him her own compliment. "He has been a great sport through it all," she said. "It is character that counts and not money."

John T. Flynn and other reporters converging on the scene of the titan's debacle found it difficult to explain the absence of bitterness toward the man who had wiped out the savings of so many. The directors of his corporations had only been dissuaded on grounds of public policy from voting him a pension of $100,000 a year; he was given instead an employe's pension of $18,000 annually. The answer, perhaps, lay in a letter written by a stockholder to Edward Brewster when Insull had reorganized Middle West utilities. "It reminds me of some of Shakespeare's plays," he wrote. "No matter how many times you read it, each succeeding time finds new beauties. . . . I take off my hat to the geniuses (or genius) that constructed that set-up. . . . We built better than either of us knew, I am sure, when we hitched our wagon to the Insull stars. All we have needed was faith and not understanding. We let Sam do it and I must say he did a mighty fine job. . . . I see no more reason for selling Commonwealth Edison at $400 than I did at $300. . . . I am still inclined to pin my faith on that genius of faith, Mr. Samuel Insull, who still commands us to 'Sail on, sail on, and on!' "

Samuel Insull's great journey, as he realized after his trial, was nearly over. Chicago saw little of him. He spent much time in Europe. In 1938, while walking across a subway platform in Paris, he suffered a heart attack and died. It was some hours before police were able to identify him as the man who bossed Chicago with an arbitrary rule, built the dynamos which gave it power and laced the countryside with the 125,000-volt lines that formed the life arteries of the Midwest.

The Paris police report before Insull had been identified was worth quoting:

An unidentified man was found in a state of collapse on the platform of the Tuileries subway station near the Place de la Concorde. He was neatly dressed in a gray suit with red stripes, wore a brown felt hat and had 7 francs, 7 centimes [about 85 cents] in his pocket. He was of medium size with white hair. He had no identification papers but the initials "S. I." were on his handkerchiefs and underclothing. Agent 2023.

A man, after all, like any other man.

SETTING THE CLOCK AT MAR-
SHALL FIELD & CO. *From a painting by Norman Rockwell*

Epilogue

More Than a Century of Progress

THE EFFECTS of the depression fell as heavily upon the city government as upon Samuel Insull. The municipal government was bankrupt and the banks refused to extend it credit. In 1930, there was no money to pay Chicago's policemen, firemen, schoolteachers, janitors or clerks. But even with these formidable problems, the city refused to abandon plans to celebrate the one hundredth anniversary of the incorporation of Chicago as a village.

The originator of the new exposition was Rufus C. Dawes, who first advanced the idea in 1923. The theme of the fair, he suggested, should be a demonstration of what mankind had been able to accomplish through a mastery and understanding of nature, a subject dramatically demonstrated by the phenomenal growth of Chicago on swampland obviously not intended as a dwelling place. Plans for the fair, inaugurated under Mayor Dever's administration, were temporarily abandoned when Mayor Thompson returned for a third term in City Hall. As soon as the city accustomed itself to living with Big Bill again, the plans for the fair were reactivated and a corporation organized to stage a fair to be known as "A Century of Progress." The organizers specified that the fair was to be built without any taxation or federal, state, city or county subsidy. It was to be wholly a project of the unofficial government of Chicago businessmen to which all matters of importance traditionally were entrusted. Though several members of the committee lost their businesses and their fortunes in the stock market crash, they did not waver in their intention of celebrating "A Century of Progress."

The fair, located on more than four hundred acres of artificially created land bordering the lake, was opened on April 29, 1933. Appropriately, it was the scientists rather than the more customary politicians who dominated the opening day. The most spectacular feat was the turning on of the lights at the fair with energy from the rays of the star Arcturus, focused on photoelectric cells in a series of astronomical observatories and then transformed into electrical energy which was transmitted to Chicago. Arcturus had been chosen because its distance of 240 trillion miles most nearly corresponded to forty light years; those at the fair liked to think the varicolored incandescent lights and miles of neon tubing at the 1933 exposition were set aglow by light which had been leaving Arcturus at the moment the Columbian Exposition was opened forty years earlier. Chicago, having only a brief century of its own history, sought by this gesture to identify itself with the infinite age of the universe.

The secretary of the new fair formed a closer link with the past. He was Daniel H. Burnham, Jr., whose father had been responsible for the architectural splendor of the 1893 fair. But the classical motif of that earlier exposition was replaced in 1933 by the severe modern architecture that had developed from the ideas of the Chicago school of half a century before. The philosophy of Louis Sullivan that "form follows function" was brilliantly expressed in a series of stark white buildings set with geometrical precision along the Lake Michigan shore line and as purely functional as the machinery on display within their walls. Rufus C. Dawes, who had been elected president of the fair, described it as "the spontaneous expression of the pride of citizenship of Chicago." The exposition illustrated, he said, "the dependence of modern industry upon scientific research"—and provided evidence of man's achievements in the realm of physical science—"proofs of his power to prevail over the perils that beset him." The words were an echo of those of the founders of the Interstate Industrial Exposition. The abstract matters of esthetics or art had little interest for the leaders of Chicago. They were practical men, proud of their accomplishments in making knowledge useful and in finding profitable applications for the discoveries of science.

A portion of the exhibits at "A Century of Progress" were reminiscent of the Columbian Exposition. Among them were the partial reconstruction of a walled city of China, a golden-roofed lama temple from Jehol, a picturesque nunnery of Uxmal representing the zenith of Mayan culture and a teahouse from Japan. Other displays, such as the bathysphere which took William

Beebe 2,200 feet beneath the surface of the ocean and the aluminum globe in which Auguste Picard soared 54,000 feet into the stratosphere, were awesome symbols of the daring exploits that were pushing out the frontiers of science. Other unusual attractions included an operating diamond mine in conjunction with a million-dollar display of diamonds, and a mechanical robot who gave lectures on diet which were illustrated by the workings of his own illuminated interior.

It was at "A Century of Progress" that Americans first became knowledgeable about dinosaurs and other prehistoric monsters. The world as it might have been a million years ago was represented in a series of dioramas before which visitors with no interest in archeological skeletons gazed with fascination at life-sized reconstructions of the hairy mammoth, the pterodactyl, the massive brontosaurus, triceratops and dimetrodon. Chicago had come a long way from the zeuglodon that once awed visitors in Colonel Wood's museum.

The Transportation Building, its roof supported by a series of fingerlike skyhooks, was one of the dominant buildings of the fair. The exhibits of America's largest automobile manufacturers underscored the accomplishments of the engineers in transforming the country into a nation on wheels. A pageant, "Wings of a Century," recounted the advances of transportation from the days of prehistory. Against the ever-changing blue, gray or green backdrop of Lake Michigan, actors on an open stage re-enacted the principal dramas in man's attempt to conquer the spaces of the earth. The pageant had a special meaning for Chicago, for it was from the city's place as a transportation center that Chicago derived its existence. First had come the Illinois-Michigan Canal, establishing Chicago as the port at the junction of America's two great inland waterways. The canal and lake traffic was followed by the engines and boxcars of the railroads; whether the trains ran south, north, east or west, Chicago was their terminal, the greatest rail center in the world. Finally had come the airplanes. Chicago became the stopover point for those who traveled by air as it had been the junction for those who journeyed by rail and water. Three times within a century one form of transportation had superseded another; yet Chicago remained for them all the crossroads of America.

Dominating the fair was an effort to anticipate another form of transportation. It was the Sky Ride, whose two gaunt towers stretched sixty-four stories high and were connected at the twenty-fourth floor by cables from which "rocket cars" were suspended. Before the possibilities of air travel were fully appreciated, it was believed the cities of the future would be joined by such suspended monorails. Although the phenomenal development of aviation outmoded such transportation, the Sky Ride gave those at the fair a view of the city as impressive as the one their parents had been able to obtain from the "bridge on an axle" that George Ferris designed for the exposition of 1893.

No Chicago fair would have been complete without a Midway. The Midway of the 1933 fair was less extensive in area but equally as provocative of comment as its predecessor of 1893. The Streets of Paris replaced the Streets of Cairo as the popular attraction; instead of Little Egypt, there was Sally Rand. Sally was an unemployed silent film actress who burst unexpectedly on "A Century of Progress" in the role of Lady Godiva astride a white horse. When this sensational bid for employment failed, she gave up her horse to buy two ostrich feather fans—on credit, she insisted later—and persuaded a manager to hire her as a fan dancer. She needed no help in publicizing her act. She first attracted attention by announcing she would not wear clothes because they interfered with the movement of the fans. The inspiration for her dance, she said, came from a childhood memory of "white herons flying in the moonlight" above her grandfather's farm. Whatever the inspiration, it was a profitable one. By the end of the summer she was drawing $3000 a week and had all but pushed into obscurity the scientific theme which was intended to dominate the fair.

There were several attempts to subdue Sally by making her don some clothing. Judge Joseph B. David was asked to issue an injunction preventing "lewd and lascivious dances" in the Streets of Paris attraction. The judge, indignantly remarking that "some people would like to put pants on horses," listened unsympathetically as an attorney charged that "one woman dances with nothing but a pair of fans about her. It's disgraceful!"

The judge interrupted. "*Honi soit qui mal y pense,*" he said. "This court holds no brief for the prurient or ignorant. Let them walk out if they wish. If you ask me, they are just a lot of boobs come to see a woman wiggle with a fan or without fig leaves. But we have the boobs and we have a right to cater to them." Denying the injunction, Judge David dismissed court with the comment that "The Streets of Paris could starve to death for all of me. I go where there is a good glass of beer."

The moralists had little luck in imposing restrictions on the Midway until the city's mayor, Edward J. Kelly, visited the Oriental Village—presumably in quest of a good glass of beer. The mayor, according to the following day's newspapers, turned a "bashful pink" at seeing a number of seductive oriental houris clad in "purely hypothetical costumes." As quoted by the reporters, he ordered that the "nudity be denuded" and instructed all managers to make their performers put on clothes. Sally Rand, after a thirty-five-minute argument with her manager, reluctantly appeared in a transparent gauze costume. Jack Hardy, production manager of the Oriental Village, sought to deprecate the importance of the mayor's order. "We're going mostly on class, not nudity," he said. "I don't think the mayor is a reliable weather vane when it comes to art and morality."

Texas Guinan, who was running a night club called The Pirate Ship, took a more realistic view. Protesting that the fair officials were "trying to put fun and pleasure on a business schedule," she closed her night club and left the fair. (Tragically, after she left, she became one of the victims of an epidemic of amoebic dysentery that marred the first summer of the fair.) Only Judge David continued in his role of defender of the arts. In September, he issued an injunction restraining the South Park Board (which had jurisdiction over the fair grounds) from draping artificial flowers over the bosom of a living model in the representation of Manet's painting, Olympia, in a peep show in the Streets of Paris. Noting that the model's bosom was already shielded by her strategically placed hand, Judge David warned, "I'll issue the injunction—but heaven help the lady if she moves her hand." As far as can be ascertained, she never did.

The well-publicized arguments over the morality of the fair's attractions increased rather than diminished the public's interest. By the end of the summer more than twenty-two million people had visited the fair grounds and it was decided to extend the exposition for another year. "However," said general manager Lenox R. Lohr, "we believe that next year the pendulum will swing to finer things." He announced that a concentration of villages—Swiss, Black Forest, English, Early American, Venetian, Spanish,

A CENTURY OF PROGRESS, 1933. U. S. Army Photograph

Irish and Tunisian—would replace much of the 1933 Midway. The Streets of Paris, an official statement promised, would be "more elaborate and more accurately representative of Parisian atmosphere than it was in 1933." In any case, the fair avoided the courts while another sixteen million visitors were drawn to the more substantial evidences of "A Century of Progress."

The South Park Board, prohibited by Judge David from acting as moral censor at the fair, made its way into the headlines with an order prohibiting members of the Chicago Artists Equity from displaying nudes in their annual outdoor show in Grant Park. The Board was compelled to withdraw its order, however, when a public protest was organized under the direction of Mrs. Frank G. Logan, wife of the honorary president of the Art Institute and one of the sponsors of the show. Though Mrs. Logan was tolerant of nudes, she was less satisfied with certain other forms of artistic expression. In particular, she disliked modernism. She was one of the principal benefactors of the Art Institute and with her husband had endowed an annual prize for work shown there. After a series of prizes had gone to paintings employing unconventional techniques or perspectives, the Logans unhappily confided to their friends that there had been "a miscarriage of artistic justice." When the Logan prize went to Francis Chapin's "Pink House," Mrs. Logan noted unhappily that it was drawn "on a bias." In 1935, when a jury picked Doris Lee's whimsical "Thanksgiving" as winner of the Logan prize, Mrs. Logan publicly expressed her dissatisfaction. "The paintings [in the show] are trash," she said. "I am incensed. After a visit to a museum one should have a glow, should be uplifted. But a sane person leaves the exhibit feeling the art unleashes the jitters or delirium tremens. I defy anyone to find more than six or eight normal pictures in the whole show."

Kate Buckingham, one of the five or six most generous donors of funds to the Institute and a woman whose philanthropies included the Buckingham Fountain with its multi-colored water displays on the lake front, echoed the views expressed by Mrs. Logan. "I haven't seen the Art Institute show and I don't want to," she said. "I don't intend to go, as from what I heard it's so dreadful that I'd be too disgusted ever to go back to the Institute." Chauncey McCormick, then the vice-president of the Institute, attempted to soothe the dissident factions. "A newspaper does not indorse murder when it prints the news of a murder," he said. "We are recording the times, giving a cross section of what is happening in America."

The explanation did not satisfy Mrs. Logan. She reprinted with approval an editorial asserting that juries gave prizes only to pictures that would stir up controversy and stimulate attendance among a public curious to discover if a painting was "as bad as they say it is." She sought to have Jules Breton's "Song of the Lark," one of the most popular paintings displayed at the Columbian Exposition, taken from a storeroom and restored to the walls of the Institute. She was as disapproving of the politics of the modern artists as of their techniques. "In Chicago today few conservative artists have been making their expenses," she complained, "and all the radicals are working for the PWA. Many excellent painters are so discouraged that they have not touched a brush for months. If insanity is essential to true art, there should be a lot of it produced." Noting that only one painting in an Institute show had been sold, she said, "That went to Philadelphia, I am happy to state."

An outgrowth of Mrs. Logan's campaign against modernism was the organization of a Society for Sanity in Art. Its purpose, according to its laws of incorporation, was to "further rationalism in painting, sculpture and allied fields and to encourage the teaching of a saneness as a constituent element of creative endeavor." Sculptor Gutzon Borglum contributed an introduction to a slim volume titled *Sanity in Art,* in which Mrs. Logan published her own ideas and correspondence from those who agreed with her. For her it was purely an artistic crusade. She firmly resisted those who wanted her to identify modernism with immorality. "Morals have nothing to do with it," she said, adding that her purpose was only "to help rid the museums of the modernistic, moronic, grotesqueries of so-called modern art." A few members of the board of trustees of the Art Institute were among those who joined the Society for Sanity in Art. A trustee who declined was Chauncey McCormick who commented, "Sanity in art—sanity in anything—is indeed a fine goal at which to aim; but the question immediately arises—whose sanity?"

Chicagoans, reading of the controversy over the Logan prizes, recalled the statement of Long John Wentworth nearly a century earlier. "Chicago has ever been noted for its sensations," he said. "And that is one of the reasons why I have never liked to leave it. You cannot find any other place that has so many of them. Why travel about when there is so much of interest transpiring at home?" Mary Borden, the novelist, revisiting Chicago during the 1930's found this characteristic ferment everywhere in evidence. "No one is ashamed of anything in Chicago," she wrote in *Harper's.* "Everything is moving too quickly, everyone is too specialized and it is all too much fun. Each one, whether crook or politician or expert gunman, is too good of his kind to be conscious of anything less positive and less exhilarating than his own power."

There were reasons for Chicagoans to be conscious of their power. The growth of their city had been unique. In the sixty years from 1830 to 1890, the population had multiplied nearly 22,000 times; from less than fifty people it had grown to more than a million. After the turn of the century it continued to grow. In 1953 its population is more than three and a half million. These are only those who live within the official city boundaries. In the suburbs, which spread in concentric waves around the city and overflow the state lines of Illinois into Indiana and Wisconsin are another two million people who are part of the Chicago metropolitan area. Chicago is still the city Americans want to see. More than twelve million visitors arrive in the city every year; nearly a million of this number come to attend a convention. Passenger trains arrive and depart at the rate of more than one a minute. Airplanes land or take off on an average of one every two minutes. The ships which sail from Lake Michigan into Chicago's harbors carry a tonnage greater than that handled by the Panama and Suez Canals combined— which explains why Chicagoans must still wait occasionally for their bridges to be put down. Chicago is the marketplace of America. Its Merchandise Mart is the world's largest commercial building. It is still the farmer's market, too. The Board of Trade is the world's largest grain market. The Chicago Mercantile Exchange is the largest market in the world for butter, eggs, potatoes, onions and other farm products. More than forty million catalogs are sent out annually from such mail-order houses as Sears, Roebuck, Montgomery Ward, Spiegel's and Alden's—enough for more than half the homes in America. Big is not a word Chicagoans use much; they prefer biggest. Chicago, they will tell you, is the biggest manufacturer in America of radio and television sets, of household goods, pictures, mirrors, window screens, shades and blinds, of sporting goods and candy, and of a range of products from tin cans to electrical machinery, railroad equipment and structural steel. If it must yield to New York in the making of fashions, it can claim pre-eminence in the manufacture of the perfumes and cosmetics which adorn the American woman.

Not all the city's energies have gone to the pursuit of the dollar. To the east, the lake front with its startlingly beautiful buildings is as much a monument to Chicago's merchants as the business institutions which bear their name. Grant Park, a long swath of green at the edge of the downtown district which the city calls its front yard, exists as it does because of the battle waged by a strong-willed merchant named A. Montgomery Ward. He was another of Chicago's self-made men. At eleven he had been working in a barrel factory and at fourteen in a brickyard. He came to Chicago in 1865 and took a position as a clerk in the store of Field, Palmer & Leiter. Seven years later he established the world's first mail-order house in the loft of a Chicago barn. When his business prospered, he bought property on Michigan Avenue for his company offices. He was shocked to find the building overlooked a wasteland of railroad tracks, dumping grounds, ugly armories that housed some of the city's national-guard regiments and other unsightly buildings. All the structures had been put up in defiance of an ordinance of 1837 that the area east of Michigan Avenue from Randolph Street to Park Row was to be kept free of buildings forever. Ward, acting as a Michigan Avenue property owner, sought the help of the courts in re-

A LION IS ON MICHIGAN AVE-
NUE, *by Commander Arthur A. Gilbert*

storing the area as a park. "Without recourse to the courts," he said, "there would be merry-go-rounds and what-nots all the way to Park Row. They have made a dumping ground of the park, allowed circuses, masked balls and anything else there." Ward, whom the *Tribune* described as "a human icicle, shunning and shunned in all but the relations of business," needed all the iron in his character to withstand the onslaught against him when he asked and secured a court injunction and order clearing the area of buildings and forcing the removal of eight railroad tracks. For thirteen years, Ward fought in the courts at his own expense to have the injunction made perpetual. Finally after the victory was won, he granted the only newspaper interview of his life to a reporter for the *Tribune*. "Had I known in 1890 how long it would take me to preserve a park for the people against their will," he said candidly, "I doubt if I would have undertaken it. I think there is not another man in Chicago who would have spent the money I have spent in this fight with certainty that even gratitude would be denied as interest. I fought for the poor people of Chicago—not the millionaires. In the district bounded by Twenty-second Street, Chicago Avenue and Halsted live more than 250,-000 persons, mostly poor. The city has a magnificent park and boulevard system of some fifty miles but the poor man's auto is a shank's mare or at best the streetcars. Here is a park frontage on the lake, comparing favorably with the Bay of Naples, which city officials would crowd with buildings, transforming the breathing spot for the poor into a showground of the educated rich. I do not think it is right." Ward did not expect any laurels for the litigation which earned him the title of "watchdog of the lake front." "Perhaps I may see the public appreciate my efforts," he said, "but I doubt it."

The court's order upholding Ward was so sweeping that at first it was feared that the Art Institute would have to be demolished. Ward indicated he was willing to let the Institute stand but it was only with the greatest reservations that he finally consented to plans to erect the Field Museum of Natural History (now the Chicago Natural History Museum) in Grant Park. The museum, with exhibits in anthropology, botany, zoology, and geology which place it among the finest institutions of its kind in the world, was founded with gifts of nearly ten million dollars from Chicago's merchant prince, Marshall Field I. Across the drive is the Shedd Aquarium, a gift to the city from a merchant who made his fortune as a partner of Marshall Field. The aquarium, first and largest of its kind in America, was given to the city by John G. Shedd, a New Hampshire Yankee who became president of Marshall Field & Co. after Field's death and a man whom Field once described to a United States Senate committee as "the best merchant in the United States." Shedd was conscious of the public responsibilities of a merchant. "The merchant is the pathfinder in art," he said. "Allow that the artist produces art, it is the merchant who exploits it, taking the initiative and taking the risks. To meet the necessities of the people is the first demand of the merchant; to lead in the demands for the artistic is the second and no less important office. Today the modern great merchandise house is international in scope and art and business success can go hand in hand. Too many men have made fortunes in Chicago and while making them have left the city to grow as it would. If some of these had found a little time for audience with men who had the welfare of the future city in mind and heart, fewer would have fancied need to take up residence in more beautiful and ripened environments."

A merchant who did have the "welfare of the future city in mind and heart," was Julius Rosenwald, who gave away sixty-three million dollars because he believed in "giving while I am alive." He began his business career as a manufacturer of men's clothing. One of his customers was Richard W. Sears, who with Alvah C. Roebuck had established a small mail-order house in competition with that of Montgomery Ward. In 1893 Rosenwald bought a half interest in Sears, Roebuck; by 1910 he was the firm's president. As Sears, Roebuck expanded under his direction, he became the richest man in Chicago. He showed little interest in maintaining any such distinction. He created the Rosenwald Foundation with a gift of thirty million dollars. Specifying that the money be used "for the well-being of mankind," he also set a time limit for its total expenditure so that no bureaucracy of officials or administrators would siphon off funds from worthy projects. He built more than five thousand schools for Negroes. He gave five million dollars to the University of Chicago. When the stock market crashed in 1929, he personally guaranteed the investments of all Sears' four thousand employes. But his visible memorial is the Museum of Science and Industry, which stands near the lake shore just east of the University of Chicago. According to Sewell Avery, Rosenwald first thought of the museum when his son, William, then only eight years old, wandered away from his parents in Munich, Germany, and was found in an industrial museum there. As the location for the museum, Rosenwald selected the Fine Arts Building of the Columbian Exposition. It had been used as a temporary home for the Field Museum but when the new edifice was erected in Grant Park it was abandoned. Rosenwald reduced the building to its original steel skeleton and brick walls and reconstructed it in permanent stone, thus preserving for future generations the architectural masterpiece of the 1893 exposition. From the 1933 fair came many of the industrial and scientific exhibits that were to be displayed, forming a single memorial to two of the proudest moments in Chicago's history. Today, as exhibits are shifted and added to keep pace with the discoveries of science, the unchanging classic lines of the museum itself remain a perpetual reminder of the durability of beauty.

The fourth great public building of the lake front, the planetarium, is a gift of Rosenwald's brother-in-law, Max Adler, also an executive of Sears, Roebuck and Co. The Adler Planetarium, like the aquarium near which it stands, was the first building of its kind in America. Adler explained his gift in simple terms. "I wanted to give some evidence of my feeling for Chicago," he said, "and of my pride in the city which made it possible for me to accumulate my modest fortune."

Montgomery Ward, Marshall Field, Sears, Roebuck—these are the names by which America knows Chicago, the names memorialized in the handsome and useful monuments of the city's lake shore. But there is more to Chicago than the fabulous titans, the builders of great businesses and the makers of great fortunes. There is the city of bungalows, of workers, artisans, hog butchers and rail workers that spreads wide across the prairie. These nameless Chicagoans have much in common with their more illustrious fellow-citizens. All are individualists. They prefer a bungalow to an apartment and when forced to an apartment, choose a "two-flat" or at most a three-story walkup. Reluctantly, as land values rise, more and more Chicagoans are forced to live in skyscraper apartments. But for every skyscraper which rises along the lake shore, another sprawling community of bungalows spreads westward across the prairie, most of the houses characterized by the face brick in front and plain brick in the other walls that is expressive of Chicago practicality—the Queen Anne front and Betty Ann back, as one visitor described the style.

Vitality is still the principal Chicago personality trait. "Make no small plans," architect Daniel Burnham counseled Chicagoans when he advanced his Chicago Plan. But the grandiose schemes of Burnham, outlined in the Wacker Manual of 1912, were outmoded in forty years, little more than a generation. In 1953, the city published a new manual, *Chicago's Tomorrow,* that included the specifications of more ambitious blueprints for the future. Chicago is a city that lives in a hurry. North of the loop the twin towers of the revolutionary apartments of steel and glass erected by Mies van der Rohe rise boldly above the brick outlines of more traditional architecture. In every direction there are outlines of the Chicago of tomorrow. Once the city was built upon swampland. It was erected a second time upon its own ashes. Now it is being rebuilt upon the debris of its slums.

Look south. The white buildings of Lake Meadows, a model community of two thousand apartments, rise above an area which had run the gamut of civic existence from millionaires' mansions to blighted slum. For twenty years, from the time of the depression until after World War II, Chicago seemed to have lost its zest to grow. But the remaking of the city, now that it has come, has been undertaken in a fashion Chicagoans recognize as typical. At Lake Meadows, valuable land was cleared until it was flat as the original prairies which Stephen A. Douglas, one of the early owners in the area, had found there. A main thoroughfare was ruthlessly shut off to provide a quiet area for residential living near the heart of the city. The

THE CHICAGO LAKE FRONT

apartments are not crowded wall to wall and window to window but stand in the middle of wide blocks of green that serve as playgrounds and school yards, giving life again to "The Garden City." Farther to the south, at the fringe of the suburban area, lies Park Forest, a new community planned and created on Illinois farmland, blossoming with sudden fertility into a self-sufficient community. Laid out according to the most modern ideas of city planning, Park Forest proudly claims the neighborly cup of coffee as its community symbol, a token of its effort to restore the neighborhood to an important role in urban life. (There are those who wonder, however, since the lawns are spacious, why the builders have banned dogs and will not permit housewives to decorate their back yards with the friendly clothesline.)

Also, on the South Side, stretching along the green Midway that owes its name to the 1893 Exposition, is the University of Chicago, still blazing new trails for American education—and for civilization. The battlements of the university's Gothic halls are symbolic of its isolation in a once fashionable neighborhood now riddled by blight and deterioration. But the battle for survival has not been allowed to interfere with the struggle for enlightenment. It was in a laboratory of the University of Chicago on December 2, 1942 that man first controlled the energy of the atom and thereby ushered in a new era for mankind, justifying the importance which William Rainey Harper attached to laboratories in the plans for the university he so meticulously outlined in his notebooks. Robert Maynard Hutchins, president of the university in 1942, was as bold an innovator in education as Harper. Hutchins was responsible for bringing the atomic-energy project to the university and risking obloquy if it should fail. When it succeeded he was equally quick to assemble the country's best scientists in an Institute for Nuclear Studies, seeking a use for the atom as dramatic in peace as its employment in war.

The city grows to the west as well. The Congress Street superhighway, a broad blade of concrete and asphalt, cuts straight through the city to the western suburbs, forming a channel that will draw the residents of the Fox River Valley into the city as they were once attracted by the lines of William B. Ogden's Galena & Chicago Union Railway. Near the Congress Street superhighway rise the enormous buildings of the West Side Medical Center District, the world's greatest concentration of planned medical resources—twenty-one public and private institutions. Among them are six hospitals, seven medical, dental, pharmaceutical, nursing and other schools associated with the practice of medicine. In 1951, one out of every four doctors practicing in the United States had taken part of his training at one of the hospitals in the nucleus of this Medical Center. Yet in 1953, the value of the buildings in the project is already three times as great as in 1951. Cook County Hospital alone treats almost 100,000 patients a year in its wards; its clinics bring its yearly total of patients to more than half a million. In the area nearby where Jane Addams founded Hull House to care for the needs of the immigrants and ameliorate the conditions of these new Americans, a program of rehabilitation under the direction of the West Side Planning Board is under way by which these once isolated groups will take their place among the proudest communities of the city.

Northward paths of concrete follow along the trails traced by the power lines of Samuel Insull. Edens superhighway, which carries the residents of the most northerly suburbs to their homes, winds through a maze of new communities. Along Insull's Skokie Valley Route, houses are mushrooming from the prairie to provide customers for the power plants he plotted a generation ago. At the west of the Loop, a double-deck boulevard now runs past Insull's Opera House to a junction with the Congress Street superhighway, carrying past the door of his skyscraper traffic that people said Insull was a fool to think would ever be there.

The reasons for Chicago's multimillion-dollar surge of superhighways, underground parking garages, skyscraper apartments and expanding clusters of new bungalows are not altruistic but economic. The time had come when reform would pay, when reform was necessary if Chicago was to remain a great city—and a good place to make a fortune. There are no titans such as William B. Ogden, Long John Wentworth, Philip D. Armour, Marshall Field I or Samuel Insull who dominate Chicago in 1953. Yet the absence of a giant willing to take on tasks properly the function of the whole community is one of the significant signs of maturity in the brash, young city. The reputation of Chicago, made in such incredible eras as those of Mike McDonald, Jim Colosimo, Al Capone and Big Bill Thompson, came in part from the absence of a sense of responsibility among a large number of the city's voters. There was always a willingness to "let Sam do it," or Big Bill or Long John or any other man ambitious enough to tackle the job. Revelations of graft still come so rapidly in the newspapers that the readers tire of them. There are reasons, however, to think that Chicagoans are ready to end a system that for nearly a hundred years has been taken for granted. The time is near when political reform as well as civic pride will pay; when that time comes there is no doubt the city will find the means to reform. The Citizens of Greater Chicago, latest of the many anti-crime groups formed in the city's history, is not wasting its efforts on the symptoms of crime but is trying to change the antiquated system of government (imposed by downstate Illinois politicians) which has permitted the alliance of crime and politics to flourish. Merchants, trying to keep pace with the rapid expansion of the suburbs by opening new community shopping centers, know that the future of their investments in the heart of the city depends directly upon the city's solvency and ability to make itself attractive for many people who in the past years have been fleeing to the suburbs. The committees of businessmen, always a Chicago prelude to an important endeavor, have already been formed. There are many reasons to believe they will succeed in making a better city.

There are many echoes of the past. Chicagoans still prefer summer concerts to the "more severe" symphonies of the winter season. In the summer Chicagoans flock to the lake front to listen to symphony concerts in numbers ranging from 10,000 to 100,000. North of the city, at Ravinia, the city's first families sit upon blankets to listen to the summer concerts as their parents once sat upon stoop rugs on Prairie Avenue—and the concerts are still interrupted by the whistle or rumble of a passing train as concerts have been since the days when Theodore Thomas conducted in the hall of the Interstate Industrial Exposition. New England morality is still dominant. When the fashionable country club of Onwentsia built its clubhouse, the structure had to be designed so that the bar would be outside the limits of Lake Forest, which still prohibits any sale of liquor. There are other echoes. Mayor Edward J. Kelly, continuing the tradition of service that William T. Stead found at the base of Democratic power in the 1890's, formed a political machine during the 1930's as powerful as any the city had ever seen. But Edward J. Kelly was a warm mayor, like the Carter Harrisons, and Chicago

AERIAL VIEW OF CHICAGO TODAY

liked him—particularly when he reflected the city's ardent patriotism and personally saw to it that Chicago was the most hospitable city in America to any soldier, sailor or marine during World War II. The rumblings of violence are not all gone. In 1937, ten men and boys were killed at the gates of the Republic Steel Corporation and the specter of the Haymarket and Pullman riots rose again. Chicago is still a city where fifty-four of its newspapers are published in a foreign language, a city of turbulence where not only alien and native born, but Negro and white, worker and manager must learn to live together.

The city is conscious of its youth, eager to claim any mark of sophistication. Marshall Field & Co. has proudly passed its centennial and Carson Pirie Scott & Co. and Mandel Brothers are nearing their own century mark. A few families can count four and five generations of Chicagoans. At the Art Institute a supercilious visitor inquires how Chicagoans can afford to buy so many Renoirs. "We did not buy them," replies Chauncey McCormick, now the Institute's president, "we inherited them from our grandmothers." But the Art Institute remains a transient home for art; except for a reflection of the taste of a few remarkable Chicagoans, it bears no more of the mark of the city than does the architecture of the building in which it is housed. Such artists as Aaron Bohrod, which the city claims, drift away, like Margaret Anderson and the writers, having had all that the city can give. The Pulitzer Prize goes to Ernest Hemingway, born in Oak Park, and to Archibald MacLeish, born in suburban Glencoe, and a son of one of the founders of one of the city's great stores, Carson Pirie Scott & Co. Chicago, seeing her sons leaving, takes consolation in a prophecy written in 1867:

"In good time," wrote an anonymous visitor, "the western bottom lands will spontaneously grow poets. The American mind will be brought to maturity along the chain of Great Lakes, the banks of the Mississippi, the Missouri and their tributaries in the far Northwest. There, on the rolling plains, will be formed a republic of letters, which, not governed like that on our seaboard by the great literary powers of Europe, shall be free indeed. . . . The winds sweep unhindered from the Lakes to the Gulf and from the Alleghenies to the Rocky Mountains; and so do the thoughts of the Lord of the prairie. . . . Some day he will make his own books as well as his own laws. . . . He will remain on his prairie and all the arts of the world will come and make obeisance to him like the sheaves in his fields. He will be the American man and beside him there will be none else."

Chicagoans are not sure that those who will fulfill this prophecy will be born in Chicago. But the city is confident that Chicago will be the crossroads where they will meet.

Index

About the Author

EMMETT DEDMON is assistant Sunday editor of the Chicago *Sun-Times* and president of the Society of Midland Authors. He has been a Chicago newspaperman (except for an interlude during World War II) since his graduation from the University of Chicago in 1939. He was formerly editor of the literary supplement of the Chicago *Sun* and subsequently was drama critic for the *Sun-Times*.

He was born in a Christian church parsonage in Auburn, Nebraska, thirty-five years ago. In 1940, he enlisted in the Air Force, serving as a navigator with the 92nd and 95th Heavy Bombardment Groups in the Eighth Air Force and as the first navigation staff officer to be assigned to Eighth Bomber Command. In 1943, while on a bombing mission to Hanover, Germany, the plane in which he was flying was set afire by a fighter attack and its crew forced to abandon ship at 23,000 feet. Dedmon parachuted to safety but was captured and held as a German prisoner of war for nearly two years. While a prisoner of the Germans, he wrote a novel on scraps of paper which was published in 1946 under the title, *Duty to Live*. He was so fond of this title (a quotation from General Robert E. Lee) that he changed the spelling of his surname from Deadman to Dedmon rather than substitute another title to avoid the collocation of contradictory words. It also offered a chance to escape a monotonous series of jokes about his name.

He is married, has one son named Jonathan and one cocker spaniel named Topper. He is constantly being reminded of the fabulous quality of Chicago. His son was born in the same hospital which sheltered Johnny Torrio when Torrio was recovering from an attempted assassination. His home, in the South Shore district, is just a few doors removed from the former residence of Sam "Golf Bag" Hunt, a Capone aide who carried a submachine gun in a golfbag on business trips, frequently took the neighborhood children to the beach on days when he was relaxing and once refused to be arrested at home on the ground that it was a "respectable neighborhood." The Chicago police department respected Hunt's wishes.

Chicago-1834